The Roots of Tantra

SUNY Series in Tantric Studies
Paul E. Muller-Ortega and
Douglas Renfew Brooks, editors

The Roots of Tantra

Edited by
Katherine Anne Harper
and Robert L. Brown

State University of New York Press

Published by
State University of New York Press, Albany

Printed in the United States of America

For information, address State University of New York Press,
90 State Street, Suite 700, Albany, NY 12207

Production by Dana Foote
Marketing by Patrick Durocher

Library of Congress Cataloging-in-Publication Data

The roots of Tantra / edited by Katherine Anne Harper and Robert L. Brown.
p. cm.—(SUNY series in tantric studies)
Includes bibliographical references and index.
ISBN 0-7914-5305-7 (alk. paper)—ISBN 0-7914-5306-5 (pbk. : alk. paper)
1. Tantrism—History. I. Harper, Katherine Anne. II. Brown, Robert L., 1944 Oct. 6–
III. Series.

BL1283.83 .R66 2002
294.5′514—dc21
2001054184

10 9 8 7 6 5 4 3 2 1

CONTENTS

ILLUSTRATIONS

Cover: A. P. Gajjar, *Yoni and Lingam,* 1975. (Private collection)

PREFACE

The study of Tantrism as a specialized academic field has been a relatively recent phenomenon, perhaps stretching over only the last three or four decades; and, in the last few years, specialized studies dedicated to this often misunderstood subject have been published and received with increasing enthusiasm. This book is an initial study addressing origins in that it attempts to seek out and understand some of the nascent forms and sources of Tantrism in ancient India. The volume grew out of two conferences held in the greater Los Angeles area in October 1989 and March 1995 that were devoted specifically to fleshing out the meager evidence on early Tantrism. It is a matter of great satisfaction that so many scholars have worked to address questions concerning the origins and have shaped careful and detailed responses, particularly given the paucity of material remnants, both archaeological and textual, known at this time. The reader will encounter various approaches to the general topic concerning roots and origins; the diversity is the result of specific disciplines and backgrounds, each scholar bringing unique insights to the general topic. By no means does this volume attempt to be comprehensive; the problems involved in uncovering inchoate elements giving rise to Tantrism and its early manifestations are far too broad to be bound in a single volume. What we hope to accomplish is to pose a body of new questions and stimulate new dialogue and research in the field of Tantric studies.

The editors wish to thank the many participants for their excellent contributions and their great patience. In addition, we would like to thank the Society for Tantric Studies, Loyola Marymount University and the University of California at Los Angeles for various forms of support along the way.

—Katherine Anne Harper

Introduction

Robert L. Brown

> Stella's personal spiritual teacher was a wandering Śaivite Tantric monk who belonged to the Aghori orders . . . He tested her through a drastic Śaiva experience in which she was to follow him to the Kalighat temple, where he had her ascend a funeral pyre and sit on a corpse that was about to be cremated. . . . Then he told her to gather the ashes, take them home, and rub them on her body.
>
> —Barbara Stoler Miller, *Exploring India's Sacred Art*

Barbara Miller describes an experience in the life of Stella Kramrisch that took place sometime in the 1920s or 1930s in Calcutta. A pioneer in Indian art history, her volumes on the Hindu temple and studies of Śiva have defined the field. Miller goes on to say, "Throughout the entire happening she [Stella] had implicit faith in its validity as a ritual that confirmed her in her fearlessness and let her understand life with a lightened heart."[1] I bring up this incident because it appears rather outside the bounds of Tantric research and scholarship. It is so highly idiosyncratic and unusual[2] that it causes one to wonder if it actually happened. It fits, however, with the individualistic and personalized nature of Tantric practices. No one would find it hard to identify the episode as Tantric, despite difficulty in associating it with a specific ritual or text. What Kramrisch derived from the experience was a sense of power and a feeling of well-being, both Tantric goals.

Almost every study of Tantrism begins by apologizing. Scholars say it is little understood, that it cannot be easily or precisely defined and that it lacks a coherent structure. André Padoux in his article in this volume (What do we Mean by Tantrism?) outlines some of what makes defining Tantrism so difficult. First, it is a term, in fact a notion, that is Western. It is not a concept that comes from within the religious system itself, although it is generally recognized internally as different from the Vedic tradition. This immediately makes it suspect as an independent category.

Second, Tantrism is not a coherent system; it is an accumulation of practices and ideas from various sources distributed unevenly in different times, places, and sects and among individuals. While the pieces of Tantrism (doctrines and practices) can be listed, none is exclusively Tantric, and all are components of other religious systems. Rather, one might see them as cumulative, with some systems having more components being weighted toward the Tantric. Thus there are levels or degrees of Tantrism.

Third, Tantric pieces can be mixed easily with other non-Tantric aspects, such as *bhakti* (devotional) worship being used alongside Tantric approaches to the deity.[3] For one who worships the deity in multiple ways, can we say he or she is at one point a Tantric practitioner, and not at another point? Thus, even to argue what it is by saying what it is not is not entirely successful.

Rather than a system, cult, or religion André Padoux speaks of a "Tantric vision" and includes among its characteristics the use of ritual, manipulation of power, transgression of norms, use of the mundane to reach the supramundane, and identification of the microcosm with the macrocosm. The reader may want as well to refer to the list of eighteen constituents of Tantrism in Teun Goundriaan's introduction to *Hindu Tantrism.*[4]

Unfortunately for the topic of this book, what is or is not Tantric is of importance. The articles in the book came from two conferences focused on the question, what were the roots of Tantrism? Scholars were asked to explore how, when, and where Tantrism began. What were the sources for Tantrism and when can we begin to speak of Tantrism as an independent religious tradition? What were the causes, historical and religious? While these questions are not answered fully in the papers of this volume, they are carefully and extensively explored from a variety of viewpoints, methodologies, and approaches. One of the book's strengths is that the questions are pursued not only from a textual viewpoint, but from art historical and historical approaches as well.

It was decided to focus on Hindu Tantrism. While Buddhist Tantrism is discussed in some papers, it is not given equal weight in the volume. This is not because we felt Buddhist Tantrism was less important or that it could not be explored for Tantra's roots, but that it would require another book.

Before turning to the papers, I want to propose a way of viewing Tantrism in terms of process rather than as a static structure of characteristics. Emphasis on process points out that Tantrism is predominantly action, either physical or mental, with less stress on belief, doctrine, or theology. It also allows identification of what is and is not Tantric in terms of application rather than in terms of the qualities and characteristics themselves. I will present the model in a diagram, and then make some comments on it:

Processes	***Accomplished by***	***Guided by***	***Goals***
visualization	ritual (*kriya*)	teacher/guru	enlightenment
verbalization	yoga, the body,	deity	*mukti*
identification	*maṇḍala, cakra,*		worldly power
internalization	*mantra, yantra,*		*bhukti*
concretization	*pūjā,* icon		
transformation			

Starting with the goals first, *both* enlightenment and worldly success are expected. These goals are frequently separated in religions, including Indian religions, with two different sets of activities expected to achieve them. Enlightenment, often seen as a difficult process of endless rebirths achievable only by advanced religious specialists, can be reached in Tantrism during one lifetime while the practitioner is still alive. On the other hand, worldly power, even of the most mundane kind, for example success in love, is also achievable at the same time as enlightenment; they are intertwined. Success in this world need not be shunned to achieve enlightenment, a position held by *śramañic* (mendicant) Buddhists, Jains, and the Brahmanic tradition of the Hindus. For non-Tantric Buddhists, Jains, and Hindus, the life of a householder is a serious impediment for full spiritual accomplishment; instead the ascetic life is needed to move forward.

The way for Tantric practitioners to reach dual goals comes by connecting themselves to a power that flows through the world, including their own bodies, a power usually visualized as female. Tantrins identify the power, locate it, activate it, and use it for their own desires. The process brings into play the other three categories of the chart above: a guide, a set of tools, and various transformational actions. The guide is above all the teacher (the guru) who is simultaneously the deity and ultimately the student as well. Indeed, the collapsing and overlapping identities of the teacher is one illustration of the transformational processes so central to Tantrism that involve the movement both toward a unity, an essence, a center, and a monism while *simultaneously* breaking into dualities and multiples that replicate (often in numbered ranks) toward the periphery.

The importance of the guru cannot be overstated, as she/he is the only way for a student to learn Tantric practice. The oft-stated idea that Tantrism is esoteric because a secret tradition is passed between teacher and student is not unfounded. It helps to explain the individual approach to worship, the lack of a temple or monastery, and less focus on a loving relationship with a deity (all characteristics of theistic Hinduism). It also brings into question the use of written texts in the Tantric tradition, the primary source for scholars of Tantrism. Is it like attempting to understand the art of auto mechanics by reading through the auto parts catalogs? We may know a great deal about the components, but how they come together and work is known only by hands-on experience.

The tools used by the teacher and student listed in the second column are not intended to be inclusive. They share, however, certain characteristics: they are all "things" or involve the manipulation of "things." I have put the word *things* in quotation marks because they can be visualized or imagined, and they can be internalized so that they are placed within the body. There is often a hierarchy imposed on them as well, so that, for example, the drawing of a physical *yantra* is of a lower spiritual power than one drawn in the heart of the practitioner. The spiritual scale going from the concrete to the more abstract is found in all Indic religions.

The tools in Tantrism are less doctrines and beliefs than concrete things that the practitioner learns to manipulate in certain specific ways, sequences, and patterns. This involves actions and processes with things being taken through time and space. Indeed, the ultimate tool in Tantra is the human body, both the outside and the inside, both the anatomical body of arms, hands, tongue, heart, genitals, and mind, and the yogic anatomy of *cakras* and *nāḍīs.* It is control of the body as a tool used to actuate processes that connects the practitioner with the universal power to reach his goals.

I have listed six processes, again not intending to be comprehensive, that the tools are used to bring about. They can be seen as paired. The first two, visualization and verbalization, involve seeing and speaking the power into being. The importance of seeing (*darśana*) in approaching the deity has often been noted in Indian religions and it is used in Tantric practice as well, but often is interiorized or envisaged rather than directed toward an icon. One of the abilities of a Tantric worshiper is to create visions of the deities (and other signs) in his mind's eye. Verbalization is of the greatest importance in Tantric worship as the recitation of sounds (*mantras*). *Mantras* are learned from the teacher and are conceived as sounds, not as written word; and, just as visualizing brings about the deities and the powers they manifest, so does the use of *mantra.*

The paired processes of identification and internalization indicate actions that make the worshiper divine, the realization of which is needed to gain access to the universal power. An example of identification has already been mentioned above, when the teacher and the deity are identified as one. Such telescoping of identities is needed to pull everything into the body of the worshiper so that the ultimate identification can be made of the deity with the worshiper. The importance of internalizing the concrete "thing" as a mental image is central to being able to create within the body what is outside it. Tantric ritual seems to be set up as a pairing of doing something involving manipulating a thing (like drawing a *yantra*) and then imagining it within through a mental image.

The last pairing consists of concretization and transformation, two seemingly opposite procedures. Once internalization is achieved, it does not mean that the process is unidirectional as the ritual always involves arranging, moving, and changing real things, even when internalization has taken place; the processes are intertwined and occilating. By concretization I mean that, for the Tantric practitioner, things (including such things as sounds or deities) have a reality that takes form in the world, cannot be abandoned, and must be used. The final process, transformation, can be applied to all the processes, as it seems to me the most essential of them all, as all involve one thing changing into another. Indeed, the ability to change one reality through ritual manipulation of things into another truer, more powerful reality may be one definition of Tantrism.

Finally, what aspects of Indian religions (Purāṇic Hinduism and Buddhism, for example) are less stressed by this Tantric view? Immediately, there are problems; to separate Hinduism and Buddhism from Tantric practices is, as noted above, difficult. André Padoux's observation that "for a thousand years, most

Hinduism has been either Tantric or Tantricized"[5] underlines the futility in attempting to categorize and divide what is and is not Tantric in current Hindu practices. Still, if we say we are talking about emphasis, not difference, we can suggest several areas less emphasized in Tantric practice than in certain other Indic religions. I will suggest five: less stress on mythology and narrative stories of deities, less stress on love for god, less stress on moral action (for Buddhism), less stress on temple worship and priests, and less stress on patronage of art, temples, and good works (on merit and therefore on *karma*). To expand and explain these would take us too far afield, but I ask the reader to keep them in mind while reading through the articles in this book. Evidence in support of this less-stressed list (and it can certainly be lengthened) is seen in part from observing that the topics are not important aspects of the discussions in the articles in this book.

The very brief and simple introduction to Tantrism given above is intended to orient the reader, particularly one who comes to the topic without much background, as discussions of Tantrism can become fairly complex and technical. The book's twelve papers are divided into five sections with the first including two papers that give overviews of Tantrism while focusing on the issues of beginnings and relationships.

Overviews

The first essay by André Padoux sets up for us (as mentioned already) some of the overall questions regarding Tantrism and why these questions have not been answered, demonstrating why the search for Tantra's roots will not be easy. In addition, Padoux points out a source of confusion—and one that is particularly important for us—between Tantric practice and its sources, what might be called its mimetic nature. Again and again, Tantrism appears to replicate or copy either pre-Tantric or local practices. The question is whether the relationship is in terms of sources or of parallel but independent origins. Padoux mentions as examples micro-macrocosmic correspondences, magic use of power, power in terms of violence and transgression, and feminine aspect of the deity, all characteristic of Tantrism but all found in either pre-Tantric or autochthonous local religion. Are these roots or merely parallel branches from the same trunk?

Padoux ends his essay by proposing two possible definitions of Tantrism that might focus its seemingly amorphous nature, both of which, however, he ultimately rejects.

> One is to confine Tantrism to the "hard core" practitioners: a system of observances (often transgressive in nature) that are given meaning by a more or less power-oriented vision of man and the cosmos, a system where power is manipulated, where micro-macrocosmic correspondences play an essential role. Also, there is usually a high degree of esotericism (the higher, the more esoteric, the more "Tantric") together with a particular type of pan-

> theon (not necessarily sexually differentiated however), and a particular and very developed type of ritual. Outside these qualifications, there may exist a varying number and proportion of Tantric traits, but not Tantrism as such.

The second definition is one frequently applied to Tantrism, "to stress its ritual aspect without omitting entirely the ideological side, but subordinating it to ritual." Padoux rejects both approaches and ends his essay saying, "I fear we still have to toil to find a solution to the problem of Tantrism."

The second essay by David N. Lorenzen, "Early Evidence for Tantric Religion," is a straightforward review of the historical evidence for the appearance of Tantrism, serving as an excellent pendant to Padoux's thematic article. Lorenzen suggests that there are two ways to define Tantrism, one is "a narrow definition [that] considers as Tantric only religious phenomena directly associated with the Tantras, Saṃhitās and Āgamas," that is texts written in Sanskrit and thus directed toward an elite. The second broader definition adds "an ample range of popular 'magical' beliefs and practices, including much of Śākta and Haṭha Yoga traditions," traditions that use predominantly vernacular languages. Lorenzen chooses the second as a definition, and then proceeds to sort through historical, textual, and epigraphical sources to locate in time and geography the beginnings of Tantrism. He concludes that Tantrism begins to be discerned in the fifth century C.E. and is clearly seen by the seventh. By the ninth it was fully manifested in both Hinduism and Buddhism. He finds its beginnings to be "primarily a northern phenomena," with its centers in Bihar, Bengal, Assam, Kashmir, Nepal, Tibet, the Punjab, and Rajasthan. While these dates and localities may seem rather conservative to some, Lorenzen's historical evidence supports them. He does not deny that there are characteristics of Tantrism that can be traced to a much earlier time. His point is that Tantrism as such ("the complex as a whole") cannot be earlier.

The History and Development of Tantra

Most of the book's essays deal in some way with developments of Tantrism through time, but the three included in this section demonstrate three distinctly different approaches to understanding development and change. The most comprehensive is M. C. Joshi's "Historical and Iconographic Aspects of Śākta Tantrism," which traces goddess worship in India from the Upper Paleolithic through the thirteenth century C.E. Joshi uses as evidence texts, inscriptions, and art to outline the major shifts and changes in the worship of goddesses, and the essay serves as an excellent survey of the historical points at which Tantric-flavored imagery and practices were added. Joshi assumes that goddess worship is, in some way, Tantric by nature, stating at the beginning that "Śākta Tantrism has its roots in prehistoric concepts of a fertile mother goddess and ancient systems for her worship." He does not suggest any one point in time or change in iconography that divides ancient goddesses from Tantric goddesses, nor contemporary non-Tantric goddesses from Tantric ones. The advantage of this is that he is never forced to propose a confining and monolithic definition of Tantrism, but outlines a continuous, cumulative development. Nor does he attempt to show why the changes he notes have taken place. In other words, he assumes that Tantrism exists in some form from the beginning of religion in India, that it is connected to goddess worship, and that the way the goddesses developed over time is in itself a history of Tantrism.

A very different approach to Śākta Tantrism is given in Douglas Renfrew Brooks's article "Auspicious Fragments and Uncertain Wisdom: The Roots of Śrīvidyā Śākta Tantrism in South India." Rather than a historical survey of practices, Brooks's study is a detailed look at a particular text, the *Tirumantiram,* written in Tamil by the seventh century saint Tirumūlar. Brooks finds that Tirumūlar knew aspects of a highly detailed and organized form of Tantric goddess worship, the Śrīvidyā. What he is able to show is that Tirumūlar—while a Śaivite and not a Tantric worshiper—knew and used essential aspects, particularly the *śrīvidyā mantra,* of the Śrīvidyā system. Since the Śrīvidyā system developed in north India, probably in Kashmir, and takes form in Sanskrit texts only in the ninth century, Brooks demonstrates that "the structure of Śrīvidyā ideology must have been in place perhaps as long as two centuries before its crystallization in Sanskrit texts." Furthermore, that Tirumūlar was familiar with this ideology and could incorporate it into his own religious system, argues for a surprisingly early India-wide awareness of "Tantric" thought that existed outside of texts and temples. Brooks's paper suggests there was a shared Tantric ideology in India that existed before codification in Sanskrit texts and that was not yet restricted to specific groups.

The third paper in this section, Thomas B. Coburn's "The Structural Interplay of Tantra, Vedānta, and Bhakti: Nondualist Commentary on the Goddess," focuses the discussion on a single passage from the sixth-century *Devī-Māhātmya.* Coburn's approach to the passage is to compare the analysis of two eighteenth-century Indian commentators, Nāgoji Bhaṭṭa and Bhāskararāya, the first an Advaita Vedāntin and the second a Tantric follower of Śrīvidyā (the system mentioned by Brooks). Coburn finds that the two use similar references, and both are involved in attempts to apply a monistic or nondual reading of the passage and of reality. But whereas Nāgoji Bhaṭṭa must ultimately say that even the goddess must be subordinate to a more ultimate reality ("Brahman-without-qualities"), the Tantric Bhāskararāya is:

> unwilling to ascribe secondary status to the physical world, or to the senses, or to the manifest diversity of the Goddess's form. The way in which [he avoids] epistemological dualism is not philosophically, but ritually—through the esoteric, experiential transformation of the world. . . . What

differentiates the two nondualisms, then, is that one—Advaita Vedānta—is of a public and profoundly philosophical sort, while the other—Tantra—inclines toward a private and ritualized experience of oneness.

Each of the authors in this section—Joshi, Brooks, and Coburn—has focused on the goddess and the development of Śākta Tantrism, but each has addressed them very differently, demonstrating the advantages and disadvantages of going from a broad historical survey to a focused and highly detailed analysis of a single moment.

The Art History and Archaeology of Tantra

The first paper in this section, that by Thomas McEvilley entitled "The Spinal Serpent," may at first appear to be neither art historical nor archeological, but I am using McEvilley's own use of the term archaeology that he introduced in his article "The Archeology of Yoga" in 1981.[6] His article in this volume can be seen as an extension of his earlier article where he argues for yogic practices in the Indus Valley culture (ca. 2800–1700 B.C.E.), using as evidence six seals showing figures in *mūlābandhāsana,* a Haṭha yoga posture used to activate the *kuṇḍalinī* and that implies the existence of the three channels (*nāḍīs*) of yogic physiology (*suṣumṇa, iḍā,* and *piṅgala*). In "The Spinal Serpent" McEvilley points out, for the first time, the startling parallels between "the Hindu doctrine of the *kuṇḍalinī* [and] Plato's doctrine in the *Timaeus.*" These correlations are so complete—even to the two subtle channels that flank the spine, the need to retain the "soul-stuff" or sperm in the head rather than expend it through ejaculation, and the visualization of this power as a serpent—that McEvilley undertakes to search for connections between Greece, India and even China. He concludes that the Tantric physiology is not exclusively an Asian element, and that "a diffusion situation probably involving some of the factors just reviewed was involved in its presence in India as well as in Greece." The roots of Tantra, according to McEvilley, seem here "to direct our gaze into the darkest depths of human prehistory."

Katherine Anne Harper argues in the next paper "The Warring Śaktis: A Paradigm for Gupta Conquests" that the Tantric notion of female power (*śakti*) was applied to a preexisting group of goddesses, the seven mothers or Saptamātṛkās, an association that brought the mothers into the mainstream of Hindu religion. She pinpoints this at ca. 400 C.E., during the Gupta Dynasty, making it among the earliest evidence we have for fully developed Tantric images, and long before we have actual Tantric texts (ca. ninth century). The association of *śakti* with the mothers was, Harper feels, done in a structured, purposeful manner by Vaidika Tantrins who:

> devised rituals meant to strengthen the king's power and protect the established order. Their reformation of older religious symbols resulted in elevat-

> ing a female septad from its shadowy past and relocating it centrally in the Hindu pantheon. At the same time, the reformers provided the newly evolved deities with attributes . . . that signified martial and spiritual empowerment, particularly for the king.

Thus, the mothers and their Tantric powers were used by the Gupta kings, a political use of Tantrism rarely argued by scholars. Her suggestion provides a new explanation for the popularization of Tantrism. Harper relies on texts, epigraphy, and art for her evidence.

The third paper in this section, Dennis Hudson's "Early Evidence of the *Pāñcarātra Āgama,*" also relies on texts, inscriptions, and art to argue that the Bhāghavata (Kṛṣṇa) tradition was a coherent religious system from the first century B.C.E. or earlier: "I shall discuss early evidence for the *Pāñcarātra Āgama.* The evidence places the Āgama in the first three or four centuries B.C.E. and connects it with a consistent ritual and theological tradition that centers on Vāsudeva Kṛṣṇa." Taking as a model the Vaikuṇṭha Perumāl Temple at Kanchipuram for the organization and identification of manifestations of Vāsudeva, Hudson applies the schema to a reinterpretation of numerous sculptures, particularly from Mathura dating to the Kushan period (first to third centuries C.E.). Furthermore, he applies the model to the exegesis of texts as well, including the *Bhagavad Gītā.* The result is a new interpretation of an early Hindu religious system, one that displays a series of overlaps with both Vedic and Tantric rituals and practices, and one in which to search for Tantra's roots.

The Vedas and Tantra

The next two essays deal with the relationships between the Vedic and the Tantric traditions. Teun Goudriaan in "Imagery of the Self from Veda to Tantra" shows that Tantrism relied on previously existing concepts and images, those found in the Vedas and the *Upaniṣads,* rather than producing new symbolic systems, and thus he stresses continuity over disjuncture. He focuses on the concept of the "self" or *Ātman,* identifying five categories in Indian thought of metaphorical imagery used to discuss the *Ātman* (soul or self): self as a person—literally a little man—in the heart; self as part of a family; self as a ruler and enjoyer; self as a mover (often as a bird); and self as the sun. This imagery forms relationships between concepts of spirituality and of the world of appearances. Tantric interpretations tend toward concretization, often with a theistic interpretation, so that the self becomes less the individual *Ātman* and more identified with God. Goudriaan writes:

> they [the Tantric practitioners] applied the images, which in the older Upaniṣads and some later texts referred to the undivided or individual self, to their conceptions of a Supreme Self, which they experienced as insepara-

> ble form the Supreme Godhead worshiped by their school or sect. We could speak of a theistic reorientation of the old auto-mystical tradition, entailing a tendency to loss of authority for the individual self.

Thus, Goudriaan demonstrates shifts in Tantric ideology but using older imagery.

A second paper that analyzes the relationship between Tantric and Vedic traditions is Richard K. Payne's "Tongues of Flame: Homologies in the Tantric Homa." Payne is arguing, as did Goudriaan, for continuity between the Vedic and Tantric traditions. He looks to *homa* rituals ("votive ritual in which offerings are made into a fire"), tracing three groups of relationships: characteristics of the ritual use of fire, identification of the fire with people, and identification of the fire with gods. His evidence includes the Shingon tradition of Japan, Tantric Buddhism that dates from the beginning of the ninth century, as well as the traditions of India. He identifies many continuities between Vedic and Tantric *homa,* with a shift from three fires to one, and then the identification of the fire with both the deity and the practitioner, as indicative of Tantric differences. He concludes that "the Tantras appear to be much more firmly rooted in the Vedas than is usually suggested."

The Texts and Tantra

The final two papers bring us to firm ground with discussions of full-fledged Tantric texts. Paul E. Muller-Ortega in "Becoming Bhairava: Meditative Vision in Abhinavagupta's *Parātrīśikā-laghuvṛtti,*" hopes:

> that this exploration of the meaning of Bhairava [in the text] will contribute to an understanding of an important ideological shift in the development of early Hindu Tantra. The intent of this essay, therefore, is not so much historiographical as it is patently hermeneutic. If we are to understand the roots of the Hindu Tantra, we need to uncover the radical and crucial interpretive shifts that contribute to its successful ideological consolidation.

One of the shifts he identifies in Abhinavagupta's texts is from Bhairava seen as an external anthropomorphic but fierce deity to the embodiment of all-encompassing reality. Muller-Ortega also stresses the importance of the interplay between ritual and meditation, along with the concomitant oscillation between external and internal Tantric practices. He ends by saying Abhinavagupta's writings (of the tenth century) show:

> that this early Hindu Tantra rejects the dry vistas of traditional philosophical debate, which seek only the representation of the Ultimate through conceptual truths. It rejects as well the self-enclosing renunciation of traditional Indian monasticism, which protectively seeks to isolate the monk

> from the imagined stain of worldliness. Transcending the dualities and distinctions of conventional thought and morality, the Tantra demonstrates an outward gesture of embracing delight in all of reality. The Tantric hero pushes outward into adventurous, spiritual exploration, into savoring and delighting the experience of so many varieties of blissful *ekarasa,* the unitary taste of consciousness.

Perhaps a more positive and eloquent statement of Tantrism's goals could not be made, particularly when they have been so darkly painted by many other scholars.

The final paper in the book is Lina Gupta's "Tantric Incantation in the *Devī Purāṇa:* the *Padamālā Mantra Vidyā."* This paper will leave the reader with a taste of Tantric ritual. The *Devī Purāṇa,* while difficult to date, is one of the earlier of the *Purāṇic* texts, and may date to around the sixth century C.E. It is in praise of the goddess, and Gupta gives a full exploration of the important *mantra* (the *Padamālā Mantra Vidyā*) in the text that Śiva uses to invoke the goddess. When the worshiper recites the mantra, he or she "changes internally as well as externally . . . The ultimate goal of human life, according to Tantrism, is to internalize the cosmos and unify the inner vibrations with the outer." Gupta discusses the ritual performance of the *mantra,* specifying what are its prerequisites, preparations, procedures, and performance.

Lina Gupta's paper leads, finally, to my brief conclusion. Gupta discusses a word used in the *Padamālā Mantra Vidyā:* "*kapālamathana,*" which means skull (*kapāla*) churning (*mathana*). She says that the *kapāla* or skull cup, an essential implement for Tantric ritual, refers to when Śiva cut off one of Brahmā's heads, only to be forced to wander in penance with the skull attached to his hand, using it to beg alms, until finally having it drop when he reached Varanasi. Gupta also tells how skulls were used in rituals, such as drinking wine from them (this is, in fact, the point of the word *churning-skull,* as it involved stirring the wine in the skull cup). Finally, she speaks of the use of skulls to predict the future by tapping on them (*kapālakoṭanī*), specifically by Atharvavedic Brahmins and Tantrins, one of whom (Vaṇgīsa) is mentioned in a Buddhist text and whom she feels may have lived in Bengal.

There are a series of reliefs from Gandhara, an area in present-day Pakistan, that date from as early as ca. 100 C.E. that actually show skull tappers. The reliefs have been discussed in an article by Maurizio Taddei,[7] one of which I illustrate here (Figure 1). The Buddha sits in the center, flanked by two skull tappers, both of whom hold a skull. The figure on his left is identified as a Buddhist monk,[8] while the right-side figure, who has his head wrapped with a cloth, is a Brahmin, identified by his hair knot showing over his forehead. Buddhist texts that discuss this story[9] tell how Vaṇgīsa was able to tell from a skull what the future rebirth of the dead person would be. Called before the Buddha, he told future births of all whose skulls were given to him except for that of a Buddhist *arhat,* one who, in other words, was not reborn having reached enlightenment.

Figure 1 Buddha flanked by skull tappers. Gandhara, Pakistan. Ca. first-second century C.E. (Courtesy of The Russek Collection)

Is this, then, a root of Tantra? We have evidence that skull tappers were known by the first century C.E. Taddei argues that the story "is the reflection of the usual controversies between Buddhists and Brahmans,"[10] and while he may be correct, it appears to me that the Buddha actually accepts the effectiveness of skull tapping, in fact using it to prove that an *arhat* could, indeed, remove himself from the round of endless rebirths. In other words, the roots of Tantra are very old and probably from the beginning predominantly nonsectarian, points made by several of the authors in this book as well.

The second reference in Gupta's paper is to the *vīra* state (*vīra* is the Tantric hero of Muller-Ortega's quotation above, an advanced Tantric practitioner). Gupta says that:

> The *vīra* state is one that requires great moral effort and the courage to confront endangering situations and steadfast pursuit of spiritual success (*siddhi*). One of the most grueling of the Vāmācāra Śākta practices performed by the *vīra sādhaka* is the *nilasadhana.* On a special night, the *sādhaka* must sit on a corpse in a deserted location such as a cremation ground, riverbank, or pond and offer an oblation of consecrated flesh (*mahāmāṃsa*) to the fire deity. Through successful completion of the rite, he transcends to the highest state where he/she is united with the deity.

This, of course, brings us back to the beginning of the Introduction, to Stella Kramrisch sitting on a corpse in Calcutta on orders from her Tantric guru. We do not know whether Kramrisch was united with Śiva, or transcended to the highest state. But it is difficult to argue that her action was somehow not "truly" Tantric. It is a cautionary note, that whatever template we create for what is or is not Tantric, ultimately what a Tantric practitioner does is by one definition "Tantric."

NOTES

Note: Standard diacritical marks are used for Sanskrit words. Sanskrit terms that occur frequently appear in a glossary with English translations. Other Sanskrit words and phrases are translated into English in the text after their initial appearance.

1. Barbara Stoler Miller, ed., *Exploring India's Sacred Art* (Philadelphia: University of Pennsylvania Press, 1983), 15.

2. The use of a corpse for a seat on which to perform Tantric ritual (*śava sādhana*) is an advanced form of worship. It is restricted in regard to place and is done with a structured ritual.

3. The notion of *bhakti* or loving devotion is not absent from Tantric texts, but is primarily directed toward the guru. See Sanjukta Gupta, Dirk Jan Hoens, and Teun Goudriaan, *Hindu Tantrism* (Leiden: Brill, 1979), 74–77.

4. Ibid., 7–9.

5. André Padoux, "Mantras—What Are They?" in *Mantra,* ed. Harvey P. Alper (Albany: State University of New York Press, 1989), 296.

6. In *RES* 1 (1981).

7. Maurizio Taddei, "The Story of the Buddha and the Skull Tapper: A Note in Gandharan Iconography," *Annali: Istituto Orientale Di Napoli* 39 (1979): 395–420.

8. René Russek, *Buddha: Zwischen Ost und West: Skulpturen aus Gandhāra/Pakistan* (Zurich: Museum Rietberg, 1987), 54.

9. See Taddei, "Story of Buddha," for reference and a summary.

10. Ibid., 406.

Part I
OVERVIEWS

1

What Do We Mean by Tantrism?[1]

André Padoux

The beginnings of the Hindu Tantric traditions are all the more difficult to find in that Tantrism is a protean phenomenon, so complex and elusive that it is practically impossible to define it or, at least, to agree on its definition. Is not this difficulty due to the fact that we see and try to define an entity that does not really exist as such? Even if we do not go that far, even if we do not endorse H.V. Guenther's remark that Tantrism is "probably one of the haziest notions and misconceptions the Western mind has evolved,"[2] the fact remains that Tantrism is, to a large extent, "a category of discourse in the West," and not, strictly speaking, an Indian one. As a category, Tantrism is not—or at any rate was not until our days—an entity in the minds of those inside. It is a category in the minds of observers from outside. To use the fashionable jargon of today: it is an *etic,* not an *emic,* entity.

The term Tantrism was coined by Western Indologists of the latter part of the nineteenth century whose knowledge of India was limited and who could not realize the real nature, let alone the extent, of the Tantric phenomenon. They believed that the practices and notions they discovered in Hindu and Buddhist texts named Tantra (hence Tantrism) were something very particular, exceptional, and limited, contrasting sharply with the general, respectable, field of Indian philosophy and religion, a particular domain one could easily circumscribe. But with the progress of studies in these fields one came to realize that, far from being a limited phenomenon, Tantrism was in fact something vast, diffuse, diverse and very difficult to define satisfactorily. Mircea Eliade was perhaps the first to point it out, when he wrote in a book published in 1948 that, after the fifth century C.E., Tantrism became a pervasive Indian "fashion" (*une "mode" pan-indienne*).[3] Neither in traditional India nor in Sanskrit texts is there a term for Tantrism; no description or definition of such a category is to be found anywhere. We know also that, more often than not, Tantric texts are not called Tantra.

As evidence that Tantrism was *not* considered a particular philosophical system, one may see that Mādhava's *Sarvadarśanasaṃgraha,* a fourteenth century text, does not mention Tantra as one of the fifteen *darśanas* (schools of worship) it describes, although this work dates to a time usually considered as that of the fullest expansion of Tantric notions and practices. There are, of course, Tantric elements in Mādhava's description of the Śaiva *darśana* where he quotes from such Tantric authors as Utpaladeva or Abhinavagupta, but Tantra as such is not mentioned. P.V. Kane explains this by saying that Mādhava deliberately ignored Tantra because it was too scandalous. But it is more likely that it was, by that time, so pervasive that it was not regarded as being a distinct system.

The usual reference to the Indian use of the term *tāntrika* derives from Kullūka Bhaṭṭa's formula when commenting on the *Mānavadharmaśāstra* 2.1, where he juxtaposes *vaidika/tāntrika* as two forms of revelation (*śrutiś ca dvidvidhā vaidikī tāntrikī ca*) and, consequently, two different approaches to the ultimate reality (the first based formally on the Veda and the Brahmanic tradition and the second on other texts). The distinction has remained a basic one throughout Indian thought, but without a particular category of "Tantrism" evolving.

We may note here the use by Kullūka of the term *śruti.* Even outside Tantric circles, apparently, the Tantric tradition could be considered as *śruti,* that is, as a revelation valid in its own sphere. In fact, Kullūka's formula shows on the one hand that, even though there is no inside definition of Tantrism, Tantrism was at least perceived by Indians outside it as different from the Vedic tradition. It evidently was similarly perceived by those inside who deprecated Vedic rites and notions. On the other hand, the quotation tends to show that the *vaidika/tāntrika* relationship was not a clear-cut one since both could be called *śruti.* Such ambiguity, in fact, goes very far because Vedic and Tantric traditions, as time passed, tended to permeate each other in ritual, in concepts, and in scriptural references. Not only are elements from the *Atharva Veda* important in some local Tantric traditions (in Orissa, for instance), but many Tantric authors quote freely from *śruti.* The assimilation went so far that, in Kashmir, some Vaiṣṇava Tāntrikas of the Pāñcaratra declared their scriptures to be the Vedic *śākhā* (school), the Ekānayaśākhā.

Concerning the Indian textual use of the term *tāntrika,* we should also take note of the fact that, in Śaiva Tantric texts, *tāntrika* often is used instead of *kaula* to refer to the more exoteric texts and practices and as a way to distinguish from the esoteric *kaula* ones. Thus, those texts and practices called Tantric are the less Tantric ones. India, it appears, far from providing us with a definition of Tantrism as something specific, rather accumulates evidence showing the interpenetration, in Hindu thought and practice, of Tantric and non-Tantric elements.

A number of traits have been listed by authors writing on Tantrism as being constituent elements. Teun Goudriaan, for instance, in his *Hindu Tantrism,* lists eighteen such traits as "some constituents of Tantrism (in its wider sense)."[4] The trouble, however, with such lists is, first of all, that there is no consensus among scholars about these elements and, second, that there are no groups or texts usually considered Tantric where all these elements are to be found; also, some, if not most, of them can be found in non-Tantric contexts. This is not surprising because "Tantrism in its wider sense" is a hazy and ill-defined sort of notion; it can cover, in fact, so vast a field as to include almost all of Hinduism. Let us, however, examine some of these traits, limiting ourselves to those I believe to be the most obvious.

The first aspect to be examined, that is, a particular Tantric ideology, I believe is important. I differ with those who consider Tantrism to be, in Jean Filliozat's words, "merely the ritual and technical aspect of Hinduism."[5] This view, however, is not to be dismissed too hastily since ritual, when the technical aspect is added to it, can go a long way toward characterizing Tantrism if you take it as a general Hindu phenomenon. Indeed, ritual may well provide one of the most practical, but surely minimal, overall definitions of Tantrism. I shall refer again to this subject later on.

The ideological aspect of the Tantric vision is the cosmos as permeated by power (or powers), a vision wherein energy (*śakti*) is both cosmic and human and where microcosm and macrocosm correspond and interact. The ideology is important because it explains such Tantric features as the concept and practice of *kuṇḍalinī,* as well as a number of yogic and ritual practices for the use and control of that power. It also explains some aspects of the speculations and practices concerning the power of the word (*vāc*), especially the nature and power of mantras, and so forth. This ideology not only colors, but orientates and organizes, and gives meaning to all Tantric practices and observances. Such an ideology is evident in the Bharirava Tantras, in those of Kālī, in such systems as the Krama and the Trika (all of the Śaiva or Śākta texts), in the esoteric Buddhist *Yogānuttara-tantras* and in the Sahajiyā traditions. It is subdued, toned down, in other traditions normally considered Tantric, such as the Pāñcaratra, or Āgamic Śaivasiddhānta. And, you would hardly find it among some dualist Śaiva authors (Sadyojyoti, for instance) even though the mantras and rituals used by these adepts are Tantric.

On the other hand, micro-macrocosmic correspondences are found in ancient, pre-Tantric texts; for example, they are fundamental in the Upaniṣads. The magical use of power is apparent in the *Atharvaveda* too and, later on, the Tantric vision permeated the Purāṇas and seeped into most of Hinduism. We must add that the ideology of power, with its aspect of violence and transgression, is essential to the cults of the feminine aspect of the divinity, cults that cannot always be considered as Tantric. In south India, for instance, the cults of local goddesses are surely autochthonous Dravidian and originally pre-Tantric. The ancient Indian practices of *tapas* (internal heat) and mastery of sexual energy (*vīrya*) for gaining supernatural powers also are examples of controlled uses of the power that are not Tantric.

In all these non-Tantric domains, there are elements identical or akin to those constituting the Tantric vision. We can say, therefore, that in the domain of ideology or doctrine, we find the same situation as in the case of the other Tantric traits. Characteristics found clearly and fully in a few groups or in some texts only are found in a wide area. Furthermore, the origin or the seeds of many traits, ideological or otherwise, can be traced back to ancient, pre-Tantric, times.

Another element generally considered characteristic or constituent of Tantrism is the use of means pertaining to this world for supramundane ends, be it *mukti* (liberation) or the lesser rewards or enjoyments classified as *bhoga.* There is the attempt in Tantric traditions to achieve liberation and to gain supernatural powers, not by renunciation of all worldly desires or pleasures, but, to use Madeleine Biardeau's words, "by harnessing desire—*kāma* [desire] in all the meanings of that word and with all its related values—to the service of liberation,"[6] a liberation that is usually *jīvanmukti* (liberation while living), a transcendental condition of unity with the deity—total freedom from the world, but also triumphal plentitude and demiurgic power.

But liberation in a Tantric context is not necessarily *jīvanmukti.* Even in such a completely Tantric work as Abhinavagupta's *Tantrāloka,* the best and highest adept, who benefits from the most intense grace of Śiva (*tīvraśaktipāta*), is instantly liberated and dies: a condition considered higher than *jīvanmukti.* The typical Tantric *jīvanmukta,* totally free of a world he dominates and transcends, is to be found in some Tantras only—for example, in the Bhairava or Kālī Tantras, in Sahajiyā Vaiṣṇavism or in Buddhism too—that can be viewed as "hard core" Tantrism. In the more staid Saiddhāntika Āgamas where the term *jīvanmukti* seldom occurs, the liberated adept acquires *śivatva,* the condition of Śiva, a condition of similarity (*sāmantā*) with Śiva, not one of total fusion (*ekatva*). This permits the liberated soul to go on loving God. It is evidently still more so in the Pāñcaratra, where devotion (*bhakti*) is essential.

Since I mention *bhakti,* I may note here that, gaining liberation while active in this world, being in this world but not of it, being entirely dedicated to God, is the basic teaching of *bhakti* from the *Bhagavad-Gītā* onward. Since, however, the love of God and the essential role of God's grace to gain liberation are insisted upon in such Tantric works as those of Abhinavagupta, where does *bhakti* end and Tantra begin? There is a problematical relationship between Tantrism and *bhakti.*

A particular Tantric way of making use of this world for supramundane ends is the ritual and soteriological use of things that are normally forbidden, that is, the transgression of norms. The main reason for this antinomian behavior appears to be the wish, by so doing, to participate in the dark, chaotic, undisciplined, and very powerful forces that are normally repressed and kept outside the pure, orderly, circumscribed world of the Brahmin. This wish, incidentally, implies a belief in a world pervaded by power, a power supposedly at its utmost in that outside world. Such transgressive practices include the transgressive ritual use of sex.

The use of sex is not found in all Tantric traditions. It is not prevalent, but present nonetheless, in the Śaiva and Śākta groups that have a Kāpālika origin or background and that have kept, if only symbolically, the Kāpālika culture of the cremation ground with its cult of the Yoginīs and its erotico-mystic rites and notions. It is also found in Sahajiyā circles, Hindu and Buddhist. But, all this is conspicuously absent from the less intensely Tantric traditions, whether Śaiva or

Vaiṣṇava. Transgression is characteristic of "hard core" Tantrism only. On the other hand, transgression is a universal category of human behavior. In India it is older than Tantrism, as proved, for instance, by the Pāśupatas and Lākulas. Erotic rites and sexo-yogic practices surely antedate Tantra. Here again, we see elements either not found in all Tantric groups or texts, or that exist outside Tantrism and have existed before it. For instance, the conception of the body as a structured receptacle of power and animated by that power and the somato-cosmic vision upon which these practices are based are certainly pre-Tantric or extra-Tantric.

The same thing can be said about most, if not of all, of the other elements considered characteristic or constituent of Tantrism. The ubiquitous use of *mantras,* for instance, together with all the notions concerning the power of the word (*vāc*) and with the relevant practices (*nyāsa, japa, mantrasādhana*) is so typically Tantric that *mantraśastra* is often taken as synonymous with *tantraśastra;* however, Tantric *mantras* are used in non-Tantric rites. Some Vaiṣṇana Saṃhitas, the ritual of which is Tantric, nevertheless, consider the Vedic *mantras* as higher than the Tantric ones. In a similar fashion ritual diagrams (*maṇḍalas, yantras, cakras*) or ritual gestures (*mudrās*) are to be found variously used in and outside Tantrism. If one looks at the Tantric ritual (*pūjā* or *dīkṣā*), one would notice some of the constitiuent elements as deriving from groups outside Tantrism also. The same applies to another element considered typically Tantric, namely the polarization of the godhead into a male pole (usually higher, but inactive) and a female one (*śakti*), which is active but theologically lower except in some Śākta traditions. Such polarization is not stressed equally everywhere. The role of *śakti* is limited not only in Vaiṣṇava Saṃhitās, but in the Siddhānta Śaivāgamas. There are, futhermore, Śaiva pantheons that are either entirely male or entirely female.

It is thus very difficult to gather traits that are both typically Tantric and found in most Tantric traditions, but not found outside these traditions when we limit ourselves to Hinduism. The difficulty becomes even greater—indeed, it becomes an impossibility—if we wish to include Tantric Buddhism as it developed in India and spread to China, Tibet, or Japan.

We could try to bypass the difficulty by choosing from among those constituent elements only a few that, when present in a text, in the practice or doctrine of a given group, would suffice for us to declare that text or group as Tantric. But, which elements ought we to choose—ideological, ritual, or practical ones? Should we limit those elements to observances (*vrata*) or cult ritual (Tantric *pūjā*)? Complicating the picture is that Tantric ritual is not always exclusive of a Vedic practice. Several texts or authors prescribe or admit both types of ritual. A Vedic public behavior may hide a Tantric domestic or secret practice. Furthermore, within the same tradition there are levels of esotericism and exclusivism, there are progressive, ascending levels of specificity (*uttarottaravaiśiṣṭyam*) and of "Tantricity." Usually the more specific and esoteric the level of the Tantra, the more Tantric it is. It is clear that there are degrees in Tantrism.

A number of other elements could be adduced to show the uncertainty of the criteria we can use to define Tantrism, the diversity within Tantric traditions and the problematic nature of the relationship of Tantrism with non-Tantric, "orthodox" Hinduism. On this last point, the judgment passed by each group on the other goes from utter condemnation to the admission of the validity of the other's scriptures within their own field and for their particular purpose. The *Sarvāgamaprāmāṇyavāda,* for instance, was upheld by such authors as Yāmunācārya. This being so, how can we concur on the definition of Tantrism?

Like Hinduism, "Tantrism" is made up of a number of groups, traditions, and texts sharing *some* common elements, especially ritual ones, and having some common beliefs and notions; the total of these elements or beliefs somehow differentiate Tantric from non-Tantric Hinduism. Tantrism, however, includes practices or beliefs found in non-Tantric Hinduism too. Hence, we are faced with the uncertainty of the limits of Tantrism, its elusive nature, and if we take it comprehensively, its apparent pervasiveness. If it is pervasive, does it not loose its identity as something specific? If, therefore, we wish to keep the notion of Tantrism, we must take it as something specific and sufficiently distinguishable in spite of its uncertain limits. If so, we can consider as Tantric those groups or texts *only* where the main Tantric constituent elements previously mentioned are found.

This would limit the category of Tantrism to a few groups of people or of texts, mainly the Śaiva-Śākta traditions with a Kāpālika background, some of the Nātha, the Sahajiyā Vaiṣṇavas, and, of course, the obvious Tantric forms of Mahāyāna Buddhism. In such "hard core" Tantrism, we find a system of observances (often transgressive in nature) that are given meaning by a more or less power-oriented vision of man and the cosmos, a system where power is manipulated, where micro-macrocosmic correspondences play an essential role. Also, there is usually a high degree of esotericism (the higher, the more esoteric, the more "Tantric") together with a particular type of pantheon (not necessarily sexually differentiated however), and a particular and very developed type of ritual. Outside these qualifications, there may exist a varying number and proportion of Tantric traits, but not Tantrism as such.

With such a definition, could we include the Pāñcarātra? Possibly we could include the Pāñcarātra of some of the older Saṃhitās and the *Lakṣmitantra,* of course, since it is heavily influenced by Śaivism. Surely, we would not include the Kashmiri Pāñcarātrins who insisted they were a Vedic *śākha,* nor the more recent Srīvaiṣṇavas. But how much of Śaivism should we include apart from the Bhairavāgamas? Is the Āgamic Śaivasiddhānta really Tantric? Yes, it is, but mostly owing to its ritual aspect and because it is the *Samānyaśāstra* of the followers of the Bhairavāgamas. What about the modern "Vedantized" Śrīvidyā of South India which traces its *guruparaṃpara* to Śaṅkaracarya and whose Tantric conceptions are so toned down in order to fit into orthodox Brahmin circles that it is hardly Tantric anymore?

Another approach to Tantrism and to its definition might be to stress its ritual aspect without omitting entirely the ideological side, but subordinating it to ritual. One would underline the particular and proliferating nature of the ritual, and its conjunction with speculations and practices concerning the power of the word (mantras, etc.). Ritual also involves the manipulation of power and a pattern that combines the assertion of the identity or fusion of worshiper and worshiped (*nādevo devam arcayet*) together with an ensemble of offerings and obeisances (*upacāra*) to the deity (or Buddhist entity), who is treated as an honored guest. It is important to stress that such rituals entail an intense inner participation—body, mind, and word—of the worshiper in the ritual he carries out. The main merit of an essentially ritual approach to the definition of Tantrism is that it applies equally well to Hindu and to Buddhist Tantrism and that it can apply not only to Indian-Himalayan-Tibetan, but to Chinese Buddhism also. Its drawback is that ritual is not only that of the cult. It includes other aspects of the Tantric adept's life and observances. Furthermore, Tantric and non-Tantric rites are often not only performed by the same person (in different circumstances), but also sometimes during the same ritual. We cannot, therefore, content ourselves with the ritual approach to Tantrism.

But are we not facing a sea of troubles simply because we want to define something that does not exist except in our minds? Having coined the term Tantrism, we want it to mean something specific. Those in India or elsewhere, whose observances were Tantric, never used the term Tantrism nor did they give the term Tantric the same meaning as we do. Some would not even describe themselves as *tāntrika.* They simply followed the beliefs and practices that were current in their times in their own social groups. What were these? Simply they were the various forms taken by Hinduism and Buddhism as they evolved over the course of centuries, mainly under the influence of the Indian, Tibetan, or Chinese spheres and/or by a process of internal transformation.

Tantrism, thus, would be quite simply the various forms taken over the course of time by large sections of Hinduism or Buddhism. Depending upon the background, the origins, and the local influences, the evolution was more or less marked by a rejection of the orthodox Vedic rules and notions; it included more or less local autochthonous cults and beliefs, local religious behaviors, and magical and/or other practices. All of this resulted in the more or less "Tantric" character of the different groups concerned. But, whatever the case, the variety of Tantra that baffles us might very well be nothing more than some of the ways in which Hinduism or Buddhism were actually understood, believed, and practiced by Indian, Tibetan, and Chinese practicioners during the last two millennia. These various religious forms we may decide to call Tantric in order to differentiate them from older or different forms of the same religions, but we ought not try to set them apart as a particular religious entity that we choose to call Tantrism, an entity that probably never existed as such.

We would thus be rid of the difficult notion of Tantrism. This would be very convenient! But is it possible? I am not sure. I fear we still have to toil to find a solution to the problem of Tantrism.

NOTES

1. An earlier draft of this paper was presented at the *Tantra Occluded: 1992—Conference of the Society for Tantric Studies* at Menlo Park, California, in May 1992.

2. Herbert V. Guenther, *The Life and Teaching of Naropa* (Oxford: Clarendon Press, 1963).

3. Mircea Eliade, *Techniques du Yoga* (Paris: Gallimard, 1948).

4. Sanjukta Gupta, Dirk Jan Hoens, and Teun Goudriaan, *Hindu Tantrism* (Leiden: E.J. Brill, 1979) 7–9.

5. In a review published in *Journal Asiatique* 256 (1968): 267.

6. Madeleine Biardeau, *L'hindousime, Anthropolgie d'une religion* (Paris: Flammarion, 1991).

2

Early Evidence for Tantric Religion

David N. Lorenzen

The history of early Tantric religion is not easy to write. Although manuscript libraries contain hundreds, even thousands of different Tantric texts, both Hindu and Buddhist, no manuscript bearing a date before the mid-ninth century has been found, a date long after the initial rise of this movement. Relevant contemporary inscriptions, a key element in any chronological and geographical reconstruction of the early stages of Tantric religion, are unfortunately very few in number. Another problem is that the range of phenomena covered by the term "Tantric religion" has been subject to different interpretations. In spite of all this, much headway has already been made in overcoming these problems and, today, scholars can speak with some assurance about at least the broad outlines of the early history of the movement. The present essay attempts to give an overview of the conclusions historians have so far reached in this field.[1]

The first problem is that of definition. Does the term "Tantric religion" cover only those cults directly associated with the Sanskrit texts known as Tantras, Saṃhitās and Āgamas, or does it also include a wide range of "popular" religious phenomena that can be broadly classified as being "magical" in character? Are the texts and followers of Haṭha Yoga tradition, especially the Nātha or Kānaphaṭā yogīs, to be considered as Tantric? Are all, or nearly all, of the Hindu and Buddhist religious traditions dedicated to female deities Tantric?[2]

Differences of opinion about these questions exist for the simple reason that two different definitions of Tantric religion are possible and indeed both are used. A narrow definition considers as Tantric only religious phenomena directly associated with the Tantras, Saṃhitās and Āgamas. Since these texts are almost all written in Sanskrit, it can be assumed that the social base of Tantric religion narrowly defined in this way has been mostly literate, upper caste, and resident in or near towns and cities.

A wide definition of Tantric religion adds to the religion based on these Sanskrit texts an ample range of popular "magical" beliefs and practices including much of Śākta and Haṭha Yoga traditions. To the extent that these popular religions are literate, many of their texts are written in vernacular languages. The main social base of this more widely defined Tantric religion can be assumed to have been less well-educated, lower caste, and generally more rural than its more Sanskritic counterpart.

In this essay I will accept a wide definition of Tantric religion, but this dual character of the movement remains a significant problem. Stated somewhat differently, there is a clear sense that the more elitist and Sanskritized manifestations of Tantric religion are more Tantric than those that are more popular and magical in character.

Even if we use a wide definition of Tantric religion, however, the epigraphic evidence for its existence is quite limited. This makes a close determination of its geographic spread and its historical chronology quite difficult. As for geography, we know that Tantric religion was primarily a northern phenomena, although it also had some following in parts of the South. Its chief centers of influence have been eastern north India (Bihar, Bengal, and Assam), Kashmir, Nepal, and Tibet, and perhaps the Punjab and Rajasthan (depending in part on whether one counts the Nāth tradition as Tantric). As for chronology, the earliest clear and datable evidence of full-blown Tantric religion appears in four literary texts written in Sanskrit of the seventh century C.E.: Bāṇabhaṭṭa's *Kādambarī* and *Harṣacartita,* Mahendravarman's *Mattavilāsa,* and Daṇḍin's *Daśakumāracarita.* The surviving Tantric texts themselves seem to nearly all date from a slightly or considerably later period, from approximately the eighth to the eighteenth centuries.

These two facts—the northern and medieval provenance of Tantric tradition—make the recovery of its history particularly difficult since the northern region was under the direct control of the Muslim rulers from about the beginning of the twelfth century. With the curious exception of the patronage given by several of the Mughal emperors, including both Akbar and Aurangzeb, to the Nāth yogis of Jakhbar in the Punjab,[3] none of the Muslim rulers of India is known to have been a supporter of Tantric religious cults. An unknown number of Tantric centers, most notably the Buddhist monastaries at Nalanda and Vikramasila, were most probably destroyed by Mulsim armies. In any case, royal patronage for all non-Muslim religions, except at the level of minor vassals and *zamindars* (land owners), evidently mostly dried up in the regions dominated by Muslim overlords. For most of the period from 1200 to 1800 C.E., this included most of the Indian subcontinent.[4]

A third major problem concerns the nature of the social institutions of Tantric religion. Surviving early epigraphs relating to religious institutions almost all register donations of land and/or money and other goods and services to temples, monasteries, and Brahmin *agrahāra* (landgrant) villages. It is known that many Tantric ascetics organized themselves into "sects," "orders," or "preceptorial lines" such as those of the Kaulas, Kāpālikas, and Nāths. It also seems to be the case that only a few of these sects and orders established large temples or monasteries. There has always been something secretive, individualistic, and countercultural about Tantric religion, rather like Gnostic Christianity in Europe and North Africa, and this has tended to discourage the creation of Tantric temples and monasteries, although Buddhist monasteries under Tantric influence such as those at Nalanda and Vikramasila, not to mention many in Nepal and Tibet, represent an obvious exception to this rule.

Most of the sources that document the early stages of Tantric religion are reasonably well known. The discussion that follows will represent a didactic review of these sources, treating separately each of the different constituent components of the wide and loosely organized complex that comes to be known as "Tantric religion." This procedure should clearly illustrate that while some components are quite ancient, the complex as a whole cannot be documented before the fifth or sixth centuries C.E. The existence of a specific Hindu Tantric sect, that of the Kāpālikas, is also first documented about that time. By about the seventh century, Tantric Buddhism seems to have been flourishing in several monasteries of Bihar. The basic categories of documentation, each relating to a major component of broadly defined Tantric religion, can be conveniently arranged as follows: (1) sources relating to shamanic and yogic beliefs and practices; (2) those relating to Śākta worship, especially worship of the Mātṛkās and demon-killing forms of Hindu and Buddhist goddesses; (3) those relating to specific schools of Tantric religion such as the Kāpālikas and Kaulas; (4) the Tantric texts themselves. Whenever possible, emphasis will be given to epigraphic documentation.

The earliest sources relating to shamanic and yogic beliefs and practices in India are mostly literary and are ancient, abundant, and widespread. This is hardly surprising since such beliefs and practices—those that aim at control over the mind, the body, and the physical world—are a virtual universal of human behavior. The most striking early evidence for shamanic-yogic practices in India is found in the famous "wild *muni*" (seer) hymn of the *Ṛg Veda* (10.136), probably dating from about the beginning of the first millennium before the Common Era. In this hymn, the *munis* are described as having ecstatic, altered states of consciousness and also the magical ability to fly on the wind.

What is perhaps more surprising than the evidence of this Vedic hymn, however, is the quite early development of a systematized set of yogic beliefs and practices that eventually became codified in the classical *Yoga-sūtras* of Patañjalī and in later Haṭha Yoga texts such as the *Haṭha Yoga Pradīpikā* of Svātmarāma. These beliefs and practices are already clearly in evidence in the *Chāndogya Upaniṣad* (8.6.6) and the *Śvetāśvatara Upaniṣād* (2.8–13), texts dating respectively from about the early and middle first millennium before the Common Era. The *Chāndogya* refers to the mystical anatomy of *nāḍīs* (veins or nerves), while the *Śvetāśvatara* describes the basic meditative posture and techniques of sense and breath control. These beliefs and practices were expounded in more systematic form in Patañjalī's *Yoga-sūtras*, possibly about the beginning of the Common Era.

Although Patañjalī's text is not usually considered to be Tantric in character, the transition to the more Tantric Haṭha Yoga involves more a shift in emphasis than a basic change in the nature of yogic beliefs and practices. Specifically, Haṭha Yoga emphasizes the development of the psychic control over the natural processes of aging and death (already a significant aim of Yoga in the *Yoga-sūtras* and the *Bhagavad-gītā*), control over the sexual organs through such practices as the *vajrolī mudrā* (retention of bodily fluids), and the interior visualization of and control over the mystical anatomy of *nāḍīs* and *cakras.* This control over the mystical anatomy is also thought to lead to knowledge of and control over the microcosmic-macrocosmic links between this anatomy and the external world of nature. This in turn leads to the acquisition of the supernatural powers known (*siddhis*). Haṭha Yoga adepts also invoke the supposed magical power of sacred oral formulas (*mantras*) and sacred diagrams (*yantras* and *maṇḍalas*). Even these formulas and diagrams, however, have a history going back to Vedic times.

This shamanic-yogic component of Tantrism first appears in a more clearly Tantric form in the seventh century texts of Bāṇabhaṭṭa and Daṇḍin. In Bāṇa's *Harṣacarita,* a "great Śaiva" (*mahāśaiva*) ascetic from the southern Deccan named Bhairavācārya is said to have befriended Harṣa's ancestor Puṣpabhūti. Puṣpabhūti assists Bhairavācārya in the realization of a powerful spell (*mahāmantra*) called the Mahākālahṛdaya. The object of the spell is to subdue a zombie (*vetāla*). Bhairavācārya is said to reside near an old temple of the Mothers (*mātṛs*). The ceremony itself takes place at "an empty building near a great cremation ground on the fourteenth night of the dark fortnight" and involves the celebration of a fire rite in the mouth of a corpse. Bāṇa's portrait of a Tantric ascetic from southern India in *Kādambarī* is more comic in tone but similar in content. Daṇḍin's *Daśakumāracarita,* on the other hand, describes its Tantric ascetic as an evil *siddha* (one with supranormal powers). Another seventh century text, Mahendravarman's *Mattavilāsa* features a Tantric Kāpālika ascetic, but he is portrayed more as a hedonistic clown than as a shamanic yogi. After the seventh century, Tantric ascetics are frequently mentioned in Sanskrit literature.[5]

A second major component of Tantric religion is the worship of female deities, particularly those who manifest a fierce character. Like the shamanic-yogic component of Tantrism, the worship of female deities has a long history in India and may be regarded as a near universal characteristic of human societies. The Vedic antecedents of goddess worship appear in a series of hymns dedicated to the goddess of the dawn, Uṣas, and a number of hymns dedicated in whole or part to river goddesses, to the goddess of speech, Vāc, or to other minor female deities. None of these hymns, however, negates the obvious fact that Vedic religion is decidedly patriarchal in character. Early hymns to the Great Goddess, the Goddess of whom all individual goddesses are merely forms or aspects, are found in the *Mahābhārata* and *Harivaṃśa,* the *Devī Māhātmya* section of the *Mārkaṇḍeya Purāṇa,* the *Caṇḍi-śataka* attributed (probably falsely) to Bāṇabhaṭṭa, and the *Gaūḍavaho* of Vākpati.[6] All these texts refer to the fierce, demon-killing forms of the Goddess, most prominently the form named Mahiṣamardinī, the destroyer of the buffalo demon Mahiṣa. The battle between this Goddess, often identified as a form of Durgā-Pārvati, and Mahiśa is mentioned in all these sources (except perhaps the *Harivaṃśa*) and is recounted in detail in the *Devī Māhātmya* and the *Caṇḍi-śataka.*

Sculptural representations of Mahiśamardinī have been found that date to the Gupta period [7] and the earlier Kushan period.[8] The earliest epigraphic mention of this goddess is probably that found in a late sixth century C.E. Nagarjuni Hill (Gaya District) cave inscription of Anatavarman of the Maukhari Dynasty.

> May the Devi's foot, its gleaming nails emitting a mass of rays, point the way to the abode of riches. Her foot challenges with its splendor the full beauty of a blossomed lotus. With its twinkling anklet it contemptuously rests on the head of Mahiṣāsura. It rewards your condition as petitioner that suits the expression of firm devotion.[9]

The same inscription mentions Katyayani and Bhāvanī as the alternate names of this same Great Goddess. This inscription and the hymns to the Great Goddess in the above-mentioned texts illustrate the relatively early development of mature Śākta religion and its increasing association with fierce, demon-killing forms of the Goddess, forms that can said to be Tantric-flavored, if not necessarily fully Tantric.

Goddess worship seems to have become more definitely Tantric in character in connection with the rise of a group of seven (or more) goddesses known as mothers or Mātṛkās. They are mentioned in the *Mahābhārata* as well as early Puranic literature, *Bṛhatsaṃhitā* and other relatively ancient texts. In Bāṇabhaṭṭa's *Harṣacarita,* the Tantric ascetic Bhairavācārya is said to stay near an old temple dedicated to the Mātṛkās. Bhāsa's *Cārudatta,* Śūdraka's *Mṛcchakaṭika,* and Bāṇabhaṭṭa's *Kādambarī* also refer to these goddesses especially in connection with offerings made at crossroads.[10]

In the present text, however, more important is a reference to these goddesses in the stone inscription of Viśvavarman, found at Gangadhar in Rajasthan and dated in 423 C.E.[11] This is often identified as the earliest epigraphic evidence for Tantric religion.[12] Two other important early epigraphic references to these goddesses appear in the Bihar stone pillar inscription of Skanda Gupta or Pūru Gupta (fifth century C.E.?)[13] and the rock inscription of Svāmibhaṭa (sixth century C.E. ?) from Deogarh in Jhansi District.[14] The Mātṛkās are also regularly invoked in the preambles of the inscriptions of the Kadambas and Early Calukyas from the mid-fifth century onward.[15]

The description of the Mātṛkās found in the Gangadhar inscription merits some discussion. The passage that refers to them in this record has been given a somewhat different interpretation by J. F. Fleet[16] and by A. L. Basham.[17] Verse twenty-three states:

> For the sake of religious merit, the king's minister had them construct this terrifying home of the Mothers, filled full of female demons (ḍākinī) . . .

these Mothers impel the great booming of the rain clouds and rouse the ocean with the mighty wind that arises from the Tantras.[18]

In this passage from the Gangadhar inscription, the words *ḍākinī* and *tantra* both clearly suggest an association with Tantric religion. According to Monier-Williams, the *ḍākinīs* are said to feed on human flesh. It is, I think, quite probable that the word *tantra* here refers to the Tantras themselves, but, as Basham points out,[19] the word has several other meanings including "a drug" and "a spell (*mantra*)." One must reluctantly agree with Basham that here "we must leave the question [of the meaning of the word *tantra*] open, recognizing that this inscription gives no proof of the existence of a developed literature of Tantrism in the fifth century A.D."[20]

The classic description of the Mātṛkās is found in the *Devī Māhātmya,* a text traditionally included as a part of the *Mārkaṇḍeya Purāṇa.*[21] It is generally accepted as the earliest and most important text of Śākta religion. Most portions of this text can be said with some confidence to have been written "before the close of the sixth century A.D."[22] The text describes the Mātṛkās as being created from the "energies" (*śaktis*) of the gods Brahma, Śiva, Skanda, Visnu (the *śaktis* Vaiṣṇavī, Vārāhī, and Nārasiṃhī) Indra, and Caṇḍika in order to help the Goddess destroy the armies of the demons Sumbha and Nisumba.[23]

An interesting Kalacuri inscription from Pujaripali, near Sarangarh, Chhattisgarh, praises several of these and other demon-killing goddesses in verses that are evidently directly inspired by the *Devī Māhātmya.* The inscription is dated either in about 1150 C.E. or in 1088 C.E. It clearly shows that, by this time, the *Devī Māhātmya* was accepted as a basic source of Śākta religion.

The early evidence for the existence of specific sects and vows of Tantric religion pertains mostly to the Kāpālikas, sometimes identified as Somasiddhātins or Mahāvratins. They are first mentioned in several literary sources including dubious references in the *Maitrāyaṇīya Upaniṣad* and the *Yajñavalkya smṛti* and a more credible reference in Hala's *Gātha-saptasatī* (third to fifth century C.E.) and in two texts of the astronomer-mathematician Varāhamihira (c. 500–575 C.E.). Starting with Mahendravaman's early seventh century farce, the *Mattavilāsa,* literary references to Kāpālikas become quite common.[24] As far as epigraphs are concerned, there are in fact only three or four that have been clearly identified as registering donations to or from Kāpālika ascetics. These are the following: (1) an Igatpuri (Nasik district) copper plate inscription of the early Cālukya king Nāgavardhana (seventh century C.E.) that registers a donation to a Kāpāleśvara temple and the Mahāvratin ascetics residing in it; (2) a Tilakwada (Baroda District) copper plate inscription (1047 C.E.) of a subordinate of the Paramāra king Bhoja that registers a donation to "the *muni* Dinkara, a Mahāvrata-dhara who was like the Kāpālin Śaṅkara in bodily form"; (3) the Kalanupaka (Nalgonda District, A.P.) inscription 1050 C.E. that registers a land grant made by a Kāpālika ascetic named Somibhaṭṭāraka to an individual named Caṇḍamayya; and (4) a sixth century C.E.

inscription from Bangalore District that registers a land grant by a king Durvinīta to a Brahman named Kāpāliśarman (who may or may not be Kāpālika). In addition, a clear reference to a Somasiddhāntin ascetic named Vāgiśa Bhaṭṭa is found in a 1171 C.E. inscription from Tiruvorriyur (Chingleput District, Tamilnadu).[25]

The 1050 C.E. inscription of the Kāpālika Somibhaṭṭaraka is particularly important since it includes a physical description of this ascetic and his vestments that agrees remarkably well with the descriptions of the Kāpālika vestments in texts by the Vaiṣṇava theologians Yāmunācārya and Rāmānuja, even to common use of the term *ṣaṇmudrā* (six insignia) to identify the key items.[26] The same two theologians also identify the Kālāmukhas as being Tantric ascetics, but this attribution of a Tantric character to them was probably willfully mistaken.[27] The numerous inscriptions registering donations to Kālāmukha ascetics and temples clearly show them to belong to a non-Tantric South Indian sect descended from the Pāśupatas. Whatever the case may be, the earliest epigraphs refer to the Kālāmukhas, dated 806 and 810 C.E., were found at Nandi Hill in Kolar District at Karnataka.[28] Another early record, the undated Tandikonda grant of the eastern Cālukya king Ammaraja II (946–970 C.E.), registers a donation to a group of Kālāmukhas located at a temple at Vijayawada (Bezwada) about sixty miles from the mouth of the Krishna River. Also worth mentioning is a short inscription found at Anaji in Dharwar District that records a gift of land to a temple connected with the Kālāmukha Śākti-pāriṣad.[29]

Epigraphic references to other Tantric sects such as the Kaulas are apparently quite rare, but systematic research on this question remains to be done. Mark Dyczkowski has, however, made considerable progress in sorting out the Kaula affiliation of many Tantric texts.[30] Also relevant in this context is a Cambodian inscription of about 1052 C.E. that tells how "king Jayavarman II's court priest Śivalakaivalya at the beginning of the ninth century (A.D. 802?) installed a royal cult based upon the four Tantric books brought from elsewhere . . . The texts in question are the Śiraścheda, Nayottara, Sammohana, and Vīṇāśikha."[31] Although these texts may not be specifically Kaula, they belong to the tradition of *vāma* (left) Tantras, some of which are associated directly with the Kaulas.

When we turn to the earliest evidence for the existence of Tantric Buddhism, we find that this consists primarily of sculptures of fierce deities such as Trailokyavijaya, Cuṇḍa, and Saṃvara and of sexually engaged (*yuganaddha*) male and female deities.[32] The principal monasteries where such Tantric sculptures have been found are those at Nalanda in Patna District, at Antichak in Bhagaipur District (often identified with ancient Vikramasila), at Paharpur in Rajshahi District, and in other sites in the northeastern region.[33] Nalanda seems to be the oldest of these monastic sites. Its foundation has been dated to the mid-fifth century C.E. It is unclear, however, whether the Tantric images found at this site belong to the earliest stages of its development.[34]

Finally, we come to the question of the dates of the earliest specifically Tantric texts, especially the Tantras, Saṃhitās, and Āgamas belonging to different

Tantric sects or schools. Apart from the somewhat dubious reference to *tantra* in the Gangadhar inscription of 423 C.E., the earliest clear reference to Tantric texts seems to occur in Bāṇabhaṭṭa's *Kādambarī*. In his description of a South Indian Tantric ascetic, Bāṇabhaṭṭa says that "he had made a collection of manuscripts of jugglery, Tantras, and *mantras* (which were written) in letters of red lac on palm leaves (tinged with) smoke."[35]

According to D. C. Sircar,[36] Buddhist tradition claims that "Padmavajra, author of the *Hevajra Tantra,* was the preceptor of Anagavajra, a son of king Gopāla who founded the Pāla dynasty in Bengal about the middle of the eighth century A.D." Sircar also notes that some scholars date the composition of this text as early as "shortly before 693 A.D." D. L. Snellgrove similarly estimates that "the *Hevajra-Tantra* [was] existing in its present form towards the end of the eight century."[37] On the other hand, Alex Wayman has ascribed another early Buddhist Tantra, the *Guhyasamājatantra,* "on a purely tentative basis, . . . to the fourth century A.D."[38] His reason for suggesting this early date does not bear scrutiny.

Hindu Tantrism is probably slightly older than its Buddhist counterpart, but early Hindu Tantras cannot be dated with any precision. Some earlier Pāñcaratra texts, insofar as these are Tantric in character, may date from the fifth century C.E., but these dates are highly speculative.[39] Much the same comments can be made about the Śaiva Āgamas preserved mostly in southern India.[40]

Goudriaan claims that the oldest surviving Tantric manuscript known, a copy of the *Pārameśvaramata,* bears a ninth century date equivalent to 858 or 859 C.E.[41] He also notes, however, that the mention of many other Tantric texts "as venerable authorities" in Abhinavagupta's great *Tantrāloka,* written sometime around 1000 C.E., "renders it at least probable that Tantric literature existed already two or more centuries before. . . ." [42]

In terms of its philosophical sophistication, Kashmiri Śaiva tradition represents the richest development of Tantric literature. In recent years there has been a veritable flood of scholarly publications in this field.[43] Its greatest traditional scholar, Abhinavagupta, wrote such Tantric works as *Tantrāloka, Tantrāsara* and *Parātriṃsikāvivaraṇa* in about the early middle part of the eleventh century.[44] A fair amount about the earlier history of Kashmiri Śaivism is known, above all from the discussions of Abhinavagupta's *Tantrāloka.* Nonetheless, few if any of the earlier sources, except for some of the Śaiva Āgamas themselves can be dated before the eighth or ninth centuries.

One interesting Buddhist Tantric school is represented by the Buddhist Siddha authors of the *Caryāgītikoṣa,* a collection of religious songs written in a language most scholars regard as an early form of Bengali. These songs, in fact represent the oldest examples of Tantric literature written in an early form of a modern vernacular language. D. L. Snellgrove[45] and Per Kvaerne[46] place most of these songs in about the eleventh century. It is possible that a few of the Siddhas to whom some of the songs are attributed may have lived a century or two earlier. In particular, Saraha may date from the ninth century and Lui (perhaps the same as Matsyendra) from the late ninth or early tenth century.[47]

Another Tantric (or Tantra-influenced) sect that has had an impressive literary output, in both Sanskrit and vernacular languages, is that of the Nāths or Kānphaṭa Yogīs.[48] Most of its texts deal with aspects of Haṭha Yoga. None can be safely dated before the tenth century C.E., however, the legendary founders of the sect, Gorakhnāth and his teacher Matsyendra, probably did not live much earlier than a century or two before this date.[49] It is notable, however, that this tradition spread throughout India in the medieval period, including even in the South where it is represented by the Tamil Siddhas. Basing himself on Zvelebil,[50] Goudriaan claims that: "the oldest Tamil Siddha, Tirumular, perhaps flourished in the seventh century A.D.; the apogee of the Tamil Siddha literature, however, lasted from the tenth to the fifteenth century."[51]

The Nāth tradition seems to have historical connections with the earlier Kāpālikas,[52] but this is too poorly documented to be of much help in dating the beginnings of Nāth tradition. The main influence of this tradition was in northern India during the later medieval period. During the early nineteenth century it became a virtual state religion in the kingdom of Mān Singh in Jodhpur, Rajasthan.[53] It also had a strong historical influence on the devotional Vārakarī tradition of Maharashtra (through the preceptorial line of Jñaneśvar), and later Kabīr, Raidās, Gurū, Nānak, Dādū and others.

In summary, it can be said that Tantric religion as a recognizable complex of beliefs and practices is first documented, in very sketchy fashion, in the fifth century C.E. and relatively rapidly increased its influence in succeeding centuries within both Hinduism and Buddhism. It became particularly strong in North India (excepting perhaps the state of Uttar Pradesh, but including Bangladesh and parts of Pakistan), in Nepal and Tibet, and in parts of southern India. By the ninth or tenth centuries, Tantric religion, both Hindu and Buddhist, had become extremely influential, perhaps even dominant, in many of these areas.

Buddhist Tantrism together with other forms of Buddhism, died out in India by the late twelfth and thirteenth centuries. It has survived in Nepal and Tibet but has lost influence in Tibet since Chinese occupation and the introduction of modern secular education. Hindu Tantrism remained popular during all the medieval period, but it seems to have lost most of its popular and intellectual support during the nineteenth century, largely as a result of the efforts of Indian reformers, both liberals and conservatives, to "purify" Hindu tradition. Nonethelss, Tantrism continued to have an active presence in at least the Benares region until the early decades of the twentieth century.[54] Today it no longer exists as a significant organized force in India or other countries (with the possible exceptions of Bali, Bhutan, Tibet, and Nepal). Nonetheless, many of its beliefs and practices are now well-integrated within more mainstream Hinduism and Buddhism. In at least this assimilated form, Tantric religion remains alive and well.

NOTES

1. The best surveys are those of Teun Goudriaan, "Introduction, History and Philosophy," *Hindu Tantrism,* ed. Teun Goudriaan, Sanjukta Gupta, and Dirk Jan Hoens (Leiden: E.J. Brill, 1979); and "Hindu Tantric Literature in Sanskrit," *Hindu Tantric and Sakta Literature,* ed., Teun Goudriaan and Sanjukta Gupta, eds., (Weisbaden: Otto Harrassowitz, 1981). See also the discussions of André Padoux, *Recherches sur la symbolique et l'energie de sa parole,* 2d ed. (Paris: Edicions E. de Boccard, 1975), and, "Tantrism," in *Encyclopedia of Religion,* vol. 14, ed. Mircea Eliade (New York: Macmillan, 1987), 273–75; P. V. Kane, *History of Dharmaśāstra,* vol. 5, pt. 2

2. Goudriaan and Padoux have written intellegent attempts to define Tantrism. See Goudrian, "Introduction, History and Philosophy," 7–91; and Padoux, "Tantrism," 14:273–75.

3. B. N. Goswamy and J. S. Grewel, *The Mughals and the Jogis of Jakhbar* (Simla: Indian Institute of Advanced Study, 1967).

4. See Sheldon Pollock for a partly opposing argument that patronage for non-Muslim culture, at least in the case of Sanskrit literature, did not dry up to the extent claimed by Alberuni and most modern historians; "Rāmāyana and the Political Imaginary in Medieval India," *The Journal of Asian Studies* 52, no. 2 (1993): 261–97.

5. The descriptions of these and other Tantric ascetics and rites found in such literary texts are quoted in translation and discussed in more detail in David Lorenzen, *The Kāpālikas and Kālāmukhas: Two Lost Śaivite Sects,* 2d rev. ed. (Delhi: Motilal Banarsidass, 1991), 16–23, 54–55.

6. J. N. Tiwari, *Goddess Cults in Ancient India: With Special Reference to the First Seven Centuries A.D.* (Delhi: Sundeep Prakashan, 1985), 61–94.

7. Thomas B. Coburn, *Devī Māhātmya: the Crystallization of the Goddesss Tradition* (Delhi: Motilal Banarsidass, 1984), 92–93; and J.N. Banerjea, *The Development of Hindu Iconography,* 3rd ed. (New Delhi: Munshiram Manoharlal, 1974), 497–500.

8. Gritli Von Mitterwallner, "The Kūṣāna Type of the Goddess Mahiṣāsuramardinī as Compared to the Gupta and Medieval Types," *German Scholars on India* (Bombay: 1976), 2: 196–213.

9. My translation. See John Faithful Fleet, *Inscriptions of the Early Gupta Kings and Their Successors, Corpus Inscriptionum Indicarum* 3 (Varanasi: Indological Book House, 1963r), 226–28. The goddess Bhadrāryā or Bhadrāyakā, possibly a form of Pārvatī-Durgā, is mentioned in the Bihar pillar inscription of Skanda Gupta or Pūru Gupta; see D. C. Sircar, *Select Inscriptions Bearing on Indian History and Civilization,* 2nd ed. (Calcutta: University of Calcutta, 1966), 1:325–28.

10. Katherine Anne Harper, *Seven Hindu Goddesses of Spiritual Transformation: The Iconography of the Saptamatrikas* (Lewiston, N.Y.: The Edwin Mellen Press, 1989); and Tiwari, *Goddess Cults,* 95–99.

11. Fleet, *Inscriptions,* 72–78; Sircar, *Select Inscriptions,* 399–405.

12. A. L. Basham, "Notes on the Origins of Śāktism and Tantrism," *Religion and Society in Ancient India: Sudhakar Chattopadhyaya Commemoration Volume* (Calcutta: Roy &

Chowdhury, 1984), 148–54; and M. C. Joshi, "Śākta-Tantrism in the Gupta Age," *Aruṇa Bhārati: Prof. A. N. Jani Felicitation Volume* (Baroda: Oriental Institute, 1983), 77–81.

13. Fleet, *Inscriptions*, 47–52; Sircar, *Select Inscriptions*, 325–28.

14. Daya Ram Sahni, "Deogarh Rock Inscription of Svāmibhaṭa," *Epigraphica Indica* 18 (1925–1926): 125–27.

15. See: J. N. Tiwari's brilliant historical study of goddess cults in ancient India, 94–181; and N. N. Bhattacharyya, *The Indian Mother Goddess*, 2d ed. (Columbia, Mo.: South Asia Books, 1977).

16. Fleet, *Inscriptions*, 72–78.

17. Basham, "Notes," 148–50.

18. I have substituted the reconstruction "[*pracu*]*dita-*" for Fleet's and Basham's [*pramu*]*dita-*." Neither Fleet's nor Basham's translation is completely satisfactory. In particular, I am not convinced by Basham's renderings of *ambhonidhi* as "cloud' rather than "ocean" and of *ghana* as "cymbal" rather than "dense," "thick," "multitude," "cloud," or "darkness." My rendering supports Basham's suggestion of a connection with rain-making better than his own translation.

19. Basham, "Notes, 149–50.

20. Ibid., 150.

21. See Thomas B. Coburn, *Devī-Māhātmya: the Crystallization of the Goddess Tradition* (Delhi: Motilal Banarsidass, 1984); and *Encountering the Goddess: A Translation of the Devī-Māhātmya and a Study of Its Interpretation* (Albany: State University of New York Press, 1991).

22. Tiwari, *Goddess Cults*, 63–64 and 74–75.

23. See especially chapters seven and eight of the *Devī Māhātmya*. The numbers and names of these Mātṛkās vary considerably in different texts; see Tiwari, *Goddess Cults*, 94–181.

24. Lorenzen, *Kāpālikas*, 13–71.

25. Ibid., 24–31, 219–22.

26. Ibid., 219–20.

27. Ibid., 4–6, 107–110.

28. Ibid., 160–61.

29. Ibid., 160–61, 141–42, 232.

30. Mark Dyczkowski, *The Canon of the Śaivāgama and the Kubjikā Tantras of the Western Kaula Tradition* (Albany: State University of New York Press, 1988).

31. Goudriaan, "Hindu Tantric Literature in Sanskrit," 21. See also ibid., 36–38.

32. Susan L.Huntington, *The Pala-Sena Schools of Sculpture* (Leiden: E.J. Brill, 1984) 7, 17–18n.

33. Ibid., 88–131, 153–54, 160–64.

34. Ibid., 96, 108–116.

35. Lorenzen *Kāpālikas*, (1991), 181.

36. *The Śākta Pithas* (Delhi: Motilal Banarsidass, n.d.[first published in 1948]), 12.

37. *The Hevajra Tantra: Critical Study*, Part 1 (London: Oxford University Press, 1959), 14.

38. *Yoga of the Guhyasamājatantra: The Arcane Lore of Forty Verses. A Buddhist Tantra Commentary* (Delhi: Motilal Barnarsidass, 1977), 99.

39. See the discussions by Goudriaan, "Introduction, History and Philosophy," 9–11, 20–21; and Sanjukta Gupta, "The Changing Pattern of Pancaratra Initiation: A Case Study in the Reinterpretation of Ritual," *Selected Studies on Ritual in the Indian Religions: Essays to D. H. Hoens,* ed. Ria Kloppenborg (Leiden: E.J. Brill, 1983): 69–71.

40. Jan Gonda, *Medieval Religious Literature in Sanskrit* (Wiesbaden: Otto Harrassowitz, 1977), 163–215; and Alexis Sanderson, "Review of N. R. Bhatt's editions of *Mataṅgapārameśvarāgama* and *Rauravottarāgama*" in *Bulletin of the School of Oriental and African Studies* 48 (1985): 564–68.

41. Goudriaan, "Hindu Tantric Literature," 21.

42. Ibid, 20–21.

43. For an up-to-date bibliography on this subject, see Paul Eduardo Muller-Ortega, *The Triadic Heart of Śiva* (Albany: State University of New York Press, 1989).

44. Ibid, 45–47.

45. See David L. Snellgrove's contribution in *Buddhist Texts Through the Ages,* ed. Edward Conze in collaboration with I. B. Homer, David Snellgrove and Arthur Waley (Boston: Shambala, 1990), I:13–14n.

46. Per Kvaerne, *An Anthology of Buddhist Tantric Songs: A Study of the Caryāgīti,* 2nd ed. (Bangkok: White Orchid Press, 1986), 5–7.

47. Ibid.

48. On the sect's early history, see the works of George W. Briggs, *Gorakhnāth and the Kānphata Yogīs* (Calcutta: YMCA Publishing House, 1938); Shashibhusan Dasgupta, *Obscure Religious Cults,* 2nd ed. (Calcutta: Firma K.L. Mudhopadhyay, 1962); K. V. Zvelibel, *The Poets of the Powers* (London: Rider, 1973); R. Venkataraman, *History of the Tamil Siddha Cult* (Ennes: 1990); and Hajariprasad Dvivedi, *Nath-sampraday* (in Hindi) (Varanasi: Naivedya Niketan, 1966).

49. David Lorenzen, "Gorakhnath," *Encyclopedia of Religions,* ed. Mircea Eliade (New York: Macmillan, 1987), 6:77–78.

50. Zvelebil, *Poets,* 18, 73.

51. Goudriaan, "Introduction, History and Philosophy," 23.

52. Lorenzen, *Kāpālikas,* 35–38.

53. Daniel Gold, "Ascenso y caída del poder de los yoguīs: Jodhpur, 1803–1842," *Estudio de Asia y Africa* 27, no.1 (1992): 9–27.

54. Goudriaan and Gupta, *Hindu Tantric,* 1991.

Part II

THE HISTORY AND DEVELOPMENT OF TANTRA

3

Historical and Iconographic Aspects of Śākta Tantrism

M. C. Joshi

The Sanskrit term *tantra* derives from the verb *tan* meaning to expand, and thus, it literally denotes anything that can be stretched or extended like threads on a loom.[1] In its developed form, Tantra refers to a complex of cultic practices, rituals, mysticism, and secret rites that are based on a philosophy and deep spiritual devotion centering on the concept of Supreme Power. That power, called Śākti, has diverse manifestations. According to traditional beliefs, the Tantras, whether associated with Śāktism or other sectarian orders of Indian origin, evolved in remote antiquity and were interwoven with an intricate mythology. Assessment of the available data, both literary and archaeological, provides information on the origin and growth of Śākta Tantrism and other similar systems. Śākta Tantrism has its roots in prehistoric concepts of a fertile mother goddess and ancient systems for her worship. Scores of her representations dating to the Upper Paleolithic, if not earlier, attest to her primary importance in India's most ancient culture.

The earliest example of an Indian mother goddess figurine dates to the Upper Paleolithic. Found in the Belan Valley near Allahabad in Uttar Pradesh by the late G. R. Sharma, the image is made of bone and is carved in the round; in shape it resembles a harpoon. On the basis of carbon 14 determinations, it has been dated between 23,840 (plus or minus 830 years) B.C. E. and 17,765 (plus or minus 340 years).[2] Also dating to the Upper Paleolithic are colorful stones marked with natural triangles. Sharma found the first of these stones resting on an area of raised ground at Baghor in Son Valley, near Mirzapur in Uttar Pradesh. According to Sharma, several similar stones now have been found in that same area; they presently are under worship as Argarimai or Mother-Fire.[3] These stones with triangles, Sharma claims, are related to a primitive mother goddess. They also may demonstrate connections to the later Tantric use of *yantras* in which triangles manifest a vital symbolism connected with fertility. While we have no specific comments to offer on Sharma's hypothesis, it should be noted that it is difficult to trace a direct link between the archaeological evidence from Belan and Baghor and those goddess figurines that have been found in later Neolithic and Chalcolithic excavations.

Of the interesting Mother Goddess figurines brought to light in recent times in Pakistan mention should be made of specimens found at Sheri Khan Tarakai in the Bannu District and Mehargarh-Nausharo. The former site, dated between 4500 and 3000 B.C.E. by the excavators, has yielded several female figurines, both plain and painted; the various examples can be placed into three broad classes: (1) examples with a pinched nose and wearing a headdress with curled horns; (2) examples with a black spot showing affiliations with a snake goddess; (3) examples showing exaggerated genitalia. Of the three groups, the most significant is the third, in which figurines with one enlarged female organ have traces of a male genital above. Excavators have identified this rare type as being hermaphroditic.[4] Related to this group is a protohistoric female fertility figure from Periano Ghundai, Pakistan, in which only the lower half is marked with a *yoni.*

Most of the protohistoric Mother Goddess figurines are executed in a primitive style with conventionalized features; those found at Harappa and Nausharo in Pakistan, however, are somewhat more refined.[5] Mother Goddess figures from Harappa and Mohenjo Daro demonstrate a variety of styles; the diversity may indicate the existence of different craft or religious traditions in Harappan culture. Two Harappan sites in India, Lothal in Gujarat and Banawali in Haryana, have yielded Goddess images that may indicate religious diversity in the Harappan population of the subcontinent as well. Representation of female deities on the Indus seals and sealings include indications of rituals involving animal sacrifice. Cultic forms of a fertility goddess appear on seals showing a female figure standing in the branches of the pipal tree. It is likely that the Mother Goddesses represented in terra-cotta and the female deities carved on seals represented two types of beliefs pertaining to worship of goddesses in at least two levels of the society that were located in the same settlement; in other words, an authoritarian class and a common class may have had two distinct modes of worship. Given our current knowledge, we are unable to understand fully the position of a Mother Goddess as a fertility deity or, for that matter, the role of other female divinities in the religious fabric of the protohistoric societies of India. It is uncertain if the Harappan population had any idea of a single supreme Goddess with or without a male counterpart or if they were governed by magician-priests or even if they had a highly developed religion.[6]

From the later Chalcolithic culture, a tiny clay figurine of a headless goddess is worthy of mention. Found in a small container at Ingamgaon in Maharashtra, the image was buried under the floor of a house (1300 B.C.E. to 1000 B.C.E.).[7] The headless figures has a parallel in the medieval form of the Tantric Devi known as Chinnamasta.

The oldest literary works in India, the Vedas, preserve some interesting elements of Śākta Tantrism. Of the Vedic female divinities, the most significant for the historical development of Śāktism are Aditi (Universal Mother), Uṣa (Dawn), Rātrī (Night), Sarasvatī (Supreme Mother and the River), Vāc (Speech), and

Pṛthivī (Earth) who together with Dyaus (Sky) represented the elements of universal parenthood as did Śākti and Śiva of later times. Sarasvatī also is called Bhāratī, a name that later became a synonym for language and speech.

Important to the growth of Śāktism was the Vedic Vāc who represented the first perception of infinite, incomprehensible and invisible Energy in the form of sound. In fact, Vāc had four stages—the subtle state called *Parā Vāc,* the internal vibrant stage called *Paśyantī,* the more developed vibrant form called *Madhyamā Vāc,* and the externally audible sound called *Vaikharī. Parā* and *Paśyantī* represented the higher stages of perception; but, according to tradition, the realization of *mantras* as divine words was possible only in the state of *Madhyamā Vāc.* Thus, in the *Atharva Veda* (19–71–1), Vāc was called Veda Mātā or the Mother of the Vedas (*Stutāmayā sahitā Vedamātā*). Similarly, the later Tantras call the Goddess *Śabdānām Jananī,* that is, Creator of Words.[8] In our search for the roots of Śāktism, we cite the important Vedic hymn called the *Vāgambhṛni Sūkta* from the *Ṛg Veda* (10.125). The hymn, was composed by Vāc, the daughter of the sage Ambhṛna. In the hymn, Vāc refers to herself as the female energy that is Supreme Power, the upholder of sovereignty and the controller of various deities such as Vasu, Soma, Tvastā, the Rudras, and the Ādityas. She also is called a source of treasures, sustainer of nature's forces, and bestower of favors. Without doubt, the hymn preserves a strong elements of monotheistic thought that forms the very basis of historical Śāktism.

Important among the later Vedic female deities is Śrī Lakśmī or Śrīmā who is mentioned for the first time in the *Śrī Sūkta,* a supplementary hymn in the *Ṛg Veda.* As the goddess of prosperity, wealth, fortune, and vegetation, she is identified as a golden doe (*hiraṇyavarṇāṃ hariṇīṃ*) decked with gold and silver threads, as a column of pleasant golden light-bearing lotus garlands; she is a royal divinity seated within a golden enclosure who derives joy from the presence of trumpeting elephants (*hastināda pramodinīṃ*). Subsequently, a common symbolic form among Buddhists, Jains, and Hindus represented Lakṣmī flanked by elephants. She also was incorporated into the Tantric pantheon as one of the ten Mahāvidyās. Even now, the *Śrī Sūkta* is recited in Śākta Tantric rituals, especially during the ceremonial bath of the Goddess. The *Śrī Sūkta,* addressed to Jatavedas or Fire,[9] demonstrates that the Goddess originally was invoked for the performance of the *yajña* (fire sacrifice). One verse of the *Śrī Sūkta* refers to Jyeṣṭhā or Alakaṣmī, the goddess of poverty and misfortune, who is identical to the Mahāvidyā Dhūmāvatī of later Tantric tradition. In the *Bṛhadāraṇyaka Upaniṣad* 7.4, there is an important reference associating Vāc with such ritualistic terminology that formed the elementary components of the *mantras* of Śākta Tantrism.

By the middle of the first millennium B.C.E., certain names and forms of the goddess, such as Umā-Haimavatī, Ambikā, Durgā, Varocanī, Sarvāṇī, Bhavānī, were known. In connection with the construction of forts, the *Arthaśāstra* of Kauṭilya referred to the worship of the goddesses Aparajitā and Madirā, both of whom were recognized later in the medieval Tantric tradition. Aparajitā (Invincible) might have been an Indianized representation of the Greek Goddess Nike. Madirā (the Goddess of Wine) also was known as Sudhā or Surādevī in Tantric rituals. In Tantric texts, she is described as a lustful young damsel of sixteen years with three eyes, wearing ornaments and red clothing.[10] According to the Purāṇic tradition, Madirā or Sudhādevī, like Lakṣmī, had her birth in the churning of the ocean. What is more interesting in Kauṭilya's *Arthaśāstra* (14.117.1), there is a sacrificial chant (*mantra*) invoking Aditi and Sarasvatī and other gods for the preservation of a fort. Kauṭilya also identifies the diverse types of fires used in sacrifices, that is, the kilns of potters or smiths, funeral pyres, houses of fallen and devoted wives, or *cāṇḍalās* (outcastes). He also mentions offerings of animal fat and flesh as being part of the magical, religious practices. He indicates too that certain *mantras* with non-Sanskritic expressions should be used for the sacrifices.[11] Certainly some of the components of the magical religious rituals and practices derived from the Śābara or other aboriginal tradition of the Tantras.

The growth of the cult of the Goddess between the third century B.C.E. and the first century B.C.E. is verified by a number of beautifully carved ring stones that have been found in various urban sites ranging from Taxila to Patna, by a stone tablet from Rajgir and by terra-cotta and metal images recovered from various historical sites. The ring stones have minute carvings of various geometric designs, scrolls, animals, birds, vegetation motifs, and palm trees in conjunction with images of goddesses (Figure 2).[12] Some of the goddesses are fixed on the points of a triangle. One ring-stone from Ropar in the Punjab is carved with the image of the goddess, a devotee, a hut-shaped temple, a priest, and perhaps another devotee (Figure 3).

While most ring stones were fashioned with a hole in the center, a few were formed as a flat disk. V. S. Agrawala called these carved stones *śrīyantras*[13] (mystical diagram of the Goddess) and they, in fact, seem to be the earliest known *yantras*. It is possible that they may have been used by a specific group of Śākta devotees. The existence of a cult of the Mother Goddess around the third century B.C.E. is suggested also by a plaque from Rajgir that depicts a Mother Goddess in various poses and a priest or devotee who holds a wine cup (Figure 4). Also, the existence of a fertility cult is confirmed in part by pots that are decorated with human figures displaying conspicuous genitalia; these were found in Śuṇga and Kushan excavations at Mathura, Purana Qila in New Delhi, and Bhita near Allahabad.

Śākta Tantrism entered a more conspicuous phase of development after the beginning of the Common Era, perhaps as the result of the increasing interaction between India and West Asia, the rise of Mahāyāna Buddhism and the growth of Pāśupata Śaivism and other Brahmanical sects. Some non-Indian goddesses such as Cybele, Ardoxsho, and Nana gradually were incorporated into Brahmanism as Bhadrakālī (then Dhumā?), Mahālakṣmī and Durgā Siṁhavāhinī. Possibly the Greek Goddess Artemis was modified into Vana Durgā who subsequently was identified with Bhilli or Kiratī in the Indian aboriginal tradition. The infiltration

Figure 2 Stone disk with Mother Goddesses. Patna, Bihar. Third century B.C.E. (Courtesy of the Archaeological Survey of India)

Figure 3 Ring Stone with relief of a Mother Goddess. Ropar, Punjab. Third century B.C.E. (Courtesy of the Archaeological Survey of India)

Figure 4 Steatite stone tablet. Rajgir, Punjab. Third century B.C.E. (Courtesy of the Archaeological Survey of India)

of non-Indian goddesses into south Asia is verified by a sliver plaque excavated from Ai-Khanoum in Afghanistan depicting Cybele on a chariot drawn by lions and accompanied by Nike and priests crossing hilly terrain. In conjunction with this, we cite the Chhoti Sadari epigraph dated 491 C.E. describing an angry Devī who rides on a chariot drawn by fierce lions.[14]

During the Kushan Period, Durgā became known as Mahiśamardinī and Katyāyanī; she was depicted as being seated on a lion and was associated with Kṛṣṇa at Mathura. In the popular tradition, she was regarded as the daughter of Nanda and Yaśodā, the foster parents of Kṛṣṇ.[15] It is possible that followers of Śāktism, during the early centuries of the Christian era, borrowed certain ideas from the Pāśupatas, particularly the concept of *pāśu* or animal (equated in Tantric terminology with an uninitiated human beings) and *pāśa* (bondage to material attachments and existence). Having incorporated such ideological notions, Śāktism required a long line of *gurus* with pedigrees relating back to the first master-teacher Śiva or Ādinātha himself. An inscription by Candragupta II found at Mathura gives evidence that a tradition of *gurus* already existed among the Lakulīśa-Pāśupatas cult at Mathura. The Śāktas also adopted the idea of unbounded compassion (as if emanating from the Mother Eternal) and the term *śunya* from the philosophy of the Māhāyana Buddhism. Images of the Mātṛkās, Saṣṭhī and Durgā Mahiṣamardinī produced at Mathura may indicate that the site was a center for followers of Neo-Śāktism. One notable sculpture from this period from Mathura is of Sarasvatī as a Jain deity; apparently the Jains regarded her as the personification of the teachings of Jina. The image is dated to c.132 C.E. In her two hands, she carries a manuscript and the *akśamālā* (rosary) that symbolizes recorded and unrecorded knowledge. Although the image is Jaina, it is carved in accordance with iconographic prescriptions of Śākta thought. The *akṣamālā* held by this image is the earliest known sculpted example; it signifies the Sanskrit alphabet from the first letter *A* to the last letter *kśa.*[16] The string of letters *A* to *kṣa* has profound meaning in the Tantric tradition. The *akṣamālā* held by this representation of Sarasvatī signifies sound/speech or Vac, the first and ancient form of Śākta conceptions. The Jain Sarasvatī from Mathura, thus, embodies the personified form of the teachings of the Jaina or Tirthaṇkara as stated by Vappabhaṭṭi (c. eighth century C.E.) in his *Śāradāstotra.*[17]

The growth of *Tantrācāra* (practice of the Tantra) is evidenced by certain references in the *Divyāvadānaṃ,* a collection of Buddhist stories datable to the second or third century C.E. Particularly relevant is the story of Ānanda, a close associate of the historical Buddha. While roaming near Śrāvastī, Prakṛti the daughter of a Cāṇḍāla (Mātaṇga), fell in love with Ānanda at first glance. Realizing that the fulfillment of her desire to have him was not possible, she enlisted help from her mother, a *mahāvidhyādharī* (an expert in magical and religious formulas). The mother prepared a sacrificial altar and offered oblations of 108 *ar* flowers and recited a *mantra* to the Goddess Amalā Vīmalā.[18] The *mantra* appears to be part of the aboriginal Śabara Mātaṇga tradition; it is composed in a mixture of Prakrit and Sanskrit. Under the spell of this *mantra,* according to the text, Ānanda lost control of himself and became highly disturbed. Thereupon, the Buddha gave him a *mantra* called *Sadāksarī Vidyā* to counteract the Goddess's magic. Afterward, the Buddha explained to Ānanda the importance of the *mantra;* furthermore, he related that the *mantra* should be used in conjunction with an amuletic cord that is tied to the arm for protection. The language of the hymn is very primitive and cannot be understood fully today. It can be determined, at least, that the *mantra* is the product of a pre-Buddhist tradition and that such practices were incorporated by early Sarvāstivāda teachers in order to popularize Buddhism. Because the *mantras* invoke only female deities such as Amalā, Vīmalā, and Kuṅkumā, they seem to have specific relevance to Śāktism.

Certainly one important milestone in the development of Tantrism was the emergence of the iconographic form of Kālī, the pre-eminent form of Śākti, sometime between the Kushan and Gupta periods. The earliest reference to her is as one of the seven flames of Agni in the *Muṇḍaka Upaniṣad* (2.4). But Asvaghosha, the Buddhist author of the *Buddhacaritaṃ* and the *Saundrarānanda,* described her as a terrifying woman (divinity?) holding a skull (*kapāla*) who, as a member of Māra's army, attempted to disturb the Buddha from his meditations. The verse indicates a somewhat prejudicial Buddhist view toward the Goddess Kālī; but it is, nonetheless, a very early reference associating the *kapāla* with Kālī. The well known Sanskrit poet Kālidāsa refers to Kālī in the *Kumārasambhavaṃ;* she attended the marriage of Śiva and Pārvatī wearing ornaments made of skulls. The *Devī-Māhātmya,* the most outstanding Śākta Tantric text, also refers to Kālī as Cāmuṇḍā (7.18) as well as Mahākālī (12.37); in these forms, she represents the dreadful and destructive aspects of Supreme Power.

The *Devī Māhātmya,* also called *Candipāṭha* or *Durgā Saptasati,* is vitally important for assessing the growth of Śāktism in the context of Indian history. It generally has been dated between the fifth and seventh centuries C.E., but the absence of any references to Gaṇeśa or Gaṇeśanī suggests that it was composed during a time when Brahma did not recognize Gaṇeśa as a Bramanical deity. Other Brahmanical gods like Śiva, Viṣṇu, and Skanda are mentioned in the text, but Gaṇeśa had not yet been admitted into the orthodox fold; therefore, the text should be dated *before* the fifth century C.E., either in the early fourth or even third century C.E. There is no doubt that the *Devī Māhātmya* has all the major Tantric characteristics—total devotion to the Goddess, fire sacrifices in her honor, a system of *japa* (mystical chants), offerings that include the flesh of the devotee and references to material enjoyment (*bhukti*) and liberation (*mukti*). The text mentions the triple forms of Supreme Power that symbolically are based on three elements; they are *tama* (darkness), *raja* (brilliance), and *sattva* (purity) and they are represented respectively by her aspects called Tamasī or Yoganidrā, Mahiṣamardinī, and Sarasvatī. These forms mentioned in the *Devī Māhātmya* symbolize the inner movement of the devotee from the darkness of ignorance to the light of knowledge.

From the Gupta Period, fifth and sixth centuries C.E., one image portrays an episode from the first chapter of the *Devī Māhātmya;* the terra-cotta plaque from Bhitargaon and now in the Indian Museum in Calcutta depicts the killing of the twin demons Madhu and Kaitabha (Figure 5).[19] Viṣṇu, who sleeps on the snake Ananta, and Brahma are shown with the two demons. In this sculpture, the Gupta artist meant to convey the idea that Viṣṇu was able to kill the twin demons only through the grace of the Goddess.[20] The *Devī Māhātmya* also contains references to Mātṛkās and other forms of the goddesses such as Śākambharī, Śivadutī, and Brahmāṇī. Elements of the monotheistic philosophy of the Śākta Tantras and the concept of *bindu* (focal point for meditation) are apparent as well.

Śākti worship and its connection to Tantrism are attested to by an inscription found at Gangadhar in Rajasthan; the inscription, dated C.E. 423–424, preserves a distinct reference to Tantric practices. It records the construction of a shrine to the Goddess and Mātṛkās by a local minister. It refers also to a Tantric ritual (*tantrodbhuta*) which perhaps is based on a left-handed system of Tantrism (Vāmācāra) because it mentions ḍākinīs and calls the temple *ugraveśma* (powerful temple where all wishes are fulfilled).[21] The somewhat obliterated inscription appears to employ the terms *kuṇapa* (corpse) and *muṇḍa,* suggesting that it is referring to a shrine dedicated to the Goddess Cāmuṇḍā and the Mātṛkās and attended by ḍākinīs. We, therefore, propose that the damaged section of the inscription mentions chanting the *mantras* for Cāmuṇḍā with her corpse that were revealed to the ḍākinīs. It is quite likely that the unknown author of this inscription wanted to indicate that, during the daily *pūjā* (worship), in accordance with Tantric rites *bali* (offering of grain) was offered in the temple of the ḍākinīs which they accepted with great joy; their presence was felt in a gust of wind. That the temple's Tantric rituals are efficacious is made clear by use of the term *veśmatyugraṃ* (most powerful or effective shrine where desires are accomplished easily). Fleet's translation of the term as "terrible abode" does not seem to be quite appropriate.[22] It is apparent that, in the Gupta Period, the goddess Durgā or Kātyāyanī was worshiped in various aspects. The Chhoti Sadari epigraph also associates Śiva's Ardhanārīśvara form with Śāktism and thus the inscriptional information conforms to later Śākta worship; such notions, in fact, appear to have served as the base for the growth of the concept of *Kāmakalā* (the triad of Śākti, Śiva and Nāda-Brahmā).

For an understanding of early Tantric practices passages from the *Harṣacarita* of Bāṇa are useful. The work describes Śākta rites performed for King Pabhakaravatdhana who was gravely ill. Worship included the use of the *mātṛmaṇḍala* or *yantra* by Kulaputras and offering of human or animal heads to the God Amardaka (Rudra) as Mahābhairava, prayers to the Goddess Caṇḍikā (ten-handed Durgā) by a priest from Andhra country and the burning of *guggula* (incense) on the devotee's head in order to propitiate Mahākāla. Bāṇa's description focuses on the performance by priests of a special *anusthana* (ritual) to please the Goddess, the Mātṛkās, Bhairava, and Mahākāla as a means of curing the king. A

Figure 5 Anantasayin Viṣṇu in *yoganidra*. Bhitargaon. Fifth to sixth century C.E. (Courtesy of the Archaeological Survey of India)

significant feature of this special Śākta ritual was the offering of the worshiper's own flesh to the Goddess which, according to Śākta tradition, is a great sacrifice. The *Harṣacarita* also preserves some notable references to a secret ritual connected with some kind of *śava* (*vetāla* or zombie); the rite was performed by a Mahāśaiva Bhairāvācarya who was South Indian by birth. At the end of the *sādhana,* Bhairavācārya became a *vidyadhara* and King Prabhakaravardhana was granted a boon by the Goddess Lakṣmī (Rajya-Lakṣmī). The *Harṣacarita* also refers to the *Mūlamantra,* a secret initiation which, according to the Śaiva system, required sacrificing a buffalo on Mahanavami (the ninth day of Aśvin) and the Tantric Śrīparvata cult. Thus, the *Harṣacarita* clearly indicates that, by the seventh century, Śākta Tantrācāra was well established. This kind of religious development presupposes a much earlier beginning for Tantra. Therefore, the reference to Tantric rites in the Gangadhar inscription is quite meaningful

India's medieval period is regarded as the golden age of Tantrism, particularly for Śāktas and Buddhists. The employment of the *Pañca Makāras* (sometimes referred to as the five M's—*madya* (wine), *maithuna* (sex), *mudrā* (ritual gestures), *matsya* (consumption of fish), and *māṃsa* (consumption of flesh) in the Tantric rituals became popular. References in such works as the *Mattavilāsa Prahasana* by Mahendravarman and *Kaipūra Mañjari* by Rajasekhara inform us of the widespread awareness of such rites. In addition, alchemy was practiced by some Tantric ascetics and teachers in order to turn base metals into gold and to attain a long and healthy life. During this period, highly developed *yantras* and *maṇḍalas* were introduced to serve as the symbolic abodes of particular aspects of the Goddess. Additional goddesses such as Tripurā, Tārā, Śaradā, Bhilli or Kiratī, Mātaṅgī Padmāvatī as well as Nityās and Yoginīs were introduced. *Yantras* were regarded as superior to images because they represented the subtle (*sūkṣma*) and gross (*sthūla*) forms of Devī. Tantric tradition regards the goddess as formless, but she may assume a form at will.

The Śākta Tantras also incorporated Kuṇḍalinī Yoga into their system sometime before the eighth century. The basic concept of Kuṇḍalinī Yoga recognizes that the Supreme Power of the universe exisits in the human body where it lies in a static or dormant state. The sole aim of Tantrins is to awaken the *kuṇḍalinī* and make it rise in the body through various practices. Such notions are clearly indicated in the *Devī Purāṇā* (10.9.7–8), Śaṅkarācarya's *Saundarayalaharī* (9.10) and Bhavabhuti's *Mālatī Mādhava* (5.1). This last work also refers to the system of *nyāsa* (purification of the body through the recitation of *mantras*) (5.21).[23]

The most significant *yantra* in the Śākta Tantric tradition is the *Śrīyantra* (Figure 6) which is first referred to in an Indonesian inscription dating to the seventh century C.E.[24] We can assume then that in India, the country of origin, the *Śrīyantra* must have existed long before the time of its introduction to Indonesia. Likewise, we can be certain that the cultic deity Śrīvidyā, the goddess associated with the *Śrīyantra,* predated the seventh century inscription; her cult, however, became popular in India after the eleventh century. The Goddess Śrīvidyā oc-

Figure 6 *Śrīyantra*

cupies an important position in Śākta Tantrism. The two principal divisions of Śākta Tantra are the Kālīkulas and the Śrīkulas; each has a complicated system of *dīkṣās* (rites),and *sādhanas* (meditations) involving a principal deity and related divinities who emerge from the ultimate source, that is, the Primordial Energy. As is evident from the names, the Kālīkulas are associated with the goddesses Kālī and destruction (*samhara*); the Śrīkulas are connected to Śrī or Śrīvidyā and creation (*ṣṛṣṭi*). The complex form of these sects seems to have been developed sometime after the ninth century.

What is most significant for students of iconography is the symbolism of the goddesses with their various attributes. We are concerned here primarily with Śrī or Śrīvidyā, a creative force whose highest form is represented by the goddess Mahātripura Sundarī or Soḍaśi. Her other forms are Lalitā, Tripurā Bhairavī, Bhuvaneśvarī, Bala Tripurā-Sundarī, Rājarājeśvarī and others. Mātaṅgī, Bagalā and Kamalā who also are connected with creative aspects of Śrīvidyā are included by the Śrīkulas. According to Tantric tradition, Śrī or Śrī Vidyā emerged from Mahākāmakalā, that is union of Mahākalā (Śiva) and Ādyā (Kālī) in a state of supreme bliss. The same idea is described in the *Lalitāsahasranāman* wherein the Goddess Śrī took her birth from the fire of consciousness (*Cidāgnikuṇḍa-Sambhūtā*). Thus, Śrī or Śrī Vidyā is a creative energy responsible for the expansion of creation. The primary forms, attributes, and colors of the principal goddesses of the Śrīkulas are earthbound—red, vermilion, or yellow, which turn white or blue in specific conceptual contexts or in connection with the ideal goal of *mukti*. The goddesses of the Śrīkulas are described as beautiful, young, and charming; they carry in their hands attributes such as the noose, goad, sugarcane bow and arrow, rosary, and book. Other hands assume meaningful *mudrās*. The noose, goad, and bow and arrow that are held by the Goddess Tripurā are symbols of worldly attachment, material desires, and things causing worldly attraction.

The *Lalitāsahasranāma* explains the symbolism of the attributes of Lalitā or Śrī; she holds the noose that symbolizes material attachment (*rāga*), the goad that represents wrath (*ahaṃkāra*), and the sugarcane bow that characterizes a mind full of desires. Because the bow and five arrows are weapons of Kāmadeva, they symbolize the five basic human faculties. Other attributes such as the rosary and book that are held by the divine female deities have significance. The rosary represents the Sanskrit alphabet from *A* to *kṣa* and is the same as the *varnamālā* (universal creative energy in the form of sound); the book symbolizes all kinds of codified knowledge including *dharma* (righteous law) and *adharma* (unrighteous law), *vairāgya* (detachment), and *avairāgya* (non-detachment), *jñāna* (knowledge) and *ajñāna* (ignorance).

The Śrīkulas who are the sectarian family of the Goddess Śrīvidyā place great significance on the *Śrīyantra* (the mystical diagram of Śrī) to which the earliest reference occurs in the *Saundarya-Lahari*. As the abode of the goddess Śrī, it consists of a central point (*bindu*) five inverted and four upward triangles within eight and sixteen petaled lotuses that are surrounded by three circles (*vṛtta*). The whole is enclosed in a square (*bhūpara*) that is marked with a projection on each side to mark the entrances to the interior. Although the *Śrīyantra,* has been interpreted by scholars in metaphysical terms, it also has tangible symbolic associations, particularly its outer enclosing perimeters (*bhūpura*) which signify city or temple walls with four portals, its central pavilion formed of jewels (*ratna maṇḍapa*), and its lion throne symbolized by the central point (*bindu*). The location of Śrī or Tripurā in the *Śrīyantra* is likened to that of a great queen (*Mahārajñī*) who rules over a country or city called Śrīpura. That place, according to the *Tripurā Mahimanstotra,* is similar to the mundane world (*Saṃsāracakrāmakaṃ*). For this reason perhaps, Śrī is worshiped in royal form with the accessories (*angas*), attributes (*āyudhās*), vehicle (*vāhana*), and family (*parivara*) that befit her royal status. The *Lalitāsahasranāma Stotram* identifies Śrī, Tripurā or Lalitā as Rājarājeśvarī (Empress) and as one who enjoys absolute power (*anulaṃghita-Śāsana*).

In this context, we need to discuss the Goddess Kālī or Dakṣinakālī. She is represented as standing naked with disheveled hair on the corpse of Śiva. Kālī is of the color of a dark cloud, has three eyes and wears earrings of the dead bodies of babies and a garland of skulls. She carries a sword and a human head in two hands; the other two hands signify welcome and blessings. Her blue-black color symbolizes the limitlessness of cosmic energy or her *mahanirguṇa-rūpa* (purest formless form) that is space itself. Her blue-black complexion also characterizes her as *sarvatattvatmikā* (all elements and colors). She is without clothing because she is above all illusion; she is Kālī because she governs and creates time. The dead and powerless Śiva below her feet represents the *Nirguṇa-Brāhman* (beyond qualities or attributes). Her three eyes characterize a trio of light, that is, the sun, moon, and fire. Her grisly earrings represent *dharma* and *adharma* and her garland of skulls represents the fifty letters in the Sanskrit alphabet (*varṇamālā*), which is symbolic of *Sabdabrāhman* (union leading to ultimate peace). The girdle of severed human arms around her waist indicates the loss of karma or the end of all action. She grants protection and boons with the word of knowledge held in the upper left hand and kills animal instincts as symbolized by the severed human head in the lower left hand. The weapons held by Śākta deities including Tārā symbolize liberation (*mukti*) in that they remove all fetters of attachment (*pāśa*). Because Kālī is the embodiment of destruction, her *yantra* has only Śākti triangles or triangles with the apex pointing downward (Figure 7). Her *yantra* has no Śiva triangles (apex upward) because she does not symbolize creation. In contrast, the *Śrīyantra* has five Śākti *trikonas* (triangles) and four Śiva *trikonas* (triangles) to indicate creation.

The last notable development in Tantric Śāktism was systematizing the important Goddesses into the ten Mahāvidyās. This development occurred after the recognition of Tārā in Śāktism in eastern India around twelfth century C.E. The ten Mahāvidyās are Kālī, Tārā, Sodasī (Sundarī), Bhūvaneśvari, Tripurā Bhairavī, Mātaṅgī, Bagalā, Chinnamastā, Dhumāvatī and Kāmalā (Lakṣmī); they

***Figure** 7 Kālīyantra*

are equated with the ten incarnations of Viṣṇu. Kālī, Tārā, Chinnamastā and Dhumā are associated with the Kālīkulas; the remaining goddesses are associated with the Śrīkula. While the Supreme Mother is regarded equally by both groups, for purposes of initiation, devotees are asked to follow one of the two systems that led ultimately to the same goal.

NOTES

1. M. C. Joshi, "Tantrism and Womanhood," *Indian Horizons* 34, no. 1–2 (1985): 40–41.

2. Govardhan Rai Sharma, *Bharatiya Sanskriti Puratattvik Adhar* (1985), 32.

3. Ibid, 33.

4. Farid Khan, J. R. Knox, and D. K. Thomas, "Prehistoric and Protohistoric Settlement in Bannu District," *Pakistan Archaeology* 23 (1987–1988): 113–75.

5. J. F. Jarriage, "Excavations at Nausharo," *Pakistan Archaeology* 23 (1987–88): 149–203.

6. Shubhangana Atre feels, however, that the Harappans had a powerful female goddess; see; Shubhangana Atre, *The Archetypal Mother* (Pune: Ravish Publishers, 1987).

7. *Indian Archaeology—A Review* 1970–1971 (New Delhi: 1974), 25–26, pl. 34-A and B.

8. See *Śrī Pañchastavi,* ed. Sri Ram Saiva (Assam, V.S. 1974), 15.

9. Munish Chandra Joshi, *Etihasik Sandarbh-main Saktatantra* (New Delhi: 1988), 26–27.

10. See *Sankshipta Tantrakamanhikam* (Allahabad V.S.2023), 98–100.

11. *Arthaśāstra* 14.178.3.2 and 14.178.3.4.

12. Sharan Agrawala Vasuveda, *Bharatiya Kala* (Varanasi: 1977), 147.

13. Ibid., 95.

14. See D. C. Sirkar, *Epigraphia Indica* 30:124.

15. See *Devi-Mahatmya,* Ch. 10.

16. M. C. Joshi, "A Note on the Sarasvatī image of the Kushan Period," *Ṛtambhara (Studies in Indology),* ed. K. C. Varma (Ghaziabad: 1986): 147–48.

17. Ibid., 147–48.

18. *Divyāvadānam,* ed. P. L. Vaidya (Mithila: 1959), 314–15.

19. M. C. Joshi, "A Note on Anantasayi: A Vishnu Image from Bhitaragaon," in *Pt. Kunjilal Dube Smriti Grantha,* ed. Dr. Rajbali Pandey (Jabalpur: 1971): 393–96.

20. M. C. Joshi, "Śākta Tantrism in the Gupta Age," *Aruna Bharati: Professor A. N. Jani Felicitation Volume,* ed. B. Data (Baroda: 1983), 77–81.

21. John Faithful Fleet, *Corpus Inscriptionum Indicarum* 3 (Varanasi: 1963), 74–76.

22. Ibid, 78.

23. M. C. Joshi, "Tantrism and Womanhood," 44–46.

24. J. G. de Casparis, *Prasasti Indonesia* 2 (Bandung: 1968), 16 ff.

4

Auspicious Fragments and Uncertain Wisdom: The Roots of Śrīvidyā Śākta Tantrism in South India

Douglas Renfrew Brooks

André Padoux, whose work on Kashmiri Śaivism has helped set the course for current Tantric studies, has said that the writing of a history of Tantrism is "impossible" given the scarcity of datable materials and the present state of scholarship on the subject.[1] Teun Goudriaan, G. Sundaramoorthy, and others have proceeded with similar caution, careful to emphasize the difference between facts and speculation when discussing the genesis of Tantric ideology and practice.[2] While there is little reason to challenge Padoux or to be sanguine about the possibility of discovering new evidence, there is much to be gained by reconstructing and re-imagining the significance of materials already known and by exploiting the potential of underutilized materials that have long laid dormant. While this will lead to more specialized and localized studies, it should not prevent us from drawing broader conclusions.

Indisputable evidence pertaining to authorship and the origins of Tantric texts and traditions is usually wanting; what must be inferred leads to the unsatisfactory conclusion that much will never be known. Rather than search for Tantrism's historical primordium, it will be more useful to consider evidence that illumines specific instances and applications of Tantric thought. Like all studies in religion, Hindu Tantrism becomes important when texts and traditions are treated contextually and comparatively.[3]

In this essay Sanskrit and Tamil materials from texts and traditions are compared in order to revise our understanding of the development of Śākta Tantrism. The comparison of Sanskrit and vernacular sources remains one of the great untapped resources for Tantric studies. While scholars are aware of the potential of such sources, few have treated them systematically or comparatively.[4]

The *Tirumantiram,* a work of extraordinary breath and poetic value attributed to the seventh century *cittar* (Sanskrit: *siddha*) saint Tirumular, is the earliest representation of Tantric thought and practice among the Tamil *cittars.* The *Tirumantiram* also establishes connections with important Sanskrit-based cults and textual canons. Although unambiguously committed to a distinctive form of Tamil Śaivism, the author of the *Tirumantiram* is knowledgeable about at least one Sanskrit-based Śākta Tantric cult, the Śrīvidyā. The *Tirumantiram* apparently understands Śrīvidyā to be compatible with its own brand of Śaivism even though it has little in common with it. Why has the *Tirumantiram* taken note of Śrīvidyā and what can be concluded from it?

My objective in this essay is twofold. First, I will demonstrate beyond any doubt that the *Tirumantiram* is familiar with important aspects of systematic Śrīvidyā, which in its Sanskritic forms appears rooted in Kashmiri traditions. References suggest that Śrīvidyā had become significant enough in South India by perhaps as early as the seventh century to warrant mention in a work that expresses only limited interest in Tantric Saktism. To understand the implications of these references to Śrīvidyā it is necessary to contextualize them within the *Tirumantiram* and to compare them in light of the historical development of Sanskrit texts on Śrīvidyā. This discussion calls into question Śrīvidyā's origins as a pan-Indian Śākta Tantric cult and in regard to its ideological roots.

Second, I will show that the evidence of the *Tirumantiram* compels us to reassess the relationship between Śrīvidyā and Śaivism. The mature Śrīvidyā presented in the Sanskrit Tantras, which may date from the same period as the *Tirumantiram,* relies almost entirely on materials originating in Kashmiri Śaivism. While there is much about South India between the seventh and eleventh centuries that suggests a context for Śrīvidyā's growth, the evidence implies that Śrīvidyā did not depend on a Kashmiri environment—be it intellectual, social, or geographic—in order to sustain and advance itself as an autonomous Śākta cult. Between the seventh and eleventh centuries, Śrīvidyā became part of a completely different cultural and religious milieu in South India. This situation may cause us to revise our understanding of Śākta Tantrism's origins in light of various types of Śaivism.

The evidence suggests that by the time of the *Tirumantiram* (seventh to eleventh centuries) certain segments within Śākta Tantrism were quasi-independent from any *particular* Śaivism. The Śāktas' cultic autonomy may be recognized in fragments of ideology or ritual liturgy that becomes part of the texts and culture of non-Tantrics or of Tantrics who do not represent themselves as initiates of the cult.

In the larger sense, the *Tirumantiram* provides an unusual opportunity to examine the relationship between Tamil influences on Tantrism and pan-Indian Sanskrit Tantras and to consider relations among different Tantric cults, texts and ideologies. This investigation also provides an opportunity to consider some of the contents of the *Tirumantiram.*

Among the Śākta Tantric traditions described in the Śrīkula and Kālīkula Tantras, the cult of Tripurā or the Śrīvidyā is arguably the most systematic and elaborately depicted. Śrīvidyā literature identifies its subjects with uncharacteristic clarity and with attention to the details of its distinctive ritual and ideology.

Further, Śrīvidyā is also among a handful of Tantric cults that have become important to those who do not regard themselves initiates.[5]

We identify Śrīvidyā by a combination of elements, ideologies, and practices that cluster together and reflect the pattern of generic characteristics that define the category "Śākta Tantrism."[6] The presence of only one of Śrīvidyā's features isolated from others will not demonstrate beyond doubt that the author is aware of its systematic presentation in the Sanskrit Tantras. However, if certain particular Śrīvidyā elements are present, as they were in the *Tirumantiram,* then one can make a compelling case for its cultic presence despite the absence of a larger intellectual or ritual context. In the *Tirumantiram,* it is the presence of Śrīvidyā's distinctive *mantra,* the *śrīvidyā mantra,* and more particularly, its mode of presentation that suggest the author has more than a passing familiarity with its teachings.

Śrīvidyā is centered on the goddess Lalitā Tripurā Sundarī, who is worshiped in iconic form, as the *śrīvidyā mantra,* and as the visually striking *yantra* known as the *śrīcakra* or *śrīyantra.* Although the anthropomorphic or physical deity (*sthūlarūpa*) commonly called Lalitā or Tripurā may be secondary to advanced forms of cultic worship, she is essential to Śrīvidyā's self-definition. The combination of the mythic goddess with the *śrīvidyā mantra* and *śrīcakra* provides the critical theological triad defining Śrīvidyā.

As her name, "Three Cities," implies, Tripurā Sundarī's cult advances a triadic conception of divinity and the universe. Within the canon of Sanskrit Tantras, the cult of Tripurā, which some adepts call the Saubhagya Sampradaya or Lineage of Prosperity, is a first cousin of the Kaula traditions of Kashmiri Śaivism. Virtually the entire store of Kashmir Śaiva speculation and vocabulary is adopted and adapted to suit Śrīvidyā's Śākta focus. For example, speculation about the triadic nature of *mantras* is adopted into Śrīvidyā with little modification; precisely which *mantras* are considered superior and most powerful becomes a means by which to distinguish Śāktas from Śaivas and Śrīvidyā from other traditions.[7]

As Madhu Khanna has shown, the earliest Sanskrit expositions of Śrīvidyā are likely Kashmiri in origin and share a common intellectual idiom.[8] These Kashmiri-rooted texts, commentators, and concepts do not appear to take written forms until at least the ninth century. Our study suggests that the *structure* of Śrīvidyā ideology was likely to have been in place perhaps two centuries before its crystallization in Sanskrit texts.

Literally, "auspicious (*śrī*) wisdom (*vidyā*)" or "the wisdom of [the goddess] Śrī," Śrīvidyā embraces the pantheon of Hindu goddesses as aspects of the great goddess (*mahādevī*). Clearly, the cult is focused on Śrī as the benign (*saumya*) consort of Śiva. Although Śrīvidyā's Śrī subsumes Viṣṇu's consort and even identifies one of her roles as Viṣṇu's Śrī, she is a goddess whose identity is rooted in the Śaivite traditions. Śrī then is symbolic of Lalitā's particular character and functions. Her embodiment as auspiciousness (*śrī*) suggests she is an intrinsically beneficent deity whose dispositional power is both self-controlled and capable of controlling others.

As the supreme deity in the form of the Śākti (*paraśākti*), she is the autonomous great goddess (*mahādevī*), and yet she accepts the empowering and sometimes subservient role of wife to Śiva. In turn, Śiva cannot even stir without her.[9] The goddess's quasi-autonomy and power to subsume all other deities, including Śiva, should be seen in the larger context of Śāktism in which goddesses retain indissoluble links to the male figures in the Hindu pantheon.[10]

Śrīvidyā's Lalitā Tripurā Sundarī is best known as Devī extolled in the Thousand Names of Lalitā (*Lalitāsahasranāma*) and as the subject of the *Lalitopākhyāna,* both texts of likely South Indian origins traditionally appended to the *Brahmāṇḍa Purāṇa.*[11] In the *Lalitopākhyāna,* Lalitā's myth is established on patterns reminiscent of Durgā and other great goddesses.[12] She is called upon to destroy the demon Baṇḍāsura and creates out of herself the weaponry and the army of lesser *śāktis* necessary to complete the task. At the conclusion of the ordeal, Lalitā once again assumes the beneficent and empowering roles of mother and wife.

In the mythic sense Lalitā achieves a stature comparable to that of Durgā or Kālī; she must be feared as well as adored. But unlike these horrific aspects of the goddess, Lalitā's power is never beyond her own control. In sum, Lalitā Tripurā Sundarī is recognizable as a great goddess inasmuch as she fulfills normative expectations and yet she is distinguished by her own myth and character. By the period of the *Lalitāsahasranāma*—certainly not much later than the ninth century—Lalitā becomes the most clearly articulated complement to the figures of Durgā and Kālī: as the beneficent great goddess of the Sanskritic tradition she is then identified with regional figures.

While the *Lalitāsahasranāma* suggests that the goddess was well known to certain Sanskritized elements of society in the region by the ninth century, the importance of the Lalitā/Tripurā cult in the larger society is hardly clear. Instead, Lalitā becomes a Sanskritic paradigm with whom the benign local goddesses, such as Kāmaksī of Kanchipuram or Śivakāmasundarī of Chidambaram, are identified, usually by association with the *śrīcakra.*

The worship of Lalitā in any form or situational context is an issue best distinguished from textual presentations. Sanskrit texts critical for understanding goddess traditions in South India form only one part of the picture. Burton Stein argued that prior to the thirteenth century separate shrines to Purāṇic goddesses in Tamilnadu were rare, although images of goddesses within temples became common from at least the eighth century.[13] Thus, before the thirteenth century the worship of Lalitā or any goddess established within temples would appear limited to Brahmanical centers, such as Kanchipuram, Chidambaram, or Tiruvorriyur.[14] While Lalitā/Tripurā is apparently important to Brahmins in the textual sense, her worship does not appear to be significant in these places either before or in the immediate centuries after the composition of the *Lalitāsahasranāma.* However, her imagery and worship is perpetuated within *sampradāyas* (sects) that are not part of the cult of quasi-public temple. The Lalitā/Tripurā cult at this time remains essentially private in practice and rooted in texts that make only ideological connections to local figures.

The earliest epigraphy from South India supports this view: Durgā, Jyeṣṭhā, the fearsome sister of the benign Lakṣmī, and the Seven Mothers (Saptamātṛkā) are the favored deities in temples.[15] It is unclear whether any connection can be made between the worship of these goddesses in South India and their northern counterparts. A. L. Basham's observation that the Gangadhar Inscription dated VS 480 (423 C.E.) is an unambiguous reference to a building constructed for the worship of the Seven Mothers confirms the suspicion that goddesses were enshrined at this time but should not be taken as evidence of comparable activity in South India.[16] By the seventh century, Durgā shrines can be identified at Mahabalipuram, and by 850 at Tanjavur. After the eleventh century, however, when attentions turn toward Amman and more benign goddesses the populartiy of the earlier terrifying godesses is eclipsed. By the thirteenth century, most Śiva temples in Tamil country have a goddess shrine while, at the same time, there is a post-Chola resurgence of folk goddess worship within temples.[17] Śrīvidyā appears to make its presence felt in temples—particularly in Kanchipuram and Chidambaram—only during this period.

Prior to the thirteenth century, Śrīvidyā as a non-temple based tradition of Tantric goddess worship was likely perpetuated within the large Brahmin settlements that pervaded Tamilnadu and were supported by the peasantry. As Stein has argued, the support extended to these Brahmin communities over time produced a homogeneous high culture centered on the Vedic gods and Sanskrit learning.[18] It is within this larger framework, I believe, that Śrīvidyā becomes widely known as a Śākta cult; Lalitā's ubiquitous power and consuming character permit her to be identified with indigenous goddesses with little effect on the local figures' distinctive mythic characters.

While Śrīvidyā's anthropomorphic goddess eventually is made a part of the larger *bhakti* movement in South India, her worship as a Tantric deity centers on her *mantra* and *yantra* forms. Since the *mantra* is not often represented visually or written explicitly, it serves as a kind of template that distinguishes Śrīvidyā's distinctive presence in the world of South Indian goddesses and their cultic worship. Unlike the *yantra* whose presence or description does not prove its ritual worship, the *mantra* is more emblematic of Śrīvidyā as a personal *sādhana* restricted by the rules of initiated transmission. In other words, the *mantra,* unlike the image of Lalitā/Tripurā or the *śrīcakra,* is the element least likely to be known to noninitiates and most likely to suggest the discourse of initiates.

Lalitā Tripurā Sundarī's *śrīvidyā mantra* appears in a number of variations—too numerous to detail here—but principally two forms usually consisting of fifteen syllables. The two *pañcadaśakṣarīs* (fifteen syllables) that are the subject of textual exegeses are the Kāmarāja *vidyā,* revealed by Śiva Kāmarāja and known as *kādi* because it begins with the syllable *ka,* and the *mantra* revealed by the female sage Lopāmudrā, commonly called *hādi* or beginning with *ha.*[19] Both versions are then divided into three parts called a *kuta* or peak; each peak is named and given its own significance. Śrīvidyā's reliance on triadic symbolism is nowhere more evident than in its *mantra.* The mantra's structure is as follows:

The *kādividyā* of Kāmarāja:	The *hādividyā* of Lopāmudrā:
ka e ī la hrīm	*ha sa ka la hrīm* [*vāgbhavakūṭa*]
ha sa ka ha la hrīm	*ha sa ja ha la hrīm* [kāmarājākūṭa]
sa ka la hrīm	*sa ka la hrīm* [*śāktikūṭa*]

Not only is the *mantra's* triadic structure consistent with the patterns of Tripurā Sundarī's symbolism, its description in this particular way becomes a normative feature of the cult's self representation. In addition to her subtle *mantra,* the *yantra* or *cakra* is added.

Śrīvidyā's *śrīyantra* or *śrīcakra* also sustains the essential triadic symbolism. Despite the important variation, the *śrīcakra's* basic structure of nine interlocking triangles surrounded by two sets of eight and sixteen lotus petals remains consistent (see figure 6). The smaller triangles created out of the intersection of nine triangles plus two sets of lotus petals and three outer lines of the rectangular perimeter are treated as nine discreet circuits. Thus, the interpretation of both the whole and its parts is seen in light of triadic structures. (The nine major triangles form forty-three smaller triangles that are taken in circuit sets of fourteen, ten, ten, eight, and one. Taking the eight and sixteen lotus petals and the outer rectangles as three separate circuits there is a total of nine circuits.) The *śrīcakra* according to the so-called Kaula Śrīvidyā is its most recognizable form. By combining the *mantra,* the *yantra* and the anthropomorphic aspects of divinity with forms of yogic ritual discipline, Śrīvidyā creates a model for a systematic and detailed Tantric cult.

To identify Śrīvidyā's presence as a Tantric cult would require confirmation of these theological elements in a ritual context. Texts usually give a clear indication of these contexts by the presuming other elements of Tantric *sādhana.* Without the supporting context, the most we can say is that elements of Śrīvidyā suggest the cult's instantiation.

The connections between the goddess's triadic forms are not always possible to verify in a given context. We may see images withouth the *śrīyantra* and *śrīyantra* with images. However, the *śrīvidyā mantra* is least frequently appropriated by those who do not worship in the context of Tantric Śrīvidyā *sādhana.* Interestingly, the first mention of Śrīvidyā's *mantra* in its familiar form and structure is likely not in the Sanskrit texts in which it is clearly part of systematic *sādhana* but in the *Tirumantiram.*

The *Tirumantiram* (or *Śrīmantra,* in Sanskrit) has yet to receive thorough and systematic study.[20] Consideration of the *Tirumantiram* has thus far focused on portions of the text most indicative of dualist Śaiva theology and the interests of

Śaiva Siddhāntins who claim him as one of their own.[21] In Tirumūlar's case, the connection between words attributed to him and his reputed behaviors remains unclear, let alone his sectarian religious identity. The connection between Tirumūlar and the dualist non-Tantric Śaiva traditions that followed him deserves further scrutiny.

Tirumūlar's legacy associates his ideas about yoga with the devotionalism (*bhakti*) of incipient Śaiva Siddhānta. There is nothing within his work to suggest that he viewed himself a Tantric. Furthermore, those who claim Tirumūlar as a spiritual preceptor do not regard him a Tantric. South Indian Tantrics, including Śrīvidyā's adepts, do not assign Tirumūlar a place in their lineages (*paramparā),* give no special attention to his work, and create no mythological connections to signify his contribution to their tradition. In short, as George Hart has observed, it appears that Tantric sources and South Indian devotionalism (*bhakti*) very likely stem from separate sources.[22] At the same time, there is little doubt that much in the *Tirumantiram* also appears as part of Tantric ideology and practice. This is quite different from asserting that *Tirumantiram* is a Tantric text. Rather, it would be more accurate to say that *Tirumantiram* shares features that are characteristic of Sanskrit texts. It would appear that the *Tirumantiram* has connections with, or at the very least knowledge of, persons who were engaged inTantric behaviors and beliefs.

Before examining the fragments of Śrīvidyā that appear in the *Tirumantiram,* it is worth considering those features most characteristic of Tamil *siddhas* that suggest at least conceptual ties to Tantric thought and practice. Kamil Zvelebil's groundbreaking work has contributed much to the general discussion of the Tamil *cittar* movement and needs not be repeated here. The *Tirumantiram* is a primary source for the system of Śaiva Siddhānta, being the tenth book of its canon. The historical relationship between the *Tirumantiram* and Śaiva Siddhānta should not detain us. Tirumūlar's notions of cosmic and ethical order (that is, Sanskrit *dharma,* Tamil *aram*) and his devotion to Śiva are important issues to later Śaiva Siddhāntins.[23] Tirumūlar is apparently the first to distinguish and compare the terms *siddhāntam* (versed in *siddha*) and *vedāntam* (versed in Vedas) as well as to explicate the theological importance of the triad *pati* (Lord), *pacu* (literally, cow, but here soul), and *pācam* (bondage).[24] Furthermore, he details the thirty-six *tattvas* or principles, the three conditions (*avastha*), and their cause, the five impurities (*mala*), all of which are basic elements of Śaiva Siddhānta. There is little about these particular aspects of the work to suggest a cultic Tantrism.

Tirumūlar and later Śaiva Siddhānta share much in common with certain strands of Tantrism—especially Trika Śaivism and Śrīvidyā—but no more a Tantric movement or sect than Patañjali's Yoga or Sāṅkhya philosophy because of later Tantric assimilations. Tantrism, we should keep in mind, is created as synthetic traditions borrow, adapt, and reinterpret ideas and practices often without explicit or self-conscious efforts to claim rights of ownership or originality.

The *Tirumantiram's* major interest in any systematic tradition or canon involves the so-called Āgamas, by which is meant the twenty-eight texts Śiva revealed to the twenty-eight celestials.[25] Also mentioned are the nine Āgamas on which arrange the nine chapters (*tantiram)* of the *Tirumantiram.*[26] The *Tirumantiram's* reference to Āgamic ideas seems indisputable, especially when one considers the fifth chapter's discussion of the four paths (*cāryā* or observe vows, *kriyā* or action, yoga and *jñāna* or knowledge) and four mechanisms for the dispensation of grace (*sattinipādam*) which are characteristics of Āgamic thought.[27]

The term Āgama is often used to gloss the term Tantra in Sanskrit texts and is sometimes used interchangeably in the titles of texts. However, the subjects and categories discussed in the twenty-eight Āgama's are not characteristic of typical Tantra, which eschews the Āgama's interest in temples and public worship.[28] What is more important here is that the Āgamas are sectarian Śaiva texts; while the *Tirumantiram's* Āgamic-based Śaivism includes a place for Śākti, it is clearly not Śākta in any way comparable to the Śākta Tantras.

The *Tirumantiram's* references to the Āgamas and use of names of Āgamas as chapter headings is somewhat confusing when compared to texts that form the heart of the Śaiva Siddhānta canon.[29] For example, the so-called *Kalottarāgama* does not appear in the canon. In addition, the twenty-eight Āgamas refer only to the doctrines of Śaiva Siddhānta although the verse cites the *Kāmikāgama* and *Karanāgama,* which are primarily texts on sculpture.[30] In short, it seems unclear precisely which Āgamas the *Tirumantiram* has in mind or which texts it wishes to exclude from the larger canon of Tantras and Āgamas. It makes no mention of the Śrīkula Tantras in which Śrīvidyā is a primary subject and which stands apart from the canon of Śaiva Āgamas.[31] Yet, unlike the staunchly sectarian and rather anti-Vedic Śaivāgamas, the *Tirumantiram's* is not hostile to the teachings of the Veda or Vedānta. Rather, it treats the Vedic traditions as distinct and implies that they are inferior to Śaiva Siddhānta.

The *Tirumantiram* does evince interest in subjects characteristic of the Tantras that are not central to the Śaiva Āgamas. This is particularly evident in chapter three where some of the esoteric and individually oriented practices involve Haṭha Yoga, such as withholding the semen (*ūrdvaretasam*), the arresting of urine and the acquisition of the eight great perfections (*mahāsiddhi*).[32] While these interests constitute only a small portion of the text, they reveal much about the *Tirumantiram's* worldview and a familiarity with traditions beyond exoteric Śaivism.

Perhaps best known as the principal exponent of yoga in Tamil, Tirumūlar equates unqualified love (*anpu*) of Śiva with knowledge (*kalvi*) of him.[33] Put differently, Śiva is both love and knowledge; any differences are purely superficial.

> Fools say: Love and God are different things. Nobody knows that God is love. When they realize that God is love, they repose in the oneness of love and God.[34]

Love consummates the individual's unmediated experience of Śiva in this world, thus distinguishing the *siddha* as one who has achieved perfection through divine light (*ọli*), power (*catti,* Sanskrit *śakti*), and the yogic concentration (*samadhi*).[35] Yoga is the method for achieving a relationship with Śiva that grants immortality and provides the means for obtaining the freedom to act as Śiva acts. As part of this yoga, Tirumūlar endorses the possibility of bodily perfection, asserts that one can attain complete control over bodily functions, and specific techniques achieve the four stages of liberation preliminary to final liberation. All of these notions are in consonance with ideologies and practices advanced in the Śākta Tantras, although none are exclusively Tantric.

In the fourth chapter of the *Tirumantiram,* the author extols the excellence and power of the five-letter *mantra* of Śiva, *civayanama.* Clearly, *Tirumantiram* is a text about *mantras* as well as other forms of devotion directed primarily at Śiva. Later, in the sixth and seventh chapters, Śaivism is extolled as the path to immortality and the worship of the *liṇga* as Śiva's principal form. Whether Tirumūlar's advocacy of *liṇga* worship reflects the situation within temples is unclear. K. R. Srinivasan has suggested that it was not until about 800 C.E. that modes of worship at Śiva shrines shifted from the anthropomorphic Śiva images to the aniconic *liṇga.*[36] It was also during this time that female as well as male deities within shrines became increasingly important for emergent popular *bhakti* movements—both Śaiva and Vaiṣṇava. Tirumūlar's influential position as a vernacular poet with links to Sanskritized Brahmanical religion may have contributed to this focusing on the Śiva *liṇga* as the primary image and, by association, his relationship to the goddess.

From the number and content of his remarks about yoga-oriented Śaivism, the *Tirumantiram's* concern for gods other than Śiva is secondary. While we hear of the sage Akattiyar (Sanskrit, Agastya) and special attention is paid to Murukan (Sanskrit, Skanda), the text places them in the larger framework of Śaivism. Yet, unlike some of the other *cittar* works, the *Tirumantiram* seems decidedly less interested in evangelism and the cause of denominationalism.

Perhaps more interesting is that the *Tirumantiram* is not only about *mantras,* but is itself a handbook of *mantras.* Some portions of the text do not fit into the mold of devotional poetry nor do they advance the exposition of Śaiva doctrines and practices.[37] Many verses are little more than obscure, mystical expressions of transcendence that appear in the form of *mantras.* Tirumūlar's relatively simple Tamil syntax belies a strong penchant for esoterism, which, in certain instances, suggests a deliberate effort to push issues of semantic meaning to the periphery. These more obscure *mantras* are rendered into a cryptic, poetical Tamil evincing strong Sanskritic influences.

Whether Tirumūlar deliberately intended the verses to function as *mantras* in addition to whatever literal or poetical meanings they may possess is uncertain. Nayanar poet-saints who followed after him, such as Sundaramurti, clearly viewed the *Tirumantiram* as *mantra,* that is, as sounds that in themselves are a source of power and serve as forms of divine revelation. At issue is the relationship created between discursive speech and *mantras.* It is in this context we should also consider his references to the goddess in the form of a *mantra.*

The *Tirumantiram* passage cited here is the first verse of the twelfth chapter of the fourth book; it begins the section entitled *bhuvanāpati cakkaram* (Sanskrit, *bhuvanāpati cakra*), that is, the *cakra* of Bhuvanāpati.

kakarāti yoraintun kanīya poṇmai
akarāti yorarattame polūm
cakararāti yornankun tancutta vēnmai
kakarati muittai kamīya muttiye[38]

Provided this verse is not an especially late interpolation—and there is nothing to suggest that it is—its reference is quite extraordinary inasmuch as it has nothing to do with Tirumūlar's Śaivism. Although there is no reason to consider this verse any more a *mantra* than the others that bear obscure semantic meanings, a familiarity with Tantra *mantraśastra* makes clear its reference. It might be translated:

The letter *ka* and [all the] five letters are golden colored.
The letter *a* [that is, *ha*] and [all] the six are red in color.
The four letters beginning with *ca* [that is, *sa*] are pure white.
The three *vidyās* [that is, *kūtas* or peaks] beginning with *ka* give desired liberation.

The verse refers to the *kādi* version of the fifteen syllable principal *mantra* (*mulamantra*) of Śrīvidyā.[39] Apparent here is the tripartite structure of the *śrī-vidyā,* the division of its fifteen syllables into three sets of five, six, and four letters. To these *kūṭas* of letters, which are called *vidyās,* another word for *mantras,* are attached a color symbolism.

While Sanskrit sources usually encode the *mantra's* syllables in order to conceal them from the uninitiated and prevent unwanted articulation beyond the confines of the ritual, the *Tirumantiram* seems not to have shared this penchant for secrecy; neither are all of the *mantra's* syllables listed explicitly.[40] Instead, familiarity with the *mantra* is presumed to such an extent that its configuration and relationship to the goddess are neither concealed nor explained.

While no further reference to the *śrīvidyā mantra* is made in the *Tirumantiram,* the Tamil rendering of the *mantra* should not mislead us. Although in Sanskrit the second *kūta* of the *śrīvidyā mantra* begins with the syllable *ha* rather than *a,* as the second line of Tamil verse begins, this is a result of the substitution in literary Tamil of *a* for *ha. Ha* is not part of literary Tamil. In the third line of the verse, the Tamil *ca* is the common letter used for all three forms of the Sanskrit sibilant and refers to the first Sanskrit *sa.*

Aware of both its fifteen syllable form and triadic structure, the text focuses on a pattern of color symbolism that may be related to *cittar* ideology. While there can be no doubt that it is Śrīvidyā's most important and distinctive *mantra* mentioned here, the symbolic description curiously fails to reappear in other Tamil texts on *mantras* or in Sanskrit Śrīvidyā texts. Contemporary adepts with whom I have had contact are either completely unaware of the verse or are unable to decipher the *Tirumantiram's* symbolism.

In the first line of the verse—in clear reference to the five syllables of the *kādi mantra's vāgbhava kūṭa*—the five letters appear gold (*poṉ*) in color, the six letters of the *kāmāraja kūṭa* are red and the four of the *śakti kūṭa* are "pure white." Elsewhere in the *Tirumantiram,* Zvelebil tells us that Tirumūlar uses words for colors (and substances) to refer to alchemical and theological concepts with well-understood symbolic meanings in Tamil; these meanings are in consonance with pan-Indian Tantric traditions.[41] It is possible then that Tirumūlar wants to connect the meanings of these technical alchemical terms to the *śrīvidyā mantra.* Thus, the *vāgbhava kūṭa* which signifies in Sanskrit Śrīvidyā texts "the essence of speech," is, according to Tirumūlar, *poṉ* or gold; in symbolic *cittar* terminology, this color refers to the combination of menstrual flow and semen, that is, the powerful confluence of Śākti and Śiva. If Tirumūlar, in fact, does mean to say that the *vāgbhava kūṭa* is symbolic of Śiva and Śākti's joining, later Śrīvidyā sources would concur. Since the *vāgbhava kūṭa* begins with the syllable *ka,* which according to later sources signifies Śiva (since it is derived according to the principles of esoteric etymology from the Sanskrit verbal root *kan,* meaning to illumine, one of Śiva's principal qualities) and ends with *hrīm,* the traditional seed-syllable (*bījākṣara*) of the goddess Bhuvaneśvarī, it is possible that Tirumūlar understands the first line of the *śrīvidyā mantra* as a reference to the joining of Śiva and Śakti.[42] Such an interpretation is in general agreement with the traditions of *mantra* interpretation offered by the important later-day Śrīvidyā writer Bhāskararāya.[43] We should note, however, that Tirumūlar makes no reference to the Śrīvidyā esoteric etymology.

In Śrīvidyā texts, the syllables of the *kāmarāja kūṭa* are traditionally understood to signify the essence or nature of Śiva in the form of Lord (or King) of desire or Kāmarāja. Following the line of reasoning suggested above, one would suspect that Tirumūlar means to signify Śiva by his reference to these syllables as red in color. Perhaps Tirumūlar means that because desire is signified by red, so Śiva's *kāmarāja kūṭa* is likewise red. Red, however, in both Tantric traditions and in *cittar* vocabulary usually refers to Śakti because it is the color of activity, blood, and the essence of the goddess; it is usually contrasted with the colors white or silver, which signify passivity, semen, the moon, and the essence of Śiva.[44] In the *Tirumantiram's* verse the six letters of the *kāmarāja kūṭa* are Śakti's color, red, while the four letters of the *śakti kūṭa,* which represent the essence of the goddess, are Śiva's color, white. There may be inverted symbolic meaning here—a situation that is not without precedent in Śrīvidyā circles.[45] In other words for the sake of identifying Śiva with Śakti and vice versa, the author has resorted to this inversion of symbolic meanings. However, it seems equally plausible that he has something in mind that we do not understand fully and that his references to color with respect to the sections of the *mantra* may not be related to the other symbolic schemes employed in the *Tirumantiram.* We may never know exactly what Tirumūlar means by assigning colors to the three *kūṭas* of the Śrīvidyā *mantra.*

More important is that Tirumūlar has an interest in and apparently a sophisticated knowledge of a *mantra* critical to the definition of a sectarian form of Śākta Tantrism. Zvelebil has noted that *Tirumantiram,* unlike later works of Śaivite *bhakti,* exhibits no preference for any cultic deity or temple cult.[46] But clearly Zvelebil cannot mean that the text exhibits no knowledge of such Śaiva or Śākta sectarian traditions. Rather, such observations about the worship of the gods in temples and in various forms, whether *mantra* and *yantra* or anthropomorphic image, advance the interests of Śaivite sectarianism. Tirumūlar's staunch Śaivism should not be construed as a narrow chauvinism. While the overwhelming majority of his references are to Śiva, the goddess and the Tamil deity Murukan are also important members of his pantheon.

Tirumantiram verses 1021–1050 describe the goddess Tripurā and a Tripurā *cakra* that is the seat of Śaktī.[47] The figure of Tripurā described here appears to be the familiar aspect of the goddess emerging in full form in the later *Lalitopākhyāna* and the *Lalitāhasranāma.* In other words, this appears to be the goddess of the Śrīvidyā cult. There is no explicit connection made between the image of Tripurā described here and the *śrīvidyā mantra* as mentioned in verse 1282; nor does he link Tripurā to the *śrīcakra.* Instead he describes a separate Tripurā *cakra* without a connection to the *śrīcakra.* The Tripurā *cakra* he describes is not part of later Śrīvidyā tradition nor does it emerge again in any Tantric literature in Sanskrit of which I am aware. Like many of the specifics in the *Tirumantiram,* this particular Tripurā *cakra* may have faded into obscurity by virtue of a more explicit identification of Tripurā with the *śrīcakra.*

We can conclude from the verses describing the Tripurā *cakra* that Tripurā in her inveterate anthropomorphic form is identified with *Paraśakti,* the supreme deity, and that her worship is popularly known in South India by the time the *Tirumantiram* was completed. She was associated with a Tripurā *cakra* but not, at least in the *Tirumantiram,* with the *śrīcakra.* On the basis of this evidence it is simply not possible to say if there are connections between the Tripurā the goddess, the Tripurā *cakra,* and the *śrīvidyā* in the *Tirumantiram.* Nonetheless, Tripurā's status as an important deity is remarkable considering the text's overwhelming Śaiva orientation.[48]

Another tentative connection between South India and Śrīvidyā may be made in a section of the *Tirumantiram* in which seven varieties of Śiva's *cakras* are described. Here the text refers to the cultic worship of Naṭarāja in the form of a *yantra* that has links to Śrīvidyā's *śrīcakra.* The *Tirumantiram* does not espouse or endorse a separate cult of Naṭarāja; neither does it assert any explicit connection between the *siddha* and the worship of Naṭarāja in Chidambaram. While the Naṭarāja cult's connections with goddess worship in Tamilnadu can be confirmed only in later sources, Tirumūlar's reference may offer an earlier connection between the Śrīvidyās and the worship in the Chidambaram temple, a contention of certain contemporary Śrīvidyā adepts.

Verses 894–978 of the *Tirumantiram* make possible reference to a Naṭarāja *yantra* in Chidambaram. In particular, contemporary adepts maintain that his reference is to a portion of the so-called *sammelana cakra* also known as the secret (*rahasya*) of Chidambaram. The *yantra,* because it is a combination (*sammelana*) of Śiva and Śākti *cakras,* is also known as the *ciddākāśarahasya* (secret of conscious space), which is identified today inside Naṭarāja's shrine. The present-day *yantra* is covered with embossed golden *bilva* leaves and attached to the wall beside the free standing image of Naṭarāja. Beneath these *bilva* leaves, according to the priests and Śrīvidyā adepts, resides the actual *sammelana cakra.* The connection between Naṭarāja's *sammelana cakra* and Śrīvidyā's *śrīcakra* is tenuous but curious when considering Tirumūlar's *Tirumantiram* and works of a later writer, Umāpatiśivācārya.[49]

There are, however, several problems in making connections between Śrīvidyā and the Naṭarāja temple in Chidambaram and Tirumūlar's reference to this particular *yantra.* First, the portion of the temple in which the *sammelana cakra* today resides almost certainly did not exist in Tirumūlar's day, that is the seventh century. The *kanaka sabha* or golden roofed sanctum that today forms the center of the temple's worship of Naṭarāja may have undergone significant renovation during the reign of Rājakesari Kulottuṅga II (1130–1150), who was responsible for expanding the importance of the goddess cult within the temple by building a separate shrine for the goddess Śivakāmasundarī called the *tirukkamakoṭṭam.*[50] Traditionalists assert that the portion of the temple with Naṭarāja's secret *sammelana cakra,* is pre–seventh century and that the *yantra* on the wall is the one to which Tirumūlar refers. This assertion is not based on any historical evidence.

From the paintings in chamber nine of the Rājarājeśvaram Temple in Tanjavur, which depict an overview of the Naṭarāja temple at Chidambaram, we can surmise that, by the time of Rājarāja I (985–1014), the Naṭarāja temple already included some kind of a *kanaka sabhā* (golden hall) as well as a *cit sabhā* (consciousness hall).[51] It is unclear whether the reference to Tirumūlar refers to either of these structures and, thus, it is impossible to verify if the reference to a *tiruvambalam cakkaram.* He may simply be referring to a Śiva *cakra* that is associated with Chidambaram.

If the Śiva *yantra* that the *Tirumantiram* describes in *sammelana cakra* can be linked to the *śrīcakra,* then there would be strong evidence suggesting the presence of all three critical elements of Śrīvidyā—the goddess Tripurā, the *śrīvidyā mantra,* and the *śrīcakra*—in Tamilnadu from as early as the seventh century and no later than the twelfth. Further, such a link would suggest the presence of the *śrīcakra* inside an established Śaiva temple. Unfortunately, the connection between Tirumūlar's *tiruvambalam cakkaram* and the *sammelana cakra* is unverifiable. Evidence suggesting a relationship between Naṭarāja's *sammelana cakra* and the *śrīcakra* comes only in the thirteenth century work of Umāpatiśivācārya.[52]

According to contemporary Śrīvidyā adepts, Tirumūlar describes only the Śiva portion of the combination (*sammelana*) *cakra*.[53] The information he offers about the identity of the *tiruvambalam cakkaram* is not particularly helpful. He makes no explicit connection between his Śiva *cakra* and the Śiva portion of the *sammelana cakra*. In verse 928, he says that the author of the *tiruvambalam cakkaram* is Śiva himself and, in v. 930, that the totality of creation in the form of the *brahmāṇḍa* is nothing other than the *tiruvambalam*. In verse 884, he supplies a description of the Śiva *cakra* that is either the *tiruvambalam cakkaram* or some portion of it.

> Draw six lines vertically and six horizontally, thus you create five squares by five and within these are written the syllables of the Śiva *mantra*.[54]

The connection between this Śiva *cakra* and the *śrīcakra* is just as uncertain as the relationship between Tirumūlar's *tiruvambalam cakkaram* and the *sammelana cakra*. There is no apparent connection between Tirumūlar's *yantra* and the so-called Śiva portions of the *śrīcakra*, that is, the four upward facing major triangles that intersect with the five downward facing Śakti triangles. This discrepancy does not prevent contemporary traditionalists from asserting that the *sammelana cakra* is actually two distinct *yantras*—one representing Śiva and one representing Śakti—which are overlain or connected with one another. They base their claim on Umāpatiśivācārya's description in his *Kuñchitāṇghristava* of the Śakti *cakra* as the *śrīcakra* and Tirumūlar's *tiruvambalam cakkaram* as the Śiva *cakra*.[55] Unfortunately, there is no way to verify independently either claim. Today the *sammelana cakra* is concealed by golden *bilva* leaves.

In sum, little can be said with certainty about the *tiruvambalam cakkaram* other than that the *Tirumantiram*'s interest in the use of *yantras* in the worship of Śiva was somehow linked to activities or deities related to Chidambaram. The evidence presented here is more important for the study of contemporary perceptions of Śrīvidyā's history than it is useful for the reconstructing the historical events surrounding Tirumūlar's life and the theological milieu of the *Tirumantiram*.

The first Sanskrit Tantra to offer a detailed exposition of the Śrīvidyā cult is thought to be the *Vāmakeśvara Tantra*, which combines two distinct texts, the *Nityaṣoḍaśikārṇava* and the *Yoginīhṛdaya*.[56] It is also generally agreed that the *Nityāṣoḍaśikārṇava* is the earlier of the two halves of the Tantra and that the first extant commentary on this portion of the text belongs to the twelfth century Jayaratha, best known for his exposition of Abhinavagupta's *Tantrāloka*.[57] Jayaratha states that the ninth-century Īśvaraśiva wrote the *Śrīrasamahodahi*, which according to Dviveda was a commentary on the *Vāmakeśvara Tantra*.[58] Provided one accepts the ninth century as the time of Īśvaraśiva, then surely the *Vāmakeśvara Tantra* comes from an earlier period. Furthermore, the text's mature and sophisticated portrayal of Tantric ritual may indicate that the tradition underwent its incipient and formative development before the text's written composition.

Interestingly, Śrīvidyā's earliest Sanskrit sources offer no suggestions about how the tradition began ideologically or ritually. Instead, the Sanskrit Tantras present the reader with a full-grown adult, as it were, one whose patterns of development are embedded in genealogy that was neither recorded nor considered important enough to rehearse. From the record of Sanskrit texts, it remains unclear precisely how old the *Vāmakeśvara Tantra* might be or what sort of Śrīvidyā may have preceded it. This situation makes the *Tirumantiram's* reference to the Śrīvidyā *mantra* all the more interesting and important.

If the *Vāmakeśvara Tantra* is any indication of the regional origins of Śrīvidyā, then it would appear that the cult of Tripurā that involved the use of the fifteen-syllable *mantra* and the *śrīcakra* is Kashmiri, or at least North Indian, in origin. This idea is supported by recent work done by Madhu Khanna on Śivānanda's trilogy.[59] If Khanna's theory of Kashmiri origins is correct, then the appearance of the Śrīvidyā in the *Tirumantiram* suggests that the tradition, or some fragment of it, had migrated south perhaps as early as these Sanskrit sources.

One can conclude certainly from the *Tirumantiram's* reference to the *mantra* that a necessary piece of Śrīvidyā was known and was present in Tamilnadu during the seventh century. Given the text's general interest in *mantraśāstra,* it is certainly plausible that it is aware of the *mantra* without knowing about the cult of Tripurā or Śrīvidyā. But that the text knows enough about this *mantra* to describe a pattern of symbolism associated with it suggests that the form, structure, and meaning of the *mantra* had undergone significant interpretation. It also seems plausible that the Tirumantiram does indeed know more about the *mantra* than it says here and that some form of systematic Śrīvidyā was being practiced in Tamilnadu by the time of its composition.

While the *Tirumantiram* does not suggest that Śrīvidyā's roots are in South India, it does advance our understanding of the intellectual and historical milieu in Tamilnadu at the time of the emergent Tantras. Our most important conclusions about Śrīvidyā in Tamilnadu are two. First, at least one portion of Śrīvidyā, its *mantra*—one of its most advanced concepts—is understood to be congenial with Tirumūlar's *cittar* Śaivism. *Mantras* like the *śrīcakra* appear not to have been restricted to those whose primary allegiance is to the great goddess or more specifically, to *Lalitātipurasundarī.* Different forms of Śaivism create environments in which Śrīvidyā can sustain itself and even flourish. Second, it appears that Śrīvidyā established itself in a cultic sense in South India as a quasi-autonomous form of Śāktism that did not require a specifically Kashmiri Śaiva context. However woven into the ideological fabric of Kashmiri Śaivism Śrīvidyā may be in the Sanskrit Śākta Tantras, its life as a *mantra* appears independent of this particular canon.

Further suggestions about the cult of the goddess Tripurā or about *śrīcakra* in the temple cult of Naṭarāja are far less certain. At this point, the story of the cult's development, either in terms of individual elements or as a systematic form of Tantric *sādhana,* shifts to texts in Sanskrit. If, in fact, Śrīvidyā sources do come from a period before or concurrent with Tirumūlar's seventh century date—an issue still not settled—then our understanding of the chronology of the Hindu Tantras must be revised. If the sources of the so-called *Kālīkula,* that is, those centered on aspects of Kālī rather than Śrī, are composed, as Teun Goudriaan maintains, well before *Śrīkula* texts which include Śrīvidyā, then these too will be affected by the evidence in the *Tirumantiram.* This evidence not only corroborates Goudriaan's point, but suggests the presence of a mature form of Śākta Tantrism well before references to the first commentaries on the Sanskrit texts.

With the evidence of the *Tirumantiram,* we can now conclude that portions of Śākta Tantrism may have been codified and disseminated orally at least two centuries *before* they are committed to written Sanskrit. While admittedly fragmentary in nature, evidence of Śrīvidyā in the *Tirumantiram* provides a beginning for contextualizing Tantrism in the history of Indian religions and establishes the presence of a form of pan-Indian Śākta Tantrism in early medieval India.[60]

NOTES

1. André Padoux, "Tantrism: Hindu Tantrism," *The Encyclopedia of Religion,* ed. Mircea Eliade (New York: Macmillan, 1987), 14:274–80.

2. See Teun Goudriaan and Sanjukta Gupta, *Hindu Tantric and Śākta Literature* (Wiesbaden: Otto Harrosswitz, 1981). (Hereafter *HTSL.*) Also see, *Arunopanisat* (*of the Śrīvidyā Tradition*), trans. Dr. G. Sundaramoorthy (Madurai: Śrīvidyā Educational Society, 1990).

3. Jonathan Z. Smith, *Imagining Religion* (Chicago: University of Chicago Press, 1982), xiii.

4. Teun Goudriaan, Sanjukta Gupta, and Dirk Jan Hoens, *Hindu Tantrism* (Leiden: E.J. Brill, 1981), 23.

5. This is the case, for example, in the Śaṅkara traditions.

6. For discussion of polythetic classification and its application in Hindu Tantrism, see Douglas Renfrew Brooks, *The Secret of the Three Cities: An Introduction to Hindu Śākta Tantrism* (Chicago: University of Chicago Press, 1990).

7. See André Padoux, *Recherches sur la symbolique et l'énergie de la parole dans certains textes tantriques* (Paris: de Boccard, 1963).

8. See Madhu Khanna, "The Concept and Liturgy of the *Śrīcakra* Based on Śivānanda's Trilogy," Unpublished Ph.D. diss. (Oxford, Eng.: Woolfson College, Oxford Universtiy, 1986).

9. See Verse One of *The Saundaryalaharī, or Flood of Beauty,* ed. and trans. by W. Norman Brown (Cambridge, Mass.: Harvard Universtiy, 1958), 48.

10. On goddesses, see David S. Kinsley, *Hindu Goddesses, Visions of the Divine Feminine in the Hindu Religious Tradition* (Berkeley: University of California Press, 1986).

11. Although an incomplete translation, see: R. Ananthakrishna Sastry, *Lalitā Sahasranāman with Bhāskararāya's Commentary translated into English* (Adyar: The Theosophical Publishing House, 1951).

12. Lalitā's myth, as it crystallizes in these appendices to the *Brahmāṇḍa Purāṇa,* follows this basic pattern with a few important variations and embellishments.

13. Burton Stein, "Devī Shrines and Folk Hinduism," *Studies in the Language and Culture of South Asia,* ed. Edwin Gerow and Margery D. Lang (Seattle: University of Washington Press, 1973), 77.

14. Ibid.

15. Ibid.

16. See A. L. Basham, "Notes on the Origins of Śāktism and Tantrism," *Religion and Society in Ancient India; Sudhakar Chattopadhyaya Commemoration Volume,* ed. Pranabananda Jash (Calcultta: Roy and Chowdhury Publishers, 1984), 148–54.

17. Stein, "Devī Shrines," 81–83.

18. Ibid., 85–86.

19. *Kādi* and *hādi* also refer to *matas* or traditional lines of interpretation. The *mantra* is part of the distinction between these lines of tradition, but it is not the only factor. For a discussion of the *hādi* school, see Khanna, "Concept and Liturgy"; and for the *kādi* line, see Brooks, *Secret of the Three Cities.*

20. All references to this work refer to volume 1 of the Tamil edition of *Thiru Manthiram of Tirumulanāyanār,* 2nd ed., ed. Thiru P. Ramanatha Pillai (Tiruneveli: The South Indian Śaiva Siddhānta Works Publishing Society, 1957). Pages in this edition are not numbered. For an important study of Tamil *siddhas* and of Tirumūlar see the work of Kamil V. Zvelebil, in particular his work *The Poets of Powers* (London: Rider and Co., 1973), 72–80.

21. The only translation of the *Tirumantiram* focuses almost exclusively on devotional verses important to Śaiva Siddhāntins; see Tirumūlar *Tirumantiram, Holy Hymns,* trans. Dr. B. Natatajan (Madras: Ites Publications, 1979).

22. See George L. Hart's cursory remarks in his work *The Poems of Ancient Tamil, Their Milieu and Their Sanskrit Counterparts* (Berkeley: Universtiy of California Press, 1978), 118, 62n.

23. For example the concepts of *pati, pacu,* and *pācam.* See Zvelebil, *Poets,* 74.

24. On Tirumūlar's relationship to Śaiva Siddhānta, see Dr. T. B. Siddhalingaiah, *Origin and Development of Śaiva Siddhānta Up to the 14th Century* (Madurai: Nepolean Press, 1979), 50–51. In verse 159, he claims the three are eternal. On the contrast between *siddhāntam* and *vedāntam,* see *Tirumanitiram,* 2329, 2331–32, 2343–44, 2346, 2354–56, 2361, and 2362–65; also Siddhalingaiah, 50. On the three basic terms of Śaiva Siddhānta, see: *Tirumantiram,* 2366–67, 2369, 2371–74, and 2380–84.

25. Ibid, 51ff; and Zvelebil, *Poets,* 74. The number of Āgamas is mentioned in verse 68 of *Tirumantiram.* For a list of the twenty-eight Āgamas and their Upāgamas, see also the introduction to the *Rudravāgama,* ed. N. R. Bhatt (Pondicherry: Pondicherry Press, 1961).

26. See Siddhalingaiah, *Origin and Development,* 50, 193n.

27. Ibid., 53.

28. This point is made clearly and in some detail by Goudriaan, *HTSL,* 7–9.

29. Siddhalingaiah, *Origin and Development,* 52.

30. Ibid., 52, 193n.

31. Mark C. G. Dyczkowski, *The Canon of the Śaivāgama and the Kubjikā Tantras of the Western Kaula Tradition* (Albany: State University of New York Press, 1988), 4ff.

32. Zvelebil, *Poets,* 75–76.

33. *Tirumantiram,* 712, 1651, 1816, 2104, and 2958.

34. Quoted from Zvelebil, *Poets,* 75.

35. Ibid., 74.

36. As cited by Stein, "Devī Shrines," 81.

37. Tirumūlar defines a *mantra* as the "perfect concentration of the mind of anything." See Kamil Zvelebil, *Tamil Literature* (Wiesbaden: Harrassowitz, 1974), 55.

38. Ibid, verse 1282, chapter 12.

39. The significance of this particular version of the *mantra* known as the *śrīvidyā mantra* in the context of the cult's history has been discussed in detail elsewhere; see Brooks, *Three Cities,* 118ff; also Khanna, "Concept and Liturgy," 96ff.

40. On the encoding of the *śrīvidyā mantra;* see Brooks, *Three Cities,* 149ff. and Khanna, "Concept and Liturgy," 96–98.

41. See Zvelebil, *Poets,* 79.

42. Douglas Renfrew Brooks, "The Śrīvidyā School of Śākta Tantrism: A Study of the Texts and Contexts of the Living Traditions in South India," Unpublished Ph.D. diss. (Harvard University, 1987), 233–35. This interpretation is based on Bhāskararāya's descriptive esoteric etymology; see *Varivasyārahasya by Bhāskararāya with his auto-commentary entitled Prakāsa,* 3rd ed., ed. and trans. Subrahmanya Sastri (Adyar, Madras: Adyar Library, 1968), 2.121–26 and 128–30. (Hereafter *VVR*).

43. Ibid., 2.121ff. and the second section of Śrīvidyānandanātha's *Saubhāgyaratnākara* (presently unedited).

44. Cf. Zvelebil, *Poets,* 79.

45. For example in Bhāskararāya's commentary on *Tripurā Upaniṣad,* he reverses the traditional attributes of Śiva and Śākti to suggest their interchangeable identities. This point is discussed in more detail in Brooks, *The Secret of the Three Cities.* 100ff.

46. Zvelebil, *Poets,* 79.

47. Pillai's *Tirumantiram* as cited above.

48. Some form of the Tripurā cult was apparently in place in South India during Tirumūlar's time. The *Tirumantiram* does not link its Tripurā with the goddess whose triadic imagery distinguishes systematic Śrīvidyā; however, the description of Tripurā as a goddess and a Tripurā *cakra* suggest that this figure was part of a cult with Tantric ritual interests.

49. Brooks, "Śrīvidyā School," 525–26.

50. Cf. *Encyclopedia of Indian Temple Architecture, South India, Lower Dravidadeśa 200*

B.C.–A.D. 1324, ed. Michael W. Meister (Delhi: American Institute of Indian Studies, Oxford Universtiy Press, 1983), 299.

51. See S. R. Balasubrahmanyam, *Middle Chola Temples' Rajaraja I to Kulottunga I* (Faridabad: Thomson Press, 1975), 33.

52. Meister, *Indian Temple Architecture,* 299.

53. *Tirumantiram,* v. 884. On the *śrīcakra* as a combination of Śiva and Śākti *cakras,* see Venkataraman, K. R., "Śākti Cult in South India," *A Cultural History of India,* 2nd ed., ed. Haridas Bhattacharyya (Calcutta: Ramakrishna Mission, 1956), 256.

54. *Tirumantiram,* v. 884.

55. The references to Śrīvidyā and the *śrīcakra* in this work will be discussed at another time. Tiksitar, in particular see verses 20, 60, 101, 109, 110, and 207.

56. See Goudriaan, *HTSL,* 59ff.

57. On the date of the *Vāmakeśvaratantra,* see V. V. Dviveda's introduction to *Yoga Tantra Granthamala,* vol. 1, *Nityāṣoḍaśikārṇava(tantra) with the Commentaries Ṛjuvimarśini of Śivananda and Arthāratnāvali of Vidyānanda* (Varanasi: Varanasesya Samskrta Visvavidyalaya, 1968).

58. Ibid., 8; and Phyllis Granoff's review of *The Kulacūḍāmani Tantra and the Vāmakeśvara Tantra with the Jayaratha Commentary,* ed. and trans. Louise M. Finn (Wiesbaden: Otto Harrossowitz, 1986) appearing in *Journal of Indian Philosophy* 17 (1989), 309–25.

59. See Khanna, "Concept and Liturgy."

60. Special thanks to my teacher and collaborator the late Dr. G. Sundaramoorthy of Madurai-Kamaraj University, Madurai, Tamilnadu for his help and insights.

5

The Structural Interplay of Tantra, Vedānta, and Bhakti: Nondualist Commentary on the Goddess

Thomas B. Coburn

One of the abiding problems for scholars of South Asian religion is how best to conceptualize the relationship between the different strands of the traditions we are trying to understand. Even if one factors out the minority traditions of the subcontinent, the problem of an adequate approach to the remainder—conventionally called "Hinduism"—looms large. The persistence of the problem is suggested by the widespread attention it has received of late, not just in scholarly circles, as a result of the convergence of religion and politics in apparently new forms. How much of the agenda of the Bharatiya Janata Party and the Visva Hindu Parishad is an expression of traditional religious sentiment, how much is a function of that sentiment in distinctly twentieth-century guise, and how much is purely political opportunism? How much truth lies in the quip that the Indians have been religious for millennia, but "Hinduism" was born in the nineteenth century? Answers to such questions are not simple nor easy to come by.

Nowhere is the problem of conceptualizing Indian religion more vexing than in trying to determine the status of Tantra and its relation to non-Tantric Hinduism. Recently we have begun to make progress on the long-standing definitional problem, and for my purposes in this article, the definition of André Padoux will suffice:

> Tantrism [is] a practical path to supernatural powers and to liberation, consisting in the use of specific practices and techniques—ritual, bodily, mental—that are always associated with a particular doctrine. These practices are intrinsically grounded in the doctrine that gives them their aim and meaning and organizes them into a pattern. Elements of the doctrine may also be associated and welded into a practical worldview, Tantrism is there.[1]

This definition acknowledges that Tantra cuts across both Buddhist and Hindu traditions, but it leaves open such unresolved questions as the historical antiquity or the social or geographic provenance of Tantrism. Opinions on these matters remain very diverse. The dominant scholarly view, of course, is that Tantrism begins in the early centuries of the Christian era and becomes a dominant feature of the Hindu landscape over the course of the next millennium. We are accustomed to thinking of Hinduism in partially overlapping historical stages—the Vedic, the epic, the Purāṇic, and then the Tantric—but we often hear an alternative voice, usually from Indian scholars, claiming much greater antiquity for Tantra. On the contemporary scene, Madeleine Biardeau indicates how very complex the situation is:

> Although tantric theory clearly distinguishes itself in its most general aspects from *bhakti,* and although it seeks to deepen this cleavage through a reversal of brahmanic values in practice as well as in a broad range of its religious literature, the gap is in fact a very small one. We find tantric themes in the *Purāṇas,* and references to the *Purāṇas* in the *Tantras* as well as authors who write commentaries in both bodies of literature. The great *Purāṇas* are read in temples in which the ritual is said to be tantric, but in which the majority of worshipers are mainstream Hindus who come to the temple with a vague notion of the meaning of ritual . . . and who would never dream of taking initiation into a tantric sect.[2]

As a modest contribution to understanding further the relationship between these concepts or texts or worldviews, I should like here to look at a particular passage from the Purāṇas and how it is interpreted by two commentators, one a Tantric of the Śrī Vidyā school, one a Vedāntin, both of whom are philosophical *advaitins* (nondualists). The passage comes from the famous sixth-century Śākta text, the *Devī-Māhātmya* or *Durgā-Saptasati,* which comprises thirteen chapters in the *Mārkaṇḍeya Purāṇa.* The commentators are two eighteenth-century figures, Nāgoji Bhaṭṭa or Nāgeśa the Vedāntin, and Bhāskararāya the Tantrin. In a recent monograph, I have explored the nature of the text and the relationship of these commentators to it in some detail.[3] What I should like to do here is look closely at a specific passage—whose discussion in my monograph is limited to one footnote because of the complexity of the commentaries on the passage—as a lens for viewing the larger conceptual issues. I leave to one side my discussion elsewhere of the commentator's biographies and of the nature and structure of their commentaries. I simply note in passing that the primary concern of both Bhāskararāya and Nāgoji Bhaṭṭa is the proper division of the verses of the *Devī-Māhātmya* into 700 *mantras* for recitation and the proper technique for reciting them. In other words, they consider it chiefly a *ritual* text, whose verbal power is to be controlled and then released, not a *philosophical* text, whose meaning is to be understood. It is all the more noteworthy, then, that both commentators do take pains to understand the meaning of this particular passage. The reasons for this are not hard to find, for it is indeed a puzzling passage, as we shall now see.

The passage comes at the very beginning of the third of the *Devī-Māhātmya*'s three episodes (*caritas*). The Goddess has previously promised to assist the gods whenever they find themselves in difficulty. The fifth chapter begins:

> Once upon a time, the two demons, Śumbha and Niśumbha . . . Took away Indra's three worlds and shares in the sacrifice. Similarly, they took away the powers of the sun, the moon, Kubera, Yama, and Varuna, . . . [Vāyu and Agni]. Then the gods, fallen from their kingdoms, were scattered and defeated [whereupon] they all . . . remembered the invincible Goddess . . . Having made up their minds, the gods went to the Himalaya, [and there] they praised the Goddess who is Viṣṇu's *māyā* [power of illusion].[4]

There follows a hymn of thirty verses, most of which designate and praise the Goddess for dwelling within all creatures in some particular form: sleep, consciousness, intelligence, hunger, etc. At the end of the hymn, the text proceeds:

> 5.37 Thus (entreated) by the gods who are filled with praise and the like, Pārvatī then went to bathe in the waters of the Ganges . . . .]
>
> 5.38 She of beautiful brows said to the gods: "Who is being praised here by you?" An auspicious (*śiva*) (form) came forth from the sheath [*kośa*] of her body (and) said:
>
> 5.39 "This hymn is made to me by those who have been vanquished by Śumbha . . . [and] Niśumbha . . . "
>
> 5.40 Since Ambikā came forth from the body sheath [*kośa*] of Pārvatī, She is sung of in all the worlds as "Kauśikī."
>
> 5.41 When she had come forth, Pārvatī became black (*kṛṣṇa*). Known as "Kālikā," she makes her abode in the Himālayas.[5]

The figure who is here called Ambikā and Kauśikī remains the central object of and the central agent in the rest of the *Devī-Māhātmya,* throughout all the proliferation of divine forms in battle. She is understood as commensurate with the Goddess with a capital *G* who has been described earlier in the text, who is also called Ambikā in her defeat of the demon Mahiṣa. However, of Pārvatī, "the black one" (Kālikā, *kṛṣṇa*), who abides in the Himalayas, we hear not a word more throughout the rest of the text. She is, quite simply, not mentioned at all.

Elsewhere I have suggested that this mysterious treatment of the forms of the Goddess is consistent with the overall spirit and apparent intention of the text. It is a *bhakti* (devotional) text. Its concern is to portray the Goddess as the fundament of the universe, to describe three of her salvific interventions in the world in some detail, and then to glorify her kaleidoscopic metamorphic potential. Like many other Purāṇic texts, the *Devī-Māhātmya* is not interested in delineating with precision how various divine forms are related to one another. Its concern is to praise, not to analyze. Indication of this is found in two facts: first, throughout the course of the narrative, the text applies over two hundred different names to the Goddess, and second, contrary to the dominant Hindu conceptualization, on one occasion the text describes *śakti* or female power as *coming forth from the Goddess herself,* not just from the male deities who are on the scene. The mysteriousness and multiplicity of the Goddess's diverse forms are not a problem for the author or compiler of the text. If anything, they enhance the wonder she evokes in her devotees.[6]

Thirteen hundred years later, however, the relationship between the several forms of the Goddess, and their bearing on pressing matters of religious truth, was the concern of our commentators. It was incumbent upon them, therefore, to dilate upon the substance of this passage. Both Nāgoji Bhaṭṭa and Bhāskararāya bring to their analysis of this passage two kinds of hermeneutical methods. They are in agreement that both of these approaches are relevant to understanding the passage, but they apply them in different ways. One is the rudimentary philosophy spelled out in the three Rahasyas or "secrets" that have been appended to the *Devī-Māhātmya* since at least the fourth century. The other is a cluster of passages drawn from the *Śiva Purāṇa.* Let us look briefly at both of these.

The Rahasyas together amount to some ninety-three verses and constitute a kind of appendix to the *Devī-Māhātmya.*[7] They are placed in the mouths of the same interlocutors as those in the *Devī-Māhātmya.* They begin with the king saying to the seer: "You have told me all about the Goddess's *avatārs.* Now please tell me about their material nature (*prakṛti*), their primary form (*pradhāna*), the Goddess's very own form (*svarūpa*), and how she is to be worshiped." The seer then proceeds to provide what one of my Indian colleagues has called "the earliest systematic statement of Śākta philosophy."[8] Charts 5.1 and 5.2 provide the important relationships in this philosophy, which is conveyed in mythological language. The important affirmations are these. The foundation of the universe is Mahālakṣmī, whose own form is both with and without characteristic marks. She is constituted of three qualities (*triguṇa*) and pervades everything. She has four arms. On seeing the universal void, she took on two other forms, in each of whom there is a predominance of one of the three qualities (*guṇas*) that are formally associated with Sāṃkhya philosophy, but that have pervaded Indian cosmological thinking since the time of the *Bhagavad Gītā.* In the form named Mahākālī, there is a predominance of *tamas guṇa* (quality of darkness), while in the one named Mahāsarasvatī there is a predominance of *sattva guṇa* (power of light, knowledge, and purity). Each of the three goddesses then produced a set of twins, one male, the other female. Mahālakṣmī proceeded to arrange three marriages—between Brahmā and Sarasvatī, between Viṣṇu and Laksmī, and between Rudra and Gaurī—and each couple was given one of the three cosmic functions of creation, preservation, and destruction. Though Mahālakṣmī has three qualities (*triguṇa*), she has an implicit predominance of the *guṇa* of *rajas* (dynamic energy) by virtue of having assigned the other *guṇas* to her other two forms. All of this activity, we should note, takes place within the realm of the unmanifest (*avyākṛtā*), as a kind of internal life of the Godhead or, more properly, the Goddesshead.

At the level of the manifest world (*vikṛti*), the Goddess also has three chief forms, "immanent" forms, if you will, with the same names as, but slightly different iconography from, their "transcendent" (*avyākṛtā*) counterparts. Each of

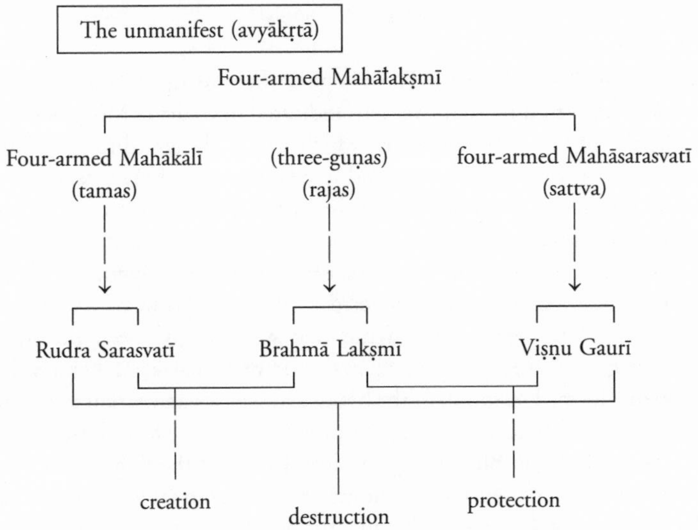

Chart 5.1 Diagram of relationships in the Prādhānika Rahasya

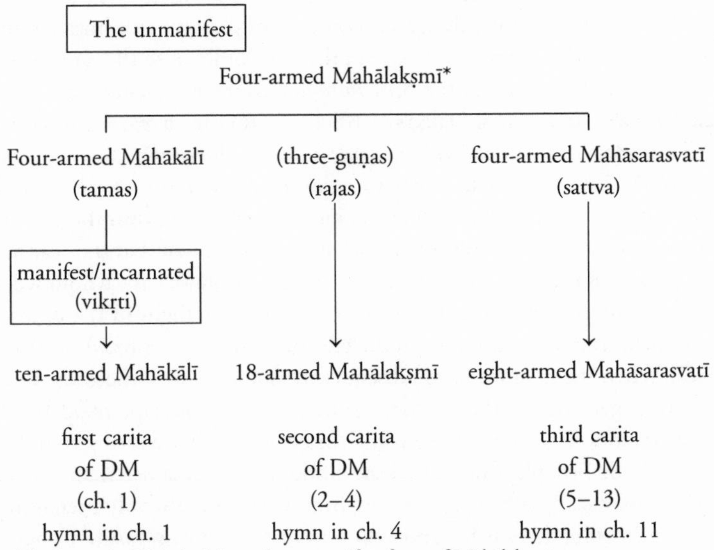

*The hymn in DM ch. 5 is to the unmanifest form of Mahālakṣmī.

Chart 5.2 Diagram of relationships in the Vaikṛtika Rahasya

these forms is understood to preside over one of the three episodes (*caritas*) of the *Devī-Māhātmya,* according to the pattern indicated in Chart 2. Moreover, each of the four hymns of the *Devī-Māhātmya,* which are widely agreed to constitute the devotional core of the text, is understood to be directed to a manifestation of the Goddess. There is one hymn in each of the first two episodes that is straightforward enough: the hymns are directed to the two *vikṛti* forms of the Goddess that preside respectively over those two episodes. Of the two hymns in the third episode, the one in chapter 11 is directed to the *vikṛti* form of Mahāsarasvatī, while the one in chapter 5—the hymn that we have just seen precedes our puzzling passage—is directed to the highest form of Mahālakṣmī, her *avyākṛtā* or "transcendent" form. The origin of the hermeneutical apparatus that the Rahasyas provide remains a mystery. For our purposes, it is enough to note that both Bhāskararāya and Nāgoji Bhaṭṭa take the assimilation of the Rahasyas to the text for granted, and one of their fellow commentators goes so far as to allege that the *real* reason Rāma slew Rāvaṇa was because the demon recited the *Devī-Māhātmya* without the Rahasyas![9]

All of the passages that Nāgoji Bhaṭṭa and Bhāskararāya cite from the *Śiva Purāṇa,* the second of the templates they use for understanding our passage, come from the first part of the seventh book, the Vāyu SaṀhitā, from chapters 24, 25, or 27.[10] In three cases, the commentators cite exactly the same passage. In two cases, they cite very similar passages, where the differences are likely mere textual variants, a common Purāṇic phenomenon. Nāgoji Bhaṭṭa then cites one further passage. There is, in other words, a common pool of passages that both commentators cite, though they do not cite them in the same order or to the same purpose.

The relevant chapters in the *Śiva Purāṇa* recount the events that follow in the wake of the destruction of Dakṣa's sacrifice, and they tell a reasonably coherent story. Śiva and his consort, called Śiva or *devī,* the Goddess, who has earlier been called Pārvatī (7.23.15), settle down to enjoy themselves on Mount Mandara. After several years two demon brothers, named Śumbha and Niśumbha, are born and through *tapas* (internal heat) gain from Brahmā the boon that they cannot be slain by a man. "Rather, let us be slain in battle by a woman with whom we have fallen in love, an invincible maiden, who has not taken delight in the touch of a man, not born from a womb, but produced from a fragment (*aṁśa*) of Ambikā" (7.24.26). When the demons have subsequently vanquished all the gods, Brahmā asks Śiva to anger or tease the Goddess so that a *śakti* (power), a maiden utterly devoid of passion, may be born from the sheath (*kośa*) that has her bodily color (7.24.26–30). So Śiva playfully teased the Goddess by calling her Kālī, "the black one," whereupon she grew angry, reviling him for apparently only pretending to love her, and reviling herself for apparently having given displeasure to her husband. Śiva apologizes, indicating that his remarks had been made in jest and that their purpose will eventually become evident. The Goddess will have none of this, saying it must be her non-lustrous form (*agauram vapuḥ*) that had prompted him to call her black; she will rectify the situation by practicing *tapas,* winning a boon from Brahma, and becoming lustrous (*gaurī:* 7.24.53). She retreats to the Himalayas and performs fierce austerities, even taming a tiger that comes to devour her. Brahmā, pressured again by the gods for relief from Śumbha and Niśumbha, has his attention caught by the power generated by the Goddess's practice of *tapas.* Approaching her and learning of her desire to shed her blackness, he is puzzled, for, as the Goddess, she can have anything she wants just for the asking. But he then chooses to make use of the power (*śakti*) she has built up, for the purpose of destroying the demons. Upon request then, "the Goddess, casting off the sheath of her skin (*tvakkośa*), became golden (*gaurī*). A Black (*kālī*) maiden with the lustre of a thundercloud, was born from the skin-sheath and called 'Kauśikī'" (7.25.38–39). This power (*śakti*), called Viṣṇu's yogic slumber (*yoganidrā*), whose nature is *māyā* (illusion) (7.25.40), bows to Brahmā and to Gaurī, who is called her mother, and immediately goes off to slay the demons. When Gaurī returns to Śiva's abode (7.27), Śiva asks if her anger has passed, says that he loves her whether she is *kālī* or any other color, and points out the many ways in which they are mutually interdependent. He repeats that it was just to assist the gods in getting rid of the demons that he teased her. The Goddess ignores this flattery, but asks if he has seen the maiden Kauśikī, whose like has never been nor will be known. Brahmā will provide him with details of that maiden's battle with the demons, she says. The faithful tiger is then installed as guardian of the household and the text moves on to other, very different concerns.

This account is of intrinsic interest for a number of reasons. It clearly understands the relationship between Śiva and Devī as a much more symbiotic one, as Ardhanārīśvara (see 7.15), than does the parallel passage in the *Devī-Māhātmya,* where the Goddess reigns virtually supreme. It is concerned to explain the relationship between the various forms of the Goddess with greater precision than is in our text, and it has a more fully developed concept of *śakti.* I suspect it was composed a good deal later than the sixth-century *Devī-Māhātmya.* Most intriguingly, the *Śiva Purāṇa* account reverses the emphasis of the name and the color of the form called "Kauśikī." The *Devī-Māhātmya,* as we have seen, has a luminous form named Ambikā arising from the *kośa* of Pārvatī, whence Ambikā gets the designation "Kauśikī." It is Pārvatī who becomes black and retires to the Himalayas, leaving Ambikā/Kauśikī at center stage. The *Śiva Purāṇa,* however, sees the figure who arises from the *kośa,* who is therefore named Kauśikī, to take the color from the *kośa,* which is black. It is she who makes the quick exit, to do battle, leaving the luminous (*gaurī*) Pārvatī, who has earlier been called Ambikā, as the dominant presence in the text. All of this, however we now leave to one side, as we turn to exploring how Nāgoji Bhaṭṭa and Bhāskararāya bring citations from this account, and from the Rahasyas, to bear on our puzzling passage.

Nāgoji Bhaṭṭa's position is a good deal easier to understand than Bhāskararāya's, in part because it is more familiar to Western scholarship, in part because he has less at stake here religiously. So let us start with Nāgoji Bhaṭṭa.[11] I have suggested above, and elsewhere, that he may be understood as an Advaita

Vedāntin.[12] Nowhere, in either his *Devī-Māhātmya* commentary or elsewhere, have I found him giving a systematic exposition of his view, but general evidence for my suggestion is that his chief claim to fame is as a grammarian, a field which, in the eighteenth century, was steeped in the culture of Śaṅkara's school. More specifically, we find him using revealing terminology throughout his commentary on the *Devī-Māhātmya.* Thus, when at the end of the final battle, the Goddess resumes all the diverse forms into herself, Nāgoji says that Ambikā then stood entirely alone "because of the lack of differentiation within the *mūla-śakti* (primal power)" (10.4). Elsewhere (4.6) he calls her the *mūla-prakṛti* (primordial substance). Similarly, it is in the form of ignorance that she causes *saṁsāra* (rebirth), but in the form of knowledge (*vidyā)* that she brings it all to an end (5.11). *Māyā* itself is to be understood as ignorance (*avidyā:* 11.4). Most telling is Nāgoji's claim that what makes the terribleness of the Goddess so great is that it cannot be "sublated" (*atirikta*) by anything other than knowledge of Brahmān, for he is here using one of the specific master concepts of Advaita Vedānta.

If we grant then that Nāgoji appears to be an Advaita Vedāntin, certain conclusions follow.[13] Adopting a dualistic epistemology, he assumes that there is a "lower" sphere of conventional knowledge (*vyāvahārika*), and a "higher" realm of ultimate truth (*pāramārthika*). What the *Devī-Māhātmya* presents, with its myths and hymns and devotional fervor, belongs entirely to the *former* realm. It offers a powerful and temporarily valid understanding of the universe, but it is not finally true, for it is sublated, or surpassed, or transcended by knowledge of a non-dual Brahmān. What Nāgoji Bhaṭṭa is about in his commentary, then, is simply the setting in order of fragments of truth, the rearrangement of approximately accurate formulations.

This turns out to be exactly what is on Nāgoji Bhaṭṭa's mind in his commentary on our puzzling passage. It is too glib to imagine him saying—"Well, it's no wonder the passage is puzzling: what can you expect from myths and other detritus from the *vyāvahārika* (ordinary) realm!"—for his search for intelligibility runs deeper than that. But he does appropriate, almost mechanically, a particular way of explaining the dynamics of the *vyāvahārika* realm in general and of this passage in particular. What he alights on is the three-*guṇa* theory of the Saṁkhya school, often used by Advaita Vedānta to explain the ordinary world and, as we have seen, introduced in the Rahasyas in association with the different forms of Mahālakṣmī. The problem for Nāgoji Bhaṭṭa here and throughout the third episode, is as follows. In the first episode of the *Devī-Māhātmya,* the association of killing with Mahākālī, in whom *tamas* predominates is comprehensible: ignorance and *māyā* are part of Mahākālī's power, and she uses them to delude the demons Madhu and Kaiṭabha into challenging Viṣṇu in this episode. Similarly, in the second episode, the association of Mahālakṣmī and *rajas* is necessary to kill the buffalo demon Mahiṣa. But how can the power of *sattva,* which logically belongs to Mahāsarasvatī in the third episode, be used to justify *any* killing? Goodness alone does not kill, so how can Mahāsarasvatī do so? This is the hermeneutical problem for Nāgoji Bhaṭṭa. The passage with which we are concerned has great potential for solving this problem and demonstrating how the distribution of the forms and qualities of the Goddess works. What is the characterization of Ambikā/Kauśikī as *Śiva,* auspicious, indicates, says Nāgoji (comm. on 5.38), is that she is a portion (*aṁśa*) of the Devī in whom the *guṇa* of *sattva* predominates. Hence the expectation that *sattva* dominates in this episode is met. Beyond that, however, because of the close connection (*sahodaritva*) between the two forms that this passage demonstrates, it is legitimate to expect that the *tamasic* qualities of the black Kālikā/Pārvatī, who retires to the mountains, will spill over into the form and actions of Ambikā, enabling her to do battle with the demons (comm. on 5.41). It makes good sense for Nāgoji to quote the *Śiva-Purāṇa* in this regard, for, as we have seen, the reversed emphasis in that text invites us to blur the distinction between light and dark forms in just the way that Nāgoji wants us to. The passage is indeed troubling, but Nāgoji makes a virtue of necessity and shows how there is indeed a logic to the forms of the Goddess that are active within the *vyāvahārika* realm. This passage demonstrates that logic by identifying the activity of the *sattva guṇa* form of the Goddess.

Bhāskararāya's commentary on this passage proceeds in quite a different fashion, for while he too is a nondualist, his nondualism is of a Tantric sort, specifically of the Śrī Vidyā school.[14] He therefore does not accept the epistemological dualism of Vedānta; his philosophy points toward the ritual actualization of the power of the unmanifest Mahālakṣmī, which is ontologically connected to, and accessible in, the *mantras* of the *Devī-Māhātmya.* He knows the power that inheres the ritual recitation of the text and he is concerned to show how that power springs from the very foundation of the universe.

There are three chief points that Bhāskararāya makes in his commentary on the verses of our passage. In typical scholastic fashion, he pays careful attention to diction and grammar, so let us meet him on his own terms with a similar kind of analysis.

His first point is that there is a kind of interchangability between the two forms of the Goddess in this passage, Kālī (ka) and Pārvatī, which is a secret (*marmatva:* comm. on 5.38). In support of this, he cites the relevant passages from the *Śiva Purāṇa* account and says that the dark maiden who emerges from the *kośa* after Pārvatī's *tapas* in the *Śiva Purāṇa* was the *vibhūti* of Pārvatī. The word *vibhūti* is a pregnant term, with a range of meanings from "beauty" and "prosperity" to "what is most important about something," its "essence." Daniel Ingalls has suggested it means something like Eliade's concept of hierophany.[15] In the *Devī-Māhātmya* itself this is the term that is used at the end of the last combat, when Śumbha accuses the Goddess of false pride for relying on the power of the other deities, and she responds: "'I alone exist here in the world; what second, other than I, is there? O wicked one, behold these my *vibhūtis* entering back into me!' Thereupon, all the goddesses . . . went to their resting place in the body of the Goddess, then there was just Ambikā, alone" (10. 3–4). Thus, like Nāgoji Bhaṭṭa,

Bhāskararāya asks us to blur the distinction between the two forms, but he does so, not to justify the correspondence of the Goddess's forms with the theory of the three *guṇas*, but to emphasize that there is, in fact , only one Goddess, one reality, no matter how many different names or labels we may apply to her.

Bhāskararāya's second and third points depend on the interpretation of a crucial half line, so let me cite again the last two verses of our passage:

> 5.40 Since Ambikā came forth from the *kośa* of Pārvatī
> She is sung of in all the worlds as "Kauśikī."
> 5.41 When she had come forth, Pārvatī became black.
> Known as "Kālikā." she makes her abode in the Himālayas.

The Sanskrit for the first half of the last verse is *tasyām vinirgatāyām tu kṛṣṇabhut sāpi pārvatī.* The clear sense, on which all other commentaries that I have seen agree, is that the first half of the line is a locative absolute, and that the "she" refers to Ambikā/Kauśikī who has just "come forth" from Pārvatī. Bhāskararāya, however, prefers a variant reading for the first half of this line *tasyāvinirgatā yā tu,* which he glosses as *tasyā vinirgatā yā tu,* yielding the translation "The one who had come forth from her, Pārvatī, became black." That is, *tasyā(ḥ)* is a feminine ablative, joined in false *saṁdhi* to *vinirgatā,* and designating the unnamed source from which Pārvatī came. Pārvatī came forth from "her," but we do not yet know who "she" is. Moreover Bhāskararāya then goes on at great length to explain what the verb *vinirgam,* "to come forth," can and cannot mean. Just what is Bhāskararāya up to, and what seems to be at stake here for our commentator?

The key to answering these questions lies in returning to the rudimentary Śākta philosophy sketched out in the Rahasyas. As noted in passing above, Bhāskararāya rejects the epistemological dualism of Advaita Vedānta, but it is comparably important to note that, for him, all the different forms of Mahālakṣmī do not designate ontologically different deities. He remains a monist. The various forms for Bhāskararāya are simply different manifestations of the same reality. That reality can admittedly be spoken about in different ways, but the differences are not of major consequence. When ultimate reality is spoken of in its aggregate (*samaṣṭi*) form, it is named Mahālakṣmī, or Caṇḍī, or Brahman. One of the first lines of his commentary declares "the deity named Caṇḍī is the highest Brahman," who is (quoting *Saundaryalaharī* 98) "the queen through whom the crown is inherited." But when this same reality is spoken of in its separate (*vyaṣṭi*) forms, it is named Mahālakṣmī, Mahākālī and Mahāsarasvatī.[16] What is crucial for Bhāskararāya is that the shifting from *samaṣṭi* to *vyaṣṭi* forms of Mahālakṣmī, that is, from aggregate to separate, or moving from the "level" of the unmanifest (*avyākṛtā*) to that of the manifest (*vikṛti*), or from the Prādhānika to the Vaikṛtika Rasasya, we are not moving to a secondary or diminished form of reality. The ultimate is still ultimate. The ontological connection is still utter, for reality is a virtually seamless web. The Goddess, the great slayer of Mahiṣa and other demons, whose activity is described in the verses of the *Devī-Māhātmya,* whose power is accessible in those *mantras,* is also the foundation of the universe.

Given the narrative and hymnic nature of the *Devī-Māhātmya,* Bhāskararāya is hard-pressed to find textual support for this interpretation. But the variant reading that he accepts for this crucial verse provides him with an important piece of evidence. It gives him a specific reference to the *avyākṛtā* form of Mahālakṣmī. She is the one whom Bhāskararāya understands to be referred to by the ablative case "her." In his own words, the form that is designated Kālikā, who is essentially the same as Pārvatī (a matter to which we shall return in a moment), this very form "came forth from the presence of the highest deity (*paradevatā:* comm. on 5.41)," that is from the unspecified "her" in the variant reading. She is the transcendent Goddess who looms behind all specific activity, who forms the backdrop and underpinning of all particular existence. Elsewhere, using a term that is deliberately reminiscent of Gauḍapāda's famous Kārikā on the *Māṇḍūkya Upaniṣad,* Bhāskararāya calls this foundational *samaṣṭi* Mahālakṣmī *turīyā,* "the fourth."[17] In developing this point, Bhāskararāya maintains that the verb *vinirgam,* to go forth, can be used either in the mundane fashion, as in "going forth to bathe," or metaphysically, to describe the relationship between the highest *avyākṛtā* form of Mahālakṣmī and her several other *vikṛti* forms. But it cannot be used, he says, with the highest form of Mahālakṣmī as the subject of the verb because it is improper to impute action to the highest deity, just as it is improper to impute color to her. Following this line of thinking on the word *vibhūti* that we noted above, he argues that this verb cannot be used to describe the relationship between Kauśikī/Ambikā and the Pārvatī from whom she sprang because there is no essential difference between them. They are, as it were, on a par with each other, virtually interchangeable *vikṛti* forms. What they have in common outweighs by far the contrast in which they both stand to the transcendent Mahālakṣmī from whom they have "come forth."

Let me conclude by suggesting that this admittedly technical discussion may help in understanding the relationship between the different strands of Hindu tradition, in particular, the strands of *bhakti,* philosophy (*darśana*) as represented by Advaita Vedānta, and the Tantra. Let me do so in heuristic fashion, with a diagram that points toward an aphorism.

The diagram asks us to think of the Hindu tradition as a conversation in which there are three participants, visualized structurally as a triangle with three vertices. At one vertex is the great mythology of popular Hinduism, as found in the Purāṇas. Its animating spirit is *bhakti,* devotion, and its narratives move unselfconsciously and unsystematically through a variety of philosophical views. Casually informed by Śaṁkhya terminology, the accounts are more or less dualistic in their ontologies, and in their understanding of the relationship between male and female deities (Rādhā and Kṛṣṇa, Pārvatī and Śiva, Śakti and Śiva). They are also casually dualistic in their varied understandings of the relationship between male and female deities and human beings and of the relationship between both of these and the material world. While Purāṇic myths may invoke the concept of *māyā* in a narrative (not philosophical) sort of way, they basically affirm a single epistemology: the commonsense world, though slippery, is more or less knowable as it is presented to us. The point throughout the Purāṇas is nurturance and expression of the devotional spirit, glorification of God, or of Goddess, or of both. Although the *Devī-Māhātmya* is distinctive in its effort to place the Goddess at center stage, it is nicely representative of this Purāṇic devotional spirit, where, as the great Bengali *bhakta* Rāmprasād, would have said it, the goal is to *taste* the sugar of the divine, not to *become* it.[18] The other two partners in the conversation, occupying the other two vertices, are concerned to resolve the tensions and philosophical problems inherent in the casually dualistic myths and hymns of devotional fervor. What we have met in the commentaries on the *Devī-Māhātmya* are two such efforts. Both of them move toward nondualism, but they do so in quite different ways, and so each occupies a different vertex of the triangle.

Advaita Vedānta, as represented by Nāgoji Bhaṭṭa, can "make sense" of the *Devī-Māhātmya,* including the puzzling passage we has been considering, by affirming an ontological monism. But it can do so only by affirming as well an epistemological dualism. Ultimately, the Goddess and her activity and the text are relegated to the realm of ordinary, less-than-ultimate knowledge. Only Brahmān-without-qualities is finally real.

Tantrics as represented by Bhāskararāya, can also "make sense" of the *Devī-Māhātmya* as a whole, and of our puzzling passage, and they, too, adopt a monistic position. But they are unwilling to ascribe secondary status to the physical world, or to the senses, or to the manifest diversity of the Goddess's forms. The way in which they avoid epistemological dualism is not philosophically, but ritually—through the esoteric, experiential transformation of the world. This is surely one reason for Bhāskararāya's preoccupation elsewhere in his commentary with the proper ritual use of the text. What differentiates the two nondualisms, then, is that one—Advaita Vedānta—is of a public and profoundly philosophical sort, while the other—Tantra—inclines toward a private and ritualized experience of oneness.[19]

My aphorism, which I offer by way of summarizing our discussion, is this:

Purāṇic *bhakti,* reflecting Sāṁkhya, affirms an ontological dualism and so is able to affirm a single epistemology. Nondual Vedānta affirms an ontological monism, but the price it pays for this is epistemological dualism. Tantric nondualism also affirms a monistic ontology, but relies on the esoteric, ritualized, experiential transformation of the material world in order to avoid a dualistic epistemology.

NOTES

Charts 5.1 and 5.2 are reproduced with permission from Thomas B. Coburn, *Encountering the Goddess: A Translation of the Devī-Māhātmya and a Study of Its Interpretation* (Albany: State University of New York Press, 1991).

1. André Padoux, "Tantrism," *The Encyclopedia of Religion,* ed. Mircea Eliade (New York: Macmillan, 1986), 14:273.

2. Madeleine Biardeau, *Hinduism: The Anthropology of a Civilization,* trans. Richard Nice (Delhi: Oxford University Press, 1989), 156.

3. Thomas Coburn, *Encountering the Goddess: A Translation of the Devī-Māhātmya and a Study of Its Interpretation* (Albany: State University of New York Press, 1991).

4. Ibid., 52–53; *Devī-Māhātmya* 5.1–6.

5. Coburn, *Encountering the Goddess,* 55.

6. See Thomas B. Coburn, *Devī-Māhātmya: The Crystallization of the Goddess Tradition* (Delhi and Columbia: Motilal Banarsidass and South Asia Books, 1984), 80n, 137, 146–53, 247–49n.

7. For fuller discussion of the Rahasyas, see Coburn, *Encountering The Goddess,* chapter 5, esp. 109–117.

8. A. N. Jani, cited in ibid., 109.

9. Ibid., 101, and 209, 8n.

10. Here I follow the Sanskrit text given in *The Śiva Mahāpurāṇa,* ed. Pushpendra Kumar (Delhi: Nag Publishers, 1981). See also the *Śiva Purāṇa,* trans. Board of Scholars (Delhi, Vanarasi and Patna: Motilal Banarsidass, 1970).

11. The commentaries of Nāgoji Bhaṭṭa and Bhāskararāya on which I draw in the ensuing discussion are those published in *Durgā-saptaśatī saptaṭikā-samvalitā* [The Durgā Saptaśatī with seven commentaries], ed. Harikrsnasarma (Bombay: Venkatesvara Press, 1916; and Delhi and Baroda: Butala and Company, 1984).

12. Coburn, *Encountering the Goddess,* 129–31.

13. See Eliot Deutsch, *Advaita Vedānta: A Philosophical Reconstruction* (Honolulu: University of Hawaii Press, 1969), 15–26.

14. See Coburn, *Encountering The Goddess,* 122–29.

15. Ingalls made this suggestion orally in 1971, in discussing the *Bhagavad Gītā*'s use of the word.

16. For more on *samaṣṭi* and *vyaṣṭi,* see Coburn, *Encountering The Goddess,* 135–39, 142–43.

17. See Bhāskararāya's comment on Prādhānika Rahasya 4, *Durgā-saptaśatī.*

18. See Coburn, *Encountering The Goddess,* 166 and 227–28, 73n.

19. The recent work of Douglas R. Brooks is very provocative in thinking about these matters: *The Secret of the Three Cities: An Introduction to Hindu Śākta Tantrism* (Chicago and London: The University of Chicago Press, 1990), particularly 93, 127–28.

Part III

THE ART HISTORY AND ARCHAEOLOGY OF TANTRA

6

The Spinal Serpent[1]

Thomas McEvilley

In the *Timaeus,* Plato describes what he calls lower soul—the appetitive part of a personality, obsessed with bodily pleasures—and higher soul—the spiritual part whose ambitions transcend the bodily realm. Somewhat surprisingly, he does not count sexual desire as among the appetites of the lower soul, but as a degenerate form of higher soul activity. The higher soul desires only to be reunited with the World Soul; this, Plato says, is the true and pure form of *eros.* When, however, the embodied soul becomes subject to external influences through the channels of the senses, a degenerate form of desire for the One, and for immortality in the One, arises. This is, on the one hand, desire of the individual to merge with the species, which, through the bewilderment of existing in time, the soul now mistakenly sees as the One, and on the other hand, desire to attain immortality through offspring. Other factors enter also, such as seeing, in a sex object, the shadow of the Idea of Beauty, and mistakenly seeking the Idea in the shadow that stimulated memory of it. Thus the true *eros*—desire for supreme knowledge, freedom, and eternality—is temporarily replaced by a false *eros*—sexual desire.

Plato proceeds to describe the physiology of sex (*Timaeus* 73b ff., 91a ff.). Soul power, he says, resides in a moist substance whose true home is in the brain, the seat of the higher soul. The brain is connected with the penis, and along the way, with the heart, by a channel that passes through the center of the spine and connects with the urethra. Under the stimulus of false *eros* the soul fluid in the brain is drawn down the spinal passage and ejaculated from the penis in the form of sperm, which is able to produce new living creatures precisely because it is soul-stuff. It may be inferred, though Plato does not speak directly to this point, that the practice of philosophy (which requires celibacy except for begetting children) involves keeping the soul-stuff located in the brain, that is, preventing it from flowing downward through the spinal channel. This inference is implicit in the Platonic doctrine, which holds that the philosopher gets beyond false *eros* to the true celestial *eros.* Since the false *eros* draws the seminal fluid down the spinal channel, the transcendence of false *eros* must end this downward flowing.

What will be obvious at once (though it has never been remarked on in any text that I have seen) is that this description applies to the Hindu doctrine of the *kuṇḍalinī* as well as to Plato's doctrine in the *Timaeus.* In the Hindu version too, the natural or proper place of the *kuṇḍalinī* (soul-power) is at the very top of the brain; when it is in this position the yogin is in the state of union with the divine (quite as Plato said of the philosopher). In an unpurified person, however, the *kuṇḍalinī* descends through the spinal channel and expresses itself, not as divine union, but as the drive to sexual union: it is expended through the penis in ejaculation. The practice of yoga causes the descended *kuṇḍalinī* power to be drawn back upward through a channel in the center of the spine. There are seven seats, or *cakras,* which the *kuṇḍalinī* may occupy, that at the base of the spine, that at the top of the brain, and five in between, while Plato mentioned only two, the throat and heart. As in Plato's version, the *kuṇḍalinī* power is especially embodied in semen, and descends in semen from the brain to the penis through the spinal channel. Various practices are recommended for forcing the semen upward through the spinal channel until it resides in the brain again;[2] there its life-giving force can express itself through giving spiritual life rather than physical.[3]

This correspondence is already so remarkable as to invite interpretation; but there is more. The Indian texts distinguish many "subtle" channels in the body. The foremost is the channel through which the *kuṇḍalinī* passes up and down the spine (*suṣumnā-nāḍī*); nearly as important are two channels that pass along the spine but outside it (*iḍā* and *piṅgala*). These two surrounding channels conform themselves to the icon of the entwined serpents. Between their origin in the upper brain and their termination at the base of the spine they cross one another five times, that to the right passing to the left, and vice versa; their points of intersection are the five intermediary *cakras.* Plato also, in the *Timaeus* (77c. ff.), knows of these two veins (which physical anatomists cannot find) that pass along the sides of the spinal column and cross one another an unknown number of times (Plato mentions only the crossing at the throat). In Plato, as in the Indian texts, these subsidiary veins are secondary carriers of the soul-power. Finally, the parallel extends to the imagery of the serpent. The spinal marrow was associated with the serpent by Aelian (*de Natura Animalium* I.51) and others, as in the *kuṇḍalinī* tradition. There the *kuṇḍalinī* power is described as a serpent that, when awakened, slithers up the spine; according to Aelian, the spinal marrow of a man leaves his body as a serpent when he dies.

That these ideas which neither the study of cadavers nor mere theorizing would arrive at should occur in both Greece and India demands special investigation. A rudimentary form of this occult physiology is attested in India as early as the *Chāndogya Upaniṣad,* which says (VIII.6.6): "A hundred and one are the arteries of the heart, one of them leads up to the crown of the head. Going upward through that, one becomes immortal."[4] (And compare *Bṛhadāraṇyaka Upaniṣad* IV.2.3.) The somewhat later *Maitri Upaniṣad* specifies (IV.21) that the name of this channel is *suṣumnā,* and that the goal of yoga is to cause the *prāṇa* (spirit-energy) to rise through that channel to the crown of the head. (And compare *Praśna Upaniṣad* III.6.) The much later *Brahma Upaniṣad* asserts that there are four seats of *prāṇa,* then appears to relate two different traditions, first naming navel, heart, throat and head, then eye, throat, heart, and head.[5] The *Haṃsa Upaniṣad* mentions a full list, loins, belly, navel, heart, neck, and eyebrows.[6] It is notable, however, that none of these passages mentions the spine, and those that refer to a channel or vein rising from the heart seem to mean the heart itself, not the heart level of the spine.

The *Śāndilya* and *Dhyānabindu Upaniṣads* describe the central channel and the two subsidiary channels, and mention the anus and navel *cakras.*[7] The *Haṭha Yoga Pradīpikā* knows of the arrangement of the three channels, and mentions the throat and brain *cakras* (III.50, IV,75, 79).[8] Matsyendra, in his *Kaulajñānanirṇaya,* summarizes the system, giving anus, gentials, navel, heart, throat, spot-between-the-eyes, and crown of the head as the *cakra* points.[9] The *Śiva Saṁhitā* spells out the entire system of the three channels and seven *cakras* (V.56–103).[10] The relative chronology of these texts is not certain, but may be more or less in the order in which I have mentioned them. If so, then the pattern with which the system emerges into articulation suggests, though it does not require, that the doctrine either entered India in stages or that it underwent indigenous development in a series of stages there. Of course, all of these texts contain materials from different ages, so no conclusion on these matters is available at present. It is equally possible that there were different versions of the system extant or that different teachers purveyed it with different emphases.

The Greek belief in the *Timaeus* can be traced to a period before Plato; the trail leads to the Sicilian and South Italian schools of medicine, which were connected with the Pythagorean and Orphic presences in the same area. These schools taught that semen comes from the brain and is of one substance with the spinal marrow, by way of which it travels to the genital organ through the spinal channel, called "the holy tube."[11] This was explicitly taught by Alcmaeon of Croton (DK 14A13). Croton, of course, was the center of the Pythagorean brotherhood, and though Alcmeon seems not to have been a member, he shared many views with the Pythagoreans.[12] In fact, the doctrine of the sperm descending through the spinal channel seems to have a special connection with the Pythagorean tradition; it is found in Alcmaeon, in Plato's most Pythagorean work, the *Timaeus,* and in Hippo of Samos (DK 38A3 and 10) in the fifth century B.C.E., probably also a Pythagorean.

The association of the spinal marrow with the word *aion,* "life" or "life-span," in a fragment of the (at least partly) Orphic poet Pindar, affirms the Orphic, as well as the Pythagorean, associations of the teaching. Pindar was influenced by West Greek mystery cults, and Aion, according to later writers, was an Orphic name for Dionysus, the divine element expressed as sexual power.[13] Heraclitus, himself very influenced by Orphism, seems also to have taught the retention of semen and a qualified sexual abstinence.[14] Diogenes of Apollonia (DK 64B6), living probably on the Black Sea in the fifth century B.C.E., had the doctrine of the spinal channel with the two surrounding "veins" and of the connection between the spinal channel and the testicles.[15] Plato, as we have seen, spoke not only of the three channels but also of the heart and throat *cakras,* which in fact he mentions earlier than any extant Indian text. Aristotle also had the doctrine of the connection between sperm and spinal fluid, and regarded the testicles not as sources of semen, but as receptacles whose purpose is to retard and "steady" its flow.[16]

There would seem to be some connection between the Indian and the Greek doctrines of the identity of spinal fluid, brain fluid, and sperm, the spinal channel connecting the brain and the penis, the surrounding channels that cross one another, the *cakras* where they cross, the value judgment that prefers the highest *cakra* as the location of the sperm-marrow-soul, the association of the marrow with a serpent, and so on.

One account would focus on the diffusion of elements of Pre-Socratic lore into Greece from India during the period, roughly the late sixth century B.C.E., when both Northwest India and Eastern Greece were within the Persian Empire. Heraclitus expressed doctrines learned directly or indirectly from an *Upaniṣadic* source—and in fact doctrines related to those under consideration here.[17] If the Tantric physiology was a part of this wave of Indian influence, then it must have entered Greece after about 540 B.C.E. The type of situation that would provide a concrete means of transmission is shown by the story of the physician Democedes of Croton. Democedes, according to tradition a contemporary of Pythagoras, spent years at the Persian court, where he met and exchanged opinions with doctors from various parts of the empire, including India, and then returned to Greece, no doubt full of foreign lore, perhaps including the physiology of the spinal channel. In fact Democedes returned specifically to Croton, where such ideas would have fed directly into the Pythagorean tradition whence, probably, Plato got them. One could hardly ask for a nicer model of a diffusion mechanism.

The main problem with this reconstruction is that Homer already has the idea that the cerebro-spinal fluid (which he calls *engkephalos*) was the container of life power. Whether he equated it with sperm is unknown, but is implied both by the fundamental idea that the *engkephalos* was life power, and because at least as early as Democritus (KD 68B32) the *engkephalos* was believed to issue forth in sexual intercourse. The connection of the spinal fluid with sperm seems present in Hesiod too, well before any known opportunity for Indian influence on Greek thought. The importation of this doctrine into the Greek tradition in the sixth century B.C.E., is unlikely, though it may have been highlighted and reinforced by material imported at that time. (The detail of the crossing secondary veins, for example, may have been passed later than the doctrine of the central channel.)

The doctrine of the *engkephalos* is not only present in the Homeric texts but seems well established there, where it is taken for granted, or treated as a given; it may, then, go back even to the Homeric tradition, which is known to contain elements at least as early as the fifteenth century B.C.E. In fact, there is some evidence that the serpent-marrow-seed-soul identity was already in place in the Minoan-Mycenean period.[18] Scholars desire some source that is earlier than

Democedes' stay in Persia, a source that could have influenced both Homer and the early Upaniṣads.

A second hypothesis is that the doctrine may have survived into the Greek and Indian traditions from proto-Indo-European times. It is indeed widespread among Indo-European traditions. "The head," R. B. Onians says, "was believed by the early Romans to contain, to be the source of, the seed,"[19] and Pliny (*Naturalis Historia* XI.37.178) describes the spinal marrow as "descending from the brain." There are hints of the doctrine in Germanic and Slavic lore,[20] and remnants of it in Shakespeare's line, "Spending his manly marrow in her arms" (*All's Well That Ends Well,* II.3.298) and in Edmund Spenser's assertion that sexuality "rotts the marrow and consumes the brain" (*The Faerie Queene,* I.4.26).

But at the same time, there are signs of this idea system in ancient Semitic texts. In various passages of the Old Testament (in Job, Psalms, Ezekial, and Isiah) and of Rabbinic literature, spirit is equated with bone marrow, with brain liquid, and with sperm, implying a system of conduits to carry it among those areas.[21] Elsewhere in the Near Eastern area, there are also suggestions of the doctrine. It has been proposed, for example, that the priests of Attis and Cybele, who castrated themselves, may have been attempting to interrupt the channel from spine to genitals and thus prevent the sperm from leaving the body and the body, consequently, from aging.[22] Similarly, Epiphanius (*Panarion* 1, 2, 9, 26), writing of the Gnostic tradition, says: "They believe the power in both the menstrual fluid and the semen to be the soul, which, gathering up, they eat."[23]

There is an Egyptian antecedent for the idea of attaining salvation or enlightenment through passing up the spine in the myth in which Osiris ascends to heaven over the spinal column of his mother, the goddess Nut, the vertebrae being used as the rungs of a ladder.[24] Onians proposes that the *djed* column, representing the spine of Osiris and worshiped "as an amulet of life," indicates the same idea.[25] The fact that the spine and phallus of Osiris were found together at Mendes in the myth of the dismemberment again implies the channel and the connection. "The vital fluid," Onians notes, "is repeatedly shown [in Egyptian iconography] as transmitted by laying the hand on the top of the spine or passing it down the spine."[26] It has also been argued that there are hints of the doctrine in Sumerian iconography, specifically in the icon of the entwined serpents and the upright figure surrounded by intertwined serpents, much as in the Tantric iconography of the "serpent power."[27] There is a strong argument for the likelihood of this doctrine occurring in the Indus Valley culture also.[28] Finally, the fundamental physiological model behind the *kuṇḍalinī* doctrine—the spinal linkage between the brain and the urethra, and the fundamental identity of the brain fluid, the spinal marrow, and the semen—seems to have been extremely widespread in the ancient world, though only the Tantric and Platonic texts speak of the two subsidiary channels surrounding the spine.

This distribution does not seem to me to invite the proto-Indo-European hypothesis; in fact, it is very problematic if the Egyptian and Indus Valley occurrences of the physiology are accepted. In this case, it is possible only on the hypothesis of early Indo-European migrations proposed by Renfrew, with the corollary of the Indus Valley being regarded as an Indo-European culture.[29]

Since the theme of causing the semen to rise to the brain is found in both ancient India and ancient China—cultures between which important diffusion transactions occurred early in the Common Era—suggests the possibility of diffusion in this case too. But the chronolgy would hardly allow diffusion from India into China. The theme of upwardization is mentioned in two Han Dynasty texts (though the full system of channels and movements is not spelled out until the Sung Dynasty), somewhat earlier than current estimates of the diffusion of Buddhism from India into China. Indeed, many scholars have proposed the opposite view: that the sexual elements of Tantra came into India from China, where they had been contextualized with Taoism.[30]

But the introduction of the Greek material into the duscussion changes this situation. The Greek and Indian forms of the physiology both involve the central channel up the spine and the two subsidiary channels that run beside the spine and cross over one another periodically, creating the caduceus configuration that is fundamental to Tantric iconography. But the Chinese version lacks this configuration. In that model, the so-called *Tu* channel runs from the perineum up the spine, like *suṣumnā-nāḍī*—but, instead of the flanking and criss-crossing *iḍā* and *piṅgala,* another chanel (*Jen*) runs down the front of the body, joining with the *Tu* channel at top and bottom. In light of this difference, it does not seem possible that the doctrine went from China into India; if Indians had received it in the Chinese configuration, it is unlikely in the extreme that they would have adapted it into the same configuration that Plato had—and with the same references to the serpent, which also are lacking in the Chinese version. The third possibility—diffusion of the doctrine from Greece into India and China (or into India whence it passed into China where they adapted the form) is chronologically possible and could conceivably turn out to have been the case; it nevertheless seems unlikely to be a popular choice, as the Indian version, at present the most complete and whole of the three, seems to many to express its parent culture most appropriately, while the Greek version still seems what Erwin Rohde, a century ago, called "a drop of alien blood."[31]

The remaining possibilty is that some fourth ancient culture diffused the doctrine into Greece, India, *and* China (where it was adapted into another form) or into Greece and India, whence it may have passed into China and been adapted. There seems no other possibility. And there *is* in fact an ancient culture that offers exactly the elements needed: one that has the caduceus icon, that associates it with the serpent motif, and that is known to have diffused other elements into Greece, India, and China.

Heinrich Zimmer argued that the iconography of the serpent power complex was diffused from Mesopotamia into India. This diffusion, if it happened, would have occurred in a number of waves, beginning with Sumerian input into the Indus Valley culture and ending with the fall of Persepolis, when many Near Eastern craftsmen carrying Mesopotamian traditions came into India. Indeed, it cannot be denied that certain Sumerian and Indus Valley icons are the same icons in different instantiations. A few examples will make the point.

The heraldic flanking composition is perhaps the most characteristic of all Sumerian visual trademarks. Where it occurs in Old Kingdom Egypt it is commonly attributed to Sumerian influence. Several cases in the Indus Valley imagery simply cannot be explained at present except through Sumer-Indus influence, whichever direction it may be presumed to have gone in, and however mediated by other cultures it might have been. An Indus seal shows, for example, an eagle heraldically flanked by serpents;[32] both the eagle and serpent motif and the heraldic flanking format uniting them are distinctively Sumerian elements. An Indus seal portraying a ritual of a tree goddess[33] shows clearly in the lower left hand corner the motif, common in Sumerian cylinder seals,[34] of a mountain or hillock flanked by two goats with their front feet on it and a tree or pole of some kind rising from its top (Figures 8 and 9). One face of a triangular seal form Mohenjo-Daro[35] shows this motif again, identical in form to many Sumerian icons. Numerous other Indus examples of this iconograph have survived.[36] Several Indus seals[37] show another of the most characteristic of Sumerian iconographs, often called the dompteur or Gilgamesh: a male hero standing between two lions who symmetrically flank him and whom he is holding in a gesture of mastery (Figures 10 and 11). A burial urn from cemetery H at Harappa[38] shows two *dompteurs,* each mastering two bulls. They have long hair and seem to be naked, like their Sumerian counterparts (some consider cemetery H to be post-Harappan, others as the final Harappan stratum). In addition, the bull-lion combat, a commonplace of Sumerian iconography,[39] occurs in the Indus Valley,[40] (Figures 12 and 13) as does the goddess in the tree[41] (Figures 14 and 15), a centrally important icon in both Egypt and Sumer.

These icons—the eagle and serpents, the mountain flanked by goats, the hero mastering lions, the lion-bull combat, the goddess and the tree—are among the central icons of Sumerian religion. Their presence in the Indus Valley city of Mohenjo-Daro in the strata that indicate Sumerian trade was active suggests that significant cultural exchanges were going on in the Bronze Age between Mesopotamia and the Indus Valley. On presently accepted chronologies, which tend to put the Sumerian flowering of civilization somewhat earlier than that in the Indus Valley, it would seem that both iconographical and conceptual elements of Sumerian religion had been assimilated in Bronze Age India. That Elamite, or some other, intermediaries might have been involved does not alter the significance of this chronology.

It must be granted, however, that this conclusion seems less certain today than it did a generation or so ago when there was a widespread scholarly consensus about Sumerian influence on the Indus Valley culture. Henri Frankfort, writing about fifty years ago, went so far as to suppose that " an important element in the

Figure 8 Indus Valley seal impression Mohenjo-Daro, showing motif of symmetrically flanking goats with feet on central tree and mountain. (Courtesy of the Archaeological Survey of India)

Figure 9 Summerian cylinder seal showing symmetrically flanking goats with hooves on tree and/or mountain. Uruk Period. (Line drawing courtesy of Joyce Burstein)

Figure 10 Indus Valley seal impression showing dompteur motif. Mohenjo-Daro. (Courtesy of the Archaeological Survey of India)

Figure 11 Achaemenian seal showing Sumerian dompteur motif with central male figure flanked by griffenlike composite monsters. (Courtesy of The Morgan Library)

Figure 12 Indus Valley painted potsherd showing lion attacking bull. Mohenjo-Daro. (Courtesy of Arthur Probsthain Publisher)

Figure 13 Sumerian cylinder seal impression showing lion attacking bull from behind. Uruk period, ca. 3000 B.C.E. (Line drawing courtesy of Joyce Burstein)

Figure 14 Indus Valley seal impression showing a goddess in a tree with a bull god and seven vegetation spirits. Mohenjo-Daro. (Courtesy of the Archaeological Survey of India)

Figure 15 Sumerian cylinder seal impression showing a goddess in a tree with a horned god. Third millennium B.C.E. (Line drawing courtesy of Joyce Burstein)

population of the two regions belonged originally to a common stock."[42] A later scholar more moderately posited "idea diffusion" from both Mesopotamia and Egypt as the proximate causes of the Indus culture.[43] Another used the more common term "stimulus diffusion."[44] Yet another doubted that the Indus culture "springs from any separate ultimate origin," and noted that, at least in the technology of writing," it is likely to be dependent, in the last resort, on the inventions of late fourth-millennium date in Mesopotamia."[45] In the 1940s, 1950s, and 1960s, then, a formidable consensus of western scholars held that influences from Sumerian culture stimulated the Indus Valley culture to arise out of the village state of the Neolithic Age into the urban planning stage uncovered at Mohenjo-Daro and Harappa.[46]

More recently, this consensus has been broken up into a series of new debates, as the increasing influence of scholars who are Indian nationals has contributed to a tendency to minimize external inputs into the Indian tradition.[47] Do recalibrated Carbon 14 dates put the Indus culture earlier than the Sumerian finds? What was the role of Elam, and what were the connections between the Elamite and Dravidian languages? Were the Indo-Europeans on the scene in India yet?

This revisionist impetus attacks the clichéd and long-held assumption of the "nuclear" Near East, especially in its Sumero-centric form. But little has actually changed in the evidence. And the revisionists have not yet accounted for the iconographic parallels.

Perhaps the key icon involved is the entwined serpents that are central to the Tantric iconography of the spinal column with its subsidiary veins. This is first encountered in Sumerian iconography, for example, in the famous Gudea Vase (Figure 16), where it seems to be the symbol of Gudea's personal deity, Ningizzida. It is not encountered in the Indus Valley iconography as presently known and, in fact, is not encountered in India at all until after the fall of Persepolis. In any case, whether this icon came with a certain doctrinal content or as an emptied vessel to be refilled is not known.[48]

It is of course possible that a complex diffusion situation obtained, parts of the doctrine descending into both Greece and India from some earlier source, other parts being passed from one of these cultures to another at a later time. But what is clear, and what should enter the general discussion of the topic, is that the Tantric physiology is not exclusively an Asian element, and that a diffusion situation probably involving some of the factors just reviewed was involved in its presence in India as well as in Greece. But there may be a still more ancient world involved.

In an essay called "An Archeology of Yoga," I investigated six mysterious Indus Valley seal images often, whether rightly or wrongly, called "Śiva." I argued that all the figures on these seals, without exception, are in a posture known in Haṭha yoga as *mūlābandhāsana,* or the closely related *utkatāsana* or *bhadda konāsana,* three variants of the same yogic function (Figures 17, 18, 19).[49] The

Figure 16 Babylonian seal showing entwined serpent pair homologized to human body. ca. 2000 B.C.E. (Courtesy of Princeton University Press)

Figure 17 Indus Valley seal impression. (Courtesy of the Archaeological Survey of India)

Figure 18 *Mūlābandhāsana.* (Digital art courtesy of Joyce Burstein)

Figure 19 *Yogāsana Vignana* demonstrated by Shirendra Brahmachari. (Courtesy of Probashi Publishing Company)

Figure 20 Australian aboriginal ritual view. (Couretsy of International University Press)

system of yogic ideas and methods that these *āsanas* (yogic postures) are involved with consistently throughout their long later history involves the occult physiology discussed here. Specifically, the function of these *āsanas* is, by pressing the heels against the perineum, to drive the sperm-marrow-soul fluid up the spinal channel. There is then some cogency to the view that where this *āsana* is found that physiology may well have been present also. It does not in fact occur in any of the places that have from time to time been suggested as providing analogues of the *āsanas*—in Egyptian sculptures of scribes, for example, or the Gundestrup cauldron,[50] or pre-Columbian seated figures. Some Sumerian cylinder seal impressions of the so-called Displayed Female are close, but the crucial element of the joined heels is never precisely found in them. This posture can, however, be observed in ethnographic photographs of Australian aboriginal rituals (Figure 20).[51] Of course, there may be no connection, but there are so few known cases in all the world's record of words and images that perhaps it is permissible to reflect upon the possibility of a connection. The obvious candidate is that this yogic position, perhaps along with certain other proto-yogic elements, may have survived from the proto-Australoid stratum of Indian prehistory.

I have said that the physiology of the spinal channel seems, in Indian cultural history at least, syntactically related to the heels-joined squatting posture. Of course, syntax varies and whether the connection would hold for earlier cultures is a guess. Still, it is plausible that the physiology of the spinal channel may also be extremely ancient and have been diffused widely at an early level of human culture—perhaps even by that hypothetical wave of migration that brought the ancestors of the proto-Australoid peoples out of Africa. The ethnographer Lorna Marshall, in her article "Kung Bushmen Religious Beliefs,"[52] writes of an occult physiological power called *ntum* that is aroused by trance dancing, which brings the *ntum* to a boil. "The men, " Marshall writes, "say it boils up their spinal columns into their heads, and is so strong when it does this that it overcomes them and they lose their senses." Indeed, when we reflect briefly on the antiquity of marrow cults, known as early as Homo Erectus, this Greek-Indian parallel seems to direct our gaze into the darkest depths of human prehistory.

NOTES

1. This research is part of a larger project on which I am working, *The Shape of Ancient Thought: A Comparative Study of Greek and Indian Philosophies.*

2. See Thomas McEvilley, "An Archeology of Yoga," *RES* 1, 1981, for discussion of these practices.

3. Modern descriptions of the system include Mircea Eliade, *Yoga: Immortality and Freedom* (Princeton: Princeton University Press, The Bollingen Series, 1971), 134, 236–49, and Swami Sivananda, *Kuṇḍalinī Yoga* (Sivanandnagar, India: Divine Life Society, 1971).

4. *The Principal Upanishads,* trans. S. Radhakrishnan (London: Allen and Unwin, 1953).

5. K. Narayanasvami Aiyar, *Thirty Minor Upanishads* (Madras: Vedanta Press, 1914), 107–109.

6. Ibid., 213.

7. Ibid., 176–77, 205–206.

8. *The Haṭha Yoga Pradīpikā,* trans. Pancham Singh (New Delhi: Munshiram Manoharlal, 1980).

9. David Gordon White, *The Alchemical Body: Siddha Traditions in Medieval India* (Chicago: University of Chicago Press, 1996), 134–35.

10. *The Śiva Saṃhitā,* trans. Rai Bahadur Srisa Chandra Vasu (New Delhi: Munshiram Manoharlal, 1979).

11. See: F. M. Cornford, *Plato's Cosmology: The Timaeus of Plato* (New York: Bobbs Merrill, The Library of Liberal Arts, n.d.), 295; R. B. Onians, *The Origins of European Thought about the Body, the Mind, the Soul, the World, Time, and Fate* (Cambridge, Eng.: Cambridge University Press, 1989), 208.

12. Alister Cameron, *The Pythagorean Background of the Theory of Recollection* (Menasha, Wisc.: George Banta Publishing Co., 1938), 37–42.

13. W. K. C. Guthrie, *Orpheus and Greek Religion* (New York: W. W. Norton, 1966), 228.

14. These points are argued, for example, by M. L. West, *Early Greek Philosophy and the Orient* (Oxford, Eng.: The Clarendon Press, 1971), 151–61.

15. It is interesting that in the *Odyssey* (5.160) Homer refers to "the sweet *aion* flowing down."

16. *De partis animal.* 656a; *de gen. animal* A 7i7a20 ff.; *Problemata* 879b and 897b23 ff.; and *part. animal.* 651b20 ff and 652a25 ff.

17. Or from an earlier source that also fed into the *Upaniśads.* See West, *Early Greek Philosophy,* 186 and elsewhere.

18. Martin P. Nilsson opines that in Minoan-Mycenaean religion "the snake represents the soul of the deceased;" see *A History of Greek Religion* (New York: Norton, 1964), 13; and *The Minoan-Mycenaean Religion and Its Survival in Greek Religion* (Lund: C. W. K. Gleerup, 1927), 273 ff. See also Jane Helen Harrison, *Prolegomena to the Study of Greek Religion* (New York: Meridian Books, 1957), 235–37, 325–31.

19. Onians, *Origins,* 124–25.

20. Ibid., 154–55.

21. Some of these passages are assembled by Onians, ibid., 287–88, 492–93.

22. This follows from the belief that the testicles were not the sources of sperm, but carriers or way stations for it. Onians argues the point, ibid., 109–10, 4n.

23. Cf. ibid., 110, n.

24. See Theodor Gaster, *Thespis: Ritual, Myth and Drama in the Ancient Near East* (New York: Harper & Row, Harper Torchbooks, 1966), 396.

25. Onians, *Origins,* 208, n.3.

26. Ibid.

27. See Heinrich Zimmer, *The Art of Indian Asia* (Princeton: Princeton University Press, The Bollingen Series, 1955), 1:66 and fig. 6.

28. See McEvilley, "An Archeology of Yoga."

29. Colin Renfrew, *Archeology and Language: The Puzzle of Indo-European Origins* (New York: Cambridge University Press, 1990). Renfrew seems to lean toward an Indo-European Indus Valley. See also J. P. Mallory, *In Search of the Indo-Europeans: Language, Archaeology and Myth* (London: Tham,es and Hudson, 1989).

30. Joseph Needham et al., *Science and Civilization in China* (Cambridge, Eng.: Cambridge University Press, 1954–1988), 2:425 and elsewhere; and Nagendranath Bhattacharyya, *History of Tantric Religion: A Historical Ritualistic and Philosophical Study* (Delhi: Munshiram Manoharlal, 1982).

31. Erwin Rohde, *Psyche, the Cult of Souls and Belief in Immortality Among the Greeks,* trans. W. B. Hillis (New York: Harper & Row, Harper Torchbook, 1966), 2:260.

32. K. N. Sastri, *New Light On the Indus Civilization* (Delhi: Atma Ram and Sons, 1965), vol. 1, 122.

33. Ernest J. H. Mackay, *Further Excavations at Mohenjo Daro* (New Delhi: Indological Book Corporation, 1938), vol. 2, 13, pl. 90.

34. E. G., Henri Frankfort, *Cylinder Seals* (London: Gregg Press, 1965), pl. 4j, 11g.

35. Sastri, *New Light,* 118.

36. See Ibid,. pl. 3.8, pl 5, 4.c, 5.c. etc.

37. See Mackay, *Further Excavations,* pl. LXXXIV, 75, 86.

38. Sastri, *New Light,* 12 and fig.13.

39. See B. M. Goff, *The Symbols of Prehistoric Mesopotamia* (New Haven: Yale University Press, 1963), fig. 260.

40. See a painted potsherd published by Sir John Marshall, *Mohenjo-Daro,* vol. 3, pl. 92, 21.

41. Mackay, *Further Excavations,* vol. 2, pl. 99, 677A.

42. Frankfort, *Cylinder Seals,* 307.

43. Mortimer Wheeler, *Civilization of the Indus and Beyond* (London: Thames and Hudson, 1966), 61–62.

44. Glyn Daniel, *The First Civilizations* (New York: Thomas Y. Crowell, 1968), 114–16.

45. Stuart Piggot, *Prehistoric India* (Baltimore: Penguin, 1950), 141.

46. The excavations conducted at Mehrgarh by Jean-Francois Jarrige and Richard H. Meadow, "The Antecedents of Civilization in the Indus Valley," *Scientific American* (August 1980): 122–33) are frequently mentioned as proof of the internal continuity of the Indus Valley culture. But it seems to me that their findings in fact show a major discontinuity just at the point when ancient Near Eastern influence might have entered in the third millennium. A sudden influx of Mesopotamian objects occurred along with significant iconographic changes and the appearance of writing. Even if Mehrgarh removes the need for external input leading to urbanization, the extensive iconographic parallels remain and seem to require some degree of formative influence from Mesopotamia.

47. The extreme example of this type of argument is found in Pramesh Choudhury, *Indian Origin Of the Chinese Nation* (Calcutta: Dasgupta & Co., 1990).

48. Onians notes, without mentioning the *kuṇḍalinī* parallels: "The union of the two

serpents round the wand might for the Greeks represent the life-power . . . by the union of male *psyche* (soul; cerebro-spinal fluid) and female *psyche*."

49. McEvilley, "An Archaeology of Yoga."

50. Timothy Taylor, "The Gundestrup Cauldron," *Scientific American* (March 1992): 84–89.

51. See, for example, Geza Roheim, *The Eternal Ones of the Dream* (New York: International Universities Press, 1969), pl. 7.

52. Lorna Marshall, "Kung Bushmen Religious Beliefs," *Africa* 32, no. 3 (1962): 138.

7

The Warring Śaktis: A Paradigm For Gupta Conquests

Katherine Anne Harper

Any inquiry into the roots of Hindu Tantrism necessitates consideration of the cult of the Goddess and an idea central to Tantrism that *śakti* is the source of all power. Tantrism traditionally has been defined in terms of specific texts called Tantras, the earliest of which cannot be dated much before the medieval period. The Tantras are systematized compilations of elaborate mixtures of psycho-experimental speculation[1] and intricate mysterious ritual. In these meticulously detailed works, we can recognize older religious ideas and practices that had been evolving over many centuries. Scholars have dated the emergence of Tantrism as early as the fifth century C.E. and reason that it was a pan-Indian movement by the sixth century.[2] Such popularity indicates that there was widespread acceptance of Tantrism long before any specific Tantras were written. This inquiry seeks to understand how Tantrism gained acceptance in Hinduism and by what means were Tantric notions promulgated. In search of inchoate manifestations of Tantrism, this study examines the Saptamātṛkās (Seven Mothers) who were the Śaktis of various Hindu gods.

Elsewhere I have demonstrated that the Saptamātṛkās emerged into the mainstream of Hindu religion as Tantric deities.[3] I contend that these Tantric goddesses were sanctioned as part of the orthodox Hindu system no later than the beginning of the fifth century C.E. The purpose of the current study is threefold: (1) to review images of the Saptamātṛkās dating to the fifth and sixth centuries C.E. as well as coeval textual and epigraphic references in an attempt to understand why orthodox sanctioning occurred; (2) to demonstrate that the Saptamātṛkās' acceptance into the orthodox Hindu pantheon was the result of notions of kingship as established by Gupta sovereigns and that the Saptamātṛkās were religio-political symbols that ensured the success of the kings' imperial program to establish *rājadharma* (righteous rule) in territories controlled for centuries by foreign invaders; (3) to identify the banners or staffs held by the Saptamātṛkās in their early imagery as essential tools for the establishment of the kings' victories against *mlecca* (barbarian) powers and their subsequent dominion over their lands.

Before investigating these materials, however, it is useful for determining our parameters to define Tantrism. To paraphrase Tuen Goudriaan, the Tantras are scriptures that expound non-Vedic doctrine and practices, especially of the Śākta denomination.[4] Tantric stands for a collection of practices and symbols ritualistic, sometimes magical, in character . . . applied as means of reaching spiritual emancipation (*mukti*) and/or realization of mundane aims, chiefly domination (*bhukti*) . . . by means of Kuṇḍalinīyoga and other psychosomatic experiences.[5] It can be characterized as the worship of Śakti or the universal and all-embracing dynamic that manifests itself in human experience as a female divinity.[6] Both the goals, *bhukti* and *mukti,* are conferred by the goddess(es). Śiva and Viṣṇu have the power to confer only *mukti.* To quote C. Mackenzie Brown, ". . . in popular sentiment . . . the *Bhagavad Gītā* yields only *mukti,* while the *Devī Māhātmya* yields both *mukti* and *bhukti.*"[7] It is the goddesses' bestowal of these two blessings that is the key to understanding Saptamātṛkā imagery as a religio-political instrument.

The central position of the cult of the Goddess and the primacy of the concept of *śakti* as the ultimate and moving force of the gods in Tantric spheres is undeniable. The antiquity of goddess worship in India, of course, is remote, and there remains today no evidence to distinguish if the ancient forms of the goddess embodied any notion of *śakti* as energy or power. Even with the emergence of a goddess cult in the early centuries of the Common Era, the evidence for the concept of *śakti* is not readily apparent. Occasional references to a Goddess named Śakti are found in the *Mahābhārata,*[8] but it cannot be determined if she fulfills the role of an all-embracing dynamis. When *śakti* finally was regarded as the sole power of the universe, it most often found its symbolic expression, both literary and visual, in the form of a divine female septad called Śaktis or Saptamātṛkās.

India had a remote history involving groups of seven goddesses in both the Vedic and the indigenous traditions. In many instances, the female septads were associated with the constellation Pleiades (Kṛttikās). The Vedic Kṛttikās functioned as an agrarian symbol of yearly and universal renewal while village female septads either inflicted disease or bestowed blessings.[9] Many Mātṛkās appeared in the *Mahābhārata,* usually as amorphous bands associated with Skanda. Their appearance in the epic marked a point in time in which aboriginal mother goddesses were being adopted into the Hindu fold, but they were without any clear definition or link to the concept of *śakti.* To date, there is no evidence to demonstrate that an evolved concept of *śakti* as an all-powerful dynamis or a formula for representing the Saptamātṛkās had crystallized during the Kushan Period, that is, by the close of the third century. By the close of the fourth century or certainly no later than the early fifth century, however, the Saptamātṛkās had made their official entry into the Hindu pantheon as the Śaktis of the gods. Coincidental to the group's formation, the mature concept of *śakti* as feminine power had evolved. Sometime in the fourth century, the ancient female septads, rife with latent symbolism, were refashioned into a new septad having omnipotent, invincible powers.

The earliest extant text to specify the nature of *śakti* was the *Devī Māhātmya* which has been dated between the years 400 and 600 C.E.[10] The story is told of the Devī Kausikī who engaged in battle with the demons Śumbha and Niśumbha during which the gods surrendered the energies of their bodies (Śaktis) to aid in the victory; thus, emerged the goddesses Brahmānī, Māheśvarī, Kaumārī, Vaiṣṇavī, Vārāhī, Aindrī (Indrāṇī) and Nārasiṃhī. Also the Devī divided her body into two halves, releasing the dark goddess Kālikā; Kālikā was renamed Cāmuṇḍa later in the story.[11] Although the *Devī Māhātmya* was the first text to have identified the Mātṛkās, those goddesses who were listed did not conform entirely to those found in the standard Saptamātṛkā iconic ensemble. Such groups, from the beginning of fifth century on, normally included six Deva-Śaktis (Energies of the Gods) and Cāmuṇḍa; Kālikā-Cāmuṇḍa, according to the text, was not the energy of any god, but rather part of the essence of the Devī herself.

In the *Devī Māhātmya,* the Great Goddess grants wealth and power (*bhukti*) and the liberation (*mukti*) only after the shedding of blood.[12] Passages in the text contain information about the concurrent state of iconic representation of these goddesses including description of vehicles and attributes. The literary depictions are so precise in fact that they seem to recount characteristics already fully conceived in art. The Tantric character of the text is indisputable, yet the *Devī Māhātmya* stood at the very center of orthodox Hinduism.[13] A second work, the *Devī Purana,* a text of unequivocal Tantric inspiration, was compiled in present form no later than the sixth or seventh centuries C.E. R. C. Hazra points out that the text's peculiar hybrid Sanskrit may date as early as the first centuries of the Common Era or even earlier.[14] In the text, Mātṛkās or Deva Śaktis are mentioned in several places in groups of seven or more. In particular, it is emphasized that the Mātṛkās should be worshiped by kings.[15] According to the text, those who desired liberation (*mukti*) would be successful in all endeavors if they worshiped the mothers with the prescribed rites.

These two texts provide the *terminus ad quem* of our search for a fully developed concept of *sakti* and a mythological structure for the Saptamātṛkās. Archaeological evidence indicates that the emergence of the Saptamātṛkās in art predated the compilation of the surviving texts. Three separate panels of Saptamātṛkā icons found at Udayagiri in Bhopal are dated in association with an inscription to the first decade of the fifth century C.E.[16] Placed in proximity to Śaivite caves, one group is adjacent to cave 4 and two groups, located side by side, are adjacent to cave 6. Although broken and eroded, we can discern important facts from the three groups. Most important are the still visible remains of staffs with emblems attached to the wall behind some of the figures. In the cave 4 panel (Figure 21), there are traces of a full-blown lotus above the head of the first figure and a trident above the head of the second figure (Figure 22). We can identify Brahmāṇī and Māheśvarī from these attributes. The emblematic staffs carried by four Mātṛkās outside cave 6 (Figure 23) are a lotus blossom, a trident (Figure 24), a spear, and a discus (Figure 25); the emblems identified the order of the seated

Figure 21 Saptamātṛkā Panel. Exterior of Cave 4. Udayagiri, Bhopal. Early fifth century C.E. (Photograph by Katherine Anne Harper)

Figure 22 Detail of emblematic banners, Saptamātṛkā Panel. Exterior of Cave 4. Udayagiri, Bhopal. Early fifth century C.E. (Photograph by Katherine Anne Harper)

Figure 23 Saptamātṛkā Panel. Exterior of Cave 6, Udayagiri, Bhopal. Early fifth century C.E. (Photograph by Katherine Anne Harper)

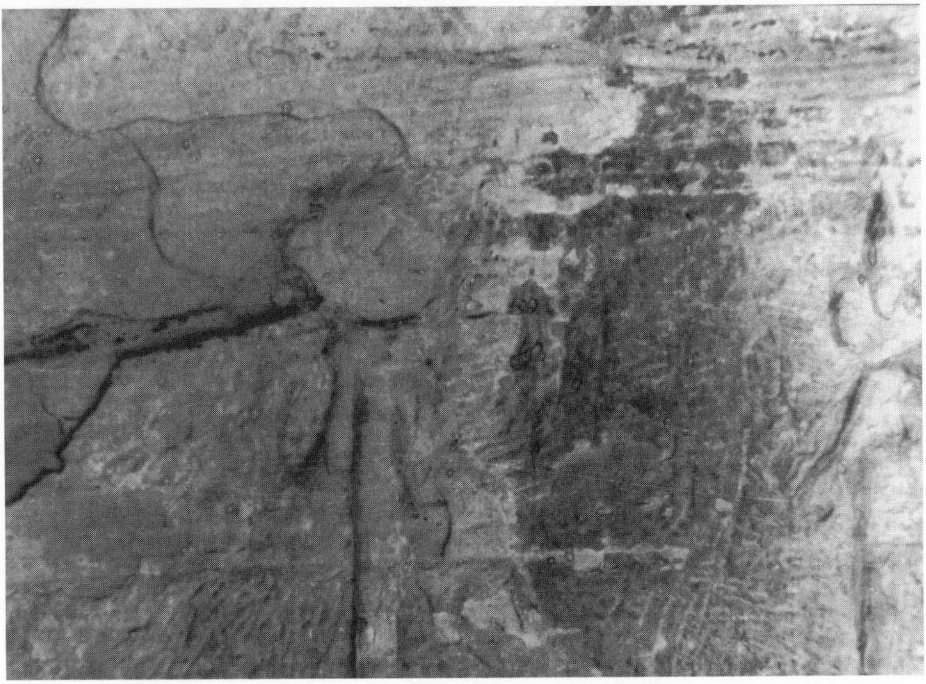

Figure 24 Detail of emblematic banners, Saptamātṛkā Panel. Exterior of Cave 6, Udayagiri, Bhopal. Early fifth century C.E. (Photograph by Katherine Anne Harper)

Figure 25 Detail of emblematic banners, Saptamātṛkā Panel. Exterior of Cave 6, Udayagiri, Bhopal. Early fifth century C.E. (Photograph by Katherine Anne Harper)

figures, specifically Brahmāṇī, Māheśvarī, Kaumārī and Vaiṣṇavī. Positioned at the beginning of each of the three Mātṛkā panels is a large image of Skanda, the God of War, identifiable by his banner displaying his emblem, the cock. The fragmentary Udayagiri panels affirm that, by the beginning of the fifth century, Mātṛkā iconography had evolved into a standardized group of seven goddesses and that their seating order had been formalized.

In order to understand the reasons why orthodox sanctioning of the goddesses occurred, we need to consider what the new Saptamātṛkās symbolized and why their inclusion was deemed necessary at Udayagiri, a site that had royal patronage. An inscription states that the King Candragupta II came in person with Vīrasena, his Minister of Peace and War, to Udayagiri in the year 401–402 in order to build a shrine to Lord Śambhu (Śiva); the Mātṛkā panels, adjacent to the Śaivite caves, were part of the original shrine mentioned in the inscription.[17] The panels of Saptamātṛkās are an important part of the iconography of the Śaivite caves. The inclusion of Skanda with the Saptamātṛkā underscored their martial associations; their weapons leave no doubt that they were conceived as warriors, a function that derived in part from an ancient association of powerful female septads placed at village boundaries to ward off peril.[18] The Mātṛkās' victory against the demons of myth was viewed as a paradigm for vanquishing earthly enemies. Inscriptional information confirmed that kings sought the favor of the Mātṛkās in military matters; for example, the fourth century Talagunda inscription of the Brahmin Kadamba King Mayūraśarman claimed allegiance to Skanda and the Mātṛkās who aided him in defeating his enemies.[19] His successors in the region, the Cālukyas, stated in several inscriptions that they were protected by the Seven Mothers.[20] The *Devī Māhātmya* declared that all the enemies of those who worshiped the Goddess perished;[21] thus symbolizing their martial aspect, Saptamātṛkā icons brandished weapons.

That the Saptamātṛkās emerged into the mainstream of Hindu tradition as seemingly violent Tantric deities was supported by paleographic evidence. The Gangadhar inscription from Western Malwa, dated 423–425 C.E., explained that a minister of a Gupta monarch built a temple for the divine Mothers who, with their companions the Ḍākinīs, stirred up the oceans with the terrible winds rising from magic Tantric rites (*tantrobhuta*).[22] Another inscription from the Patna District of Bihar dated to 455–467 C.E. was written on a sacrificial post (*yupa*) erected for a bloody ceremony involving the worship of the Divine Mothers.[23] It is worthy of mention also that the inscription was recorded by a member of the royal family, the brother-in-law of the king Skandagupta.

Worship of the Saptamātṛkās as Tantric deities had both exoteric and esoteric implications. Recalling the promises of the *Devī Māhātmya* and the *Devī Purāṇa* that the Śaktis conferred both *bhukti,* an exoteric aim, and *mukti,* an esoteric aim, artistic renderings of the goddesses give clues about how these goals were actualized. The Goddesses' conferment of *mukti* synthesized the ancient, primary function—life-giver/mother—and added to it esoteric symbolism with transcendental applications. The Saptamātṛkās were worshiped for personal and spiritual renewal, that is, birth on an entirely different plane of existence, that of nonexistence (*mukti*); they liberated devotees from the endless cycles of rebirth. A fuller exploration of their liberating function is available elsewhere;[24] here we are concerned with the Saptamātṛkā's other function, that is, to fulfill the human urge to control and to aspire to power (*bhukti*).

As noted previously, inscriptional and textual evidence verified that patronage of the warring goddesses was sought by kings. In turning to supernatural forces, they sought positive reinforcement for secular and communal interests as well as assurances of victory. As part of their sacerdotal responsibilities, priests who served as advisers to the king cultivated foolproof methods to ensure victory. Undoubtedly, such a motive contributed to the development of the magical component of Tantrism and the inclusion of Tantric images among those of a more orthodox nature. State ministers who were vedic-oriented Brahmins (Vaidika Tantrins),[25] authenticated the Saptamātṛkās for royal empowerment in response to state exigencies. Goudriaan elaborates on this matter; he reasons that the public responsibilities of advisory Brahmans must have induced them to search for ever newer and stronger methods of safeguarding the welfare of the ruler, the subjects, and as a matter of consequence, also themselves. "Such intellectuals were active in systematizing originally unconnected rituals and designing new methods of existing traditions. Those with mystical leanings who were in contact with yogins—or who served aristocrats of that type—came to develop interiorized variants of external rituals by a process not unlike that which led to the speculations recorded in the Upaniṣads . . ."[26]

In considering the Saptamātṛkās and their relationship to the desire for domination, let us regard the Guptas, the earliest known dynasty of kings to sanction their worship in iconic form. As I have stated, at Udayagiri, there are three prominent panels of Saptamātṛkās. Nowhere in India do we find so many examples in such close proximity; indeed, they are very conspicuous deities, more common than Durgā and as common as Viṣṇu and Śiva. It is also a place where they made an emphatic statement by bursting upon the scene with all the powers one would expect of warring Śaktis. While we may take for granted the goddesses' ability to influence the tides of mortal battles, how they affected for better or worse the dynastic ambitions of their Gupta petitioners merits scrutiny.

The beginning of the Gupta Empire traditionally has been assigned to the year 320 C.E. when Candragupta I took control of a small kingdom somewhere possibly in Bihar or Bengal. It is thought that his marriage to the Licchāvi princess Kumāradevī strengthened his position and increased his land holdings; perhaps, after this territorial extension, he assumed the imperial title *Mahārajādhirāja* for himself and his successors. His son, Samudragupta, in addition, adopted the imperial ideal of *Dharṇībandha* or *Digvijaya*—the conquest in all directions to bind the country as a single unit.[27] The notion of unifying the geography of Bhārata had been established by Aśoka Maurya more than 600 years before. The founders of the Mauryan and Gupta lines shared the same name, Candragupta, and ruled from the same capital, Pataliputra. There is evidence to suggest that the Gupta concept of empire was directly inspired by the Mauryas.[28] During his reign of forty-five years, Samudragupta made great strides in fulfilling the dynastic aspiration to unite the land of Bhārata. The Allahabad pillar inscription (which coincidentally was carved on an old Aśokan column) related that the king brought under his control tracts of land reaching from modern-day Assam and Bangladesh in the east to the border of the present Punjab State in the north and subjugated twelve kings in the Deccan.[29] He died, however, before the conquest of the west was completed; the Śakas still controlled Malwa, Gujarat, and Kathiawar nearly 300 years after their original invasion of India.

It was Samudragupta's successor, Candragupta II, who finally realized the imperial dream to exterminate Śaka rule in the west and extend the empire from sea to sea, as had his predecessor Candragupta Maurya centuries earlier. There is every reason to believe that Chandragupta II sought to exploit any visionary connotations engendered by association with the historical accomplishments of the first Mauyran king. An allegorical play written during the reign of Candragupta II enumerated the merits of the earlier king and his able minister Kauṭilya, writer of the *Arthaśāstra.* The play, *Mudrārākśasa,* was written by Viśākhadatta, a minister of Candragupta II[30] who, in literary disguise, equated the victories of the two kings against *mlecca* invaders. Reconquest of western India, land crossed by the major trade routes, meant increased revenues, particularly through possession of important ports and harbors connecting India with the outside world. Also the long-held city of Ujjayini in western Malwa was so strategic to trade that Candragupta later designated it as his second capital after he conquered the region.[31]

Perhaps an even more important reason for the expulsion of foreign rule meant the establishment of dominion by a righteous king. The *Arthaśāstra, Manusmṛti, Yajñavalkyasmṛti* and Kamandakiya's *Nītisāra,* four ancient texts on governance, set down the ideal standards for sovereigns and designated that conquest and the extension of territories were primary obligations of a king. The *Manusmṛti* instructed that a king should strive for gain with his army and bestow the bounty of conquest on the worthy[32] and that the king's special duty was conquest.[33] The *Yajñavalkyasmṛti* emphasized a monarch's duty to preserve the purity and the integrity of Hindu society and culture: "The king is the master of all, with the exception of the Brahmanas . . . He shall protect the classes and shall lead orders [sic.] in accordance with justice."[34] The *Nītisāra,* dated to the close of the fourth century C.E., was written by a Brahman adviser for Candragupta II.[35] The text specifically stated that those who desecrated gods and Brahmins and foreign invaders were to be overthrown by a righteous king.[36] Gupta kings sought to extend the empire of Bhārata and, at the same time, responded to a divine mandate to ensure the purity of Bhārata as well as uphold the caste system.[37] Certainly verification of the Guptas' commitment to establishment of a Hindu order was the celebration of *aśvamedha* sacrifices. Such rituals, as well as the law texts, affirmed that royal domination was subordinated to the concept of the welfare of the people and *dharma.* The king's duty to safeguard the commonweal was accomplished in different ways, notably diplomacy, warfare, or any number of devious means.

Centuries before, Kauṭilya in his *Arthaśastra* laid the groundwork regarding the methods for conquest of one's enemies, either through direct combat or through subversive and/or magical means. In fact, he expounded at length on the delusive contrivances used to terrorize, confuse, defeat, and kill the enemy. A long list of spells, potions, medicines, and *mantras* was provided to aid in subjugating enemies.[38] That such a discussion occurred in the text attests to an early and widespread acceptance of manipulative means for domination; the descriptions in fact may be viewed as an early form of *bhukti.* Actual implementation of magic was the particular purview of the king's Imperial Chancellor (*mantri pariṣad*); the title itself indicated that, at least originally, the advice given by him to the king had a magico-religious aspect. J. Gonda reminds us that *mantrin* was the one who "knew those sacred or potent formulas which were called *mantras:* apart from the rhythmic parts of the Vedas, the sacrificial, mystical or magical formulas, the term included also charms and incantations, secret plans and designs, hence *mantrin-* in the sense of 'enchanter' or 'conjurer'."[39] The *Yajñavalkyasmṛti* advised that enemies were to be injured or destroyed by incantation.[40] The *Nītisāra* actually praised Candragupta himself for his power in using magical spells to decimate the enemy.[41] Moreover, the text advised use of *rahasyakaran*—spells with malevolent intent, including the Marana ceremony for destruction of enemies,[42] and the *Nirājana* rite for expulsion of enemies.[43] References to sorcery for the purposes of righteous governance abound in the text; while there was no specific mention of the word *bhukti,* the implementation of magic as a device for royal domination was unmistakably validated.

That Tantric goals and practices were acceptable in royal and orthodox circles by the end of the fourth century C.E. was made eminently clear by the writer of the *Nītisāra.* His legal text used the word *tantra* to mean royal prerogative or royal authority [44] and *tantrakusala* to mean the science of polity.[45] By implication these two reference connote *bhukti.* Furthermore, the writer addressed Candragupta as Lord of the Earth, the one who ruled by virtue of his three "Śaktis" or regal powers[46] and explained that the king, "swelling with the *Śaktis,*" marched into battle.[47] Of these powers, *mantra śakti* (power of charms) was superior to the other two powers, *prabhu śakti* (preeminent position of the king himself) and *utsaha śakti* (strength of will) because, according to myth, Bṛhaspati used *mantra śakti* alone to overcome the ruler of the *asura* (demons).[48] Given these references, one cannot dispute the primacy of Tantrism in its relationship to kingship among Gupta monarchy. Apparent likewise was the relationship of the king to female power (*śakti*). Let us return now to the mute stone Śaktis at Udayagiri with an eye toward reading more clearly any remaining signs of religio-political portent.

It is important to acknowledge that the selection of the site of Udayagiri and the selection of the deities placed there were not random acts. The cave temples with their icons and their location had religious as well as political importance. The Udayagiri inscription indicated that Candragupta II, "who was seeking to conquer the whole world" embarked upon his campaign against the foreign enemies to the west from this very spot.[49] With their base camp located in the vicinity, Candragupta's forces battled for nearly a decade to overcome Śakas adversaries who controlled the stategic city of Ujjaini and the lands beyond. Lending support at the army's rear flank were the images of the Saptamātṛkās with their accompanying icons of the War God Skanda. In post-Vedic literature, Skanda gradually replaced Indra as the divine Commander in Chief. That he was particularly important to the martial ambitions of the Guptas is evinced by the names Skanda and Kumara given to two great Gupta kings. Skanda's affiliation with the Divine Mothers was affirmed also by the Bihar Stone Pillar inscription.[50] Each of the three large Skanda icons at Udayagiri, like the adjacent Mātṛkās, carried a signifying banner standard. Critical to understanding the power of Skanda and the Saptamātṛkās to confer *bhukti* are the emblematic standards they carry.

Divine or royal battle standards (*dhvaja-dana* or *jarajara*) had a distinctive history in ancient India and were of the greatest significance in ensuring a king's victory and the well-being of his country; they gave evidence of the alliance between the conception of sacredness and political authority.[51] Such staffs were charged with holy powers. Originally given by Indra to an earthly king, the war banner was an attribute essential for validating the authority of a ruler; in addition, it was an invigorating device by which he thwarted malevolent forces. The conferring of the banner (Indramahotasava ceremony) was an important rite, celebrated by monarchs from the Vedic period on. For the celebration, a special tree was selected, felled, purified, removed to the capital city, decorated, and worshiped. The king fasted, bathed, and recited auspicious stanzas that ensured his subjects of contentment, plentiful food, and freedom from danger and illness.[52]

One story in the *Mahābhārata* is particularly instructive. Indra gave King Vasu a bamboo pole that was to be driven into the ground, decorated, and worshiped to honor the God. So pleased was Indra with Vasu's pious veneration of the pole that he made Vasu "an invincible universal monarch."[53] When Skanda assumed Indra's title as Commander in Chief of the Gods, he inherited Indra's throne and duties.[54] Indra also gave Skanda his blood red war banners.[55] Kauṭilya recommended that a king's war banners should be smeared with a magical potion for protection.[56] So important were war banners that the *Bṛhatsaṃhitā* devoted an entire chapter to the subject; the author claimed that Indra originally received the banner from Viṣṇu to help trounce on demons.[57] Erection of the battle standard was tantamount to the destruction of enemies. As part of the Indramahotsava seven minor banners were made of strong and unbroken wood and ornamented. The additional banners, called Indra's Sisters, were presented with emblematic offerings which the *Bṛhatsaṃitā* equated with the different gods presenting garments, ornaments, and weapons to the Goddesses who was created to fight the asuras in the *Devī Māhātmya.* Thus, the equation linked the old Vedic ceremony to a revised rite that included the Śaktis and, thereby, extended the ancient paradigm to embrace certain features of the Tantric milieu.[58] Although the *Devī Māhātmya* was silent on the subject of the war banners, the *Devī Purāṇa* furnished vital information including elaborate descriptions of the Indramahotsava ceremony and the seven minor banners (in this text they are called Indra's Daughters).[59] In addition, this same text contributed additional information on the connection of Mātṛkās to war banners including instructions for their making, specifications for their insignia, and methods for their proper worship by kings:

> The king who joins in the meditation obtained through *pūjā* shall know neither fear of his enemies nor illness. Through *Devīpūjā* he will not be destroyed and there will be no arising of sorrow. Slaughter of his troops will be held in abeyance. There will be no destruction from enemy weapons. There will be no destruction of good, auspiciousness or happiness. All danger will be destroyed.[60]

Subsequent verses provided information on the boons and types of protection afforded the king who possessed the seven banners of the Goddesses:

> The king who has the banner with the lion of Umā shall know no fear of his enemies. For one who has the banner with the monkey king, his enemies will be destroyed and his best desires will be fulfilled. The purpose of the swan banner is to bestow knowledge, pleasure, and progeny on the king. All disease will be destroyed for the king who has the Garuda banner. The king who has the banner with the *triśula* of the destroyer of the demon Mahiṣa accomplishes all deeds. The banner with the lotus confers *dharma, kāma, artha* and *mokśa.* The banner with the symbol of the skeleton will be eternally free of fear from animals.[61]

Additional verses instructed that the king who worshiped Indra and Devī and possessed their banners had an increase in fortune and pleasures; also the king was certain to possess the rightful symbols of kingship.[62] It is obvious that the power once invested solely in the Vedic Indra to influence a king's fate later was shared or transferred to the Goddess. Another chapter of the *Devī Purāṇa* reiterated nearly identical information; however, the emblems on the seven banners were the swan, bull, peacock, conch, discus, elephant, and skeleton. The text, furthermore, stressed that a king who desired power should install the banners and institute the proper ritual for worship of the Goddesses. By doing so, he received fulfillment of all earthly desires (*bhukti*) and liberation (*mukti*).[63]

Discrepancies between the two lists of appropriate attributes need not concern us in that a number of variable emblems were assigned to each Śakti. What does warrant notice, however, is that the banners were vitally important attributes of the Saptamātṛkās. Considering these references and the concurrence of the literary and archaeological data, it stands to reason that, sometime in the fourth century C.E., revisionist Vaidika Tantrins who were connected with the ruling class realized the *a priori* significance attached to powerful female septads in ancient India and also the weighty authority of Indra's war banners. They synthesized the older symbols and imbued them with new significance in an effort to create ever more potent devices to rid the world of unworthy rulers. The importance of war banners in Gupta society was corroborated by an inscription made by an official of Candragupta II who boasted that he "acquired banners of victory and fame in many battles."[64]

The significance of emblematic staffs or banners held by the Mātṛkās and Skanda at Udayagiri now comes into focus. Their political implication was great in that they connoted divine authority invested in the king; they were symbols of state and ownership and they were the conduit for the divine powers needed to decimate enemies. That at least some stone icons had political import to the Guptas has been argued convincingly by two scholars recently, both of whom identify the giant Varāha image at Udayagiri as an allegorical figure representing Candragupta II after his final conquest of the Śakas and the political unification of India north of the Vindhya mountain range and from ocean to ocean.[65] Similarly, the Gupta Saptmātṛkās played an important role in Śaka extermination and restoration of a righteous empire, but they were more than allegorical figures. Not only did their victories against demons have paradigmatic consequence, but the Śaktis were a means by which the mandate of the Gupta monarchs to establish *rājadharma* was accomplished. The king's regal powers, as stated in the *Nītisāra,* were his Śaktis; the Mātṛkās were his Śaktis realized in tangible forms. Their emblematic banners were visual confirmation that Indra's or Skanda's ominous might had been transferred through the goddesses to the king. For the king to go to war or to rule without these banners was unthinkable; to do so was to invite catastrophe. A king who was forced to relinquish banners in battle conceded defeat; collecting enemy banners meant subjugation and appropriation of the opponent's powers. As symbols of the sovereign state, they were the very tools of skillful manipulation and control.

Recall that the *Devī Māhātmya* states that the Goddess confers both *bhukti* and *mukti;* it is important to discuss the latter within the context of a royal mandate. Both the *Devī Purāṇa* and the *Nītisāra* stressed that a sovereign, for the welfare of all, must embody a fourfold ideal (*caturvarga*) which included *mukti.*[66] Specifically the king had to be so accomplished in his religious duties that he achieved liberation. The ideal demanded the king's realization of the quintessential spiritual state; to achieve *mukti* in actuality, however, would have created a difficult a paradox for the king, given the demands of ruling a vast empire particularly while launching large-scale wars. To achieve liberation, normally, one had to renounce all earthly connections and obligations; however, the Saptamātṛkās conferred liberation on the king and in doing so, circumvented the paradox. Candragupta realized his spiritual goal, if even symbolically, as witnessed by his title "great royal sage among kings" (*rājādhirājarṣi*) given in the Udayagiri inscription; in other words the "king's spiritual power was equal to his martial strength and moral superiority."[67]

Thus, the answers to the questions why and by what means did Tantrism gain acceptance in an orthodox Hindu context are linked, at least in part, to the Gupta quest to establish righteous order in Bhārata. They did so by emulating a model set down originally by Candragupta Maurya and formulated by Kauṭilya. The Gupta empire not only attempted to rival the earlier Mauryan empire in its geographical expanse, but elaborated upon Kauṭilya's methods to gain and maintain control over enemies by subversive means. Certainly one resonant note in the parallel between the two empires was the desire to eradicate foreign rulers in Bhārata by any expedient means. Building on older models, royal advisers who were Vaidika Tantrins devised rituals meant to strengthen the king's powers and protect the established order. Their reformation of older religious symbols resulted in elevating a female septad from its shadowy past and relocating it centrally in the Hindu pantheon. At the same time, the reformers provided the newly evolved deities with attributes that signified martial and spiritual empowerment, particularly for the king. The path to understanding the sophisticated and polyvalent symbolism of the Saptamātṛkās is circuitous indeed; however, the scarcity of archaeological and literary evidence is not necessarily caused by loss, but rather the Tantric character of the goddesses themselves. Securing the favor of such enigmatic divinties undoubtedly was guarded vigilantly. Their rites were shrouded in secrecy, obscure mimetic magic, and cryptic language passed on in weighty oral traditions.[68] Only by use of such camouflage could astute rulers and royal advisers protect the empire from abuse of the Mātṛkās' magical powers by the unworthy. Once the Saptamātṛkās found a place in the Hindu pantheon and the formula for their worship was established by the Vaidika Tantrins, icons of the beguiling deities were located in Śaivite temples as a matter of course. In later artistic renderings, the goddesses did not always carry banners; but by then the efficacy of the deities in promoting the welfare of the state was taken for granted with or without banners. Thus, Hindu kings in succeeding centuries sought the sponsorship of the Saptamātṛkās for conquest, control, and liberation.

NOTES

1. Agehananda Bharati, *The Tantric Tradition* (Garden City, N.Y.: Anchor Press, 1965), 15.

2. Mircea Eliade, *Yoga: Immortality and Freedom,* 2d ed. (Princeton, N.J.: Princeton University Press, 1970), 200.

3. Katherine Anne Harper, *The Iconography of the Saptamātṛikās: Seven Hindu Mothers of Spiritual Transformation* (Lewiston, N.Y.: The Edwin Mellen Press, 1989).

4. Teun Goudriaan, "Introduction, History and Philosophy," *Hindu Tantrism,* ed. Sanjukta Gupta, Dirk Jan Hoens, Teun Goudriaan (Leiden: E. J. Brill, 1979), 5.

5. Ibid., 6.

6. Ibid., 6.

7. C. Mackenzie Brown, *The Triumph of the Goddess* (Albany: State University of New York Press, 1990), 172.

8. *The Mahābhārata,* trans. J. A. B. van Buitenen (Chicago: University of Chicago Press, 1973, 1975, 1978), 3.25.10–12; 3.217.10–15.

9. Harper, *Iconography,* 13–45.

10. R. C. Hazra, *Studies in the Purāṇic Records on Hindu Rites and Customs* (Dacca: University of Dacca, Bulletin no. 20, 1940), 12.

11. *Devī Māhātmya,* trans. Swami Jagadisvarananda (Madras: Sri Ramakrishna Math, 1972), 7.1–26 and 8.1–63.

12. *Ibid., 13.1–25.*

13. Thomas B. Coburn, *Devī Māhātmya: The Crystallization of the Goddess Tradition* (Delhi: Motilal Banarsidass, 1984), 173.

14. R. C. Hazra, *Studies in the Upapurāṇas* (Calcutta: Sanskrit College, 1958), 2:77.

15. *Devī Purāṇa* 23.12–20 as cited by Pratapaditya Pal, "The Mother Goddess According to the *Devī Purāṇa,*" *Purāṇa,* 30, 1, All-India Kashiraj Trust, Varanasi): 142.

16. John Faithful Fleet, *Inscriptions of the Early Gupta Kings and their Successors. Corpus Inscriptionum Indicarum* (*CII* hereafter) (Varanasi: Indological Book House, 1963r), 3:21–25.

17. Ibid., 3:72–78.

18. Harper, *Iconography,* 33–45.

19. D. C. Sircar, *Select Inscriptions Bearing on Indian History and Civilization* (Calcutta: University of Calcutta, 1942), I:450–55.

20. John Faithful Fleet, "Sanskrit and Old Canarese Inscriptions," *The Indian Antiquary* 6 (1877): 72–76, 7 (1878) 161–64, and 13 (1884): 137–38. See also: V. V. Mirashi, *Inscriptions of the Kalachuri-Chedi Era, Corpus Inscriptionum Indicarum* 4, pt. 1 (Ootacamund: Government Epigraphists for India, 1955), 123–31 and 137–45.

21. Jagadisvarananda, *Devī Māhātmyam* 12.6; 12.14–25.

22. Fleet, *CII,* 3:72–78.

23. Ibid., 3:49.

24. Harper, *Iconography,* 153–167.

25. Douglas Renfrew Brooks, *The Secret of the Three Cities: An Introduction to Śākta Tantrism* (Chicago: The University of Chicago Press, 1990), 4.

26. Goudriaan, et al., *Hindu Tantrism,* 30.

27. Sarla Khosla, *Gupta Civilization* (New Delhi: Intellectual Publishing House, 1982), 5.

28. For elaboration on this point see Joanna Williams, "A Recut Aśokan Capital and the Gupta Attitude Towards the Past," *Artibus Asiae* 25 (1973): 225–40.

29. Fleet, *CII* 3, 1.

30. M. R. Kale, *Mudrārākshasa of Viśākhadatta* (Delhi: Motilal Barnarsidass, 1976), xiii–xv.

31. V. R. R. Dikshitar, *The Gupta Polity* (Delhi: Motilal Banarsidass, 1993r), 228.

32. *The Laws of Manu,* trans. Georg Buhler (New York: Dover, 1969), 7.98–101.

33. *Ibid.,* 10.119.

34. *Yajñavalkya Smṛti,* trans. J. R. Gharpure (Poona: Principal Law College, 1937), 12.308.10–15.

35. Dikshitar, *Gupta Polity,* 13. See also *Kamandakiya Nītisāra,* trans. Manmatha Nath Dutt (Varanasi: Chowkhamba Sanskrit Studies, XCVII, 2nd ed., 1979), 1.2–6.

36. *Dutt, Nītisāra* 9.35–38.

37. *Ibid.,* 2.35.

38. *Kauṭilya's Arthaśastra,* trans. R. Shamasastry (Mysore: Padam Printers, 1988), 416–56.

39. J. Gonda, *Ancient Indian Kingship from the Religious Point of View* (Leiden: E.J. Brill, 1969), 135.

40. Gharpure, *Yajñavalkya Smṛti,* 12.308.20–25.

41. Dutt, *Nītisāra* 1.2–6.

42. Ibid., 10.11.

43. Ibid., 3,65–67.

44. Ibid., 8.61.

45. Ibid., 8.20.

46. Ibid., 1.1.

47. Ibid., 8.55.

48. Dikshitar, *Gupta Polity,* 142.

49. Fleet, *CII,* 3:34–36.

50. Ibid., 3:49.

51. Gonda, *Ancient Indian Kingship,* 22.

52. Ibid., 74.

53. Van Buitenen, *Mahābhārata* 1.57.17–32.

54. Ibid., 1.131–132.

55. Ibid., 3.218.

56. Shamasastry, *Kauṭilya's Arthaśastra* 14.426.

57. M. Ramakrishna Bhat, *Varāhamihira's Bṛhatsaṃitā* (Delhi: Motilala Barnarsidass, 1986), 345–60.

58. Ibid., 356–57.

59. *Devī Purāṇa,* ed. Pushpendra Kumar Sharma (New Delhi: Sri Lal Bahadur Shastri Kendriya Sanskrit Vidyapeeth, 1967), 12.15–20 and 12.45–52.

60. Ibid., 23.12–16.

61. Ibid., 23.12–16.

62. Ibid., 23.17–20.

63. Ibid., 35.12–32.

64. R. C. Majumdar and A. S. Altekar, *The Vakaṭaka-Gupta Age* (Delhi: Motilal Banarsidass, 1986), 167. See also Dikshitar, *Gupta Polity,* 349.

65. Fredrick M. Asher, "Historical and Political Allegory in Gupta Art," *Essays on Gupta Culture,* ed. Bardwell L. Smith (Delhi: Motilal Banarsidass, 1983), 53–66; and Heinrich von Stietencron, "Political Aspects of Indian Religious Art," *Visible Religion* 4–5 (1985–1986): 16–36.

66. Sharma, *Devī Purāṇa* 23.12–16 and Dutt, *Nītisāra* 2.1–17.

67. Barbara Stoler Miller, "A Dynasty of Patrons: The Representation of Gupta Royalty in Coins and Literature," *The Powers of Art: Patronage in Indian Culture* (Delhi: Oxford University Press, 1992), 5.

68. Brooks, *Secret,* 6.

8

Early Evidence of the *Pāñcarātra Āgama*

Dennis Hudson

Those Hindus who believe Kṛṣṇa to have been the full descent of God into our realm of space and time (*brahmāṇḍa*) have called themselves Bhāgavatas, "those who belong to the Possessor of Glories (*Bhagavān*)." Among their narrative and theological texts most notable are the *Mahābhārata,* its central theological work; the *Bhagavad Gītā;* and the *Śrīmad Bhāgavata Purāṇa.* Other works include Purāṇas such as the *Viṣṇu* and the whole corpus of Veda and its culmination in the Upaniṣads of the Vedānta. Bhāgavata liturgical texts consist of Veda as interpreted by the Āgamas. Among the schools of the Āgamas, the Pāñcarātra describes itself as using a mixture of Vedic and Tantric elements. H. Daniel Smith has summarized the Pāñcarātra texts (*saṃhitās*)[1] and Sanjukta Gupta has discussed them.[2]

In this essay, I shall discuss early evidence for the *Pāñcarātra Āgama.* The evidence places the Āgama in the first three or four centuries B.C.E. and connects it with a consistent ritual and theological tradition that centers on Vāsudeva Kṛṣṇa. Bhāgavatas believe that, Kṛṣṇa, together with his kinsmen, is the full manifestation of the Bhagavān known in differing contexts as the supreme Person (*puruṣa-uttama*) named Nārāyana and Vāsudeva. My discussion will focus on data contained in two admirable studies by Doris Meth Srinivansan, "Early Vaiṣṇava Imagery: Caturvyūha and Variant Forms"[3] and "Vaiṣṇava Art and Iconography at Mathurā."[4] Srinivansan's aesthetic and historical analyses of the early evidence for the crucial Pāñcarātra doctrine of the *vyūhas* (formations) are subtle and rich. Here I want to build on her thinking.

I will do so, however, with two different assumptions. One is that this early evidence reveals a consistent Bhāgavata system of thought and practice from the beginning, and not, as she and others have assumed, a gradual synthesis of differing streams (Viṣṇu of the Veda, Vṛṣṇi heroes of the Bhāgavatas, and Nārāyana of the Brāhmaṇas and Āraṇyakas).[5] The other is that the paradigmatic orientation for the four-*vyūha* form (or *maṇḍala*) has Vāsudeva facing the west, not the east as is usually assumed. I will argue from an eighth century model, admitting the danger of imposing later developments onto the past. Yet I think the explanatory power of the model will justify the risk. The Bhāgavata tradition itself believes it has always been a coherent whole and it is worth taking that claim seriously to interpret the data we have.

The following discussion is based upon my recent analysis of the Vaikuṇṭha Perumāl Temple at Kanchipuram.[6] The temple was completed about 770 C.E. as the imperial Viṣṇu-house for the Pallava emperor, Nandivarman II Pallavamalla (731–796). It was constructed according to the *Pāñcarātra Āgama* and illustrated the *Bhāgavata Purāṇa* in the form it was then known. Its connection to Pallavamalla's imperial (rather than kingly) status, which he gained in 745–746, is expressed by the temple's original name recorded in inscriptions and in a Tamil poem: "the Viṣṇu-house of the Supreme Lord [who is King of Kings]." Among the important things revealed by that monument, the following are relevant to this exploration.

First, the Vaikuṇṭha Perumāl Temple faces west as do all the Viṣṇu-houses built by the Pallavas in their capital, Kanchipuram. In contrast, the shrines they built for Śiva face east.[7] The west-facing direction of a *garbhagṛha* (inner sanctum) and of a standing or sitting icon inside it, means that worshipers face east. Such an orientation has important Vedic precedence. In the *Śatapatha Brāhmaṇa* 1.2.5 of the *Yajur Veda,* the sacrifice of the new and full moon is portrayed as Viṣṇu in the form of a dwarf (Vāmana). With that dwarf, the gods wrested the earth from the *asuras* (demons). Signifying the rescued earth, the dwarf became the sacrificial ground (*vedi*) oriented east-west with the fire for offerings (*āhavanīya*) on the east. The east side of the *vedi* signified the realm of the *devas* (gods), the north side the realm of humans, and the south side the realm of deceased ancestors. *Asuras* were left with the west side. In case of an *asura* victory, the *devas* transferred an imperishable place of sacrifice to the moon where they could flee to regain power, a place now seen as the moon's black spots in the shape of a hare (*śaśa*).[8]

In *śrauta* (Vedic) rites, that eastern fire was in the square raised altar (*uttara vedi*) that represented heaven. If the deity to whom the oblation was offered by a priest on the northwest facing east were to be depicted by a sculpted figure, the figure would be facing west. That west-facing heavenly fire contrasted the domestic fire (*gārhapatya*) in the round altar on the west side of the sacrificial arena that represented earth, and contrasted the fire in the half-circle altar to the south (*dakṣiṇa*) that represented the atmosphere between heaven and earth.

A figure important for our later discussion is the man who played the role of the supervising Brāhmin during *śrauta* rites.[9] According to H. G. Ranade, in *Ṛg Veda* ritual he was apparently a *purohita* (priest) to the king or to a poet. He later appeared as the fourth of the original three priests (the Hotṛ of the *Ṛg Veda,* the Udgātṛ of the *Śama Veda,* and the Adhvāryu of the *Yajur Veda*) and was connected with the *Atharva Veda.* Ranade summarized the elements of his duties relevant to our discussion as follows: (1) he sits to the south of the fireplace during the sacrificial performance and supervises silently the performance of other priests; (2) he gives consent to proceed with particular rites; (3) he offers expiatory oblations on the three sacred fires and makes up for any losses caused by faulty performance; (4) he occasionally recites certain *ṛcs* (praises) and *stomabhāgas* (*soma* sacrificial verses) and even chants particular *sāmans* (praises); (5) he has to participate in the philosophical dialogues (*brahmodya*) that take place during the sacrificial performance.[10] Interestingly, he made his offerings into the fire from the northwest, facing east, and addressed *mantras* to Viṣṇu as the primary authority for the rites.[11]

In my opinion, if we coalesce the Brahmin on the south with the dwarf form of Viṣṇu as the sacrifice that takes over the whole earth, and both with the full moon (*śaśi*), we have the *ācārya* (spiritual guide) of the *Pāñcarātra Āgama.* Bhāgavatas traced their narrative and liturgical lineage from Brahmā through the Lunar Dynasty, signified by Soma the moon, made of deathlessness (*amṛtamaya*).[12] In the Vaikuṇṭha Perumāl Temple, that Lunar lineage was connected with the south side of the *vimāna* (temple).

As I understand Pāñcarātra thought and practice, during consecration rites (*dīkṣā*), the *ācārya* "took over" the initiate as refugee (*prapanna*) and made him or her a "slave" to Vāsudeva Kṛṣṇa, the "black man" of the Lunar Dynasty. The relationship of master to slave was illustrated narratively by the relationship of Kṛṣṇa to members of the Lunar Dynasty, beginning with the Vaiśya caste cowherds in Gokula, then moving to the Kśatriyas (warrior caste) in Mathura, and ending with the Pāṇḍavas and Kauravas.

The paradigmatic Bhāgavata "slave" appears to have been the ruler, as was the case with Pallavamalla. The relevance of Pāñcarātra *ācāryas* as the *purohitas* of kings is found in their powerful *dīkṣās* by which they could purify any properly motivated person of any caste. Once purified, they could be initiated into Āgamic rites and through them be linked to Veda. Many kings were either classified as Śūdras or barbarians (*mlecca*), something that made Pāñcarātra *ācāryas* quite relevant to kingship. The Guptas and Pallavas, for example, had low ritual status yet were great builders of Āgamic temples. Evidence indicates that they used Bhāgavata rites in their kingship and represented their *ācāryas* with the figure of Vāmana Trivikrama.

Second, the emperor Pallavamalla appears to have built the Vaikuṇṭha Perumāl Temple as an architectural and liturgical *summa theologica* of the *Pāñcarātra Āgama* of the Bhāgavatas. Although oriented east-west, the *vimāna* and its surrounding *prakāra* form a *maṇḍala.* The meanings of the *maṇḍala* are revealed by the central mountainous tower (*vimāna*) which is divided between exoteric and esoteric dimensions.

The exoteric dimension is the *vimāna*'s sculpted outer wall at its bottom, the western side of which has been extended to form a porch (*ardhamaṇḍapa*). The temple sculptures face outward toward the surrounding wall (*prakāra*) that delimits the temple area. Among other things, the temple sculptures signify the geographical and chronological elements of space-time (*brahmāṇḍa*). They face sculpted panels on the inside of the *prakāra* that depict Pallava history. The figures on the *vimāna*'s four sides gaze at the sculpted Pallavas across a surrounding drain that appears to have served as a moat. The *vimāna* surrounded by the moat represents White Island (*Śveta dvīpa*) in the Ocean of Milk. The Pallava kings on the *prakāra* facing it represent the initiated slaves of the Bhagavān who resides in and on the mountainous White Island.

The esoteric dimension of the *vimāna* is hidden by its outer bottom wall. Inside, it consists of three *garbhagṛhas* arranged vertically (Chart 8.1). The bottom *garbhagṛha* reveals the connection of each side of the *maṇḍala* with a formation (*vyūha*) of glories within himself that the Bhagavān brings about in order to make space-time exist. Each *vyūha* corresponds to Kṛṣṇa or to one of his kinsmen (Chart 8.2). Sitting inside the *garbhagṛha,* facing west, is a black stone icon (*arca*) of the Bhagavān in his complete *vyūha* form, Vāsudeva, who once descended into space-time as the dark blue or black man, Kṛṣṇa. On the outer north *garbhagṛha* wall gazing through a window in the enclosing *vimāna* wall is a seated figure of the *vyūha* Saṃkarṣaṇa, slightly inebriated; a five-headed cobra rises behind his head. He once descended as Kṛṣṇa's elder brother, the white-bodied Balarāma fond of

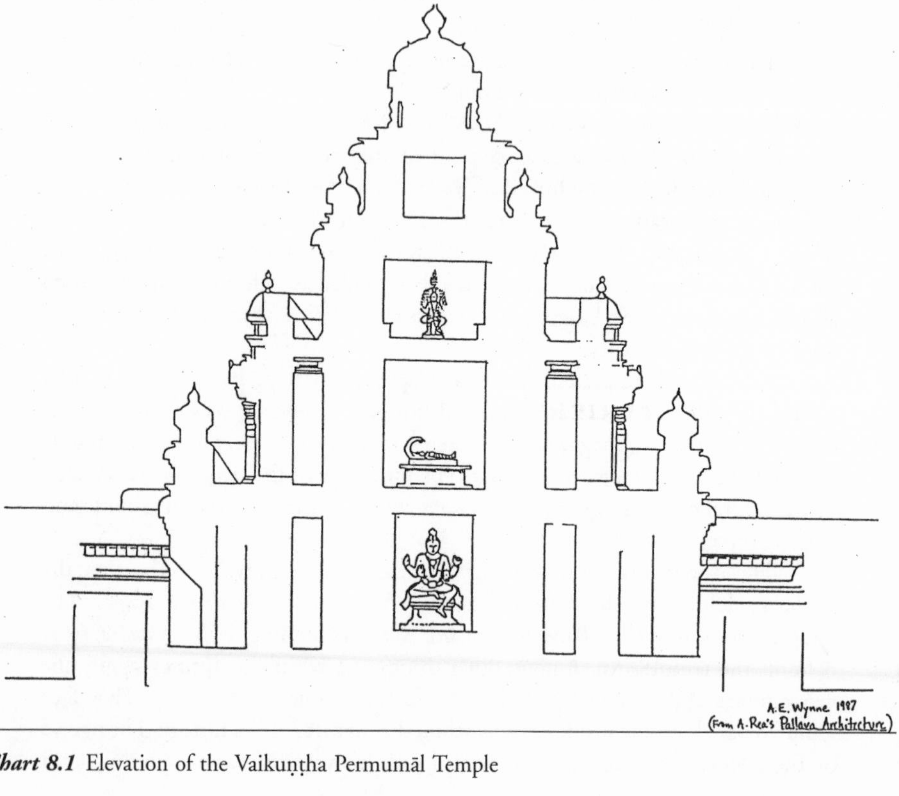

Chart 8.1 Elevation of the Vaikuṇṭha Permumāl Temple

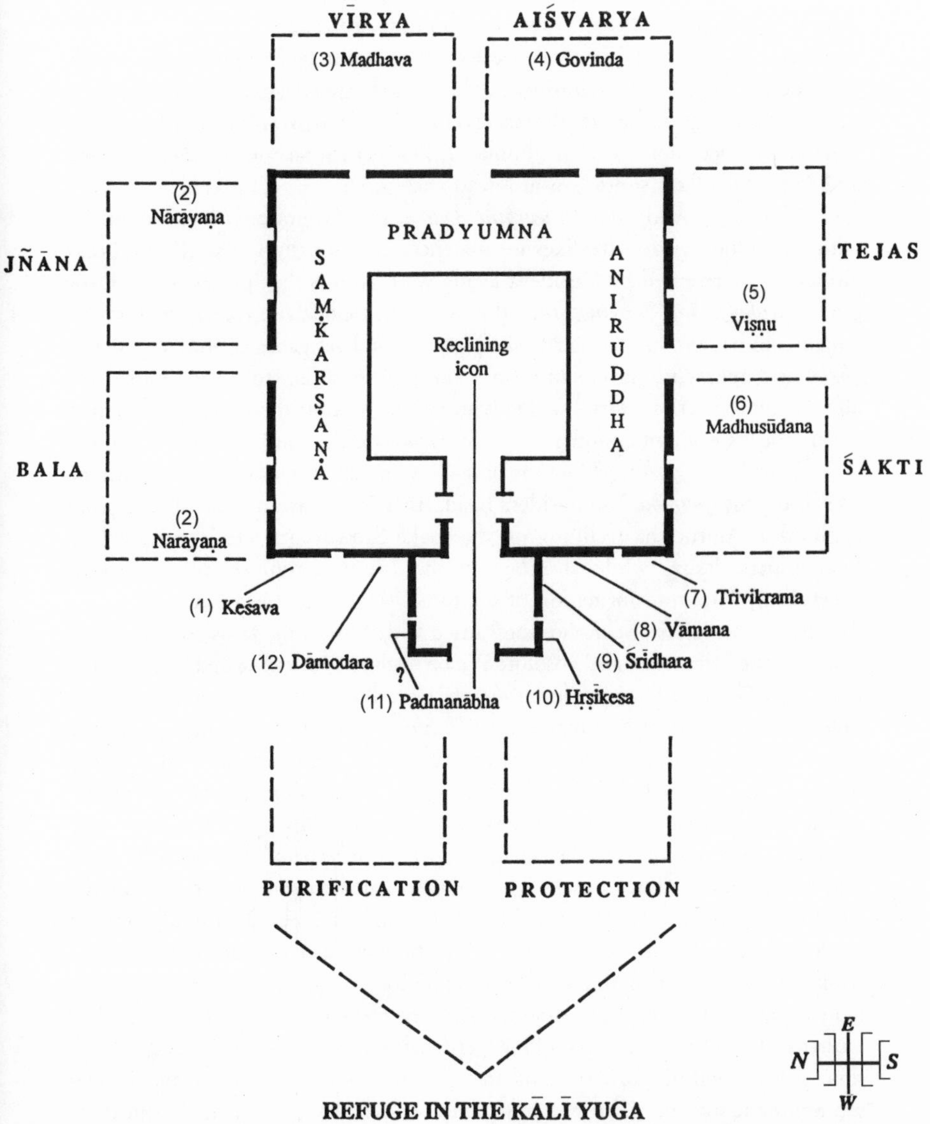

Chart 8.2 Garbhagṛha on the Middle Floor: The Six Glories (Bhaga) and Twelve Mūrtis

drink. Seated figures of the other *vyūhas* similarly face outward from the other sides of the *garbhagṛha,* Pradyumna on the east and Aniruddha on the south. Pradyumna, "the pre-eminently mighty one," is the origin of Kāma among the *devas.* He descended as Kṛṣṇa's son by Rukminī, also called Pradyumna. Aniruddha, "the unobstructed," descended as Kṛṣṇa's grandson by Pradyumna, also called Aniruddha. The *vyūha* sculptures of the bottom *garbhagṛha* thus identify the primary meanings of the *maṇḍala's* sides: Vāsudeva faces west (toward the *asuras*), Saṃkarṣaṇa faces north (toward humans), Pradyumna faces east (toward *devas*), and Aniruddha faces south (toward dead ancestors).

Third, following the *Pāñcarātra Āgama,* the six glories (*bhaga*) identified with those four *vyūhas* are likewise matched directionally (Chart 8.2). All six glories are represented by Vāsudeva facing west, who is the "possessor of all the glories" (*bhagavān*). Moving from the north in a clockwise direction, they are paired: omniscient knowledge (*jñāna*) and its indefatigable conquering power (*bala*) as Saṃkarṣaṇa; sovereignty (*aiśvarya*) and its ability to act without being affected by the action (*vīrya*) as Pradyumna on the east; the potency of mantra (*śakti*) and its brilliant conquering power (*tejas*) on the south as Aniruddha.

Fourth, the *garbhagṛha* on the floor above reveals other associations with the *vyūhas* on the *maṇḍala's* four sides. Inside that shrine is an icon of Bhagavān depicted as Aniruddha reclining on the snake Saṃkarṣaṇa. He is pervaded by Pradyumna's desires while absorbed in the "sleep of unified consciousness" (*yoganidrā*). That transformation of the three *vyūhas* exists as a fetus within the dark placental waters of consciousness fused with matter; the fetus reclines in the womb of the primordial and absolute Person (*parama puruṣa*) seated below in the bottom *garbhagṛha.* The middle *garbhagṛha* represents the womb (*yoni*) that Kṛṣṇa called the transcendent Brahmān (*mahad brahmā*) into which Vāsudeva plants the embryo (*garbha*) from which all created beings arise (*Bhagavad Gītā* 14.3–4 and *Śrīmad Bhāgavata* 3.26.1–31). Vāsudeva is the father of all forms (*murtayaḥ*), which arise from the womb that is the transcendent Brahman. The reclining scene depicts the fetal son of the father imagining those forms before they actually come into being from within himself. The sculpted panels on the outer sides of the *garbhagṛha* portray some of what "Puruṣa the son" imagines, his mind propelled by Pradyumna's desiring force (Chart 8.3). Those events take place only when he awakes to birth by emanating space-time at his lotus-navel. That realm, which is a reorganization of the newly born son, is represented by the *garbhagṛha* above. (The lotus-navel signifies the fire-pot of the sacrificial altar in the east *uttara vedi.* Space-time develops within that "lotus of fire," or womb.)[13] The west and north sides symbolize the span of nighttime, from sunset at the southwest corner to sunrise at the northeast corner. Daytime is illustrated by the east and south sides (Chart 8.4).

The west side of the middle *garbhagṛha,* the side facing the *asuras* in the darkness of night, depicts themes of nighttime and of purification and refuge. Nighttime and rule of the *asuras* represent the condition of human life in the Kālī Yuga (Dark Age). The black stone icon represents the color of the Bhagavān's

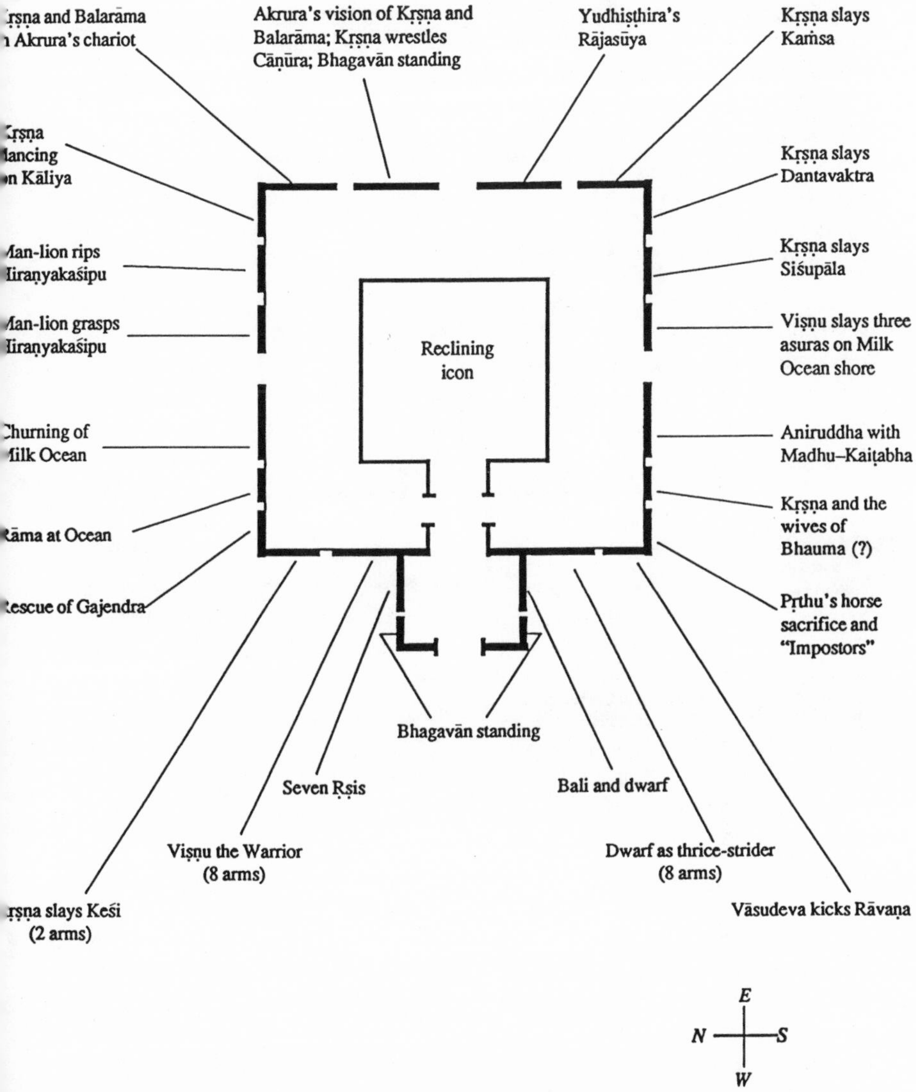

Chart 8.3 Garbhagṛha on Middle Floor: The Panels Identified According to the Bhāgavata Purāṇa

body of Light that humans in the Kālī Yuga see owing to their impassioned consciousness.

The north side faces the human realm and corresponds to the last of night as the sun prepares to rise (*brahmamuhūrta*). Relevant to omiscient knowledge (*jñāna*) and its power (*bala*), the north side's sculptures depict themes of initiation

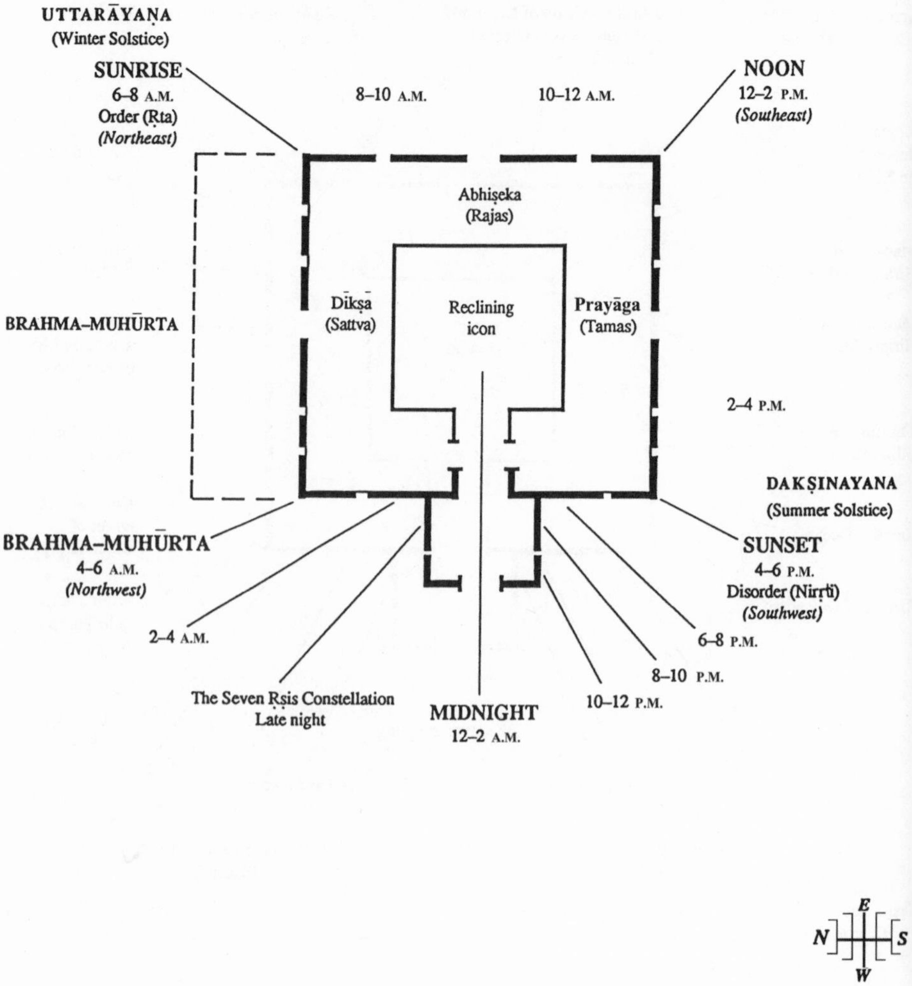

Chart 8.4 Garbhagṛha on the Middle Floor: Time and Ritual Action

into *mantra* (*dīkṣā*), the deathlessness (*amṛta*) it bestows, and the goal of waking up to omniscient knowledge befitting that predawn ritual hour. Water, representing varying states of consciousness, unifies all the panels. Significantly, after initiation (represented by Danvantari emerging from the churning of the Milk Ocean with deathlessness just stolen by the *asuras*), the penultimate stage in that waking up is represented by the Man-Lion slaying Hiraṇyakaśipu in the Ocean of Milk, and the ultimate stage by Kṛṣṇa dancing on the snake Kāliya in a Yamunā pool.

The east side, the side facing the *deva* realm, corresponds to the time from sunrise until noon, the main time for liturgical activity. Appropriately, it depicts themes relating to the initiate's sovereignty (*aiśvarya*) and nonclinging action (*vīrya*).

The south side faces Yama's realm of dead ancestors and corresponds to the period from noon to sunset in the west, when shadows lengthen and "language in the manner of twilight" is appropriate.[14] Its sculptures depict the use of *mantra* to destroy polluting enemies as nighttime approaches. Notable are the portrayals of the *cakra* (wheel) as a weapon of brilliant conquering power (*tejas*) and the depiction of *mantra's* potency (*śakti*). Sculptures on the *vimāna* outer wall below make other apsects of Aniruddha's south side clear. A sculpture of a Boar holding the Earth signifies the Bhāgavata ruler's potency (*śakti*) for "rescuing" and protecting his realm through rites guided by his *ācārya.* Next to it, Mohini, Viṣṇu's female form, holds the vessel of *amṛta* that she has taken back from the *asuras* by playing on their erotic lust.

In the discussion that follows, two sets of connections are important: (1) the lion, snake and drunkenness to consecration (*dīkṣā*) into omniscient knowledge and its power on the north; (2) the boar, the *cakra,* and the vessel of *amṛta* held by Mohinī to the initiate's application (*prayoga*) of mantraic knowledge on the south. We may also keep in mind that the Brahmin assigned the south side of the fire sacrifice (the direction of dead ancestors) corresponds directly to the ruler's *ācārya* who performed mantraic rites to manifest the power (*tejas*) needed to defeat the ruler's enemies and to keep the vessel of deathlessness (*amṛta*) in his possession. As noted by Frederique Apffel Marglin, in certain later temple rites at the Jagannātha Temple in Puri, the king's *ācārya* dressed as Mohinī when dealing with *tejas* in the night.[15] If the middle floor *garbhagṛha* represented the raised altar (*uttara vedi*) and the firepot within it, the southern side would indeed be the side related to the ruler's *purohita,* his *ācārya.*[16]

Fifth, the top *garbhagṛha* that once contained a standing icon facing west reveals that in his entirety the Bhagavān Vāsudeva entered into the space-time he created at his fiery lotus-navel in his Kṛṣṇa avatar. The standing Kṛṣṇa on the top is the erotic and heroic mode of Vāsudeva sitting on the bottom. The watery placental realm represented by the shrine in the middle mediates between the two. Those three *garbhagṛhas* standing above one another in the middle of a *maṇḍala* expanding in all directions replicate the complete body of God. It is a three-dimensional *yantra* through that one can walk all around and by which one can employ the senses of the body to see the Paramātman, the Puruṣa Nārāyana, the Bhagavān Vāsudeva Kṛṣṇa, as he truly is: "The Supreme Self, the Person (*puruṣa*) who is the abode or refuge (*ayaṇa*) of men (*nāra*), the possessor of glories (*bhagavān*) who is the shining one (*deva*) dwelling in all things (*vasu*) and in whom all things dwell (*vasu*), the blessed one (*bhagavān*) who is a black man (*kṛṣṇa*), the son of Vāsudeva."[17]

To sum up the meaning of the *maṇḍala,* we may diagram it this way:

NORTH
Saṃkarṣaṇa/Balarāma
Predawn
Jñāna/Bala
Initiation
Waking up
Lion

WEST
Vāsudeva Kṛṣṇa
Nighttime
Six glories
Purification
Refuge

EAST
Pradyumna
Morning
Aiśvarya/Vīrya
Nonclinging action

SOUTH
Aniruddha
Afternoon
Śakti/Tejas
Sudarśana-cakra
Mantraic Rites
Boar

In her article of 1979, Doris Srinivasan discussed a stone sculpture illustrating the four *vyūhas* of the *Pāñcarātra Āgama.* A tall sculpture (167cm), it was found in Bhita, Uttar Pradesh. She dated it to the Śuṅga Period, perhaps as early as the first quarter of the second century B.C.E. The dominant figure is a four-armed crowned male figure with a decorated body. To his right, facing in the next cardinal direction, is a standing male figure with a seated lion between his legs. To his right, facing in the next cardinal direction and opposite the crowned figure, is a standing male figure without a decorated body and holding what may have been a flask; he appears to be an ascetic. To his right, facing in the last cardinal direction, is a standing male figure with a boar facing toward the dominant crowned figure. As we now find it, that four-sided sculpture is outside the cultic context for which it was created. There is no external evidence to indicate its intended orientation. Srinivasan assumed that the crowned four-armed figure faced east and she cited the later *Viṣṇudharmottara Purāṇa* 3.44.9–12 as evidence.

To my mind, use of that Sanskrit text to identify the orientation of an icon found out of its cultic context poses a problem because the words it uses for the cardinal directions depend on the perspective of the subject. As commonly interpreted, they represent the point of view of a person facing east: *dakṣiṇa* means to the right and south; *uttara* means to the left and north; *pūrva* means before and east; and *paścima* means behind and west. If, however, the perspective is that of a figure facing west (such as the deity worshiped by someone facing east), then the right is to the north (*uttara*) and the left is to the south (*dakṣiṇa*); the west is in front (*pūrva*) and the east is behind (*paścina*). The *Dharmottara Purāṇa* text tells us that the *vyūhas* move to the right (*pradakṣiṇa*) in relation to each other, but it does not necessarily tell us their orientation.[18]

If, however, we apply the model provided by the west-facing Vaikuṇṭha Perumāl Temple, the meaning of the four sides of the Bhita sculpture is clear. The dominant crowned figure is the Bhagavān Vāsudeva Kṛṣṇa facing west. The male to his right with the lion facing north is Saṃkarṣaṇa Balarāma. The ascetic male facing east is Pradyumna. The male facing south with the standing boar is Aniruddha. According to the model, the north is associated with the lion, with *jñāna* and *bala,* and with Saṃkarṣaṇa Balarāma. The south is associated with the boar rescuing the Earth and with the *śakti* and *tejas* of rites guided by the *ācārya.* In the Vaikuṇṭha Perumāl Temple, the east is not represented by an ascetic, yet the meaning is appropriate and the west-facing Viṣṇu temple at Deogarh used the ascetics Nārāyana and Nara to signify Pradyumna.[19] Furthermore, the model makes sense of a variant arrangement that Srinivasan described (her figure 14). A male figure stands with the lion emerging at his left shoulder and the boar emerging at his right shoulder. The two back arms that usually hold the *cakra* (left) and *gadā* or club (right) instead hang to his sides and connect to standing figures that personify those weapons. The two hands of the natural arms rest at the hips, but are broken.

Again, the intended orientation of the sculpture is not known. Yet, according to our model, the figure is probably Pradyumna. Since Pradyumna faces east, the north and lion are to his left and the south and boar are to his right. The inactive positioning of the *cakra* and *gadā* and the graceful pose suggest the detached and nonclinging posture of Pradyumna coupled with his desirable and desiring nature. In that context, the inactive *cakra* and *gadā* may have specific meanings. Because the basic *mantra* is generated from the *cakra-maṇḍala,* the inactive *cakra* on his left and to the north suggests that the *dīkṣa* (of the north) has been completed. Since the *gadā* signifies power put into action, the inactive *gadā* on his right and to the south suggests that the practical application of *mantra* (of the south) is suspended. Among the *devas* whom he faces in the east, Pradyumna represents Kāma. Other examples of that placement of the lion and boar in later centuries may also be interpreted as the Pradyumna *vyūha* of the Bhagavān facing east.[20]

Similarly, the model explains a fragmentary four *vyūha* figure from Mathura dated to the Kuṣāṇa period, discussed by Doris Srinivasan and by T. S. Maxwell.[21] Although found out of its cultic context and pieced together, it appears to have been intended for frontal viewing, which explains its mode of depicting the *vyūhas.* A crowned male figure with four arms faces directly forward with one right hand resting on a mace. He is Vāsudeva Kṛṣṇa. From his right shoulder emerges a smaller figure with a canopy of snake heads and holding a drinking cup. He is Saṃkarṣaṇa Balarāma. From behind the central figure's crown emerges another male, whose head is broken, but as T. S. Maxwell has suggested, it resembles a Kuṣāṇa Bodhisattva figure: "the robe over the left shoulder and arm, the water flask held at waist level, and the raised right hand are all features derived from contemporary Buddhist iconography."[22] It is designed so as to appear as if it "stands within, or rises from the interior of the principal god below it."[23] He is Pradyumna who is the form-imagining consciousness inside the reclining Aniruddha sleeping on Saṃkarṣaṇa. His portrayal in the manner of a Bodhisattva with a flask suggests Pradyumna's non-clinging relationship to forms and echoes the ascetic figure that represents him on the Bhita sculpture. As noted, Pradyumna was similarly represented by the ascetics Nārāyana and Nara in the early sixth century in Deogarh. From his left shoulder another figure emerged, but it is missing. No doubt it was Aniruddha.[24] With such an arrangement, the devotee did not need to walk around the sculpture to trace out the clockwise sequence of *vyūhas;* they could be viewed simultaneously and still keep their relationship to one another.

Let us turn to another early piece of evidence that Doris Srinivasan has brought to our attention. It is a group of six coins issued by the Indo-Bactrian king Agathocles, who ruled 180–165 B.C.E.[25] They are rectangular and are made of bronze. On the obverse, a legend in Greek reads *basileos* to the right and *agatokleous* to the left. It appears to mean either the coin of the king Agathocles, or the coin of the king of Agathocles. In the middle is a standing male, holding in his right hand a club and in his left a plow. That figure corresponds to Saṃkarṣaṇa Balarāma, the representative of *jñāna* and *bala.* The club may signify his indefatigable conquering power (*bala*), because the plough appears to signify his omniscient knowledge (*jñāna*) in the following way. *Saṃkarṣaṇa* means the act of drawing together, contracting, attracting, ploughing, furrowing. *Balarāma* means the power (*bala*) that is pleasing (*rāma*). The Bhagavān's omniscienct knowledge (*jñāna*) must voluntarily obscure itself if the world based on ignorance is to exist. That obscuration is signified by the liquor that Saṃkarṣaṇa drinks, represented elsewhere by a cup. Saṃkarṣaṇa Balarāma signifies the Bhagavān's pleasing and indefatigable power of omniscient knowledge that ploughs the field during the pleasure of drinking liquor. The agricultural metaphor is used to describe sexual pleasure, which in turn signifies the primoridial conception of everything within the Bhagavān's omniscient knowledge based on self-imposed delusion. Kṛṣṇa made those ideas perfectly clear in the *Bhagavad Gītā* 13, 14, and 15. Vāsudeva is the knower of the field and the field is his transcendent womb. Into it he plants the seed that grows into space-time and all beings within it. The plant that emerges from that ploughing is the cosmic tree that he told Arjuna to cut at the root with the ax of nonclinging. We shall return to those teachings later.

On the reverse of the coin is an inscription in Brahmi script. On the right it reads *rājane* and on the left *agathuklayeśa;* it appears to mean [the coin] of the king [*rājane*], the lord [*iśa*] of Agathocles [*agatuklaya*]. That reading suggests that the figures on both sides represent the Bhagavān whom the barbarian (*mlecca*) Agathocles served as an initiated slave (*dāsa*). As far as I know, the only Bhāgavata rites that could clean up a *mlecca* for Bhāgavata initiations were those of the *Pāñcarātra Āgama,* notably the Man-lion consecration (*Narasiṃha dīkṣā*).[26] A male figure standing between the two words is identical to the figure on the obverse except that he holds in his right hand a pear-shaped vase (*maṇḍala*) and a large *cakra* in the left. The *cakra* is interesting for numerical reasons; it possesses eight spokes and five knobs that emanate from one half of its rim. What the knobs are is not clear; the numbers, however, can be interpreted plausibly according to Āgamic ideas. The *cakra* is a version of the Sudarśana-*cakra* called the Nārāyana-*cakra yantra* in the *Ahirbudhnya-saṃhitā* 22.[27] Its eight spokes no doubt mean many things, among which are the eight syllables of the basic Bhāgavatas *mantra* (*Om namo nārāyaṇāya*), which literally means, "Om, veneration to the abode (and refuge) of man." Sudarśana, the text says, should be worshiped especially by kings because it signifies both desire (*icchā*) and the ability to accomplish ends (*kriyā*), and from it come the *mantras* that infuse the weapons of the king's army. The *yantra* form of the *cakra* concentrates the *mantra*'s verbal and spellbinding protective power. In other words, the *cakra* signifies the potency (*śakti*) of mantraic rites to produce brilliant conquering power (*tejas*) characteristic of Aniruddha on the south side. It appears then that this figure does not represent Vāsudeva Kṛṣṇa, as has been assumed, but the Bhagavān as the *vyūha* Aniruddha. In that light, it is perhaps significant that the *vyūhas* Saṃkarṣaṇa and Aniruddha are on opposite sides of the same coin, just as they are on the opposite north and south sides of the model *maṇḍala.*

What about the five knobs? That number points toward the five in the teaching known as "that which has come down (*āgama*) [to us] regarding the rites of the five (*pañca*) nights (*rātri*)," the *Pāñcarātra Āgama.* There are various sets of five that could be intended, particularly the Bhagavān's five modes of being relevant to humans: the transcendent mode (*para*); the *vyūha* through which the supreme develops space-time and everything within it; the incarnations he takes within space-time (*vibhava*); the iconic embodiments for worship (*arcā*); and the form he takes as the Self dwelling in the self of each conscious being (*antaryāmin*). The list makes clear what Āgama means by Vāsudeva, that is, the shining indweller of all beings who dwell within him. The five could signify also the categories of worship that initiates were expected to perform, most of which took place from the predawn time (*brahmamuhūrta*) until noon. They spent the afternoon and evening in study and in various disciplined devotional practices (yoga).[28] Five might also refer to the five central chapters of the *Bhagavad Gītā.* But let us consider them later.

As an initiated king, what would Agathocles have done as a Bhāgavata? In all likelihood, he probably followed Arjuna's model and took refuge in the Bhagavān rather than attempt the ritual and yoga that led to the fully awake status of the man of true being (*sat*) described in *Bhagavad Gītā* 14 and elsewhere. He no doubt had an *ācārya* who served as his *purohita* and performed the rites necessary for the Bhagavān to protect his rule. He also no doubt engaged in devotional acts befitting a Bhāgavata possessing kingship, including patronizing *ācāryas,* building Viṣṇu temples and sponsoring festivals for forms of the Bhagavān, especially Kṛṣṇa. As Srinivasan noted, we know from Pāṇini and from Patañjali's commentary on Pāṇini that, in the fourth-second century B.C.E., such worship of Kṛṣṇa took place.[29] We know about the events celebrated then from the *Śrimad Bhāgavata,* the Purāṇa "pertaining to the slave of the Bhagavān who possesses kingship." Evidence for the type of religious activity Agathocles engaged in also is found in epigraphy and in the Purāṇas. We know from epigraphy that the Bhāgavata Heliodorus, the son of Dion, was sent by the king Antialkidas of Taxila as the Yavana ambassador to the ruler at Vidisa in central India. Sometime in the second century B.C.E., he sponsored the creation of a Garuḍa-*dhvaja* (flagpole) for Vāsudeva, the God of gods.[30] According to M. D. Khare, the flagpole with Garuḍa on top was one of eight in front of the Vāsudeva temple,[31] which faced east on a northeast-southwest axis. The pillar is octagonal, a smaller portion above divided into sixteen facets and then an even smaller portion divided into thirty-two facets, the pillar ended in a rounded top.

The eight facets ending after multiplication in a Garuḍa image may tell us what the pole signified for Heliodorus. Kṛṣṇa explicitly identified himself with the number eight in *Bhagavad Gītā* 7.4 when he drew Arjuna's attention to himself as the human form of Vāsudeva. Eight represents the eight modes of matter (*prakṛti*) that make up the Bhagavān's gross body (*sthūla śarīra*), which is our universe (*brahmāṇḍa*); and they make up the essential elements of our inividual embodiment within that universe: earth, water, fire, wind, space, mind, intelligence, and the sense of I.

Then, in 10.30, Kṛṣṇa identified himself with Garuḍa, in a set of identifications that matched the "unclean" yet purified status of the Yavana donor at the time of his unction (*abhiṣeka*) as ruler: "Of the daityas [demons] I am Prahlāda [saved by Man-lion], of those who seize the Kālī die [in the unction rites], I am Time, and of wild animals I am the Indra of beasts [the lion], and of birds I am the son of Vinatā [Garuḍa]." In light of *Srimad Bhāgavata* and *Mahābhārata* lore,[32] that sequence suggests the purification and unction of an unclean devotee: Prahlāda represents the devout rebirth of the demonic ego covered with gold (*Hiraṇyakśipu*) that knowledge finally rips apart; Time decides who loses the ritual dice game during the royal unction ceremonies; the lion's roar represents the authority of the *ācārya* to teach the initiated ruler; and Garuḍa, made of vedic hymns, released his mother Vinatā from slavery to snake-like darkness by stealing deathlessness (*amṛta*) from Indra—a symbol of the ruler's protected status as a Bhāgavata.[33]

Perhaps, then, the multiplication of the number eight upward to Garuḍa signified the movement of Heliodorus' consciousness in consecration from his gross physical body (*sthūla śarīra*) signified by the number eight, to his unmanifest physical body (*sūkṣma śarīra*) signified by the number sixteen, to his causal unmanifest body (*kāraṇa sūkṣma śarīra*) signified by the number thirty-two, to the fourth (*turīya*) represented by the rounded end topped by Garuḍa. In Pāñcarātra Bhāgavata thought, however, the fourth is, like Garuḍa, the servant of the Bhagavān, because Vāsudeva is beyond the fourth (*turīya atīta*). He is the transcendent fifth, the absolute supreme Person, the God of gods residing inside the *garbhagṛha* before which this pillar stood.

Another inscription, from the second half of the first century B.C.E., suggests the coherence of the Bhāgavata religion into which the *mlecca* Yavanas, Agathocles and Heliodorus, had been initiated. An inscription from Ghosundi in Rajasthan tells us that the Bhāgavata king Sarvatāta performed a horse sacrifice and built "the Nārāyaṇa enclosure as a stone surrounding wall for the worship (*pūjā*) of the untouched (*anihata*) dual lords of all, the Bhagavāns Saṃkarṣaṇa Vāsudeva."[34] The contrast of *pūjā* as the mode of worship in which priests touch the iconic body of God (*arcā*) to the Bhagavān's "untouched" status was probably intended, indicating an Āgamic concern for the purity of the iconic lords of all and of the priests who served them. The stone wall called the Nārāyaṇa enclosure preserved that purity for the *pūjā,* and its name (the abode of man) plays upon the human kinship relations of the elder and younger brothers housed within it. They were the human modes of the abode of man (Nārāyaṇa) depicted as dwelling within that womblike abode (just as the Vaikuṇṭha Perumāl Temple's top floor standing icon depicted Kṛṣṇa dwelling within space-time inside the womb of the sitting icon on the bottom floor).

Srinivasan noted that Saṃkarṣaṇa is mentioned first suggesting that the kinship relationship of Saṃkarṣaṇa Balarāma and Vāsudeva Kṛṣṇa was the focus of the resident icons, rather than their metaphysical relationship as *vyūhas,* which would have reversed the sequence. It means, we may presume, that the representation of Balarāma stood to the right of Kṛṣṇa. Those two brothers implied the other kinsmen that make up the five Vṛṣṇi heroes (the half-brothers Pradyumna and Sāmba, and Pradyumna's son, Aniruddha) who may or may not have been explicitly represented.

Representing Balarāma and Kṛṣṇa as brothers, however, is also a way of representing the *vyūhas* Saṃkarṣaṇa and Vāsudeva. Balarāma standing to Kṛṣṇa's right replicates Saṃkarṣaṇa's emanation in the direction of *pradakṣiṇa* (circumambulation) from Vāsudeva as the first *vyūha* to escape (*ādiśeṣa*). Rather than assume as Srinivasan did, that the Vṛṣṇi heroes fused with a *vyūha* doctrine from another tradition (that of Nārāyaṇa), the evidence suggests instead that the story of the Vṛṣṇi heroes, Kṛṣṇa and his kinsmen, illustrated the *vyūha* doctrine. Their narrative represents the manner in which the *vyūhas* operate in the lives of the initiated (*sādhakas*). Let me point out only one example of this interpretation, one from the story of their birth.

The story of Saṃkarṣaṇa's and Kṛṣṇa's birth as humans by means of Vāsudeva and Devakī (*Śrīmad Bhāgavata* 10) may be read as illustrating the processes that take place within a devotee when receiving *mantras* from an *ācārya.* The ego-centered sense of I (*ahaṃkāra*) that dominates waking consciousness is represented by Kaṃsa. It vehemently opposes the Bhagavān's takeover of the initiate until it is killed by him. The white Saṃkarṣaṇa Balarāma was the first to escape (*ādiśeṣa*) from that threatened I's imprisonment of Vāsudeva and Devakī. Transferred embryonically across the Yamunā River to Gokula, he prepared the way for the later arrival of Vāsudeva Kṛṣṇa. In that way, he was elder in birth to Vāsudeva Kṛṣṇa as a kinsman, yet was subordinate to the *vyūha* Vāsudeva as the first of the three that manifest the pairs of his six glories.

In ritual terms, Saṃkarṣaṇa Balarāma's embryonic transfer signifies the *ācārya*'s preparation of the initiate's causal body (*kāraṇa sūkṣma śarīra*) by using the power (*bala*) of omniscient knowledge (*jñāna*). The causal body is represented by Gokula and the Vaisya population of cowherds. Once that domain of the initiate was prepared, the *ācārya* imparted the complete mantraic form of the Bhagavān through waking consciousness into that deepest level of embodied consciousness. The dark bodied Kṛṣṇa represented that primary *mantra,* probably the eight-syllable *Oṃ namo nārāyaṇaya.* It first had to cross the raging waters of consciousness that separate the gross body from the subtle, represented by the Yamunā River. Once in Gokula, however, that embodied *mantra* began to take over the *sādhaka* completely. The remainder of the story depicts the dynamics of that takeover, ending with the slaying of the deluded sense of I (Kaṃsa) and the establishment of the embodied *mantra* at the doorway (*Dvārakā*) in the ocean of waking consciousness. That doorway probably corresponds to the place on the forehead where the subtle body links to the gross body when the *sādhaka* is awake.

According to this reading, the stories about Kṛṣṇa and his family based in Dvārakā depict the processes by which the Bhagavān protects the devout *sadhaka.* Kṛṣṇa's two sons by different wives, for example, illustrate the *vyūha* Pradyumna, whose glories have to do with sovereign nonclinging action. Pradyumna, the preeminently mighty one, the son of the chief queen Rukminī, and Sāmba (a weapon), Kṛṣṇa's son by Jambāvati, illustrate the answer to Arjuna's question in the *Bhagavad Gītā* 3.36: "By what, then, is a person impelled to do evil (*pāpam*) even though unwilling, o son of Vṛṣṇi, is he driven as if by force?" The cause, Kṛṣṇa said, is desire (*kāma*) and anger (*krodha*), which arise from the material thread of *rajas* (passion) woven into one's bodies (3.37).

According to the *Śrīmad Bhāgavata* 3.1.28–30, Kṛṣṇa's son Pradyumna was the rebirth of Kāma (desire), and his son Sāmba was the rebirth of Skanda (anger). Sāmba's (and Skanda's) secondary status reflects anger's secondary yet useful status, because it is the frustration of desire that produces anger. Yet anger may be useful to the Bhagavān, and through Sāmba the entire Vṛṣṇi clan was destroyed.[35] Sāmba (or Skanda) was not forgotten by Bhāgavatas, merely implied by Pradyumna, because anger is under the control of the sovereign lord of desire. (In the directional *maṇḍala* explained to Arjuna by Kṛṣṇa in the *Bhagavad Gītā* 10.21–24,

Skanda is in the west, the direction of the *asuras,* and opposite Pradyumna of the east, the direction of the *devas*). In the eighth century, Pradyumna and Sāmba were sculpted together at the southeast corner of the Vaikuṇṭha Perumāl *vimāna,* and in the ninth century the Tamil poet Aṇṭal invoked both in her poetry.[36]

The Yavana Bhāgavata evidence reveals that at least by the second century B.C.E., barbarians received *dīkṣā,* probably by means of the *Pāñcarātra Āgama.* Evidence from early Tamil literature indicates that the same was true among the Tamils, who according to the *Laws of Manu* (10.44) had the same ritual status as Yavanas: Drāviḍas and Yavanas were among those dynasties born of Kṣatriyas who had fallen to the status of Śūdras because they had given up the sacred rites of Veda.

The *Śrīmad Bhāgavata* provides the narrative explanation for such *mlecca* conversions and illustrates the purification that converts underwent. Significantly, the story is directly connected to the establishment of the doorway (*Dvārakā*) discussed above and to the theme of refuge taught in the eighteenth chapter of the *Bhagavad Gītā.* The Yavana Bhāgavata king Agathocles, we noted, was probably such a refugee (*prapanna*).

According to the story, after Kaṃsa was slain, Jarāsaṃdha (joined by old age) waged eighteen battles against Kṛṣṇa and Saṃkarṣaṇa at Mathura where Ugrasena ruled over the Yadus. Just before Jarāsaṃdha's eighteenth attack, however, a Yavana hero entered the scene.[37] He had learned from Nārada that the Yādus were equal to him in battle and so he attacked Mathura with three and one-half crores of *mlecca* troops. That prompted Kṛṣṇa and Saṃkarṣaṇa to move their people into an impregnable fortress (*durga*) they called Dvārakā in the ocean to the west (the direction of Skanda and anger).

Kṛṣṇa then left Dvārakā on foot without weapons but wearing a garland of lotuses. When the Yavana saw him walking, stunningly beautiful with his dark color and four arms, he recognized him from Nārada's description and decided to follow him, likewise on foot and without weapons. Kṛṣṇa, whom even yogins cannot capture in their minds, appeared to run away from him and to avert his face. By keeping himself just out of grasp, Kṛṣṇa led the Yavana to a distant mountain cave, and all the while the Yavana hero berated him for his unheroic behavior. Kṛṣṇa then hid himself inside the cave. When the Yavana entered he saw a man sleeping. Thinking him to be Kṛṣṇa pretending to be asleep, he kicked him. The sleeper awoke, opened his eyes, saw the Yavana standing there, and with his angry look emitted a flame of fire from his body that burned the Yavana to ashes.[38]

The sleeper was named Mucukunda, a son of Māndhātā from long ago in the Ikṣvāku lineage (of Rāma and of the Śākyamuni Buddha). Because Mucukunda had been devoted to Brahmans and to truth, Indra and the *devas* had asked him to protect them from the *asuras,* which he did, but after Skanda was born to be their protector, Mucukunda was allowed to leave that position. In the meantime, Time had eaten up his family and kingdom and he had nothing to which to return, so the *devas* granted him any boon except that pertaining to the absolute (*kaivalya*), which only the Bhagavān Viṣṇu can grant. Choosing sleep, he entered a cave where the *devas* gave him the boon that anyone interrupting him would be reduced to ash by his gaze. Now, however, he was awake in the cave and Kṛṣṇa made his beautiful form visible to him.[39] Mucukunda recognized him as the bull of men among the three *devas* of *devas,* the *trimūrti* named Brahmā, Viṣṇu, Śiva. He saw his brillant form dispelling the darkness of the cave and knew that whoever had awakened him was now ash because of his own vileness (*pāpman*).[40]

After identifying himself as Vāsudeva, Kṛṣṇa explained that Kaṃsa and others were now dead and that because Mucukunda had adored him in the past, he had made himself visible to him. He offered Mucukunda a boon. Because Mucukunda had once learned about the *deva* Nārāyana, he now recognized the son of Vāsudeva to be him and was joyous.[41] He confessed that, infatuated by Māyā, he had forgotten the Bhagavān, and that immersed in the householder life of a king he had become subject to the Bhagavān as Time. Yet he was able to detach himself from the royal life and now desired to serve his feet. He renounced all things bound up with the *sattva, rajas,* and *tamas guṇas* and sought shelter with him, the Person beyond the *guñas.*[42] In response, Kṛṣṇa told him to go into the world with his mind absorbed in him, for he would have unwavering devotion. Yet, as a Kśatriya, he had committed sins not connected with his *dharma* (duty), so he should now purify himself through *tapas* and submission, and in another birth he would be born a twice-born male, compassionate toward all beings, and then he would attain the absolute (*kevalam*).[43]

Mucukunda left the cave and saw that people, animals, trees, and plants were all smaller than when he had gone to sleep; he concluded that the Kālī Yuga was near. He walked northward to the Gandamadana mountain, "austere, full of faith, having the senses under control and the mind concentrated on Kṛṣṇa."[44] There he halted in Badri at the dwelling place of Nārāyana and Nara and worshiped Hari, pacified in the face of all dualities.[45]

The story, it appears, is about a single person with two identities, like the Yavana Bhāgavata king Agatocles. His Yavana identity, entranced by Kṛṣṇa, was burned up in the cave of his innermost consciousness and his older and truer identity as Mucukunda was revealed. His long sleep represented a fall from the status of Kṣatriya to that of Śūdra when rites had been forsaken. The fact that the Yavana was a king reflected his inherently Kṣatriya nature, but his ritual status as *mlecca* reflected his fall or sleep. Now that the Kālī Yuga was near, he was qualified to become a refugee and required only one more birth before he could attain the absolute.

The position of that story before the eighteenth and final battle that Kṛṣṇa waged with Joined-by-old-age connects it explicitly with the teaching Kṛṣṇa gave Arjuna in the the *Bhagavad Gītā* (18.65–66) as he was about to start fighting:

> Focus your mind on me, be devoted to me, sacrifice to me, perform veneration of me, and so you will come to me, I promise you truly, for you are dear

to me. Give up all dharmas and turn to me alone as refuge, and I will free you from all evil (*pāpa*), do not worry.

The story about Yavanas in the northwest is related directly to similar stories about barbarians in the southeast. The Yavana's connection to the number eighteen is paralleled by a Tamil king's connection to the number eighteen, also in a battle context where other connections are made to the number eighteen.[46] Furthermore, Mucukunda was not only embodied by a Yavana king, but also a Tamil king. According to the *Cilappatikāram,* Mucukunda had been a Cōḷa king in Puhār who had left to protect Indra's realm while he was absent. That identifies Mucukunda with a non-Āryan who was like the Yavana.[47] It seems, then, that the meeting of the Yavana with the sleeping Mucukunda inside the cave where he had been led by Kṛṣṇa is a metaphor for the process by which non-Aryan rulers became Bhāgavatas. It is a story about *mleccas* discovering their true inner selves. Conversion was merely awakening to the remembrance of what had been known all along, a knowledge dimly signaled by one's fascination with Kṛṣṇa, even as an enemy.

Let us return to the plough, *cakra,* flask, and conch. In her second article, Doris Srinivasan analyzed a wide range of damaged sculptures from the Mathura region of the Kuṣāṇa period (c.105–173 C.E.), with a few from earlier centuries. As she noted, over three-quarters of the icons she discussed are clearly Bhāgavata, which suggests that Vaiṣṇava as a label for sculptures may need to be refined. It may be, in fact, that in these early centuries, iconographically speaking, Vaiṣṇava is Bhāgavata. I would like to discuss some of her findings, arguing again that a coherent Bhāgavata tradition explains them.

Among the pre-Kuṣāṇa sculptures, Srinivasan discussed "the earliest known multi-armed Vaiṣṇava image," from Malhar in Madhya Pradesh.[48] It depicts a four-armed male holding a *cakra* in the upper left hand and a club (*gadā*) in the upper right, on the shaft of which is a first century B.C.E. inscription. The natural hands hold a conchlike object close to the chest. A long sword hangs from the left hip. She suggests that it could represent a Vaiṣṇava hero (*vīra*) and perhaps was connected to Mathura's cult of ancestral Vṛṣṇi hero-gods, although, as she noted, in Mathura no pre-Kuṣāṇa Vṛṣṇi hero icon can be identified with certainty.[49]

If we apply the model from the Vaikuṇṭha Perumāl Temple, however, it appears that the figure depicts the *vyūha* Aniruddha. Indeed, its *cakra* in the left hand and the conch-like object held close to the chest, together with the warrior identity of the sword, resembles the attributes of Aniruddha on the obverse of the Agathocles coin, dated a century or so earlier. As Srinivasan later discussed, the conch-like object and the flask seem to represent the same thing and the conch eventually replaced the flask altogether.

The combination of flask and conch is also found on the south (Aniruddha) side of the Vaikuṇṭha Perumāl *vimāna.* Mohinī holds the vessel containing deathlessness (*amṛta*) and, as we noted earlier, rites in the Jagannātha Temple in

Puri, as discussed by F. A. Marglin, revealed that her distribution of *amṛta* to the *devas* implied the ritual use of the conch in the darkness of night—it served as the body of Kālī for her worship in rites of *tejas* performed by the king's *purohita* dressed as the courtesan, Mohinī. (That is surely ritual language "in the manner of twilight" appropriate to Aniruddha on the *maṇḍala's* south side.) The *Śrīmad Bhāgavata* tells us that Kṛṣṇa's conch represents the principle of water (*apām tattvam*) (12.11.14) and signifies his lordship over the righteous administration of Yama, lord of the ancestral dead and supervisor of the purgatorial watery realms of the south (10.45.36–50). In other words, in a southern context, the conch signifies the deathlessness of a prosperous life of one hundred years, if the Bhagavān wills it for his slaves. The Sudarśana *cakra* in the upper left hand represents the principle of *tejas* (12.11.14) that expresses itself through mantraic rites to ensure the possession of deathlessness.

The Purāṇa also tells us that the club (*gadā*) represents "the *prāṇa,* the vital energy, which includes the strength of the senses, mind and body."[50] Following the pattern established by the first century B.C.E. multi-armed image just discussed, it is held in the upper right hand throughout the Kuṣāṇa sculptures Srinivasan described. As she observed:

> The most frequently represented Vaiṣṇava deity [within the Kuṣāṇa period in Mathura] is a four-armed standing male who holds a *gadā* and *cakra* in the extra raised right and left hands, respectively. . . . The natural right is in *abhaya mudra* and the natural left may hold either a flask (*kamaṇḍalu*) or the conch (*śaṇkha*). . . . This type is also found on a series of kinship triads recently studied. Within the context of the kinship triads, this figure can be identified as Vāsudeva-Kṛṣṇa; as such, he is always shown as the last member of a group representing three deified Vṛṣṇi ancestors, that is, Vāsudeva-Kṛṣṇa stands to the left of his older sister Ekānamśā and to her right stands the older brother, Saṃkarṣaṇa/Balarāma.This placement affirms genealogical rather than theological status. Theologically, Vāsudeva-Kṛṣṇa is the most important of the three deities, yet in these triads his terminal position or lesser height than Saṃkarṣaṇa/Balarāma emphasizes his status as the younger brother. To date, certainly five, perhaps six kinship triads are known.[51]

The kinship triad, she also observed, correlates with the basic features of *śrāddha* rites performed for dead ancestors.

The main object of worship, however, was a single four-armed figure Srinivasan identified as Vāsudeva-Kṛṣṇa, of which over thirty representations are known, apart from depictions of him as part of a group. She writes:

> In these single representations, as in the kinship triads, Vāsudeva-Kṛṣṇa epitomizes a deified ancestral hero. The *gadā* and *cakra* bespeak of a warrior's strength and power, as does the conch which is used for signalling in

battle. No halo surrounds him; the *lakṣaṇas* [holy marks] of a Cakravārtin or a Mahāpuruṣa hardly ever occur. Instead he stands garlanded, crowned and ornamented. He is also shown with the multiplicity convention, reserved for some special Hindu deities alone.[52]

Without discussing each of the items Srinivasan describes, I suggest that, in those cases where the male figure holds a club in a right hand and a *cakra* in the left, accompanied by a flask or a conch, we think of it as Vāsudeva Kṛṣṇa manifesting the *śakti* and *tejas* of Aniruddha. The theological basis for that is the *vyūha* doctrine, that the Bhagavān contains within himself all three pairs of glories. The narrative and kinship basis is that before Kṛṣṇa gave birth to Pradyumna and, through him, to Aniruddha, he contained them hidden within his dark (*kṛṣṇa*) body. Their later births merely made exoteric what had all along been esoterically within him. As a Cowherd, after all, he was both the desirable lord of desire (Pradyumna) and the hero of brilliant conquering power (Aniruddha). That means then, that in the kinship triad, Ekānamśā is flanked by Balarāma to her right and by Kṛṣṇa as Aniruddha to her left, a pairing that matches our discussion of Agathocles' coin. It expresses the north-south axis of the model *maṇḍala;* and Nārāyana's Śakti, Ekānamśā, unites the two. Accordingly, Ekānamśā, "she who is single or portionless," appears to represent the Bhagavān facing west; hidden by her, then, is Pradyumna facing east. If the *maṇḍala* were fully depicted, Pradyumna might emerge from the top of her head, as in the sculpture discussed earlier.[53] Ekānamśā, then, suggests Mohinī. The connection of the kinship triad to the theme of death rites for the ancestors appears to confirm this identification. The kinship triad signifies the *dīkṣa* and rites that preserve deathlessness even in the face of Death's legitimate authority.

It is reasonable that much sculptural attention would have been given to Balarāma and Aniruddha together, because the former signifies initiation (*dīkṣa*) and the latter the practical application (*prayoga*) of it. The practical use of mantraic rites for the sake of prosperous longevity (*amṛta*) no doubt has been the concern of most Bhāgavatas throughout the religion's history. The *Pāñcarātra Āgama* makes those concerns legitimate, even if they are not the ideal goal of the fully awake devotee of true being (*sat*), always a virtuoso at any time in India's religious history.

It is notable that some of the depictions of Saṃkarṣaṇa Balarāma discussed by Doris Srinivasan explicitly bring the lion and Saṃkarṣaṇa's plow together, revealing that they do indeed signify his omniscient knowledge (*jñāna*). Describing his appearance in a kinship relief, Srinivasan wrote, "The god has four arms. He holds a mace in the upper right and a plough surmounted by a small lion in the upper left hand. The natural right is in *abhaya* and the natural left hand rests at the waist." In another portrayal, "Wearing the triple crested turban and single earring, the god is shown resting his extra right hand on top of a heavy mace. To his left is seen a plough surmounted by a small lion."

In yet a third, a two-armed portrayal, "The right hand is . . . raised in front of the protective serpent hood. The left hand holds an object, probably a goblet close to the chest. To the right is a mace; on the left is a staff crowned with a miniature lion."[54] Here we have a full statement of the Pāñcarātra theology about the *jñāna* and *bala* he represents. The snake hood identifies him as Āḍi Śeṣa, the first [*vyūha*] to escape from Vāsudeva and the self-deluding basis (couch or bed) for all subsequent self-transformations. From that primordial snake come the individual snakes (like Kāliya) in each person's pool of consciousness. The mace signifies the power (*bala*) of his omniscient knowledge in the *sādhaka* when effected through *dīkṣā*. The *jñāna* itself is represented by the staff crowned by the miniature lion; and in other examples, the staff is a plough, which refers to the meaning of *saṃkarṣaṇa* and alludes to the *Bhagavad Gītā* 13–14, as noted earlier.

> One final architectural fragment is worth discussing from the vantage of our model: The relief shows two figures: a small, possibly crowned male kneeling before a much larger god who has four arms and wears a broad, floral garland. The *gadā* rests on its narrow base and is supported by the extra right hand placed on top. The *cakra* is held by the extra left hand which is suspended downward. The natural left holds the *saṅkha* at the waist, while the natural right hand extends downward in a gesture approximating *varadā mudrā*. The *dhoti* clad deity displays neither nimbus nor headgear. The hair is worn in snail-shell curls, usually seen on the Buddha and Jinas. This feature, together with the suspended left hand and kneeling devotee are unique to Kuṣāṇa Vaiṣṇava iconography. That this fragment may be a late Kuṣāṇa piece is indicated by the treatment of the hair, the suspended hands and the appearance of the *varadā mudrā*.[55]

Srinivasan included this in her discussion of avatars from the Mathura region, noting that N. P. Joshi suggested it might depict Trivikrama, the dwarf (*vamāna*) as thrice-strider. I suggest instead that it depicts the Bhagavān as the *avadhūta* (radical renouncer) Dattātreya with Kṛṣṇa's ancestor, King Yadu. The club may in fact be the *daṇḍa* (sceptre) characteric of *avadhūtas,* which was sometimes composed of three pieces of bamboo.[56]

On the south side of the Vaikuṇṭha Perumāl *vimāna,* the side of twilight, dead ancestors and deathlessness, two panels portray Kṛṣṇa's instruction to his friend Uddhava before Kṛṣṇa went off to die. The story is the major portion of the *Śrīmad Bhāgavata* 11, and Kṛṣṇa's instruction, called "The Summary of the Doctrine of Brahman" is among other things a commentary on the *Bhagavad Gītā* 12–18. Among its teachings is the use of normally *adharmic* (unrighteous) acts as means to the highest goal, a method appropriate to the twilight concerns of the south side. Kṛṣṇa in fact concluded the Summary by stating the perspective of such *adharmic* rites concisely: "This is the perception of the intelligent and of the prudent, that here one attains true being by means of the unlawful, and by means of the body that will die attains the righteousness that is me."[57]

The first panel depicts Kṛṣṇa teaching Uddhava the Summary. The other panel depicts the first teaching of The Summary, the story of Kṛṣṇa's ancestor, King Yadu, when he encountered the *avadhūta* Dattātreya in the forest.[58] The *avadhuta* represents the radical renunciants that Kṛṣṇa introduced and then set aside in the *Bhagavad Gītā* 12, because Kṛṣṇa's chief concern in that text was with the religious life of householders. Nevertheless, Dattātreya's appearance on the south side in the context of *tejas* was relevant because Dattātreya is elsewhere connected with the *tejas* generated by sexual rites. The *amṛta* of those rites is represented on the same south wall by Mohinī holding the vessel of *amṛta,* and perhaps in this Kuṣāṇa figure by the conch held at the waist. According to H. S. Joshi, accounts of the *avadhūta* Dattātreya describe him as attached to wine and women yet not defiled by them, indicating that he represented Tantric rites of the left hand (*vāmācāra*) that use the drinking of wine and sexual intercourse as methods of transcendence. The woman, he suggested, symbolizes self-experience and wine the pleasure arising out of it.[59]

Significantly, the Vaikuṇṭha Perumāl portrayal depicts Dattātreya tonsured in a manner that suggests a Buddha or Jina. Like the Kuṣāṇa image, his right hand extends downward toward Yadu in a gesture of giving. That gesture apparently refers to his name, "Given (*datta*) by means of Atri (*atreya*)" which, in the manner of twilight, alludes both to the Bhagavān's self-giving and to the giving (*dāna*) of people who are themselves given to (like mendicants and *avadhūtas*). It may also allude to the important Buddhist story of Viśvaṃtara or Vessantara (who gave everything away), the last birth of the Bodhisattva before he became Śākyamuni Buddha. His perfection of giving led directly to his complete awakening as the Buddha.[60] It may also allude to the non-Buddhist version, Tāravaloka (Starlight or Light of She Who Carries Across),[61] which may have appeared already in Guṇādhya's first century Paiśāci version of "The Great Romance."[62] Because the late Kuṣāṇa image the left hand holding the *cakra* hangs down in a manner that hides it suggests that the figure represents just what Kṛṣṇa taught about such radical renunciants, who move beyond the *maṇḍala-*, image-, and temple-centered rites signified by the Sudarśana *cakra.* In R. C. Zaehner's translation, when asked about those who seek the Imperishable Unmanifest, Kṛṣṇa said:

> . . . those who revere the indeterminate Imperishable Unmanifest, unthinkable though coursing everywhere, sublime, aloof, unmoving, firm, who hold in check the complex of the senses, in all things equal-minded, taking pleasure in the weal of all contingent beings, these too attain to Me.[63]

In discussing the origin of the *vyūha* doctrine, Srinivasan rightly turned our attention to two references to Nārāyana in the *Śatapatha Brāhmaṇa.*[64] Let us consider each in light of Bhāgavata thought. In 12.3.4, Nārāyana appears as Puruṣa Nārāyaṇa, which literally means, the person who is the abode and refuge of man. Prajāpati, the lord of progeny, told him to offer sacrifice. Having done so, he said, "All the worlds have I placed within mine own self, and mine own self have I placed within all the worlds," with the same pattern repeated for the gods, the Vedas, and the vital airs.[65] The worlds, the gods, the Vedas, and the vital airs thereby were made imperishable, as was "the All." Whoever knows that, the story ends, "passes from the imperishable unto the imperishable, conquers recurrent death, and attains the full measure of life."

That story illustrates a portion of the important "Hymn to the Person" (Puruṣa-Sūkta), *Ṛg Veda* 10.90, notably the portion from the fifth stanza to the concluding sixteenth. The first four stanzas describe the Person as absolute. The fifth stanza records the absolute Person's transformation of himself to produce the limited realm of directional space whose time is measured by the sun and moon. He did it by inseminating his own womb, Virāj, thereby giving birth to himself as his son. The son then served as the victim who was sacrificed and turned into space-time and its components. In Zaehner's translation, the fifth stanza reads: "From [Puruṣa] was Virāj born, from Virāj [Puruṣa] again: once born,—behind, before, he reached beyond the earth."[66] The sixteenth stanza concludes, "With sacrifice the gods made sacrifice to sacrifice: These were the first religious rites (*dharma*), to the firmament these powers went up where dwell the ancient Sādhya gods."

Returning to the *Śatapatha Brāhmaṇa* story, several important ideas connect it with the *Bhagavad Gītā*. First, it says that by understanding the rite properly, the patron (*yajamāna*) who plays the role of Puruṣa becomes like the absolute Puruṣa and is transcendent to the changing processes of space-time even while participating in them. He will live a full measure of life, which presumably matches the lifetime of the absolute imperishable Puruṣa, who is simultaneously the sacrificial process, the victim sacrificed, and the person to whom sacrifice is offered. Second, that teaching is the content of Kṛṣṇa's most secret (*guhyatama*) teaching about himself in *Bhagavad Gītā* 9. There he described himself as the absolute Puruṣa who repeatedly impregnates his own womb (*prakṛti, virāj*) watching the resulting processes with indifference, unlimited by them in the way that the absolute Puruṣa is unlimited by the sacrificial transformation of himself as his son. Kṛṣṇa repeated that secret teaching again in *Bhagavad Gītā* 14. Moreover, Kṛṣṇa said, he is the absolute Puruṣa who has entered as a human into the space-time to which he has given birth, and they are fools who do not believe it (9.11). Kṛṣṇa, in other words, illustrated the teaching of the *Śatapatha Brāhmaṇa* about the Person who is the abode of man. (We note in passing that in the most secret realm of the Vaikuṇṭha Perumāl *vimāna,* the sitting icon in the bottom *garbhagṛha* represents the absolute Puruṣa; the reclining icon in the middle *garbhagṛha* represents the womb in which he has planted his seed as embryo; and the standing icon in the top *garbhagṛha* represents the human form of the absolute Person whom fools refuse to recognize.) Third, the story illustrates the meaning of the name Vāsudeva, the shining one (*deva*) who dwells (*vasu*) in all things and in whom all things dwell. It also illustrates the meaning of Viṣṇu, the pervading actor. Kṛṣṇa identified himself with both names and their meanings when he taught Arjuna.

In the *Bhagavad Gītā,* where he first drew Arjuna's attention away from family concerns and to himself as *ācārya,* Kṛṣṇa said, "At the end of many births, he who has omniscient knowledge (*jñāna*) takes refuge in me, saying 'Vāsudeva is everything,' [and] he is a great Self hard to obtain" (7.19). Kṛṣṇa then described Vāsudeva, who is not only the unmanifest reality beyond this realm of space-time, but is the Unmanifest beyond that unmanifest. In terms of the Puruṣu-sūkta, Vāsudeva is the absolute Person who is the unknowable Unmanifest, his womb Virāj is the unmanifest matter (*prakṛti*) that he inseminates, and this realm of space-time (*brahmāṇḍa*) is the transformed son born of it. Into this manifest realm of the son, the Father entered as Kṛṣṇa, son of Vāsudeva and Devakī.

Kṛṣṇa then identified himself three times with Viṣṇu (pervading actor). He did so first in chapter ten, at the beginning of his identification with elements that make up our manifest realm of space-time, apparently following the guide of a *maṇḍala.* In 10.21 he said, "Of the sons of Āditi I am the pervading actor (*Viṣṇu*), of the radiant lights I am the sun (*ravi*), of the Maruts I am the ray of light (*marīci*), of the constellations I am the moon (*śaśi*)." Those elements describe the north side of the *maṇḍala.*[67] They all suggest the breaking light of the predawn *brahmamuhūrta* concluding the night of the full moon, and they bring together snake and lion with the Brahmin supervisor of the sacrifice: Viṣṇu the *ācārya* is like a lion waking and roaring in the mountains to the north,[68] while the sun's radiant light dimly emerges in the east, the Maruts shine in the mountains with the brilliance of serpents,[69] and the full moon, whose spots signify the sacrifice, moves toward the west.

Viṣṇu's identity as a son of Āditi (*aditya*) is telling. On the one hand it connects him to the sun emerging in the east, who was an Āditya. On the other, it connects him to the sacrifice represented by the dwarf (*vāmana*) who took all three realms of the universe relevant to humans (earth, atmosphere, heaven) away from the *asuras* in the west. In the *Śrīmad Bhāgavata,* that dwarf form of Viṣṇu is described as the son of Āditi (8.16–23), and he appears to represent the *ācārya.*

The *Bhagavad Gītā* stanza (10.21) thus begins with the dwarf and ends with the moon, replicating the beginning and the ending of *Śatapatha Brāhmaṇa* 1.2.5, where the preparation of the sacrificial arena (*vedi*) is described. The supervisor of those preparations, we recall, was the Brahmin who sat to the south and faced north, a *purohita* whom I suggested appears as the Pāñcarātra *ācārya.* By identifying himself with the pervading actor, son of Āditi, right at the beginning, Kṛṣṇa suggested that he was that Brahmin priest/*purohita*/*ācārya.* Like the dwarf, the *ācārya* held within himself, by means of *mantra,* the entirety of the sacrifice.

The other two uses of Viṣṇu occur in the next chapter, when, with a divine eye, Arjuna perceived the all-consuming nature of the Puruṣa. In terms of the Puruṣa-sūkta and the *Śatapatha Brahmana* story, he saw the Person who is the abode of man (*purūsa nārāyaṇa*) as Time, the sacrificial process eating up what he had begotten. Twice Arjuna named that terrifying process Viṣṇu, the pervading actor (11.24 and 11.30).

Let us now turn to the second appearance of Puruṣa Nārāyana in the *Śatapatha Brāhamaṇa.* In 13.6.1–2, we are told that Puruṣa Nārāyana wanted to pass over all beings and alone be everything in the universe. He did it by means of a five-day sacrifice called the Puruṣamedha. In it, the Puruṣa is the victim (*medha*), who is born from a forty-day rite identified with Virāj. The five-day ceremony, then, illustrates Puruṣa-sūkta 5–16. Throughout the discussion of the rites, the number five controls the symbolism (13.6.1.7) and alludes to the crucial fifth stanza of the Puruṣa-sūkta. We may assume that the five days of the ceremony are determined by the phases of the moon, so that five nights (*pānca rātri*) determine the five days. On the middle day, when victims are sacrificed, the rites take place all night (*atirātri*). The five-fold sequence of the Puruṣamedha thus appears to constitute the source of that regarding the five nights (*pāñcarātra*) which has come down to us (*āgama*). The meaning of Puruṣamedha, the text explains, is that the Puruṣa who dwells within this universe eats whatever is here as its food (*medha*). Moreover, since the five-fold sequence symbolically sacrifices humans (*puruṣa*) that are fit victims (*medha*) on the middle day, it is also called the Puruṣamedha (13.6.2.1–2). The five days are arranged like a barley-corn, it says, with the largest sacrifice occurring in the middle (the all-night Atirātra); the less complex Ukthya sacrifices occur on the day before and the day after it; and the even less complex Agniṣṭoma sacrifices occur at the beginning and at the end.[70]

The emergent pattern important here is this: The first and fifth days share the same theme; the second and fourth days share the same theme; and the most important third day is unique, extends through the night, and involves a litany called the Puruṣa Nārāyana. The pattern is two plus two plus one. Four is transcended by a fifth and that fifth is the center. Pāñcarātra, then, may refer specifically to that unique fifth night, and the *Pāñcarātra Āgama* may then be understood as that which has come down to us regarding the fifth night (that is the center).

On that central day, the Brahmin sitting on the south praises the four men who have been bound to the sacrificial stakes as the victims. (Later in the ceremony they are replaced by animals.) They represent the four classes (*varṇa*) that emerged from the head, shoulders, abdomen, and feet of the newly born Puruṣa when he was sacrificed. The Brahmin praises them with the Puruṣa Nārāyana, a litany consisting of the Puruṣa-sūkta (*Ṛg Veda* 10.90) and the Uttara Nārāyana (*Taittirīya Araṇyaka* 3.13). The patron will also use the latter at the end of the five days.[71]

Significantly, after the five days of rites were complete, if the patron was a Brahmin, he had two choices. He could place the two fires of the *śrauta* rites into his own self, worship the sun with the Uttara Nārāyana, and go off to the forest without looking back. He then became a radical renunciant, a *sannyāsin,* no longer attached to Vedic rites. Or, he could stay in the village, place the two fires back into his churning sticks, and after worshipping the sun with the Uttara Nārāyana, live at home and offer whatever sacrifices he could afford (13.6.2.20). In both cases, the patron passed over all beings and became everything in the universe. Presumably, he lived with the faith that he now possessed the lifetime of the absolute Puruṣa and was ultimately beyond the many deaths signified by the movements of the sun and moon within directional space.

When we apply the information from that account of Puruṣa Nārāyana to the *Bhagavad Gītā,* important patterns emerge in that text. Let me suggest what some of them are. In chapters 7 and 8, Kṛṣṇa (the *ācārya*) drew his disciple Arjuna's attention to himself and his own identity as Vāsudeva who is Puruṣa Nārāyana, the Shining One who indwells all things and in whom all things dwell, the Person who is the abode (and refuge) of man. In chapters 10 and 11, Kṛṣṇa began to instruct Arjuna in the mysteries of the Bhagavān (apparently) by revealing the various meanings of the *cakra maṇḍala,* among which were the directions and realms of space-time within himself. Then he enabled the initiate to see Puruṣa Nārāyana as Puruṣamedha, the Person who eats his own creations, the Person who eats humans. Awestruck by that preparation, the disciple Arjuna was now prepared for the central teachings of the Bhāgavata religion. Those central teachings consist of the next five chapters, 12–16. At the beginning of chapter 12, Kṛṣṇa discussed two alternatives with which the five-part Puruṣamedha ends, that of the radical renunciant and that of the householder. The teachings that follow correspond in pattern to the five-fold sequence of the Puruṣamedha ceremony, chapter 14 matching the all-night sacrifice and its Puruṣa Nārāyana litany.

Indeed, at the beginning of chapter 14, Kṛṣṇa told Arjuna that he would now tell him the highest knowledge of omniscient knowledge that leads its knowers to a mode of being equivalent to his own; as Kṛṣṇa said in stanzas one and two:

> Further, I shall proclaim the supreme, the highest knowledge of omniscient knowledge, knowing which, all sages passed to the supreme attainment. Taking refuge in this knowledge, they reached a rank equal to mine, and in the emanation they are not born and in the dissolution they are not distressed.

In other words, what he taught here corresponds to the content of the Puruṣa Nārāyana litany and leads to the goal promised by both accounts of Puruṣa Nārāyana in the *Śatapatha Brāhmaṇa.* The sages had become free of the son and had become like the father, the absolute Person. Not surprisingly, then, in the next two stanzas of the central chapter 14, Kṛṣṇa turned immediately to the meaning of the crucial fifth stanza of the Puruṣa-Sukta, where Virāj is the Person's womb. Here, Kṛṣṇa called that Virāj "my womb, transcendent Brahman" (*mama yonir mahad brahma*):

> My womb is the Great Brahman and I plant the embryo in it: the origin of all living beings arises from that, O son of Bhārata. In all wombs, O son of Kuntī, whatever forms originate, of them the Great Brahman is the womb and I am the father who gives the seed.

Consistent with the five-fold Puruṣamedha barley-corn pattern, the chapters surrounding chapter 14 share themes in the following way: The immediately enclosing chapters 13 and 15 treat the theme of the knower of the field and the field he knows (13), and then of the cosmic tree that grows from his planting the seed in that field (15). Kṛṣṇa told Arjuna to cut it at its root with the ax of nonclinging. The outer encompassing chapters 12 and 16 treat the theme of differing kinds of people, the sons of light (*daiva*) (12) and the sons of darkness (*asuras*) (16).

Let us consider how these patterns relate to phases of the moon and to the model *maṇḍala*. We assume that the crucial middle sacrifice of the Puruṣamedha went through the night because that was the night of the full moon. The rites began on the day of the fourteenth moon and continued throughout the appearance of the full moon, ending with the beginning of the next day's rites before sunrise, those of the full moon and fifteenth day. That most important sacrifice corresponding to the full moon was signified by the moon itself: It bore the marks of sacrifice (*śaśi*) that could be seen when the moon was full. Following that lead, we can see that the discussion of the sons of darkness in the sixteenth chapter falls on the first day of the dark half (*kṛṣṇa pakṣa*) of the month, which is the sixteenth moon. Moreover, the important transition of the eleventh chapter corresponds to the important ritual role that the eleventh (*ekadaśi*) day plays in the monthly calendar of Bhāgavatas. Furthermore, the first chapter of the *Bhagavad Gītā* corresponds to the day after the new moon night, while the ending of householder issues with the sixth chapter corresponds to Śaṣṭhi (the Sixth), a day and a goddess concerned with progeny and Skanda's birth and maturation.

When we apply the *maṇḍala* model of the Vaikuṇṭha Perumāl to these crucial chapters of the *Bhagavad Gītā,* we see the following. The teachings on the householder fire in chapters 1–6 took place in the west, because that was the location of the *gārhapatya* fire in the sacrificial arena. In chapters 7–11, when Kṛṣṇa (the *ācārya*) began teaching Arjuna about Vāsudeva, they likewise remained on the west side of the *maṇḍala* that represented the eastern raised altar (*uttara vedi*), focussed on a *cakra-maṇḍala* that generated the fundamental mantra, *Om Namo Nārāyaṇaya.*

In chapter 12, Kṛṣṇa the *ācārya* began the teachings regarding the five nights or regarding the fifth night (*pāñcarātra*) that explain the four-*vyūha maṇḍala.* In chapter 13, he deepened those teachings referring still to the west side and the *vyūha* Vāsudeva, the possessor of glories. Those two chapters corresponded to the first two days of the Puruṣamedha sequence.

In chapter 14, Kṛṣṇa explained the north side. There the *jñāna* and *bala* Saṃkarṣaṇa Balarāma are represented by the snake, lion, and the *brahmamuhūrta,* and the concerns are with humans waking up through *dīkṣā* and its consequent way of life (*sādhana*). In the five-day Puruṣamedha sequence, that instruction corresponded to the central all-night sacrifice that ended with the *brahmamuhūrta* and its concluding sunrise. In chapter 15, Kṛṣṇa explained the east side. There the initiate's *aiśvarya* and *vīrya,* expressing Pradyumna, are represented by the morning between sunrise and noon, by the *sādhaka's* liturgical activity (*karma*) addressed to the Devas, and by a nonclinging relation to their fruits. It corresponded to the fourth day of the Puruṣamedha.

In chapter 16, Kṛṣṇa explained the south side where the *śakti* of Aniruddha may be used to generate *tejas* under the guidance of the supervising *ācārya* (Brahmin of the *śrauta* sacrifices). *Tejas* would be used to keep deathlessness (*amṛta*) on the side of the *sādhaka,* a son of light (*daiva*) in danger of being overwhelmed by the sons of darkness (*asuras*) as twilight turns to night. The guide for that son of light, Kṛṣṇa said, is *śāstra* (scripture) (16.23–24). Its prescriptions counter the whims of desire (*kama*). Included in that *sastra,* presumably, would be the type of rites found in such Pāñcarātra texts as the *Jayākhyā Saṃhitā, Ahirbudhnya Saṃhitā* and the *Pādma Saṃhitā,* which are alluded to in panels on the south side of the Vaikuṇṭha Perumāl Temple. It corresponded to the fifth and final day of the Puruṣamedha sequence.

In chapter 17, Kṛṣṇa returned to the west side. With the central mysteries now revealed, he addressed issues posed to initiated Bhāgavatas who live in the western darkness of nighttime where *asuras* dominate. Accordingly, Arjuna asked Kṛṣṇa about religious people who rejected *śāstra* yet performed acts resembling those of Bhāgavatas. How were they to be understood? Kṛṣṇa explained that it depended on the nature of their faith (*śraddhā*). Among them were householders dominated by *sattva guṇa* who sacrificed to the *Devas,* householders dominated by *rajas guṇa* who sacrificed to the *yakṣas* (local gods) and *rākṣasas* (demons), and householders dominated by *tamas guṇa* who sacrificed to the dead and to gatherings of the living. There were also people who mortified themselves savagely against the rules of *śāstra* (17.4–6). They all practiced religious rites relating to food, sacrifice, *tapas,* and giving, he explained. Interestingly, in each case, the practices of those dominated by *tamas* in Kṛṣṇa's explanation appear to correspond to those of the householder patrons of the *śramaṇas* (ascetics). They worshiped dead heroes (*pretān*) in funeral mounds (*stūpas*) and sacrificed to gatherings of the living (*bhūta gaṇām*) through alms given to *bhikṣus.*[72] In Bhāgavata thought, the Buddhist, Jaina, and Ājivika *bhikṣus* were judged to be sons of darkness deluded by the Bhagavān himself. Kṛṣṇa concluded by instructing Arjuna in the *mantra* Bhāgavatas recited when performing rites of food, sacrifice, *tapas,* and giving. That *mantra* (*Oṃ tat sat*) states that the faith (*śraddhā*) from which the act arose is true and therefore the act is true, even though it resembles the acts of others who worship the *Devas, yakṣas, rākṣasas* and dead and living people (17.23–28).

In chapter 18, Kṛṣṇa returned to the theme of chapter 12, the alternatives with which the Puruṣamedha story had concluded: The performer of the five-day ceremony who placed the fires within himself and went out into the forest (*sannyāsin*) had renounced all ritual acts based on desires, while the performer who stayed in the village as a householder and performed whatever sacrifices he could afford had surrendered all their fruits. Kṛṣṇa urged Arjuna to follow the householder. He then launched into a discussion of metaphysics that suggests the philosophical dialogue that the Brahmin priest was to participate in during the *śrauta* rites. First he discussed the three-fold nature of the surrendering of fruits (18.1–12), then the five-fold causes by which all ritual acts performed by such a householder succeed, and then the role of the *guṇas* in that action (18.13–48). Next he described how such a householder lives and becomes Brahma and attains Vāsudeva (the absolute Puruṣa Nārāyana as in the *Śatapatha Brāhmaṇa*) (18.49–56). Finally, he brought Arjuna back to his immediate situation, the one with which the *Bhagavad-Gītā* began: Arjuna must act now. Since he had to act, Kṛṣṇa told Arjuna to love Vāsudeva, to take refuge in him, to give up all *dharmas,* and Vāsudeva would free him from all evils (*pāpam*) (18.57–66). The *dharmas* he was to give up, we note, correspond to the *dharmas* with which the Puruṣa Śūkta ends in stanza 16, the religious rites on which space-time depends.

In other words, Kṛṣṇa, who embodied Vāsudeva, embodied the Puruṣa Nārāyana and he took reponsibility for the *dharmas* that uphold and move space-time born from his body. He was in charge. Arjuna's task was not to attain the status of Puruṣa Nārāyana, as the patron of the Puruṣamedha would have (and as the sages in 14.1). Instead Arjuna relied on the potency of the man who already had that status, Vāsudeva Kṛṣṇa his *ācārya.* Any *ācārya* who, through *mantra,* embodied Kṛṣṇa embodied that Puruṣa Nārāyana and was a similar source of refuge. It seems likely that the Yavana Bhāgavata Agathocles had taken refuge in such an *ācārya.*

One last query may be addressed. How reliable is the *Śrīmad Bhāgavata Purāṇa* for understanding Bhāgavata tradition in the centuries B.C.E. if it took the shape it now has only in the eighth century C.E.? We cannot answer that question here, but an answer will need to consider two points. First, as J. A. B. van Buitenen once wrote, the *Bhāgavata Purāṇa* is unusual among Purāṇas for the archaic nature of its Sanskrit.[73] He conjectured that its writers purposely imitated an archaic style in order to give it authority. While it is true that the text as we know it is compiled from various sources and has been added to over time, the archaism of its language may in fact express the archaic nature of its lore. It may in fact be lore about Bhāgavatas that dates to the time when the *Mahābhārata* was being formulated, and perhaps earlier. Second, in its use of the *Bhāgavata Purāṇa,* the Vaikuṇṭha Perumāl Temple reveals the text's exoteric and esoteric structure. With few exceptions, the panels on the bottom floor *vimāna* depict material from Books 1–6 and 11–12. As we noted, those panels face the exoteric realm of the temple *maṇḍala.* With few exceptions, the panels on the middle floor *garbhagṛha,* within the esoteric realm of the *maṇḍala,* depict material from Books 7–10. Given that organization, "the Purāṇa of the Bhāgavata possessing Kingship" (*Śrīmad Bhā-*

gavata Purāṇa) may indeed possess esoteric lore (Books 7–10) relevant to a Bhāgavata ruler encompassed by more publically available lore (Books 1–6, 11–12).

Those esoteric teachings relating to the *sādhaka* as king may explain why such ancient teachings did not come into public currency until quite late. They may also explain why the lore was illustrated elaborately on the imperial Viṣṇu-house of a Bhāgavata emperor in a dynastic lineage judged to be Śūdra. That, in turn, may exemplify the need for the powerful *mantras* and *dīkṣās* of the mixed Vedic and Tantric rites of the Pāñcarātra in the centuries B.C.E. when monarchy became the paradigm for government and the monarchs were not Kṣatriyas.

It is significant, finally, that at the center of the Puruṣamedha (the third day and night), at the center of the *Bhagavad Gītā* (chapter 14), and at the center of the Vaikuṇṭha Perumāl *vimāna* (the bottom floor *garbhagṛha*), there is an absolute Person, the primordial Father and Mother, who inseminates his own womb. The use of *maṇḍala, mantra,* and *dhyāna* to identify the human body with that primordial androgynous Person—a goal characteristic of Āgama or Tantra—appears to be very old indeed.

NOTES

Chart 8.1 is an adaptation by A. E. Wayne from A. Rea's *Pallava Architecture.* The square box at the summit of the *vimāna* is completely enclosed. Charts 8.2, 8.3, and 8.4 were made by Carol Reck.The copyright for all the illustrations is retained by the author.

1. H. Daniel Smith, *A Descriptive Bibliography of the Printed Texts of the Pāñcarātrāgama,* 2 vols. Gaekwad's Oriental Series, 158 and 168 (Baroda: Oriental Institute, 1975 and 1980).

2. See Sanjukta Gupta, "The Caturvyūha and the Viśākha-yūpa in the Pāñcarātra," *Brahma Vidya, Adyar Library Bulletin* 35, 3–4 (1971); Gupta "The Pāñcarātra Attitude to Mantra," *Mantra,* ed. Harvey P. Alper (Albany: State University of New York Press, 1989), 224–48; and Gupta, "Yoga and *Antaryāga* in Pāñcarātra," *Ritual and Speculation in Early Tantrism: Studies in Honor of André Padoux,* ed. Teun Goudriaan (Albany: State University of New York Press, 1992), 175–208.

3. *Archives of Asian Art* 32 (1979): 39–54.

4. See *Mathura: The Cultural Heritage* (New Delhi: American Institute of Indian Studies and Columbia: South Asia Books, 1989), 383–92.

5. Doris Meth Srinivasan, "Early Vaiṣṇava Imagery: Caturvyūha and Variant Forms," *Archives of Asian Art,* 32 (1979): 48–49.

6. Dennis Hudson, *The Body of God: Text, Image, and Liturgy in the Vaikuṇṭha Perumāl Temple at Kanchipuram* (forthcoming).

7. See Dennis Hudson, "Kanchipuram," *Temple Towns of Tamil Nadu,* ed. George Michell with photographs by Bharath Ramamrutham (Bombay: Marg Publications, 1993 and 1997), 18–39; Hudson, "Arjuna's Sin: Thoughts on the *Bhagavad-Gītā* in its Epic

Context," *Journal of Vaiṣṇava Studies,* 4/3 (Summer 1996): 65–84; Hudson, "The *Śrīmad Bhāgavta Purāṇa* in Stone: The Text as an Eighth-Century Temple and Its Implications," *Journal of Vaiṣṇava Studies,* 3/3 (Summer 1995): 137–82; Hudson, "Vraja Among theTamils: A Study of the Bhāgaatas in Early South India," *Journal of Vaiṣṇava Studies,* 3/1 (Winter 1994): 113–40; Hudson, "Vāsudeva Kṛṣṇa in Theology and Architecture: A Background to Srīvaiṣṇavism," *Journal of Vaiṣṇava Studies,* 2/1 (Winter 1993): 139–70.

8. *Śatapatha Brāhmaṇa* 11.1.5.3 calls the moon The Hare in the Moon. See *Sacred Books of the East,* vol. 44, trans. Julius Eggeling (Oxford: Clarendon Press, 1882–1900), 10.

9. *Brahmatva-Māñjarī (Role of the Brahman Priest in the Vedic Ritual),* ed. and trans. H. G. Ranade (Poona: H. G. Ranade, 1984).

10. Ibid., 11.

11. Ibid., 4–5.

12. *Śrīmad Bhāgavata Purāṇa* 9.14.3.

13. Another west-facing Bhāgavata temple in Kañchipuram illustrates that idea. See K. V. Raman, *Sri Varadarājaswāmi Temple—Kañchi: A Study of its History, Art and Architecture* (New Delhi: Abhinav Publications, 1975), 159–60.

14. For "language in the manner of twilight," see Alex Wayman, *The Buddhist Tantras: Light on Indo-Tibetan Esotericism* (New York: Samuel Weiser, 1973), 128–35.

15. Frederique Appfel Marglin, *Wives of the God-King: The Rituals of the Devadāsis of Puri* (Oxford: Oxford University Press, 1985), 217-28; and Marglin, "Refining the Body: Transformative Emotion in Ritual Dance," *Divine Passion: The Social Construction of Emotion in India,* ed. Owen Lynch (Berkeley: University of California Press, 1990).

16. In the Varadarājaswāmi Temple in Kanchi, for example, at the southwest corner of the south side of what appears to signify the *uttaravedi,* there is a sculpture of Gaṇeśa and at the southeast corner a sculpture of Danvantri (Danvantari); see Raman, *Śrī Varadarājaswāmi Temple,* 45.

17. These meanings of the names are found in the *Sri Vishnu Sahasranama: With the Bahashya of Sri Parasara Bhattar,* trans. A. Srinivasa Raghavan (Mylapore, Madras: Sri Visishtadvaita Pracharini Sabha, 1983).

18. T. S. Maxwell has discussed the *vyūha* figures, but his discussion must be read critically; see *Viśvarūpa* (Delhi: Oxford University Press, 1988), 123–43 and plates 40–56.

19. Dennis Hudson, "The Viṣṇu Temple at Deogarh: A Bhāgavata Viṣṇu-House of the Pāñcarātra Āgama," presented to the Fifth Symposium of the American Committee for South Asian Art, Freer and Sackler Galleries, Washington, D.C., 19–21 April 1991.

20. For example, plates 40–45 in Maxwell, *Viśvarūpa.*

21. Ibid., 17–35, pls. 10–13.

22. Ibid., 23.

23. Ibid., 21.

24. Ibid., 42. Maxwell unconvincingly identified the figure emerging from the top as Aniruddha and the missing one on Vāsudeva Kṛṣṇa's left as Pradyumna.

25. See A. K. Narain, "The Two Hindu Divinities on the Coins of Agathocles from Ai-Khanum, " *The Journal of the Numistic Society of India* 35 (1973): 73–77.

26. *Sātvata-saṃhitā* 17, as cited in Smith, *A Descriptive Catalogue* 1, 527–28.

27. Ibid., 53.

28. *Jayākhya-saṃhitā* 22, as cited in Smith, *A Descriptive Catalogue,* 125.

29. B. N. Puri, *India in the Time of Patañjali* (Bombay: Bharativa Vidya Bhavan, 1968), ch. 7–8.

30. *Dines Chandra Sircar, Select Inscriptions Bearing on Indian History and Civilization,* vol. 1, 2nd ed. (Delhi: Motila Banarsidass, 1983), 88–89.

31. "Comments" on John Irwin's "The Heliodorus Pillar at Besnagar," *Puratattva* 8 (1975), 166–76.

32. *Śrīmad Bhāgavata* 3.30.38. Kapila uses the same words for Time as are used here, *kalaḥ kalayatam,* and his entire teaching (3.25–33) appears to be a commentary on *Bhagavad Gītā* 2–11. For Prahlāda, see 7.1–10. For Garuḍa as made of Vedic hymns, see 8.3.31. *Ṛg Veda* 1.54.2 describes Viṣṇu as a ferocious wild beast in the mountains.

33. The story of Garuḍa and Vinatā occurs in the context of the churning of the Milk Ocean in "The Tale of Astika," *Mahābhārata* 1.14–53.

34. *Select Inscriptions* 1, 90–92.

35. *Śrīmad Bhāgavata* 11.1 and 30.

36. Nācciyār Tirumoḷi 1.1.

37. 10.50.44–58.

38. *Bhagavad Gita* (Bh.G.) 10.52.9–12.

39. Bh.G. 10.51.23–35.

40. Bh.G. 10.51.28–35.

41. Bh.G. 10.51.45–58.

42. Bh.G. 10.51.45–58 (Tapasvananda 3: 259).

43. Bh.G. 10.51.59–64.

44. Bh.G. 10.52.3 (Tapasyananda 3: 260).

45. Bh.G. 10.52.4.

46. The fifth century Tamil epic *Cilappatikāram* used Bhāgavata tradition in its story of the Tamil Cera king who defeated the Āryan kings in a battle that lasted eighteen hours. See: V. R. R. Dikshitar, *Cilappatikāram* (Madras: South India Saiva Siddhanta Works Publishing Society, 1978), 353 and 355 and notes; and *Shilappadikaram* (*The Ankle Bracelet*) trans. Alain Danielou (New York: New Directions, 1965), 169–71.

47. *Dikshitar, Cilappatikāram* 6.8–13 (and *urai*). See also: Dikshitar, *Cilappatikāram,* 134 and notes, and Danielou, *Shilappadikaram,* 26.

48. Doris Meth Srivivansen, "Vaiṣṇava Art and Iconography at Mathurā," *Mathura: The Cultural Heritage* (New Delhi: AIIS, 1989), 383.

49. Ibid., 383–84.

50. *Śrīmad Bhāgavata: The Holy Book of God,* 4, trans. Swāmi Tapasyananda (Madras: Sri Ramakrishna Nath, 1982), 209], 12.11.14.

51. Srinivasan, "Vaiṣṇava Art," 384.

52. Srinivasan, "Vaiṣṇava Art," 384.

53. For discussion of Ekānamśā, see Dennis Hudson, "Piṇṇai, Krishna's Cowherd Wife," *The Divine Consort: Rādhā and the Goddesses of India,* ed. John Stratton Hawley and Donna Marie Wulff (Berkeley: University of California Press, 1982), 238–61, esp. 254–55.

54. Srini vansan, "Vaiṣṇava Art," 389.

55. Ibid, 387.

56. *Śrīmad Bhāgavata* 11.18.17; 11.18.40; 11.23.34.

57. Ibid., 11.29.22.

58. Ibid., 11.7–9, especially 11.7.19–23.

59. H. S. Joshi, *Origin and Development of Dattātreya Worship in India* (Baroda: Maharaja Sayajirao Universtiy, 1965), 66–71. See also *Mārkaṇḍeya Purāṇa* 17.15–16 and 23–25.

60. Margaret Cone and Richard F. Gombrich, *The Perfect Generosity of Prince Vessantara: A Buddhist Epic* (Oxford: Clarendon Press, 1977); *Ārya Śūra, Jātakamālā 9* (*Once the Buddha Was a Monkey: Ārya Śūra's Jātakamālā,* trans. Peter Khoroche (Chicago: University of Chicago Press, 1989), 58–73.

61. *The Katha Sarit Sagara or Ocean of the Streams of Story,* trans. C. H. Tawney (Delhi: Munshiram Manoharlal, 1968), 2: 497–503; and the Sanskrit text, *Kathāsaritisāgara* 16.3 (Patna: Vihara-Rastrabhasa-Parisad Edition, 1963) 3: 902–916.

62. According to R. Vijayalakshmy, *The Great Romance* appeared around the first century, probably at the Sātavāhana court at Pratiṣṭhāna in the region of the Vindhyas. See R. Vijayalakshmy, *A Study of the Perunkatai* (Madras: International Institute of Tamil Studies, 1981), 24–36.

63. *The Bhagavad-Gītā,* trans. R. C. Zaehner (London: Oxford University Press, 1969), 322–325 (12.3–4).

64. Srinivasan, "Early Vaiṣṇava Imagery," 47–50.

65. *The Śatapatha-Brāhmaṇa,* 5: 172–174.

66. *Hindu Scriptures,* trans. R. C, Zaehner (London and New York: Knopf, 1966), 8–10.

67. As I read *Bhagavad Gītā* 10:19–42, Kṛṣṇa explains the fundamental details of Vāsudeva's bodily form as space-time (*brahmāṇḍa*). He begins the *maṇḍala* exposition with the spatial directions in heaven. Starting in the center and then in the clockwise direction from north, east, south, and west, he describes the elements relevant to life and the rites of refuge and initiation by the *ācārya* in the west (20–31). Then in the counterclockwise direction (*prasavya*), he relates the *ācārya*'s explantion of the *maṇḍala* beginning on the west and ending with the seed in the center (32–39). That *prasavya* movement anticipates the vision of Time as destroyer in chapter 11. The teaching seems to explain a form of the *cakra maṇḍala* that prepares initiates for the mysteries expounded in chapters 12–16.

68. *Ṛg Veda* 1.154.2. The wild beast in the mountains is connected there to Viṣṇu's three strides, another indication of the sacrificer/dwarf/Brahman as *ācārya.*

69. *Ṛg Veda* 1.172 and 8.7, cited by A.A. Macdonell, *The Vedic Mythology* (Varanasi: Indological Book House, n.d.), 78.

70. See *Ṛg Veda* 13.6.1.9, 405, 2n.

71. The "Puruṣa Nārāyana litany" in *Vājasanīya Saṃhitā* 31.1–22, in Paul Deussen, *Sixty Upaniṣads of the Veda,* vol. 2, trans. V. M. Bedekar and G. B. Palsule (Delhi: Motilal Banarsidass, 1980), 893–96.

72. In *Śatapatha Brāhmaṇa* 13.8.1.5 and 13.8.2.1, those who are of the *asuras* make funeral mounds that are circular and on a foundation (like *stūpas*). In contrast, those of the *Devas* make them four-cornered and without a foundation.

73. "On the Archaism of the *Bhāgavata Purāṇa*" in *Krishna; Myths, Rites, and Attitudes,* ed. Milton Singer (Honolulu: East-West Center Press, 1966), 23–40.

Part IV
THE VEDAS AND TANTRA

9

Imagery of the Self from Veda to Tantra

Teun Goudriaan

Although much time and paper have been spent on discussions of the concept of Ātman (hereafter translated as the self) in the Hindu tradition, the intellectual efforts of scholars have not resulted in an explanation of its real nature. Nor could this be expected, since the self, this innermost spiritual core of the person, is held to be beyond the reach of mind or reason. True spirituality cannot be described, only directly experienced in blissful consciousness, such is the prevailing Hindu position.

Indian religious leaders and philosophers themselves had different ideas about the self's status, characteristics, stages of development, destination, size, or quantity (unique cosmic Ātman or plurality of separate self monads?). Also the terminology is multiform and the mutual distinctions are of a subtle nature and not always clear. To my knowledge, no satisfactory encompassing monograph about the Hindu tradition of the self (in philosophy as well as religion and art) has yet appeared, despite the existence of useful introductory studies such as those by Emil Abegg in 1945 and Troy W. Organ in 1964. Here lies a real challenge, because insight into the self has been expressed to be the real purpose of life,[1] the "goal of the internal quest."[2]

It is not my intention to add to the existing literature on the philosophical interpretations of the self. Instead, I shall concentrate (on a less technical level) on selected aspects of the verbal imagery by which religious teachers, philosophers and poets have built up a "multiple denomination" in the course of their attempts to give expression to the inexpressible. Surprisingly, these varied approaches to a typology of the self have also not been made the topic of a comprehensive study. The mystery of the self has been approached and obliquely referred to with remarkable variety and insistence, also with consistence, in Indian literature, in Sanskrit as well as in the rich traditions of the vernaculars. In the following pages, I shall restrict myself to some illustrative examples in Sanskrit literature from the Vedas onward, with special reference to some Upaniṣads and early Tantric sources. The Upaniṣads most often referred to are the *Bṛhadāraṇyaka* (BĀUp), the *Chāndogya* (ChUp) and the *Maitrāyaṇīya* (MaiUp), the latter being of a later date than the first two; the Tantric or literature with a Tantric orientation is rather varied, but some emphasis is laid upon the *Lakṣmī Tantra* (LT; Pañcarātra, that is,

Vaiṣṇava), the *Tantrasadbhāva* (Tsb; Northern Śaiva), and the *Kulālikāmnaya* or *Kubjikāmata* (KMT; Śākta), all three are dated to the early medieval period. An intermediate stage is represented by the *Mahābhārata* (Mbh). As a deep cleft seems to exist between the findings and the theorizations of modern psychology and the classical Hindu tradition, all attempts at comparison between the two will be avoided at this stage.[3] It is also beyond the scope of this paper to try to demonstrate the existence of points of contact in this sphere between the Indian tradition and early Western esotericism.

Being unfamiliar with modern theoretical developments in the field of semiotics or science of literature, I shall not try to keep up with this discussion. There are different types of verbal imagery, for which I use the terms metaphor, simile, and allegory. For practical reasons, a metaphor may here be understood as a word or expression applied (with preservation of its conventional meaning) to another object for the purpose of elucidating or suggesting a particular aspect of that object's nature. Very often, the metaphor or simile will serve to realize a process of concretization, exteriorization, or even personification, in order to facilitate human understanding of abstract notions. The use of a metaphor to express an aspect of spirituality implies a kind of paradox: the spiritual is present as the concrete although it is not identical with it; the identification evokes a certain tension, this in contradistinction to the simile, where such an identification is avoided.[4] In our context, there is, however, an important countertendency toward abstraction of originally concrete, archaic concepts such as *puruṣa* "(little) man" (see below).

Certain types of metaphor (in most cases those derived from visionary or dream experience) or simile may develop into allegory, that is, a literary structure in which, in the words of H. E.Taylor, "all statements or expressions [which are constitutive toward that structure] are intended to carry, beside their palpable meaning, another which is veiled and more spiritual. . . . "[5] The allegory may serve as a suitable tool to express "dynamic" psychagogic aspects of mystical realization that concern the self's soteriological history. Instances of allegorical set-up, however, will not feature prominently in the present article. It must be emphasized that, in a context like ours, the scope of literature and the literary cannot be restricted to the aesthetic sphere, but extends to the psychagogic; still Monroe Beardsley's well-known definition of literature as "a discourse with important implicit meaning"[6] continues to serve our purpose.

In attempting a survey of the literary imagery of the self, we must be aware that the different themes occur independent of entirely different socioeconomic, cultural, and religious contexts, literary genres, and the ritual, soteriological, ethical, or poetical aims of the author or transmitter. Beside the trend toward concretization there occurs, as noted above, a tendency toward sophistication, speculative abstraction, and spiritual reinterpretation of older conceptions.

The imagery may be based on one of the following thematic clusters:

1. Archaic or primitive: especially in Vedic literature we find a number of

coexisting ideas about a plurality of selves or souls such as *asu* (life force), *prāṇa* (breath), *jīva* (life principle) or *puruṣa* (man or soul being). A matter of special concern for Vedic man was the question of how to imagine that entity that leaves the body in the process of dying, and how this entity would find its way toward its destination, wherever that might be. On the other hand, one asked oneself how the same entity entered the unborn babe and from where it came (such questions are asked in the *Praśna Upaniṣad* 3.1).

2. Body or senses: in late Vedic sources (especially the Upaniṣads) where a nonmaterial, controlling self has made its appearance, images come to the fore that try to denote the relation of this self (whether called *ātman, puruṣa* or otherwise) to the bodily and sensorial functions.

3. Estrangement: several images are expressive of the self's essential difference from the body and the mental functions. They interpret the self's incarnation in terms of an estrangement, a captivity or a banishment and try to outline the way by which it may succeed to return to its original and real abode and destination. Here, similes or metaphors tend to develop into allegorical tales such as that of the lost king[7] or the banished prince (known from the *Sāṃkhyasūtras*).[8] One can also compare visual symbols such as the labyrinth.[9] As a special variety of this type, we may consider the allegorical descriptions of the plight of deserted and lonely maidens, cowherdesses, or princesses.

4. Purity: certain similes or metaphors are expressive of the recognition by the self of its own purity, or its return toward its pristine state, such as recognizing one's pure self in a cleaned mirror (*Śvetāśvatara Upaniṣad* 2, 14; LT 7, 18)[10] or they emphasize the self's innate freedom, for instance, the bird metaphor discussed below.

5. Experience: the last group of images conveys a philosophical or religious message based upon direct experience of the self's real nature. It is sometimes difficult to distinguish here between the simile (type: the self is like . . .) and what one might call the identive metaphorical statement directly expressive of the author's insight concerning the inner self (type: the self is . . .; or: one should meditate on the self as . . .). We must also be aware that such images may refer to the Universal Self, the individual self, or to a nonspecified conception. In the theistic milieu (to which the majority of Tantric sources belongs), the relation between these two selves generally is expressed not unlike that between the soul and God. In principle, the following instances refer primarily to the individual self, unless otherwise indicated.

The range of subjects with which the self has been compared or by means of which its nature has been denoted is nearly infinite. Several such comparisons (such as that with a king) have been applied in subtly different ways. A tentative survey according to subject headings might include the representation of the self as:

1. a man ("little man," family man, king, actor, charioteer, etc.)

2. a woman (princess, bride, etc.)
3. a god or goddess;
4. an animal (bird, fish, sacrificial animal, beast of prey, etc.)
5. a grain or plant (seeds, lotus, etc.)
6. an inanimate object (crystal or pearl, gold, etc.)
7. a primary element (fire, sun, space, etc.)
8. a sound or *mantra*

Only some of these items testify to a direct continuation of Vedic imagery into Tantric literature; others have come up, to our knowledge, only after the Vedic period. In general, however, the incidence is amply sufficient to show that many Tantric *gurus* relied on the older Sanskritic tradition (orally transmitted or studied by means of written texts) to express their conceptions of spirituality and its relation to the world of appearances.

The way in which this process went on in practice is outlined below by means of a few selected instances.

An interesting instance of development from a concrete toward an abstract conception is furnished by the image of the self (or soul) as a "little man." The most famous literary presentation of this idea is the legend of Sāvitrī and Satyavān in the *Mahābhārata* (3.281.17).[11] We read how the God Yama forcibly extracts from Satyavān's body the *puruṣa* with the help of a noose (which proves the *puruṣa's* material character). This little being is the size of a thumb: a clear reference to late Vedic statements such as in the *Śvetāśvatara Upaniṣad* 5.8, in the last instance going back to a primitive concept.[12] In fact, the idea of a self of small or minute size has become an ever-recurring and constantly varied feature of the Indian mystical tradition. It is also very often represented in religious literature influenced by Tantrism. In the ChUp (8.12.4), a text that in several respects presents evidence of what may be somewhat one-sidedly called "proto-Tantric" ideas, the little man is localized in the (right) eye;[13] he is not "the person with the eye."[14] However, the usual location of the self is in the heart, often conceived as the "space of the heart"[15] or, metaphorically the "heart-lotus" in one of the later Upaniṣads.[16] That the heart is the usual residence of the "thinking soul" in archaic cultures was argued with many illustrative references by Ernst Windisch.[17]

It is stated also by means of a simile that the real Puruṣa is invisible and cannot be found even if one were to dissect the body.

> Just as nobody who takes an axe (and dissects a log of wood) will see smoke or fire within the log, in the same way those who dissect a body, hands or feet, observe nothing else than that.[18]

Apart from denying the material nature of the self, the simile also suggests a certain relation in the nature between the self and fire. It may be remarked also that Sri Aurobindo, in his allegorical epic *Sāvitrī,* abstracted the appearance of Satyavān's soul in his own way by saying that ". . . another luminous Satyavān arose . . . the silent marvel stood between mortal man and god."[19]

A remarkable use of the concept of the "soul-man" in the Tantras is the "man of evil" (*papapuruṣa*) that should be burned by the worshiping priest in the course of his meditative ritual of *bhūtaśuddhi* "purification of the elements," a necessary precondition for his obtaining a pure and divine nature with which he can worship God. According to the Sanskrit commentary to the *Arcanakhaṇḍa,* a ritual guide to the Vaiṣṇava (professedly non-Tantric) Vaikhānasa community of temple priests, the "man of evil" is present in the navel. He should first be dried out by enclosing him with a *maṇḍala* of Vāyu while reciting a Ṛg Vedic stanza (10.137.3) and afterward burned up by means of the seed syllable of the fire god Agni. The "man of evil" has the following form: his head consists of brahmin-murder, his arms of theft, his heart of alcoholism, his hips of violation of the teacher's bed (consorting with the teacher's wife), his feet of the combination of these four deadly sins. His other limbs consist of minor sins, he has a red beard and red eyes; he is, in short, a little devil who implicitly is assumed to live in every person whose karma has not been exhausted. The older Vaikhānasa Āgamas, relatively free of Tantric influences, do not mention him.

The image of the self as "family man" can be classified as an aspect of the representation of the self as a male human being, as mentioned above. The expression of the self's situation in terms of a family relationship might seem paradoxical from the viewpoint of Advaita or Sāṃkhya because these schools insist upon its uniqueness or isolation. However that may be, there is no such contradiction in the early Upaniṣadic occurrence of this image. It gives us a realistic image of the Ātman, to be meditated upon by the adept (especially the Vedic sacrificer) who strives for completeness in the present life and the hereafter.

The *locus classicus* is BĀUp 1.4.7: *"ātmaivedam agra āsīd eka eva / so 'kāmayata: jāyā syād atha prajāyeyātha vittaṃ me syād atha karma kurvīya,"* that is, "The self only existed here in the beginning, all alone. He desired: 'may there be a wife (for me), that I may beget offspring, and may there be possessions for me, that I may perform activities'." Here the self quite frankly is stated to be still unsatisfied, a position that is unthinkable in classical texts. But, the text itself gives already an exegetical turn to the image. Admittedly, the self's inner urges are expressed "in bodily terms"[20] or, I would prefer, in terms of male patriarchal self-realization; but the author proceeds by explaining that one should consider the Ātman as one's mind (*manas,* here corresponding to the "psyche"), his wife as one's speech, his child as one's breath, and his possessions as the sensorial faculties; these together make up one's completeness. Thus, one's status as a successful householder is projected, so to say, onto the mystical plane of interiority by way of explicit allegory. No distinction is made between cosmic and individual planes; the whole "spiritual family" can be realized in the here and now. A little further (BĀUp 1.5.7), the family relation is rendered in even more homely terms—mind is presented as the father, speech as the mother and breath as the child. A cosmic dimension is added, however, in the BĀUp (1.5.11–13) where mind, speech, and breath have as their respective bodies: heaven, earth and water, and sun, fire (earthly representation of the sun) and moon as their "luminous forms." The only child, breath, has according to the BĀUp (1.5.12) a secret other name, viz. Indra. Thus, the "king of the gods" plays a role in mystic speculation that corresponds with that of the individual self in an earlier tradition (see below).

This spiritual allegory of the self expressed in terms of a family relation already contains what one might call "proto-Tantric features" and has counterparts in several Tantric passages. One might even think of it as the prototype of the later development of the term *kula* "(spiritual) family" in all its implications, which plays such an important role in Tantric religion. There, however, has occurred an important shift in the "allegorical sense" as a consequence of the developing distinction between the cosmic and the individual self; in the Tantric view, the former is now designated by the "father" (who stands somewhat aloof from the pettiness of ordinary family life), the latter by the "child." The mother's role is occupied by the cosmic Śakti. The blissful togetherness of the little family also is realized by the Tantric adept in the course of his meditation. In the first stanza of his *Tantrāloka,* Abhinavagupta adroitly refers to this mystical truth while he pays honor to his own parents on the surface level; the mother obtains the epithet *sṛṣṭimahāḥ* "whose greatness is occasion," the father is *guptaruci* "of hidden glow," while his own heart or spiritual core is denoted as their "emission" (*visarga*).

From the monastic point of view, this situation which suggests a consciousness of separation should be transcended in a realization of cosmic unity. On an allegorical level, this may be represented by the ascetic ideal (implying internal self-realization) versus the "external" existence as a householder, as is suggested in the *Tantrasadbhāva:*

> Representation is of (the nature of) living in Saṃsarā
> which is a house; the self of representation
> becomes a householder; the One who is inside it
> does not possess a family.[21]

Actually, some texts give prominence to the mental and/or real separation from family ties as a prerequisite for the *sādhaka* (initiate) who is to actualize his progress towards final release.[22] Already the BĀUp (4.4.22) states: "knowing this . . . , the wise men of old did not wish progeny (asking themselves): 'What shall we do with progeny when the self is this our world?' "

It is clear that this interpretation of the time-honored image of the householder fits easily into a theistic worldview, as exemplified by the *Liṅga Purāṇa* 2.9.55; "Having made one syllable *OṂ* your lamp, search for the Master of the house, the Subtle One Who resides in the interior . . . behold the Gracious One (Śiva) residing in the body."[23] The eternal desire for self-expression and the reverse direction toward the original unity is formulated in Kaula in the *Siddhsiddhān-*

tapaddhati (4.11.9)[24] ascribed to Gorakṣanātha; "the Single takes to himself the family (*kula*), the family desires the Single," which is explained in the text in this way, that "(Śiva) of unique form, possessing immeasurable power, although abiding in his own blissful state, enjoys a state of plurality, but (afterward) of His own initiative again assumes His former base."

The status of the ruler is allotted to the Ātman in a variety of images and metaphorical expressions. Usually they function in a context where the self's relation to lower mental and bodily functions is discussed. According to a well-known expression, the self "rules by means of his ruling powers" (*īsata īsanibhih,* BĀUp 1.4.11); and "ruler" (*īsana*) is given as the appellation of the Ātman (BĀUp 4.4.15 and 4.4.22); "he is present in the hollow space of the heart, master of all, ruler of all, Lord of all," he is "Lord and king of all beings" (BĀUp 2.5.15). Also the MaiUp (6.8) knows the term "ruler" as one of the epithets of the self. The BĀUp (2.1.18ff.) depicts a specific situation in which this rulership is effectuated: during dream experience, the self can wander about in full freedom everywhere it likes. In this capacity, it is compared to a king who, on an inspection tour through his empire takes his officials and servants with him (the officials are *prāṇas,* here the vital functions).[25]

These activities of the self, experienced in dream, are essentially false, as Śaṅkara points out in his commentary.They are lingering impressions (*vāsanā*) that mirror earlier experiences under the influence of desire and karma. However, in the next stage of interiorization, that of deep sleep (BĀUp 2.1.19), the self is again compared to a king (also to a child and a stately brahmin). This time, the king is inactive and has retreated, as it were, to his inner apartments where he enjoys the highest bliss. Because the details of this passage involve intricate difficulties, their discussion can be better postponed to another occasion.

The royal image is taken up again in the BĀUp 4.37–38 and connected there with the phenomena of birth and death.When the self has decided to inhabit a body, the vital functions are said to await it eagerly, just as the impending visit of a king is awaited eagerly by several local functionaries such as the head of police. And, when it is about to depart, all these vital functions gather around it, just as the functionaries gather around the king at the end of his official visit. We conclude that the images of the "royal self" are polyvalent in the Upaniṣads; it can be applied in different situations and by means of different subtypes.

The *Mahābhārata* uses exactly the same imagery:

> Just as several councilors of a king,
> enjoined (by him) proclaim their separate decrees—
> in the same way (do) the five (senses) in the bodies;
> He is superior to them, the sole repository of insight.[26]

The idea is that the king is the only person who can make real political decisions because only he surveys the whole situation. In a similar fashion, the fundamental text of the Sāṃkhya school, the *Sāṃkhyakarika* states that the ten senses, the mind, and the ego, like lamps, illumine objects for the self's benefit and then deposit them in front of the Buddhi (intelligence or reason).[27] As is usual in Sāṃkhya, the self is here called Puruṣa. The commentator Māṭhara clarifies that the relation between the self and the functions is like that between a king and his dignitaries with the Buddhi acting as chief minister. The earlier commentary *Sāṃkhyatattvakamudī* even specifies that this psychic process can be compared to a system of gradual taxation. The image is not unknown to Tantric literature. The *Lakṣmī Tantra* gives a similar description; although complicated by the addition of three spheres of application (divine, psychic, and material), here it is the Buddhi that offers the impressions of the senses to the self (called Kṣetrajña).[28] The Buddhi is supervised (*adhiṣṭhitā*) by the self (LT 7.32); in the same way the self is called the supervisor (*adhiṣṭhatṛ*) of the vital functions in Ādiśeṣa's *Paramārthasāra.*[29] Although Tantric literature in general is perhaps less concerned with describing the relations between the various psychic and sensory functions, the lordly nature of the self is often emphasized. Thus, the *Jayākhya Saṃhitā,* perhaps the oldest Pāñcarātra Āgama, in the context of the worshiper's self purification, states:

> He beholds in the space of the heart
> that unmoving (self), of solar brilliance,
> permeated by flashing splendor,
> the lord, the supreme Pervader[30]

This seems to refer to the individual self (*jīvātman,* cf. 59d *jīvam ātmānam*), but similar descriptions in related sources are applied to Viṣṇu/Nārāyaṇa who is present in the human heart as Supreme Self and inner controller (*antaryāmin*), also according to the JS itself (4.106). Another instance is found in the Vaikhānasa ritual text *Samūrtārcanādhikaraṇa* (*Treatise on Worship by Means of an Image*) ascribed to the sage Atri (31.33ff.). A more detailed treatment can be found in Marīcī's *Vimānārcanakalpa* (*Guide to Temple Worship,* ch. 84).[31]

Such statements about God's presence in the heart or about the divine nature of the self give expression to a theistic reorientation of the Ātmanic tradition in most of the schools with Tantric orientation. In the passage from the LT (7.33) discussed above, the self is said to be the "divine sphere" (*adhidaivatam*) for the Buddhi. The Śaiva or Śakta sources generally hold that the individual self is Śiva (or a Śiva, in dualistic tradition) who is fettered within a body.[32] For the *Kulārṇava,* one of the most authoritative of the Kaula Tantras, "the body is a temple, and the soul (*jīva*) is God Sadāśiva."[33] The dedication of one's own being to this divine self is a popular theme in Tantric as well as *bhakti* (devotional) sources; it long has been elaborated in allegorical guise in the well-known stanza *Ātmā tvam,* which describes human activity as a continuous act of worship to Śiva:

> Thou art my self, the Mountain's Daughter my mind,
> Thy retinue of gods my vital breaths, my body Thy mansion;
> enjoyment of sense-objects is mere worship of Thee,
> in sleep I abide in *samādhi* (profound meditation).
> Walking by foot in circumambulation,
> my words are all songs of praise;
> whatever I do, O Gracious Lord
> It is all adoration to Thee.[34]

Similarly, we read in the *Prapañcasāra Tantra:*

> The activities of mind, speech and body
> should be meditation, praise and acts of worship;
> O Lord of gods, all my work should be adoration of Thee.[35]

The divine self's residence is described in typically Tantric fashion in the Tsb. (1.49c–51a): in the region of the heart, a lotus should be imagined with eight petals and a sixteen-fold filament. Within it, a pericarp "like Mount Meru" resting upon a quadrangle. "In its center, the self abides blissfully like Śiva; pure, of minute size like the hundredth part of a hair's tip. This is the Supreme Self in the body . . ."[36] In the so-called Kashmir Śaiva tradition, the illuminated self is represented by the god Bhairava, the "Lord of all" (*viśveśvara*).[37] In Tantrism, a widely known allegorizing image is that of the "Isle of Gems," where the Goddess is enthroned in the worshiper's heart.[38] The divine representation of the self in the body dates already from the Upaniṣadic period, although it is by no means prominent there. In MaiUp, a passage of strikingly proto-Tantric character, Indra is identified with the Puruṣa who resides in the right eye (see above), and his unnamed wife resides in the left eye; their union finds place within the hollow of the heart.[39] This is, at the same time, one of the earliest and clearest instances of the realization of the self's bisexuality.

The lordly Ātman or Puruṣa is often said to reside in a stronghold (*pūr, pura*). The BĀUp (2.5.18) plays upon the similarity of the words *puruṣa* and *pura:* the Puruṣa is said to bear this name because, formerly (*puras*), he entered the strongholds in winged form and continues to abide in them. But, the idea of a "mystic stronghold of *brahman*" (*brahmapura*) is found already in the *Atharvaveda Saṃhitā* (10.2.18ff.); also here, an etymological connection is established with the word *puruṣa.*

> Of eight rings and nine doors
> is the gods' invincible stronghold;
> within it, a golden treasure-room
> reaching the sky, surrounded by splendor.
> Within that golden treasure-room

of the three beams and threefold base—
the self-possessing appearance within it,
that only the knower of Brahman knows.[40]

In this famous passage, the self is described as a strange, "self-possessing," presumably dwarfish being (*Yakṣa*), a "monster," that lies hidden in a kind of golden cage.[41] A variant of the second stanza occurs in AV 10.8.43:

A lotus of nine doors, covered by three strands;
the self-possessing appearance within it,
that only the Brahman-knowers know.

The Kaula Tantric Kubjikā school possesses a still unedited *Kubjikā Upaniṣad* that very clearly attaches itself to the *Atharva Veda* tradition. Notwithstanding its notably apocryphal character, it quotes an astonishing number of stanzas from the *Atharva Veda,* among them the present stanza, which is an oblique reference to the "royal *yantra*" of Kubjeśvara, Goddess Kubjikā's male partner. The "lotus" is not interpreted as the body, but is said to be an eight-petaled lotus *maṇḍala* of conventional type; the "nine doors" are not the nine apertures of the body, but a figure of nine angles (*navakoṇam*); and the "three strands," which Whitney surmises to be the three temperaments, are three circles (*vṛttatrayam*). The Yakṣa is, in this exegesis, a *binducakra* (which suggests that the Ātman is possessed by the *bindu* or central dot that plays such a prominent role in Tantric *maṇḍalas*); the whole is characterized as a *Brahmacakra* (*cakra* here representing *pura*). This is certainly an interesting instance of "abstractive" Veda-exegesis; several more related cases are found in the *Kubjikā Upaniṣad.*[42]

The idea of a stronghold is continued in the well-known term *puryṣṭaka* "the eight-fold stronghold," which usually denotes, in Hindu tradition, the five objects of the senses, together with the mind, ego function and reason. It is also frequent in Tantric literature, such as the LT (7.23) and Bhaṭṭa Nārāyana's commentary on the *Mṛgendra Āgama.*[43]

From the above remarks, one should not conclude that the individual self is motionless. On the contrary, many references and descriptions, especially in Tantric texts, testify to its all-pervasive nature, its innate pulsation, or its capacity of movement. A passage translated above, the JS (10.60) refers to the self's quality as "supreme pervader." The Tsb (1.50ff.) distinguishes two states of the inner self, that is, pervasive (*vyāpin)* and nonpervasive. The latter state, says the text, is that of *paśu* (sacrificial animal), in accordance with the usual Śaiva terminology; in this state, the self's innate freedom is blocked and bound to the wheel of rebirth. The pervasive state, we can conclude, is a function of the self's ethereal nature which is often proclaimed.[44] Of similar intention is the insistence on the self's being minute in size as well as immeasurably large.[45] The minute size tends to be associated with the *jīvatman* and pervasiveness with the Supreme Self;[46] the

Lakṣmī Tantra considers the minute size as one of the defects of the unredeemed soul.[47] Also, according to the Śaiva Siddhānta, the state of being *aṇu* "minute" inheres the *paśu.*

This self or soul of small size can be set into motion by the meditator through yogic practices. One of these procedures is generally known as *kuṇḍalinīyoga,* but mutually differing descriptions occur. An interesting Vaiṣṇava practice, during which the self is led upward from a fiery *maṇḍala* in the abdomen toward a lunar *maṇḍala* in the head, is described in the *Marīcisaṃhitā.*[48] An important application is the redemptive manipulation during a Śaiva *dīkṣā* ceremony of the initiate's self by the guru who has identified himself with Śiva; we refer to Brunner's interpretation.[49] There is clearly a widespread conviction of the individual self's mobility in the sectarian ritual traditions with Tantric orientations; and its passiveness and liability to manipulation stands in remarkable contrast to the all-powerful Ātman that was proclaimed in the earlier Upaniṣads. However, also in these Upaniṣads the "moving self" is well known; thus, according to the BĀUp (2.1.18), as noted above, the self in the dream situation performs internal journeys. Birth and death are the occasions of the self's arrival into and exit from the body; the same text (4.4.2) describes how the Ātman leaves the body though a beam of light issuing upward from the tip of the heart,[50] through the eyes, the fontanel, or by another way. This is followed in the text by the famous simile in which the contracting and leaving of the self is compared to a caterpillar that moves from the tip of one leaf toward another.

Very frequent is the representation of the bodiless, moving self as a bird. This may be a continuation of the very old conception of the bird soul,[51] but Indian culture has developed a rich imagery of its own, usually expressive of the central principle of unbound freedom as the soul's natural and pristine privilege. In the *Atharva Veda,* we find, in a magical context (counteracting jealousy), a remarkable reference to that which is "nestled within the heart, the little winged spirit" (*manaskaṃ patayiṣṇukam*); here *manas* has its old meaning of "spirit-power."[52] As Abegg notes, birds that approach the sacrificial ground may represent the ancestors' souls.[53] The Vedic sacrificer is said to be a bird who flies upward to heaven.[54] These time-honored conceptions are then connected in the Upaniṣads with the developing views on the self. In winged form, the self (*puruṣa*) entered the body, says the BĀUp. The self's contraction into its own essence during sleep is compared to the return toward its nest of "a hawk or eagle after its flight, tired and putting together its wings."[55] In a related image in PraśnaUp (4.1.7), the senses coming to rest in the self are compared to birds who return to their nest. A different association is evoked by two stanzas in the BĀUp:

> Putting off the bodily (cage) by dream,
> not sleeping, it observes the sleeping (functions).
> Taking the bright (essence) along, it returns to its abode,
> the golden self, the unique swan.

> By means of breath protecting its lower nest,
> immortal, it roams outside it;
> it goes along at will, out of the reach of death,
> that golden self, the unique swan.[56]

From the early Upaniṣads onward, the conception of the *haṃsa* or "swan soul" has remained in vogue. It is, to my knowledge, generally presented as a metaphorical expression, not as a simile, and it always evokes the freely moving, emancipated self that "has emerged from the cage of the material elements" (*niḥsṛtam bhūtapañjarāt*).[57] This does not mean, however, that freedom is always realized in practice: "he binds himself like a bird by a net," says the MaiUp (3.2 and 6.30), without actually using the term *haṃsa.* An early theistic instance of this imagery is SvetUp (1.6) where the *haṃsa* is said to wander in the "circle of Brahman" (probably the round of existences; the commentator Upaniṣadbrahmayogin interprets the circle of Brahman as *nānāyoniṣu* (through several rebirths), in a misconception of difference between itself and the divine cause that sets it into motion; it needs God's grace to enter immortality.

In the yogic tradition, the idea of *haṃsa* obtained another dimension associated with the etymological analysis of the word *haṃsa* as I (*ham)* and He *(sa),* which was understood to express, by its very linguistic form, the unity of the individual and the universal self. In addition, these two aspects were connected with the outgoing and the ingoing breath, respectively. The syllables *ham* and *sa,* thus, came to represent a continuous *mantra* uttered by each living being through respiration and was stated in clear terms in one of the earlier Upaniṣads, the *Dhyānabindu Upaniṣad:*

> By the syllable *ha* he leaves, by *sa* he enters again;
> "*haṃsa, haṃsa,*" this *mantra* the soul recites continually[58]

The *haṃsa* symbolism is further enriched by the Tantric doctrine of the identity of the phonetic system with divine emanation. Thus, in the *Jnānārṇava Tantra,* we find:

> The syllable *ha,* O Goddess, is the formal representation
> of the Void, eternally undecaying;
> the syllable *sa,* being the form of Śakti,
> denotes the Supreme in combination with the visarga;
> She is called Śakti because She is the cause of creation .
> O Fair One, yoga enables (the yogin) to behold the self
> by means of the utterance "He am I" (*so 'ham).*[59]

In this way, the original archaic conception of the self as a bird developed into a mystically loaded metaphor, overlaid in the Tantric phase with yogic and mantric esoterism. But Tantrism is by no means monolithic. The KMT offers a threefold interpretation of *haṃsa* as "the supreme seminal sound that is present in the heart." *Haṃsa* contains the three conscious principles of Śiva, Śakti, and the (individual) Ātman, appearing as "separation" (*viyoga*), union (*saṃyoga*), and sound (*nāda;* produced by the union).[60] The terms "separation" and "union" suggest the principles of *akula* and *kula* mentioned above. Divine *haṃsa,* says the text, is worshiped by the (realization of) communion between these three principles. The Ātman exists in the middle between "contraction" (in-breath, Śakti) and "expansion" (*vikāsa,* Śiva). The union between the latter two is formulated in the ritual-sexual terminology as "friction" (*mathana*) in the naval, that is, the Maṇipura center and its product as the self as well as the "fire of wisdom" (*jñānāgni*) of unknown brilliance and accompanied by supreme happiness. We are reminded here of Vedic descriptions of the Puruṣa as the God Agni Vaiśvānara in the belly.[61] The kindling of the "fire of wisdom" is a clear reminiscence of the ritual kindling of the sacrificial fire, remembered by these Tantric *gurus* as a powerful store of spiritual imagery.[62] There is another old element in the description of the mystical *haṃsa* in the KMT: the friction of Śiva and Śakti also creates *amṛta* (Water-of-Life), in which one should imagine the self as bathing (as a swan bathes in lake Mānasa, a well-known image for the bliss of spiritual freedom).[63]

The discussion of the *haṃsa* brings us to another type of imagery in which it is difficult to distinguish between metaphorism and the application of the natural simile, on the one hand, and description of mystical reality on the other. The statement that the self is a sun or like the sun may be considered a metaphor or simile, but such an enunciation at the same time serves as a direct pointer to the self's fiery and universally pervasive nature. An immediate connection with solar imagery was already met with in a quotation from the BĀUp (4.3.11–12) that mentions the "golden self"; gold has an ancient association with the sun.[64] A combination of "bird," "gold" and "sun" is presented in MaiUp:

> The bird of golden hue, established in the heart
> and in the sun; diver and swan, the glow of heat, a bull;
> he is in this fire, (him) we worship.[65]

The self that abides in the heart is "like a blazing fire, multiform" (MaiUp 7.7), but it is also "the fire which has its abode in heaven, solar, called Time" (MaiUp 6.2). There are numerous statements about the self's fiery nature that we cannot deal with here. According to Erich Frauwallner, this fiery nature was imagined originally in a literal fashion, but afterward this idea was abandoned. Instead, a "spiritualization of the concept of the soul" ("*Vergeistigung des Seelenbegriffs*") occurred, which led to the recognition of knowledge (*vijñānam*) as the soul's characteristic.[66] Such an interpretation, although essentially right, is somewhat simplistic. The conception of the soul or self as an entity of fiery nature with solar associations has held its ground right into Tantric culture, notwithstanding the tension which may have existed between it and the doctrine of the soul's immateriality. It must not be forgotten that such concretizing images were also meant as meditational aids, but still they served as approaches to the essence of what was being meditated upon.

The sun, the cosmic representative or repository of the all-powerful consuming and re-creating force that is fire, is often referred to in images of the self. The sun itself is described as the "Ātman of all that moves and stands" in a beautiful stanza of the *Ṛg Veda.*[67] According to the *Jaiminīya Brāhmaṇa,* the sun is the secret repository and destination of the sacrificer's self.[68] The thumb-sized self is equal in form to the sun *(aṅguṣṭhamātro ravitulyarūpaḥ)*, says the SvetUp (5.8). In the Tantric Tsb (1.50), the internal movement of what it calls the "Supreme Self" is compared to the daily movement of the solar orb (*bhramate sūryabimbavat*). The solar image is applied several times in relevant images, for instance:

> Just as this world of beings after sunrise
> performs its works, without these being done
> nor caused to be done by the sun itself, just so
> the self also (remains inactive and aloof).[69]

In preceding sections, the relation between the self and the vital functions was said to be expressed in the older Upaniṣads in terms of a householder and his family, or a ruler and his functionaries or subjects. When the self is compared to fire or sun, the minor functions obtain the status of emissions of fire or light, spread out by the central source of power; in this way, the images emphasize the fundamental unity of what has evolved and the source:

> Just as from fire the sparks, and from the sun the rays,
> likewise of him, the breath and other (functions) ever again
> emerge outwards from him, in due arrangement.[70]

The same image is applied still more explicitly in a passage of the *Praśna Upaniṣad* (4.1.2): "to him, he (Pippalāda) said: 'Just as, Gārgya, the rays (*marīcayaḥ)* of the sun which approach the place of his setting all unite within that circle of fire, and time and again come forth when he rises; in the same way, this whole (system of the senses) unites within the chief power (*pare deve*), the mind, and that is the reason why the Puruṣa (during deep sleep) does not hear . . . (nor executes the other functions)." The central repository in this typical instance of older Upaniṣadic psychology is the *manas,* which acts as the self's immediate associate and is equated (in 4.1.4) with the sacrificer.[71]

The teachings of Bhīṣma in the twelfth book of the *Mahābhārata* contain several instances of the same image, but applied with minor variations:

> As shafts of fire, impetuous gales of wind,

> rays of the sun, and currents riverine
> role forward and return in streams continuous;
> likewise the bodies of embodied (selves).[72]

Although the activities inaugurated by the self are expressed in these instances in the form of similes, the underlying suggestion is nevertheless that these similes contain a transference in the concreteness of the self's very nature, which is one of potential powerful movement (an idea very close to the Tantric conception of the Supreme). The active nature of the senses (cf. also the "metaphoric" term *indriyaraśmi* (the sensorial rays) in the Mbh. (12.197.14) is also brought forward in the interpretation by the Nyaya school of visual perception as *nayanaraśmi* "a ray of fire atoms which proceeds from the eyeball."[73] And similarly, the Gauḍapādakārikās (1,6cd) teach us: "the Prāṇa generates all things. The Spirit [generates] the rays of intelligence as separate . . ."[74]

At the same time we can observe the tendency to reserve the solar position for a Supreme Self distinguished from the embodied self. Already according to the MaiUp (6.1), the "external self" is located in the sun, as a "golden Puruṣa;" a still earlier instance of the line of thinking, intimately connected with archaic experience, was mentioned above (*Jaiminīya Brāhmaṇa,* 1.17f). In the sectarian sources under Tantric influence, the tendency has developed into theistic imagery. Thus, in Sadyojyoti's *Mokṣakārikā,* the metaphorical expressions are "Śiva-sun: and "Śakti-splendor":

> By the Śakti-ray of the Śiva-sun
> its eye of consciousness is realized, and thus
> the self, its cover gone, beholds
> God Śiva, with His Powers manifold.[75]

In the *Lakṣmī Tantra* (14.35), the pure essence of the Goddess, abstracted from her executive powers, and realized without accessories within the space of the heart, is compared to the brilliant sun that rises in the clear sky.

Tantric sources often make mention of the rays (most often *marīci*) emitted by the Supreme; as a rule, they are concretized as goddesses. Thus, when the *Yoginīhṛdaya* (2.81) uses the term *marīcayaḥ,* the commentator Amrtananda paraphrases the *kulamātaraḥ* "the Mothers of the (spiritual) Family." Kṣemarāja, the eleventh-century theoretician of nondualistic Śaivism, explains the word *mātṛḥ* (the Mothers) occurring in the *Svacchanda Tantra* (1.36) as referring to the Seven Mothers Brāhmī, etc., taking the shape of "Bhairava's ray" in different directions in the sky. The surrounding deities (*āvaraṇdevatāḥ)* of the Tantric Goddess Śrī (Lalitā) symbolized by the *śrīcakra* are likewise designated as her rays.[76] In the monastic view, the sensorial process should be meditated upon as nothing else than the emission by the Śiva-self of the circle of rays (*marīcicakram*) that presides over the activities of the sense organs.[77]

The "rays" are the means by which the self, statically existing as unspecified pure consciousness, concretizes or condenses its essence into powerful activity, or renders it imaginable and approachable. Already the *Atharva Veda* refers to protection afforded by Indra's beams (*aktu*).[78] Divine favor is felt and evoked as blessing sunshine. But the rays in the proto-theistic view, also establish contact with, and realize ascension toward, the supreme deity in heaven (Mbh 12.290.70); in an early and somewhat different image, the subsidiary powers as seasons act as door guardians who lead the sacrificer, released from the bonds of time, to the sun as a final abode.[79] The contact between the Puruṣa in the eye and its counterpart in the sun is established through rays (*raśmibhiḥ*) according to the BĀUp (5.5.2); when the person is dying, this contact has become unnecessary because of the leaving of the internal Puruṣa, and that is why one at the moment sees the pure solar orb without rays. This latter specification has found its way into traditional prognostications of impending death. We find, for example, exactly the same stipulation in the KMT (23.19), with the only difference in interpretation being that death is to be expected only after two years.

But the rays also fulfil a more aggressive function. In the MaiUp (2.6 and 6.31), five vital faculties are characterized as the rays by which the self consumes the objects of the senses (just as we may presume, the sun by its rays consumes the moisture of the earth); verse 6.31 implicitly gives an "etymological" connection between Ātman and *atti* "he eats" (the connection was missed by Van Buitenen in his translation). The consumption of the sense objects by the pure mind is expressed from the non-dualistic Tantric viewpoint in the *Tantrasadbhāva:*

> Just as the water on the surface of a stone
> is soon reduced to naught by solar rays
> —(how strange!) Nobody drank it yet it disappeared—
> And found no more; thus (stilled) is the enlightened mind.[80]

This is the Bhairava state, in which the all-producing and all-consuming Self has made an end to all appearance of pluriformity. Again, the KMT (23.13) presents the same image in a less sophisticated context of impending death (*kṛtāntaḥ;* identical twin with Time) "soon takes toward himself the water which is life, and dries it up incessantly, acting by moonbeams and solar rays"; the passage needs a contextual discussion which we cannot pursue here. The drinking of moisture by the solar rays is beautifully expressed by Bhāravi in his *Kirātārjunīya* (9.3):

> By means of rays as hands, extremely thirsty,
> he tasted the brim the sweet draught born of flowers;
> and as in drunkenness to the earth approaching,
> his countenance all red—thus was the setting sun.[81]

In the KMT, the Marīcis are practically identical with the Yoginīs in their function as guardian deities, and their fear-inspiring, consumptive nature is emphasized.

Impelled by the guru's wrath, they burn the aspirant who irritates his guru (3.57); the self-willed person who modifies a mantra given him by the guru becomes an object of their hate (7.26). We are told that anyone who goes against the guru's wishes or breaks secrets, will be eaten by the Yoginīs. The adept who is ripe for immediate release might (really or symbolically) offer his being to the Marīcis, according to a ritual described with mantras in the KMT (23130ff). The ceremony, characteristically, also can be performed with variations for gaining magical powers.[82] These goddesses are also called Yoginīs (23.143). They consist of a group of six, headed by Ḍākinī (in principle identical with the presiding goddess of the six *cakras* described in Avalon's *Serpent Power*), and a seventh leading deity called Kusmamālinī (the Flower-garlanded), who here replaces Kubjikā as the representation of the all-consuming Self. At the end of the KMT (25.196), however, the rays once more appear in their benign nature; the adept who conducts the worship of the Kubjikā tradition in the right way, will be worshiped by them in return.

At the end of this rapid survey of some ways of imagining the self in selected Sanskrit sources, it might be useful to reformulate a few inferences. These are preliminary only because of the limited material studied and the restricted period involved in the preparation of this article.

1. The self is described by means of a varied imagery divisible according to a number of traditional themes. Within these themes, a remarkable degree of multifunctionality has sometimes been realized over the centuries.

2. The selections from the texts of Tantric character make it abundantly clear that the formulators of this literature knew the earlier revelation (especially the important Upaniṣads) very well; in many ways, they continued and developed the time-honored imagery. Some of them eagerly took up and expanded the Vedic tendency toward linguistic speculation.

3. In many cases, they applied the images, which in the older Upaniṣads and some later texts referred to the undivided or individual self, to their conceptions of a Supreme Self, which they experienced as inseparable from the Supreme Godhead worshiped by their school or sect. We could speak of a theistic reorientation of the old auto-mystical tradition, entailing a tendency to loss of authority for the individual self. Although it would be wrong to consider Tantrism as a monolithic block, most of the very different schools or movements seem to have this tendency in common. The adepts of the monastic Śaiva school, however, tried to harmonize the "auto mystical" and the "theistic" traditions.

4. Many of the similes and allegories, and especially the metaphors, seem to have been applied in the religious context not merely as literary devices, but in a more or less "identive" function as a means to approach the suprasensual, as guides to contemplation and enlightenment.

5. The didactic or psychagogic applications of figurative expression in religious or philosophical contexts deserve close attention from specialists within the context of the modern theory of literature.

6. A sustained study of the Tantric forms and principles of exegesis of Vedic revelation is worthwhile and might lead to interesting results.

NOTES

1. See for instance, Glyn Richards, *The Philosophy of Gandhi* (London: Curzon Press, 1982), 13

2. Troy W. Organ, *The Self in Indian Philosophy* (The Hague: Mouton & Co., 1964), 44.

3. The philosopher N. G. Damle complains about the unsatisfactoriness of modern psychology regarding the study of the self; see *Contemporary Indian Philosophy,* 4th ed., eds. S. Radhakrishnan and J. H. Muirhead (London: Allen & Unwin, 1966), 183ff. Sudhir Kakar says, "The I, as Hindus would say, is pure consciousness, the ātman . . . ;" see *The Inner World* (Delhi: Oxford University Press, 1978), 59. Cf. Śaṅkara's characterization *ātmā ahampratyayaviṣayaḥ* "the self is the object of the notion I," quoted by Paul Hacher in "Śaṅkara's Conception of Man," *Studia Missionalia* 19 (1970): 24.

4. Gerard Kurz, *Metapher, Allegorie, Symbol* (Gottingen: Vandenhoeck and Ruprecht, 1982), 21ff.

5. Henry O. Taylor, *The Medieval Mind. A History of the Development of Thought and Emotion in the Middle Ages,* (Cambridge: Harvard University Press, 1959), vol. 1, 67. See also Kurtz, *Metaphor,* 30.

6. Monroe C. Beardsley, *Aesthetics: Problems in the Philosophy* of *Criticism* (New York: Harcourt, Brace and World, 1958), 127. Compare Wiliam P. Harman's remarks on religious metaphorism, in *The Sacred Marriage of a Hindu Goddess* (Bloomington: Indiana University Press, 1989), 4ff. and 148ff.

7. Cf. Wendy Doniger O'Flaherty, *Dreams, Illusions and Other Realities* (Chicago: University of Chicago Press, 1980), 127ff.

8. S. N. Dasgupta, *Yoga as Philosophy and Religion* ((London: Kegan Paul, Trench, Trubner, 1924), 15.

9. J. A. Schoterman, "Indiase Labyrinthen," *Het Kosmisch Patroon. Het vele en het ene in de godsdiesten,* ed. T. Chowdhury (Tilburg, Netherlands: 1989), 117–32.

10. A Mahadeva Sastri, *The Śaiva Upanishads,* 2nd ed. (Madras: Adyar Library & Research Centre, 1950), 175–234; *Lakṣmītantra,* ed. V. Krishnamacharya (Adyar: Adyar Library & Research Centre. 1959); and *Lakṣmī Tantra,* trans. Sanjukta Gupta (Leiden; E.J. Brill, 1972).

11. *Mahābhārata,* ed. Vishnu S. Sukthankar (Poona: Bhandardar Oriental Research Institute), 3:277–83.

12. Emil Abegg, *Indische Psychologie* (Zurich: Rascher Verlag, 1945), 7, n.9; Jan Gonda, *Aspects of Early Viṣṇuism* (Utrecht: Oosthoek, 1954), 92; Sir J. G. Frazer, *The Golden Bough* (London: Macmillan, 1957), I:235ff.

13. *Chāndogya Upaniṣad, with the commentary by Sankaracarya,* 2nd ed. (Gorakhpur: Gita Press, 1955).

14. Karel Werner, "Indian Concepts of Human Personality in Relation to the Doctrine of the Soul," *Journal of the Royal Asiatic Society* (1988): 81.

15. BĀUp 2.1.16–20; see *Bṛhadāranyaka Upaniṣad, with the commentary of Śaṇkarācarya,* 2nd ed. (Gorakhpur: Gita Press, 1955); and the Pāñcarātra text *Jayākhya Saṃhitā* 10.60; *Jayākhyasaṃhitā,* 2nd ed., ed. Embar Krishnamacharya (Baroda: Oriental Institute, 1967).

16. *Dhyānabindu Upaniṣad,* in *Iśādiviṃśottarasatopaniṣadaḥ,* ed. N. R. Acharya (Bombay: Nirnaya Sagara Press, 1948), Ātmanirṇaya, prose after 93.

17. Ernst Windisch, "Uber den Sitz der dendenden Seele, besonders bei Indern und Griechen." *Berichte uber die Verhandlugen der Koniglich Sachsischen Gesellschaft der Wissenschaften, Phil.-hist. Klasse,* Leipzig, 43, (1981): 155ff. For its continuation in monastic Śaivism, see: Paul Muller-Ortega, *The Triadic Heart of Śiva: Kaula Tantricism of Abhinavagupta in the Non-Dual Shaivism of Kashmir* (Albany: State University of New York Press, 1989).

18. MBh 12.195.12. An "experimental" investigation after the self by dissecting the living body of a criminal is mentioned in the Buddhist canon.

19. Sri Aurobindo, *Sāvitrī,* Pt. 3, vol. 2 (Madras: Sri Aurobindo Ashram, 1951), 211.

20. J. A. B. van Buitenen, "The Large Ātman," *History of Religions* 4 (1965): 103–114.

21. *Tantra Sadbhāva,* verse 1.399. *Tantrasadbhāva,* ms. 1–136, fol. 20b; and ms. 5–445, National Archives of Nepal, Kathmandu, fol. 11b.

22. *Svacchanda Tantra* 11.113ff.; *Kubjikāmatatantra* 23.101, see: *Kulālikāmnaya* Version, ed. Teun Goudriaan and Jan A. Schoterman (Leiden: E.J. Brill, 1988).

23. *Liṇga Purāṇa* (Bareli: Samskrti-samsthana, 1969).

24. The text quotes the *Lalitāsvacchanda* for the first part of the citation; see Kalyani Mallik, *Siddhasiddhāntapaddhati and other works of the Nātha Yogīs* (Poona: 1954), 19, and her Introduction for the distinction *anāmā-akula.* A connection of the Kula ideology with Vedism on the ritual level has been argued by Frederique Marglin in *The Divine Consort: Rādhā and the Goddesses of India,* ed. John S. Hawley and Donna M. Wulff (Berkeley: Graduate Theological Union, 1982), 310ff.

25. The passage has been translated by O'Flaherty, *Dreams,* 139.

26. MBh 12.195.10. The stanza is part of a teaching imparted by Manu to Bṛhaspati, and reproduced by Bhīṣma in the cadre of his instruction of Yudhiṣṭhira from his famous bed of arrows.

27. *Sāṃkhyakārika* 36.

28. *Lakṣmī Tantra* 7.33ff.

29. *Paramārthasāra,* verse 11. *Paramārthāsara by Ādiśeṣa,* ed. and trans. Henry Danielson (Leiden: E.J. Brill, 1980).

30. *Jayākhya Saṃhitā,* 10.60. There is a subtle difference from the ChUp 8.1.3 *Yāvān vayam ākāśas, tāvān eṣo'ntar hṛdaya ākāśaḥ* . . . Śaṅkara on 8.1.5 notes that the space within the heart itself is the Brahma (Ātman). See also note 34.

31. Gerard Colas, "Le Yoga de l'officiant Vaikhānasa," *Journal Asiatique* 276 (1988): 253.

32. *Paraśurāmakalpasūtra* 1.5.

33. *Kularnava Tantra,* 3rd ed., ed. T. Vidyaratna (Delhi: Motilal Banarsidass, 1975), 9.4.1.

34. From the *Śivamānasapūjāstotra* (21.68) that is ascribed to Śaṅkara; quoted by Gopinath Kaviraj, *Tāntrik Vaṅmay meṃ śāktadṛṣti* (Patna: Bihar Rastrabhasa Parisad, 1963), sub 9.27. Cf.also ChUp 3.17.1ff.

35. The *Prapañcasāra* is likewise ascribed to Śaṅkara; see *Hindu Tantric and Śākta Literature,* ed. Teun Goudriaan and Sanjukta Gupta (Weisbaden: Otto Harraassowitz, 1981), 131.

36. Tsb, fol. 2b. *Tantrasadbhāva.* Manuscript no. 5–445/185 National Archives of Nepal, Kathmandu. Compare also Krishna Sivaraman, "The Śivadvaita of Śrīkantha: Spirit as the Inner Space Within the Heart," *Hindu Spirituality: Vedas through Vedanta,* ed. Krishna Sivaraman (New York: Crossroads Publishing, 1989), 291ff.

37. Abhinavagupta, *Tantrāloka* 1.123. See: Alexis Sanderson, "The Visualization of the Deities of the Trika," *L'Image Divine: Culte et Méditation dans l'hindouisme,* ed. André Padoux (Paris: Editions du Centre National de la Recherche Scientifique, 1990), 70.

38. Arthur Avalon, *Principles of Tantra. The Tantrarattava of Śrīyukta Śiva Candra Vidyārṇava Bhaṭṭacārya Mahodaya,* 3rd ed. (Madras: Ganesh, 1960), 1153f.; Heinrich Zimmer, *Myths and Symbols in Indian Art and Civilization,* 5th ed. (Princeton, N.J.: Princeton University Press, 1972), 197ff.

39. Verse 7.11. *Maitrāyaṇīya Upaniṣad,* ed. and trans. J. A. B. van Buitenen (The Hague: Mouton, 1962), 121.

40. AV 10.2.31–32. A slightly different version occurs in AV 10.8.43. Brahman is also introduced as a Yakṣa in the *Kena Upaniṣad* 3.2.

41. *Atharva Veda Saṁhitā,* trans. William Dwight Whitney (Delhi: Motilal Banarsidass, 1971r), 571.

42. For the Kubjikā school, see Goudriaan and Gupta, *Hindu Tantric,* 52ff. On the traditional iconography of *Yakṣas,* see Ananda K. Coomaraswamy, *Yakṣas* (New Delhi: Munishiram Monoharlal, 1971). Cf. also F. D. K. Bosch, *The Golden Germ. An Introduction to Indian Symbolism* (The Hague: Mouton, 1960), ch. 4.

43. *Kriyāpāda* 3.4. See *Mṛgendrāgana, Kriyāpāda and Caryāpāda,* trans. Hélène Brunner-Lachaux (Pondicherry: Institut Français d'Indologie, 1985), 39.

44. For example, BĀUp 3.2.12; MaiUp 2.6.

45. For example, ChUp 3.14.3; Kaṭha Up 1.2.20 "more minute than the minute, greater than the great . . ."; and echoed by Mbh 12.294.22.

46. For Rāmānuja's views on the matter see Julius Lipner, *The Face of Truth* (Albany: State University of New York Press, 1986), pp. 64ff.

47. *Lakṣmī Tantra,* 726ff.

48. *Marīcisaṃhitār,* Ch. 84; see Colas, "The Yogar," 252ff.

49. Hélène Brunner-Lachaux, *Somaśambhupaddhati: Le Ritual Quotidien dans la Tradition Śivaite de l'Inde du Sud selon Somaśambhu* (Pondicherry: Institut Français d'Indologie, 1977, 3:118ff.; and Brunner, *Mṛgendragama,* 238ff.

50. S. R. Belvalkar, *History of Indian Philosophy* (Poona: Bilvakunja Publishing House, 1927), 2:374.

51. Frazer, *Golden Bough*, 239.

52. AV 6.18.3. In his translation, Whitney renders *manaskam* with "mind." Emil Abegg uses "*das Geistlein*" (the little mind); see his *Indische Psychologie* (Zurich: Rascher Verlag, 1945), 8. Windisch prefers "die Seele" (the soul), 164.

53. This is in reference to the *Baudhayana Dharmasūtra* 2.14.9.10; see Abegg, *Indische*, 9.

54. Brian K. Smith, *Reflections of Resemblance, Ritual and Religion* (New York: Oxford University Press, 1989), 105.

55. BĀUp 4.3.19.

56. BĀUp 3.4.11–12. Note that "putting off" (*abhiprahatya*) is hypothetical; here I follow Heimann's use of "*abwerfend*." See Betty Heimann, "Die Tiefschlafspekulation der alten Upaniṣaden," *Zeitshrift fur Buddhismus* 4 (1922), 263. In his commentary, Śaṅkara rightly notes that the text establishes an etymological connection between *haṃsa* "swan," literally "goose," and the root *han* (to strike), which is the base of the form *abhiprahatya*. Of course, "etymology" here means something like mystical verbal connection given the "divine Sanskrit language," not mere "linguistic prehistory."

57. JS 10.58d.

58. *Dhyānabindu Up.*, 60–61.

59. *Jñānārṇava Tantra*, ed. G. S. Gokhale (Poona: Anandasrama Sanskrit Series, 1952), 10.6–7. In 9ab, the *ha* is identified with Śiva. The *viṣarga* has a double meaning: as a sound, it stands for the guttural spirant that represents *s* or *r* at the end of a syllable and traditionally is listed as the sixteenth and last vowel; and it can also mean creation. For the linguistic speculation see André Padoux, *Vāc: The Concept of the Word in Selected Hindu Tantras* (Albany, N.Y.: State University of New York Press, 1990).

60. KMT 12.54ff.

61. For example, MaiUp 2.6.

62. For the late Vedic identification of *prāṇa* and ritual fire, see Henk W. Bodewitz, *Jaiminīya Brāhmana I.1–65. Translation and Commentary: With a Study Agnihotra and Prāṇāgnihotra* (Leiden: E.J. Brill, 1973), 220ff.

63. KMT 12.54–67. In verse 67, the process is called Śaktityāga "leaving the state of Śakti behind (as separation from Śiva)."

64. For an example, see Bodewitz, *Jaiminīya*, 201.

65. MaiUp 6.34. Van Buitenen, in his translation, unhappily rendered *haṃsa* as "duck." The idea is probably that the self is able to dive into the depths as well as to soar into the heavens; van Buitenen, 149.

66. Erich Frauwallner, *Geschichte der Indischen Philosophie* (Salzburg: Otto Muller, 1953), 1:70ff. Other related popular concepts are those of warmth or heat. Cf. Laurence A. Babb, *The Divine Heirarchy* (New York: Colombia University Press, 1975), 99. Referring to light (*jyotis, prakāśa*), for instance, Śaṅkara on ChUp 8.1.2 states that the self in the heart as a reflection of Brahman is *vijñana jyotsḥivarūp āvabhāsa* "shining in its essence of being light of knowledge."

67. RV 1.115.1.

68. JB 1.17ff; see also, Bodewitz, *Jaiminīya*, 52ff.

69. Paramārthasāra by Adiśeṣa, verse 13. The *Bhagavad Gītā* (13.33) mentions the illuminating nature of the self as comparable to that of the sun.

70. MaiUp 6.26. In 6.31 of the same text, the self's expressive functions (*liṅga*) are again compared to sparks (*visphuliṅga*).

71. *Praśna Upaniṣad* 4.1.4.

72. Mbh. 12.195.11. In 12.292.28, the emission of experienced objects by the self, as of rays by the sun, is said to be realized as a fantasy for the self's own amusement (*krīḍārtham*). See also 12.197.13–15, discussed in my article "The Pluriform Ātman from the Upaniṣads to the Svacchanda Tantra," forthcoming in the *Wiener Zeitschrift fur die Kunde Sudasiens.*

73. H. Isaacsson, *A Study of Early Vaiśeṣika: the Teachings on Perception,* M.A. thesis (Groningen: Indiological Institute, State University, 1990), 58.

74. The translation is by Paul Hacker, *Kleine Schriften* (Wiesbaden: Steiner 1978), 263.

75. *Moksakarika,* 11. In *Aṣṭaprakaraṇam,* ed. Vraj Vallabh Dviveda (Varanasi: Sampurnanand Sanskrit University Press, 1988), 268. The commentator Rāmakantha emphasizes that the process is nothing but an act of Śiva's grace extended to the worshiper by the Śakti of Wisdom (Jñānaśakti).

76. *Varivasyārahasya* by Bhāskararāya (see Goudrian and Gupta, *Hindu Tantric,* 170), verse 83; cf. also the autocommentary. The cadre is meditation on the Kaulikārtha: identity of self, Guru, and Goddess.

77. *Kṣemarāja, Spandanirṇaya* on *Spandakārikaḥ* I, 6–7. ed. Jaideva Singh (Delhi: Motilal Banarsidass, 1980), 52.

78. AV 17.9; see also Gonda, *Aspects,* 28.

79. JaimBr. 1.18; see Bodewitz, *Jaiminīya Brahmana,* 54.

80. Tsb 1.305ff. (ms. 5–445, fol. 16a).

81. *Kirātārjuniya* 9.3 Quoted by M. Winternitz, *History of Indian Literature,* trans. Subhadra Jha (Delhi: Motilal Banarsidass, 1963), 3:71.

82. Cf. Teun Goudriaan, "Some Beliefs and Rituals Concerning Time and Death in the Kubjikāmata," *Selected Studies on Ritual in the Indian Religions, Essays to D. J. Hoens,* ed. Ria Kloppenborg (Leiden: E.J. Brill, 1983), 92–117.

10

Tongues of Flame: Homologies in the Tantric *Homa*

Richard K. Payne

Japan has been described as "the extreme eastern limit of Indian cultural diffusion."[1] Part of that diffusion is the Shingon tradition, which is a Buddhist form of Tantra. Shingon was formally established in Japan at the beginning of the ninth century by the monk Kūkai (Kōbō Daishi). He reports that during his journey to China (804 to 806), he received initiation into the two main ritual lineages of Tantric Buddhism that were at that time present in China.[2] One of these is associated with the *Vajradhātu Maṇḍala,* while the other is associated with the *Mahākarunagarbha Maṇḍala.* Kūkai consciously worked to create a new synthesis, based on an integration of these two ritual lineages.[3]

There is a great distance then, both geographic and cultural, between Shingon and the Hindu forms of Tantra. Examination of the ritual practices of Shingon, however, reveals a number of significant similarities with Hindu Tantra. Indeed, ritual themes, such as the use of fire, can be traced back to the Vedic ritual tradition.[4] Some ritual themes can be traced even farther back to Indo-European forms of ritual practice.

This essay will focus on the *homa* (Jap.: *goma*), a votive ritual in which offerings are made into a fire. The *homa* plays a very important part in Shingon and is widely performed in contemporary Japan. It was brought to Japan along with many other Tantric rituals as part of the Shingon ritual corpus.[5] The Shingon *homa* is important to the study of the roots of Tantra because it is found in both Buddhist and Hindu Tantra and because it has Vedic and Indo-European antecedents. The Shingon tradition in Japan is a living tradition, having a voluminous body of literature, including detailed ritual manuals and both classical and contemporary exegeses of the rituals. As such Shingon provides an important body of materials for the search for the roots of Tantra.

In the Shingon tradition a three-way identification is made as part of the *homa* ritual. The three terms of the identification are (1) the altar, hearth, and fire; (2) the deities evoked in the ritual; (3) the practitioner himself. The mouth of the hearth is at the same time the mouth of the deity[6] and the practitioner's own mouth. The various offerings placed in the fire are identified with the deity and with the practitioner's delusions.[7] Just as the fire transforms the various physical offerings, the visualized offerings are transformed within the body of the deity into limitless offerings made to all deities. At the same time the practitioner's delusions are purified into the fundamentally pure consciousness that is inherently the practitioner's own. Given this three way identification, the practitioner feeds himself, offering aspects of himself to himself, and transforms himself through the power of his own flaming wisdom. The tongues of flame rising from the hearth are at the same time the deity's tongue and his own.

The *homa* and the three-fold identification provide a means for elucidating the continuities between the Shingon ritual tradition, the Vedic ritual tradition and the Indo-European roots of Vedic ritual culture. The continuities examined here can be grouped under three rubrics: (1) characteristics of the ritual use of fire; (2) identification of the ritual fire with people; (3) identification of the ritual fire with the gods.

Across the range of Indo-European, Vedic and Tantric ritual use of fire, one of the continuities is the significance given to the shape of the hearth upon which the fire is built. Georges Dumézil has elucidated the structural similarities between the Roman fires and the Vedic. The Vedic ritual tradition typically uses three fires, one built on a circular hearth, one built on a square hearth, and one built on a demilune hearth.[8] The circular *gārhapatiya* (domestic fire) hearth corresponds to the householder and to the earth. Its fire must be kept burning at all times. If it goes out, it can only be lit again "from a fire produced by friction, saved from an earlier sacrificial fire, or taken, regardless of the rank of the sacrificer, from the house of a *vaiśya*."[9] Similarly, in Rome the fire of Vesta is kept on a circular hearth, is maintained perpetually, and if extinguished, may be lit again only from a friction-born fire.[10] Rather than the earthly existence of some individual householder, it is the earthly existence of Rome as a social unity to which the circular fire of Vesta corresponds.[11]

In the Vedic ritual enclosure, the *gārhapatya* is at the western end of an east-west axis, while the *āhavanīya* (seat of the deity) is at the eastern end of this axis. The *āhavanīya* is lit from the *gārhapatya* and is kept on a square hearth and corresponds to the heavenly realm of the gods, for "it is this fire whose smoke bears the gifts of men from this world to the gods."[12] In some instances the fires devoted to various deities were temporary, rather than perpetual fires, and they were lit before square (or at least quadrangular) temples. The function of these fires is the same as the *āhavanīya*, for their purpose "is only to carry the offering to its invisible recipient."[13]

The third, the *dakṣināgni* (southern fire), of the Vedic complex corresponds to the fires of the Roman god Volcanus. The function of the *dakṣināgni* is to protect the ritual performance from demonic influences. The association with the southern direction has been explained by reference to the geopolitics of the Indo-European nomads' movement from west to east across north India.[14] The south was the direction of the indigenous, non-Aryanized population; the southerly direction continues to have an inauspicious association in present-day Hinduism. "The Roman god Volcanus . . . is the fire which, for good or evil, devours and destroys. Thus, useful and dangerous at the same time, he has his temple outside the walls."[15] Dumézil thus finds the *dakṣināgni* fire and the fires of Volcanus can be equated both by function and by location.

Just as the fire of Vesta served to represent the unified whole of Rome, so, according to Walter Burkert, the "ever burning hearth in the temple at Delphi was sometimes seen as the communal hearth for the whole of Greece."[16] Hestia is ambiguous, being an anthropomorphized deity, while at the same time Hestia "is the normal word for hearth, the centre of house and family. . . . The hearth is an offering place for libations and small gifts of food."[17] The same ambiguity is present in the figure of Agni as well, for he is both a deity and the fire itself.

Staal has pointed out the structural similarities between Vedic and Iranian ritual practices: "The Iranian fire ritual is in many respects similar to the Vedic. Fires are installed on three altars. The domestic altar is circular, the offering altar, square . . . In Iran, fires were also transported."[18] One example of movement of the fires in the Vedic context is in the complex series of rites of the Agnicayana. During the first twelve days of the Agnicayana the ritual fire is first transported from the home of the *yajamāna* (sacrificer) to the ritual enclosure and is then moved from one hearth to another during the course of the ensuing ritual.[19]

The use of differently shaped hearths continues into the Tantric Buddhist tradition. There are five kinds of rituals known to the Shingon tradition, and there is a form of the *homa* found in each of these five categories. The five categories of rites are the *śāntika* for "stopping calamities," the *pauṣṭika* for "increasing merit and obtaining prosperity," the *ābhicāraka* for "subduing devils and adversaries," the *vaśīkarana* for "achieving love and respect from others," and the *aṅkuśa* for "'summoning" sentient beings to enable them to attain higher states of existence."[20] The altar hearth for the *śāntika homa* (Jap.: *soku sai*) is circular; that for the *pauṣṭika homa* (Jap.: *zo yaku*) is square; that for the *ābhicāraka* (Jap.: *go buku*) is triangular; that for the *vaśīkarana* (J: *kei ai*) is shaped like an eight-petaled lotus; and that for the *aṅkuśa* (Jap.: *ko sho*) is either a demilune or *vajra* shape.[21]

Another set of homologies with the shape of the hearth is discussed by Wayman in his work on the *Guhyasamāja Tantra,* a Tantra that seems to count four types of *homa,* in contrast to the five employed in the Shingon tradition. Wayman has asserted that the shape of the hearths is also the shape of the *cakras* visualized within the body of the practitioner: "the fire-disk at the throat (or neck) is shaped like a bow [that is, demilune, R.K.P.]; the water-disk at the heart is circular in shape; the wind disk at the navel is triangular; and the earth disk in the sacral place is square."[22] In addition, they are also linked to the four elements and "the shapes of the four continents of Purāṇic mythology."[23]

There is continuity from the Indo-European tradition, through the Vedic to the Tantric concerning the significance of the shape of the altar-hearth. What is less clearly continuous, however, is the specific meaning attributed to individual shapes. As indicated by Wayman's comments, further exploration of this may well require the introduction of many other kinds of homologies.

In addition to the significance given to the shape of the hearth upon which the ritual fire is built, Indo-European, Vedic, and Tantric traditions also share the image of fire as being that which conveys the offerings from the world of men to the world of the gods and ancestors, while at the same time purifying those offerings. A. L. Basham has described succinctly this aspect of the Indo-European ritual use of fire, noting the well-known Vedic tradition that "It is through Agni that the sacrificial offerings are brought to the gods, and as an intermediary between gods and men he has a very important function."[24] As mentioned previously, Dumézil sees a functional unity between the Vedic *āhavanīya* and the Roman offering fires that were lit temporarily for various gods. The former is the "fire whose smoke bears the gifts of men from this world to the gods,"[25] and the latter functions "only to carry the offering to its invisible recipient."[26]

In the Vedic tradition one of the epithets of Agni is Vahni, the "Conveyer." While Agni is all kinds of fire, he is most important as the sacrificial fire that, consuming the offerings, conveys them to their recipients. It is this which makes Agni so central to the Vedic ritual tradition. Agni retains this primacy of place in the Shingon *homa.* The tradition has known *homas* organized into as many as nine sets of offerings, or as few as one. The first set of offerings is invariably made to Agni or, if there is only one set of offerings, it is made to him. Although Agni is by no means a figure of veneration in the popular cult, he is recognized to be an essential part of the ritual process.

At the same time that Agni as the ritual fire conveys the offerings, he also purifies those offerings. A well-known expression of this dual function of Agni as both conveying and purifying the sacrificial offerings is found in the *Viṣṇu Purāṇa:*

> Legend relates that one day Bhrigu cursed Agni. A woman named Puloma was betrothed to a demon, and Bhrigu seeing that she was beautiful fell in love with her and, after marrying her according to the Vedic rites, secretly abducted her. But thanks to Agni's information, the demon discovered the place where the woman promised to him was hidden, and brought her back to his dwelling. Furious with Agni for helping the demon, Bhrigu cursed him, saying: "Henceforth thou shalt eat of all things." Agni demanded of Bhrigu the reason for this curse since he had only told the demon the truth. He pointed out that if a man is questioned and tells a lie he is cast into hell, along with seven generations of his ancestors and seven generations of his children. Moreover, the man who fails to give information is equally guilty. And Agni went on to say: "I too can hurl curses, but I respect the Brahmans and I control my anger. In truth I am the mouth of the ancestors. When clarified butter is offered them, they receive it thanks to me, their mouth, so how can you tell me to eat all things?" Hearing these words, Bhrigu agreed

to change his curse and said: "As the sun purifies all Nature with his light and heat, so Agni shall purify everything which enters his flames."[27]

There is continuity in the Indo-European ritual tradition, and Vedic and Tantric ritual traditions in the use of fire as the means by which offerings are made; this continuity includes the shape of the hearth. As might be expected, specific correlation between the shape of the altar-hearth and the symbolic value attributed to that shape converge the closer the traditions are to one another. While the use and meaning of fire and altars in Roman religion are only loosely linked to those in Tantric religions, within the Tantric traditions themselves, such as between the Buddhist Tantric practices in Tibet and Japan, they are much more closely related. Also, the way in which fire is conceived to function in the ritual process within the south Asian religious context shows continuity over an extended period. In particular, the Vedic and Purāṇic conceptions of Agni as both conveyer and purifier of offerings seems to explain a great deal concerning the continuing centrality of Agni in the ritual semantics of both Hindu and Buddhist Tantric *homa.*

In addition to the function fulfilled by fire in Vedic and Tantric rituals, there is another complex of themes clustering around the identification of fire with people. These themes include the ideas of fire as having sexuality, of fire being associated with digestion, of the Brahmin filled with *tapas* (internal heat) as being equal to a ritual fire, of the sacrificer as identical with the ritual fire, of the sacrificer himself as the offerings that are made into the fire, and of the funerary fire in which the sacrificer's breathing is identified with the ritual fire.

The sexual qualities of fire were expressed by the ancient Greeks when they referred to the hearth as the goddess Hestia. While the hearth is feminine, the Greeks identified the fire as a phallic force.[28] This relation at the same time recalls the masculine fire deity Agni and later the relation between *liṅga* and *yoni* in the Śaivite tradition. The motif of masculine fire and feminine hearth is explicitly used in Tantric rituals as well; and in Tantrism, the offerings have seminal symbolism.

Wendy O'Flaherty finds the origin of attributing sexuality to the ritual fire in the technology of fire production: "Springing from the natural physiological analogy, the tie between Agni and Kama was supported by the Vedic symbolism of the two fire-sticks, the upper one male and the lower one female, whose friction is described in anthropomorphic terms."[29] Given this context, we are able to connect ritual *tapas* with *kāma* (desire).

The Upaniṣads also identify ritual with sex. The *Bṛhadāraṇyaka Upaniṣad*[30] states for example:

> A woman's lower part is the (sacrificial) altar: (her) hairs the (sacrificial) grass, her skin the *soma*-press. The two labia of the vulva are the fire in the middle. Verily, as great as is the world of him who performs the Vajrapeya sacrifice (so great is the world of him) who, knowing this, practices sexual

> intercourse; he turns the good deeds of the woman into himself but he, who without knowing this, practices sexual intercourse, his good deeds women turn into themselves.

One of the characteristics of identifications, or homologies, of this kind is that the identification seems to run in both directions. As described above, the body of a woman and sexual intercourse is identified with the altar and the sacrificial ritual. Elsewhere in the *Bṛhadāraṇyaka Upaniṣad*[31] the sacrificial fire is identified with the sexual organs of a man's wife.

> If a man's wife has a lover and he hates him (wishes to injure him), let him put fire in an unbaked earthen vessel, spread out a layer of reed arrows in an inverse order, and let him offer (in sacrifice) in inverse order these reed arrows soaked in clarified butter (saying), "You have sacrificed in my fire, I take away your in-breath, and out-breath, you so and so. You have sacrificed in my fire, I take away your sons and your cattle, you so and so. You have sacrificed in my fire, I take away your sacrifices and meritorious deeds, you so and so. You have sacrificed in my fire, I take away your hope and expectation, you so and so. Verily, he departs from this world impotent and devoid of merit, he whom a Brahmana who knows this curses. Therefore one should not wish to play with the wife of one who is learned in the Vedas, who knows this, for indeed he who knows this becomes preeminent.

Similarly, in another place the same Upaniṣad, while discussing the five fires that constitute the round of rebirth, says that:

> The woman, verily, Gautama, is fire. The sexual organ itself is its fuel; the hairs the smoke, the vulva the flame, when one inserts, the coals; the pleasurable feelings the sparks; in this fire the gods offer semen. Out of this offering a person arises.[32]

The equation of sacrificial fire and sex continues into the Purāṇas as well. Vettam Mani quotes the following description of a sacrificial fire pit from the *Agni Purāṇa:*

> On the western side is a yoni (receptacle) 10 x 15 aṃgulas should be made. Its depth should gradually decrease in the descending order of 6, 4, 2 aṃgulas. In shape the yoni will be of the shape of the peepal leaf. The priest performs the rites, himself seated to the west of the yoni and his head turned to the east.[33]

Mani goes on to make the symbolism explicit: "Yoni is that of Śakti; the Kuṇḍa is her stomach. The conception about Śakti is that of a woman lying on her back, head towards the east." In other words, the priest is seated between the woman's legs and faces toward her vagina, into which he makes offerings.

Similar symbolism is found in the Hindu Tantras as well. In the *Tantra of Great Liberation,* there are instructions for the construction of an altar that includes drawing a *yoni yantra.* A fire is lit outside the *yantra* and the *sādhaka* (petitioner) is to:

> . . . take some fire in both palms, and wave it thrice in a circle over the *sthandila* [symbolizing Śiva's erect phallus, R.K.P] from right to left. Then with both knees on the ground, and meditating on Fire as the male seed of Śiva, the worshipper should place it into that portion of the Yoni yantra which is nearest him.[34]

The symbolism of impregnation is continued in the Tantric fire rituals of Bali through the symbols of pregnancy and childbirth. The text of a fire ritual translated by Christiaan Hooykaas says that the goddess's "pregnancy has a serious meaning; this is called Homa."[35] In this case it is the birth of a son which is identified with the kindling of the fire, referred to as the Śiva fire. Other sexual and reproductive symbols are used elsewhere in the ritual as well.

In addition to identifying ritual fire with sexual energy, digestion is also understood as a kind of fire, particularly the digestion of those invested with *tapas,* that is, the Brahmins. In the section on the responsibilities of a householder, the *Laws of Manu* equates the ritual fire with the Brahmins. For example, "An offering in the mouth-fire of Brahmanas rich in sacred learning and austerities saves from misfortunes and from great guilt."[36] In the Shingon *homa,* the imagery of digestive fire is explicitly employed, that is in the equation of the three mouths. In India, being filled with *tapas,* not only is the digestive fire of a Brahmin equal to a ritual fire, but the whole person becomes identified with the fire. According to the *Laws of Manu,* a Brahmin may substitute for a ritual fire: "If no (sacred) fire (is available), he shall place (the offerings) into the hand of a Brahmana; for Brahmanas who know the sacred texts declare, 'What fire is, even such is a Brahmana.'"[37] In Book 4 of the *Laws,* the same strictures concerning certain kinds of behavior are applied equally to fires and Brahmins. One is neither to defecate nor urinate while looking at either a fire or a Brahmin.[38] Similarly, one who is impure must touch neither a fire nor a Brahmin.[39]

The Brahmin "rich in sacred learning" is one who knows the Vedas as a result of the *tapas*[40] generated by his own initiatory austerities. Walter O. Kaebler points out that, "Relatedly, the Brahmanas continually inform us that the entire corpus of revelation and sacred knowledge, namely the Veda, rests upon a foundation of *tapas.*"[41] The *tapas* that forms the base of the Vedas and is the source of the Brahmin's knowledge, is also central to Agni. "Agni, the personified and ritual fire, helps generate wisdom, vision, and knowledge for those who toil devotedly in his presence. As noted so often, *tapas* is inherent in Agni's very nature. He both possesses and radiates *tapas;* he is clearly a *tapasvin.*"[42] While Kaebler has taken *tapas* as the center point for his examination, the homology is one that interconnects *tapas,* the transformative, experiential knowledge of the Vedas, the ritual fire, Agni, and the initiatory transformation of the Brahmins. It is this homology that allows for a Brahmin to substitute for a ritual fire, and which leads to the requirement that they be treated in the same fashion.

Not only is the class of Brahmins identified with the ritual fire, but the consecrated sacrificer is also identified with the fire as well. In discussing the initiation ceremony (*dīkṣā*) of the Agnicayana, Ian Gonda cites the following: "In like manner (that is, as the gods who strode the Viṣṇu strides through these worlds);"[43] "the fire is the sacrificer's divine body;"[44] and "the *dīkṣita* is Agni."[45]

In the same fashion, the Shingon practitioner is to identify himself with the fire. At the very beginning of the offering sequences the practitioner is to perform the following meditative identification:

> The heart of the Tathāgata is identical with ultimate reality; ultimate reality is identical with the fire of wisdom; the hearth is identical with the body of the Tathāgata; the fire is identical with the Dharmakāya fire of wisdom; the mouth of the hearth is identical with the mouth of the Tathāgata; the fire is identical with the wisdom inside the practitioner's body. Thus, the mouth of the Tathāgata's body are all three identical with one another.[46]

In addition to being identified with the fire itself, the practitioner may be identified with various aspects of the offering ritual. In the Vedic ritual, the sacrificer and the victim of the sacrifice are identified with one another, the victim substituting for the sacrificer. The identification is not total, however. As explained by Charles Malamoud, "the sacrificer seeks to show that he is at once identical to, and different from the victim. By offering up the victim, it is himself he wishes both to offer and avoid offering. Victim and sacrificer are united *nidanena,* 'by esoteric identification'."[47]

Thematically, the practitioner as sacrifice parallels the significance given the material offerings made in the Shingon *homa,* though given here new significance consonant with Tantric soteriology. Each of the offerings is identified with the practitioner's own delusions. Just as the offerings are purified by the fire, so the delusions are purified. Concerning this aspect of the Shingon *homa,* Taiko Yamasaki states that, during the sacrifice, the practitioner visualizes delusions entering the Buddha's wisdom-flame, where they immediately reveal their essential nature as the fuel of wisdom.[48]

The idea of oneself as the sacrifice becomes especially concretized in the funerary uses of fire sacrifice. Richard H. Davis, speaking of the traditional Vedic conceptions of cremation of the dead, suggests that, "If death sets in motion a passage to the realm of the ancestors, cremation is a sacrifice that conveys one there. The funerary fire Agni is the divine power that releases the spirit, the sacrificial offering, from its earthly body and begins to transport it to the heavenly domain of gods and ancestors."[49] Here again we find the dual function of Agni as both purifying the offering and transporting it to the realm of the deities.

Citing Madeleine Biardeau, Davis calls attention to cremation as "the only sacrifice where the sacrificer himself becomes the victim physically consumed in the fire."[50] This is true not only in the Vedic context, but also for contemporary Śaiva initiates: "The Śaivas, like the Vedic ritualists, consider the incineration of the physical body as a large scale oblation in the sacrificial fire."[51]

In the Buddhist *Sarvadurgatipariśodhana Tantra* there are two sections dealing with *homa* rites. In the first it is stated that if the practitioner uses the "flesh, bones, hair, ashes" or other similar items from the body of the deceased as a part of the *śāntika homa* (the *homa* for "pacification"), then the deceased "becomes freed from every sin."[52] More dramatically, one section gives a set of directions for performing a *homa* using the entire corpse of the deceased. "In order to eliminate evil rebirths," the practitioner places the corpse "on a mat in the center of the hearth. Then the *mantrin* should cover it with a cloth blessed with the *mantras.* Kindling the Consumer of Offerings and summoning Agni, whose body blazes with thousands of flames and who resembles the white moon, tranquil and limitless, he should arrange the offerings."[53]

Another form of identification of the practitioner with the ritual fire takes place in the *prāṇāgnihotra,* a Vedic ritual in which the practitioner's breaths are identified with the fires of the *agnihotra* rite. There is a reversal of identifications between the *agnihotra* and the *prāṇāgnihotra,* just as in the case of the identification of sex and fire. Through one sequence of identifications the twice-daily performance of the *agnihotra* came to be equated with breathing. This identification reaches the point that knowledge of this identity becomes a key aspect of reestablishing the fires, should they become extinguished.[54] The *prāṇāgnihotra* is an ever-present sacrifice that can substitute for the daily performance of the *agnihotra* rite itself. The reversal takes place when the *agnihotra* is explained as being concerned with the maintenance of the sacrificer and his continuous breathing of the *prāṇāgnihotra.*[55]

The internal quality of the *prāṇāgnihotra* recalls the interior *homa* of the Shingon Tantric tradition. According to Bodewitz, "The connection between the *prāṇāgnihotra* and some forms of Tantric *pūjā* is based on the fact that both represent an interiorization (of the Vedic rites and of the external *pūjā*)."[56] For example, in his commentary on the *Mahāvairocana Sūtra,* the Chinese monk I-Hsing asserts that "in general the meaning of Homa is with the fire of wisdom to burn the kindling of the *kleśas* until all are entirely consumed."[57] The development of the *prāṇāgnihotra* involves an interiorization of the *agnihotra* offering that is at least thematically similar to the relation between the inner *homa* and the outer *homa.* However, Bodewitz has noted: "In using the term 'interiorization' one should be aware of the fact that several disconnected phenomena are covered by this rather vague word."[58]

Beyond what the two rites share concerning the interiorization of ritual, in both cases this interiorization does not involve the rejection of ritual per se. Summarizing I-Hsing's instructions concerning the *homa,* Michael Strickmann says: "If one is able to provide the requisite offerings, it should be carried out in conjunction with the meditative rite. Otherwise, the Inner Homa may be performed by itself. Yet it is illicit solely to realize Homa in the heart if one *does* have the wherewithal to accomplish the outer rite."[59] In connection with the *prāṇāgnihotra* Bodewitz has said, "The development is not (exclusively) from Vedic ritualism to non-Vedic or post-Vedic non-ritualism and anti-ritualism. The ritualism generally remains in one or other form. Its object and consequently its performance and external features change."[60] Bodewitz's conclusions concerning the continuation of ritualism make the ritualism of the Tantras appear less as a curious regression than a part of an ongoing, developing ritual tradition.

Thus, in a variety of ways people are identified with the ritual fire. Sex and digestion, *tapas*-filled Brahmins and *tapas*-filled consecrated sacrificers, the practitioner as an offering and the practitioner's corpse as an offering, and finally the practitioner's breath have all been equated with the ritual fire.

Perhaps the very oldest of the components found in the Tantric *homa* is the view of fire as a god. Such a notion may be both prehistoric and universal since fire is such a great transformative force. The existential significance of fire is so great that it may be the origin of religion itself. The sacrificial use of fire is known throughout the entire range of Indo-European religions and in the Vedic tradition fire is known by the name Agni, which is clearly reflected in many Indo-European cognate words.[61] As mentioned previously, Agni is ambiguously both a deity and elemental fire. Fritz Staal says:

> Though considered a god, he is never disconnected from his element, fire, until later Hindu mythology, where he appears in more anthropomorphic terms. In the *Ṛgveda,* Agni is brilliant, golden, has flaming hair and beard, three or seven tongues, his face is light, his eyes shine, he has sharp teeth, he makes a cracking noise, and leaves a black trail behind. He is fond of clarified butter . . . , but he also eats wood and devours the forest. In fact, he eats everything (*viṣva-ad*). He is in particular a destroyer of demons and a slayer of enemies.[62]

The centrality of Agni to Vedic ritual is well-known. From the simplest, the Agnihotra, in which libations are made into fire twice daily, to the most complex, the Agnicayana, which after weeks of preparation requires twelve days and the services of seventeen priests to perform, the making of offerings into fire forms a consistent theme. This practice continues in the *homa* of the Tantric traditions, both Hindu and Buddhist, and the figure of Agni himself retains his importance in both traditions as well. In the Shingon *homa* the first set of offerings is made to Agni. The Fire Deity is invited to receive the offerings, and to manifest in the flames of the hearth. Placing a flower on top of the burning wood in the hearth, the practitioner makes a meditation *mudrā* and visualizes the flower going to the center of the hearth. The visualization continues with the flower transforming into a lotus seat for the deity. Above the seat the syllable *raṃ* is visualized in Siddham script. The syllable *raṃ* changes into a wish-fulfilling jar and then the wish-fulfilling jar changes into the four-armed form of Agni. "His first right hand forms the *mudrā* of fearlessness, in the second is held a rosary, in his first left hand is grasped a sage's staff, in the second is grasped a water bottle (*kuṇḍikā*). Surrounding his body is a blaze of flames."[63]

Agni takes similar place of primacy in the *homa* of the Śaiva tradition of south India. At the beginning of the *homa* described in the *Somaśambhupaddhati* the following directions are given:

> IV. 10. The officiant then completes the union of the three fires; the fire of the stomach, the fire of the *Bindu,* and the terrestrial fire; then he places (into the fire) the consciousness of Vahni, by means of the *bījā* of Vahni (HRUM): "Om Hrum, before the consciousness of Vahni I bow!"[64]

Here Agni is addressed by his epithet Vahni, the Conveyer.[65] However, beyond the simple continuity provided by the presence of Agni in his role as Conveyer of Offerings in this Śaivite Tantric *homa,* we find a similar threefold identification as in the performance of the Shingon *homa.* The ritual identification of the practitioner with the deity involves the union of the three fires, that of the fire of the stomach, the fire of the *bindhu* (ritual dot), and that of the ritual fire, referred to in the text as the terrestrial fire. Following this threefold identification, Agni is made present in the ritual fire. According to Hélène Brunner-Lachaux, it is this which changes the fire from an "inert fire" into a "divine fire."[66] The importance of projecting the consciousness of Agni into the ritual fire following the visualized union of the three fires is that it makes the fire actually effective, Agni is present, ready to transmit the offerings. The importance of the inner *homa* mentioned previously is much the same in the Shingon tradition. I-Hsing says that if one were to perform only the outer *homa* and not the inner, then "One would simply be burning the kindling and vainly using up the offerings. Not only would one be committing a profane act, but moreover it would be devoid of efficacy."[67]

Not only is Agni made present in the flames of the ritual fire, but so are many other deities. In other words, the fire may be the physical body in which a deity temporarily abides. A classic and dramatic example of a deity becoming present in the body of a ritual fire is found in the opening of the *Rāmāyaṇa.* This occurs when king Daśaratha is sacrificing in order to gain an heir. Vālmīki tells us:

> . . . as he sacrificed, there arose from the sacred fire a great being of incomparable radiance, enormous power, and immense might. He was black and clothed in red. His mouth was red, and his voice was like the sound of a

> kettledrum. The hair of his body, head, and beard were as glossy as that of a yellow-eyed lion. He bore auspicious marks and was adorned with celestial ornaments. His height was that of a mountain peak, and his gait that of a haughty tiger. His appearance was like that of the sun, and he looked like a flame of blazing fire.[68]

This theme of the fire as the physical form through which a deity manifests himself continues into the *homa* practiced in Shingon. Not only are Bodhisattvas, guardian deities, celestial deities, and earthly deities invited to the altar-hearth, but the body of the fire is identified with that of the deity. Taiko Yamasaki gives an alternate description of the ritual process for evoking Agni (Jap.: *Ka-ten*) already discussed above:

> The practitioner visualizes the wisdom-flame as a syllable that changes into a triangular flame, which then becomes the figure of Ka-ten [lit. "fire god," that is, Agni; R.K.P.]. White in color, with four arms, the body of Ka-ten is cosmic flame. Placing a "floral tassel" on the burning fuel, the practitioner visualizes above it a throne surmounted by a syllable that first transforms into a ritual vase and then into the figure of Ka-ten, forming the *mudrā* of fearlessness, holding a rosary, a wand, and a vase in his several hands, his body filled with flame. Performing the *mudrā* and *mantra* of summons, the practitioner visualizes Ka-ten being drawn into the hearth, and recites verses of invocation and welcome. The offerings then begin . . . The practitioner performs the *mudrā* and *mantra* of universal offering to transform the offerings into the universal dimension, and empowers them by reciting the verse of the three universal powers. The mouth of the hearth [which is also simultaneously the mouth of Agni and the mouth of the practitioner, R.K.P.] is rinsed again, and a "floral tassel" tossed into a corner of the hearth to serve as the vehicle of Ka-ten's return to his essential realm. With the *mudrā* and *mantra* of dispatching the deity, Ka-ten is visualized departing from the hearth.[69]

The same kind of ritual procedure is followed for each deity evoked in the flames. Within this same basic structure, the only significant modifications are in the *mantra* employed and, in some cases, the kinds of offerings made.

Divining the presence of a deity from the character of the fire would seem related to the idea that the deity is physically present in the fire. The Vedic tradition maintains specific guidelines for interpreting the significance of fires that appear differently from one another. In relation to the twice daily Agnihotra ritual, the *Kathakasaṃhita*[70] says "The flame which has a golden colour is sacred to Bṛhaspati. When it is neither golden nor red, then it is sacred to Mitra. When it is red, then it is sacred to Varuṇa. When it is enveloped in smoke, then it is sacred to Varuṇa. When it is enveloped in smoke, then it is sacred to All-gods . . . Where the flame flickers as it were in the coals, that is his (Agni's) mouth, Avi by name. That is Brahman. Therein should be offered."[71] Note here the motif of the fire as the mouth of the deity as well as discerning which deity the fire is sacred to according to the fire's color.

According to the *Mahāvairocana Sūtra,* one of the two texts central to the Shingon tradition, there are twelve acceptable fires. Drawing some examples from Strickmann's summary of this section of the *Mahāvairocana Sūtra,* the first is "named Mahendra, dignified and golden, of increasing awesomeness, coifed with flames and in a state of *samādhi* [deep meditation], manifesting the plenitude of wisdom." The second is identified as "Fullness of Action" and it "sends forth its rays like the autumn moon, is surrounded by an auspicious wheel, and wears a pearl adorned chignon and a pure white garment." The sixth is named "Furious" and is described as "squint-eyed, fog-colored, with an upright shock of hair and an earth-shaking bellow, powerful, and displaying four fangs in his mouth."[72] Although it is not clear if the descriptions given in the *Mahāvairocana Sūtra* are intended for divinatory purposes or not, the descriptions certainly do represent personified forms of deities as different kinds of fires. Thus, not only is the ritual fire identified with Agni, but it serves as the physical body by which many other deities are manifest. In some cases the character of the fire itself is examined to determine which deity is present.

Several themes have been explored here that demonstrate continuity from the Indo-European through the Vedic to the Tantric ritual tradition. The shape of the hearth is symbolically significant, though the specific significance given changes, perhaps as a result of the differences between the various soteriological conceptions. A second factor affecting the change of symbolic value is change in ritual practice, such as the movement from the Indo-European and Vedic three fires to the Tantric single fire. The idea of fire as both conveying and purifying the offerings carries across from the Vedic to the Tantric, while the imagery of fire as both sexual and digestive continues as well. Fire is identified with people in a variety of ways—those filled with *tapas* are identical with the ritual fire, while the sacrificer may be identified with the offerings made into the flames. At the extreme, the corpse as a whole is an offering. While the physical body may be an offering, the life force of the breath (*prāṇa*) is homologized with the ritual fire.

Deities are identified with the fire as well, the most important being Agni. Agni is central to the ritual semantics in his dual role as conveyer and purifier of the offerings. In addition, the body of the fire may become the temporary abode of many different deities, the mouth of the hearth being identified with the mouth of the deity, the flames within the hearth being identified with the digestive fires of the deity.

The identification of the deity evoked with the fire is compounded by a third identification, that of the practitioner himself with both the fire and the deity. This threefold identification occurs both in the Shingon Tantric Buddhist tradition of Japan and in the Śaivite Tantric tradition of South India. It appears to be the case that this threefold identification marks the division of the Tantric ritual tradition from the Indo-European and Vedic traditions. The Indo-European and Vedic sacrificial offerings into fire are votive in character; the ritual logic of this relationship leads to the identification of the practitioner with the deity, and hence the ritual logic of the *homa* leads to the threefold identification of the fire with both the deity and the practitioner.

A final point that has emerged from this examination of the practice of making offerings into fires in the Vedic and Tantric traditions is the reversal of identifications. Once identification is made from one thing to another, the reverse identification also becomes possible. This is the case with the sexual fires, the digestive fires, and the breath fires.

In conclusion, it can be determined that the roots of the Shingon *homa* ritual are traceable back through China to the early medieval formation of Tantra in India. While many elements of the *homa* can be traced farther back to Indo-European ritual practices, the Tantric *homa* seems specifically to develop out of Vedic ritual and the meta-ritualistic speculations of the Brāhmaṇas, that is, the Tantras appear to be much more firmly rooted in the Vedas than is usually suggested.

Perhaps because of the long-standing tendency in Western scholarship to interpret the Upaniṣads as a radical break from the Brāhmaṇas, the connection between the ritual speculations of the Brāhmaṇas and the philosophic speculations of the Upaniṣads has been overlooked. As Brian K. Smith has said:

> It is a remarkable fact about the Western reconstruction of the Vedic religion that whereas the great identities of the Vedantic Upaniṣads (linking the microcosmic true self to the macrocosmic One in and expression of mystical unity) have always seemed to inspire admiration, statements of equivalence in the ritualistic Brāhmaṇas are often scorned and disdained as so much mumbo jumbo from the imagination of priests.[73]

One begins to suspect a hostility toward ritual per se as the cause of distinctions between the Brāhmaṇas and the Upaniṣads. However, the continuities between the Brāhmaṇas and the Upaniṣads seem to be part of the larger continuity between the Vedic and the Tantric tradition.

Some scholars have suggested that the Tantras represent a resurgence of pre-Āryan religion. This seems to be what Snellgrove is suggesting, for example, when he asserts that Tantra should not be seen as a decadent form of Buddhism. Rather, "One might even claim that these new elements far from issuing in a degeneration brought about a rejuvenation, nourished in the hidden well-springs of Indian religious life."[74] Kvaerne, citing Eliade, is more explicit, suggesting that the positive evaluation of women found in Tantra is "an aspect of a general resurgence of the non-Āryan religious substratum, manifested in the Tantric movement, Hindu as well as Buddhist, that is, a resurgence of a religious universe in which the role of the female creative force, manifested in every woman, comes to the fore."[75]

While it may well be that some or many of the important elements of Tantra can be traced back to pre-Āryan, indigenous forms, two problems remain. First, there are many other important Tantric elements that can be traced back to Vedic sources. Concerning one of the most important elements, interiorization, was pre-Vedic."[76] Thus, Tantra as a self-conscious movement cannot simply be seen as a resurgence of pre-Āryan, indigenous religious forms. Second, so little is known definitely about pre-Āryan, indigenous religion that it seems to approach the quality of an inkblot—the meaning found there is drawn from the observer rather than from the object. There is a danger in attributing the meaning of objects and practices that are known from a later period to objects and practices from an earlier period that appear to be similar.

Perhaps the suggestions that Tantra arises from a resurgence of pre-Āryan religion—rather than seeing it simply as a development within Indian religious culture—result in part from the actual history. Once periods are identified, they seem to cry out for characterization. How the religious traditions of periods are characterized is all too vulnerable to the subtle influence of our own expectations. Then again, once a tradition at a given point in time is identified and characterized, the "problem" arises of how to explain its transition into another period. Thus, the Vedic period is typically described as ritualistic, while the period of the Upaniṣads, Buddhism, and Jainism are characterized as non- or anti-ritualistic. The challenge then is how to explain such an apparent transition. Similarly, the period of the Upaniṣads, Buddhism, and Jainism is characterized as philosophic and meditative, while the Tantric period, both Buddhist and Hindu, is characterized as superstitious, decadent, and ritualistic. How can one then explain this transition? Such problems may in fact be only the appearance of a problem, a pseudo-problem resulting more from the way in which the traditions and periods have been characterized, than from what is revealed by a detailed examination of the continuities. While we may not be able to escape from periods and their characteristics, I suspect that the vast majority of them are only heuristic in quality—useful devices whose conventional character must be kept in mind. Within Buddhism one of the metaphors for the teachings of the tradition is that of a raft. Having reached the shore, one should leave the raft at the water's edge. Although as scholars our task is different from that of the individual seeking enlightenment, the cautionary note of the tale may prove a useful device for us as well.

The Tantric *homa* demonstrates a relatively high degree of continuity with earlier ritual practices. The rich complex of homologies, which serves as the cognitive base for much religious practice in India, seems to provide ample resources for the development of the threefold identification of the Tantric *homa* out of the existing tradition, once the catalyst of the identification of the practitioner and the deity is added. In the absence of clear evidence that such a soteriological concept is to be found in pre-Indo-European Indus civilizations, the unique threefold identification of the Tantric *homa* is perhaps best understood to be a novel creation.

NOTES

1. Michel Strickmann, "Homa in East Asia," *Agni: The Vedic Ritual of the Fire Altar*, ed. Frits Staal (Berkeley: Asian Humanities Press, 1983), 2: 418.

2. *Kūkai: Major Works,* trans. Yoshito S. Hakeda (New York and London: Columbia University Press, 1972), 141.

3. For a critique of the effectiveness of Kūkai's attempt, see Tsuda Shin'ichi, "The Hermeneutics of Kūkai," *Acta Asiatica* 47 (1985): 82–108.

4. Alex Wayman, *Yoga of the Guhyasamājatantra* (Delhi: Motilal Banarsidass, 1977), 52.

5. See Musashi Tachikawa, "*Homa* in Vedic Ritual: The Structure of the Darsa-purnamasa," *From Vedic Altar to Village Shrine,* ed. Yasuhiko Nagano and Yasuke Ikari, Senri Ethnological Studies, 36 (Osaka: National Museum of Ethnology, 1993), 239–67; Musashi Tachikawa, "An Ancient Indian Homa Ritual: Pavitresti, a Modified Form of Darsapurnamasa," *Studia Asiatica* 8 (Nagoya: The Department of Indian Philosophy, Nagoya University, 1985).

6. See Brian K. Smith, *Reflections on Resemblance, Ritual and Religion* (Oxford, Eng.: Oxford University Press,1989), 197.

7. Skt.: *kleśa,* Jap.: *bonno.* Hisao Inagaki with P. G. O' Neill, *A Dictionary of Japanese Buddhist Terms Based on References in Japanese Literature* (Union City, California: Heian International, 1988).

8. For a discussion of the theme of five fires, see David M.Knipe, *In the Image of Fire, The Vedic Experiences of Heat* (Delhi: Motilal Banarsidass, 1975), 1–18.

9. Georges Dumézil, *Archaic Roman Religion,* trans. Philip Krapp (Chicago: The University of Chicago Press, 1970), 1:313.

10. See Fritz Staal, *Agni, The Vedic Ritual of the Fire Altar* (Berkeley: Asian Humanities Press, 1983), I:279.

11. Dumézil, *Archaic,* 1:315.

12. Ibid., 1:313.

13. Ibid., 1:315.

14. Staal, *Agni,* 1:96.

15. Dumézil, *Archaic,* 1:320.

16. Walter Burkert, *Greek Religion,* trans. John Raffan (Cambridge, Mass.: Harvard University Press, 1985), 170.

17. Ibid.

18. Staal, *Agni,* 1: 93.

19. Ibid., 1.:56–8.

20. Inagaki, *Dictionary,* s.v. "*goshuho.*"

21. Richard K. Payne, *Feeding the Gods: The Shingon Fire Ritual,* Ph.D. diss. (Berkeley: University of California, 1985), 79.

22. Wayman, *Yoga,* 66–7.

23. Ibid.

24. A. L. Basham, *The Origins and Development of Classical Hindiusm* (Boston: Beacon Press, 1989), 13.

25. Dumézil, *Archaic,* 1:313.

26. Ibid., 315.

27. *New Larousse Encyclopedia of Mythology* (London: Hamlyn Publishing Groups, 1968), s.v., "Indian Mythology."

28. Burkert, *Greek Religion,* 170.

29. Wendy Doniger O'Flaherty, *Asceticism and Eroticism in the Mythology of Śiva* (London: Oxford University Press, 1973), 90.

30. *Bṛhadāranyaka Upaniṣad* 6.4.3.

31. *Bṛhadāranyaka Upaniṣad* 6.4.12.

32. *Bṛhadāranyaka Upaniṣad* 6.2.3.

33. Vettam Mani, *Purāṇic Encyclopedia: A Comprehensive Dictionary with Special Reference to the Epic and Purāṇic Literature* (Delhi: Motilal Banarasidass, 1975), s.v. "*Homakunda.*"

34. *Tantra of the Great Liberation (Mahānirvana Tantra),* trans. John Woodroffe (Arthur Avalon) (New York: Dover Publications, 1972r), 127.

35. Christiaan Hooykass, "Agni-Offerings in Japan and Bali," *Agni: The Vedic Ritual of the Fire Altar,* ed. Frits Staal (Berkeley: Asian Humanities Press, 1983), 2:385.

36. *The Laws of Manu,* trans. Georg Buhler, Sacred Books of the East, vol. 25 (1886; reprint, New York: Dover Publications, 1969), 3:98.

37. *Manu,* 3.212, 114.

38. *Manu,* 4:48, 136.

39. *Manu,* 4:142, 151.

40. See: Mircea Eliade, *Shamanism: Archaic Techniques of Ecstasy,* trans. Willard R. Trask (Princeton, N.J.: Princeton University Press, 1964), 412–44.

41. Walter O. Kaebler, *Tapta Marga: Asceticism and Initiation in Vedic India* (Albany: State University of New York Press, 1989), 61–62.

42. Ibid, 65.

43. *Śaṭapatha Brāhmaṇa* 6, 7, 2, 11 as cited in Jan Gonda, *Change and Continuity in Indian Religion* (The Hague: Mouton and Co., 1965), 333, 49n.

44. *Śaṭapatha Brāhmaṇa* 6, 6, 4, 5 as cited in Gonda, ibid.

45. *Apastamba Srautasutra* 10, 13, 1 as cited in Gonda, ibid.

46. *Ritual Directions for the Santika Homa Offered to Acala,* trans.Richard K. Payne (Koyasan, Japan: Department of Koyasan Shigon Foreign Mission, 1988), 38–39.

47. Charles Malamoud, "Paths of the Knife: Carving up the Victim in Vedic Sacrifice," *Indian Ritual and Its Exegesis,* ed. Richard F. Gombrich, Oxford University Papers on India, vol. 2, pt. 1 (Delhi: Oxford University Press, 1988), 3.

48. TaikoYamasaki, *Shingon: Japanese Esoteric Buddhism,* trans. Richard and Cynthia Peterson (Boston and London: Shambhala Publications, 1988), 172.

49. Richard H. Davis, *Ritual In An Oscillating Universe: Worshiping Śiva in Medieval India* (Princeton, N.J.: Princeton University Press, 1991), 44–5.

50. Ibid., 45.

51. Ibid., 47.

52. Tadeusz Skorupski, *Sarvadurgatiparisodhana Tantra, Elimination of All Evil Destinies* (Delhi: Motilal Banarsidass, 1983), 69–70.

53. Tadeusz Skorupski, "Tibetan Homa Rites," in Staal, *Agni,* 2:415.

54. *Jaiminiya Brahmana,* 1, 1–65. trans. H. W. Bodewitz. Orientalia Rheno-Traiectina, 17 (Leiden: E. J. Brill, 1976), 222.

55. Ibid., 225.

56. Ibid., 328.

57. Strickmann, "Homa in East Asia," 2: 444.

58. Bodewitz, *Jaiminīya,* 330.

59. Strickmann, 443.

60. Ibid., 330.

61. Staal, *Agni,* 1: 73.

62. Ibid.

63. Richard K. Payne, trans., *Ritual Directions for the Santika Homa Offered to Acala* (Koyasan, Japan: Department of Koyasan Shingon Foreign Mission, 1988), 43.

64. My translation from the French; see *Somaśambhupaddhati: Le rituel quotidien dans la tradition sivaite de l'Inde du Sud selon Somasambhu,* 3 vols., trans. Hélène Brunner-Lachaux, Publications de l'Institut Français d'Indologie (Pondicherry: Institut Français d'Indologie, 1963, 1968, 1977), 1:238.

65. cf. Alain Danielou, *Hindu Polytheism,* Bollingen Series, no. 73 (New York: Pantheon Books, 1964), 89.

66. Brunner-Lauchaux, *Somaśambhupaddhati,* 238, 1n.

67. Strickmann, "Homa in East Asia," 2: 444.

68. Chapter 15, verse 9–12. Swami Venkatesananda, *The Concise Rāmāyaṇa of Vālmīki* (Albany: State University of New York, 1988), 155–56.

69. Yamasaki, *Shingon,* 174–75.

70. H. W. Bodewitz, *The Daily Evening and Morning Offering (Agnihotra) According to the Brāhmaṇas.* Orientalia Rheno-Traiectina, 21 (Leiden: E.J. Brill, 1983), 6.11, 88.

71. Regarding the name Avi, see ibid., 91, 1n.

72. Strickmann, "Homa in East Asia," 2: 438.

73. Smith, *Reflections,* 32.

74. David Snellgrove, *Havajra Tantra* (London: Oxford Univewrsity Press, 1959), 1: 40.

75. Per Kvaerne, "On the Concept of Sahaja in Indian Buddhist Tantric Literature," *Temenos* 12 (1975): 106.

76. Bodewitz, *Jaiminīya,* 328.

Part V
THE TEXTS AND TANTRA

11

Becoming Bhairava: Meditative Vision in Abhinavagupta's *Parātrīśikā-laghuvṛtti*

Paul E. Muller-Ortega

In Tantric *sādhana,* deity and deification are synergistically intertwined.[1] What is prescribed in any particular *sādhana* for the purpose of deification very much depends on the deity the sādhaka wishes to become. In this essay, I explore two related, though separable, symbolic contexts for the Hindu Tantric deity Bhairava, as well as the interaction between two varieties of *sādhana* for achieving deification as Bhairava. The exploration of what is involved in "becoming Bhairava" in these two contexts not only reveals an important shift in the meaning of "Bhairava," it also allows an approach to the very rich notion of the *khecarī* or *bhairavīmudrā* (ritual gestures). I hope that this exploration of the meaning of Bhairava will contribute to an understanding of an important ideological shift in the development of the early Hindu Tantra.

The intent in this essay is not so much historiographical as it is patently hermeneutic. To understand the roots of the Hindu Tantra, we must uncover the radical and crucial interpretive shifts that contribute to its successful ideological consolidation. Thus it is useful to examine the symbolism of the Tantric deity, Bhairava, a figure who straddles two domains in early Hindu Tantra. On one hand, the symbolism of Bhairava is connected to *āveśa-sādhana,* that is, the cremation-ground culture of possession by hordes of demonic female deities led by the frightful, fanged deity known as Rudra-Bhairava.[2] On the other hand, and especially in the hands of the brilliant early expositor of Hindu Tantra, the Kashmiri Śaiva teacher Abhinavagupta (tenth century C.E.), Bhairava is reinterpreted in terms of what could be called the *samāveśa-sādhana,* the Tantric-yogic exploration of the nondual consciousness.[3] Here, Bhairava comes to mean the unencompassable and exquisitely blissful light of consciousness that is to be discovered as the practitioner's true inner identity.

These two aspects of Bhairava may be examined using as a locus text in which the boundary between these two domains is clearly discernible. This is the short Āgamic work usually termed the *Parātriṃśikā* or *PT* that connects itself somewhat problematically to the *Rudra-yāmala-tantra* (see Table 1).[4] The *PT* verses were deemed sufficiently important by Abhinavagupta that he commented on them twice, once in his *Parātrīśikā-laghuvṛtti (PTlv)* and once in his *PTv.*[5] In fact, it is in these commentaries that we find important evidence for the process by which what we are calling the *āveśa-sādhana* mutates into what may be termed the *samāveśa-sādhana.* In this process, the demonic figure of Bhairava mutates and expands to include the apparently benign philosophical concept of a Tantric absolute reality. The attempt here will be to exploit selectively the thematic richness of a passage drawn from this work to explore several important symbolic themes related to this absolutizing transformation. Moreover, the exploration of this passage and the sequence of development within the early Hindu Tantra that it typifies illustrate aspects of the complex and problematic interplay between the domain of ritual techniques and the realm of meditative practices.

A standard scholarly gambit attempts to drive useful interpretive wedges in the gap between a text and its commentaries. It is, however, quite difficult to exploit these interstices when the only context we have for a text *is* its commentary. An example of this in the study of *darśana* (viewing) is the attempt to read the *Yoga-sūtras* outside of Vyāsa's *Yoga-bhāṣya* and other subcommentaries. If these attempts have shown us anything, it is that it is difficult to do so in anything more than a speculative fashion.[6] In the case of the *PT* verses, we have even less to go on than the *Yoga-sūtras.*

It is even more difficult to explore this gap when such a commentary establishes a new and subsuming paradigm that encompasses the original text in a plausible way. Such is the case with Abhinavagupta's commentary entitled *The Short Gloss on the PT* (*Parā-trīśikā-laghuvṛtti*).[7] Here, the seamless continuity of Abhinavagupta's encompassing commentary on the *PT* verses tends to obscure the original ritual and experiential context of these verses. With ingenuity, Abhinavagupta overlays a doctrine of non-dual consciousness on the original and much less clearly doctrinal Āgamic text. In his synthetic Trika-Kaula elaboration of the doctrine of Recognition (that Abhinavagupta inherited from his predecessor, Utpaladeva), he doubles back to the *PT* verses to weave them into a sophisticated system. Thus, he embeds them in the complex ideology of the Heart with its related notions of the *kula* or Embodied Cosmos, the *viṣarga-śakti* or Emissional Power of the continuous cosmogony, and the esoteric language philosophy of the *mātṛkā* (sound).

The PT verses relay the secret teaching of a particular *mantra* (verse or *śloka* 9), the so-called Heart-*mantra* (*Hṛdayabīja*), *SAUḤ.* They then describe in the next seven verses, the visionary engulfing of the consciousness of the practitioner by the *śaktis* (powers) that the *sādhaka* courts. Having received the impelling and initiatory descent of energy (*śaktipāta*)[8] from the Guru, the *sādhaka* who diligently remembers the *mantra, S-AU-Ḥ,* progressively penetrates into a condition of meditative absorption (*samāveśa*) in which he comes face to face with a host of divinized beings: the Mothers (*Mātṛs*), the Mistresses of Yoga (*Yogeśvarīs*), the Heroes perfected by the practice of the secret ritual (*Vīras*), the Lords of the Heroes

(*Vīreśvaras*), the powerful *Siddhas*, and the *Śākinīs*, such as the *Khecarīs*. These beings are experienced as inhabiting the *sādhaka*'s body and appearing before him ready to do his bidding, to foretell the future, reveal the past, or grant any desire.[9]

In his commentary on the verses, Abhinavagupta states that when meditative absorption is sufficiently strong, the meditator achieves a vision of the deity he desires by placing the *mantra* connected with this deity in his Heart consciousness.[10] Thus, for Abhinavagupta, meditative vision constitutes a process of drawing near (*ā-kṛ*) or attracting the divine beings already resident in the body of the *sādhaka* by coalescing their form or shape (*ākṛti*) out of consciousness through the use of a *mantra*. Attracted in this way, the deity will appear before the *sādhaka*, drawn there by the Powers of Rudra, and will become identical with the practitioner's own body.[11]

Abhinavagupta clarifies that the divine beings reveal themselves because the *sādhaka* has become Bhairava, the Lord of the Wheel of Powers (*śakticakreśvara*), the *kuleśvara*, the Lord of the Embodied Cosmos. The *sādhaka* becomes identical to Bhairava who is at once the supreme consciousness and the naked beggar. This dual identity of Bhairava as both anthropomorphic and non-anthropomorphic or as both *sakala* (the composite form of the personified deity) and *niṣkala* (the transcendent form of nondual consciousness) circumscribes the complex and ambiguous nature of the meaning of deification for this Tantric environment.[12]

In Abhinavagupta's formulation which emphasized the *niṣkala* but does not exclude the *sakala*, this intense form of meditative *sādhana* represents an interiorized ritual of worship that centers on the production of the blissful nectar (*ekarasa*) of nonduality, and combines a method for liberation with the achievement of supernatural powers. At the core of this method is the notion of remembering (*smṛ*): the recognitional process of anamnesis by which the *sādhakā* recuperates the essential and preexistent identity with Śiva-Bhairava.[13]

A key term that underscores the apparent exegetical divergence of the commentary from the text is the notion of *āveśa* (verse 11), which in the original text seems to mean something like demonic possession. In Abhinavagupta's commentary, *āveśa* appears to be reinterpreted to mean a state of yogic and meditative absorption, that is, *samāveśa*. Thus, in the shift from text to commentary, two levels seem to be discernible—in the original *PT* verses, the *sādhana* of possession emphasizing the encounter with external anthropomorphic deities separate from the *sādhaka* and, in terms of Abhinavagupta's gloss, the *sādhana* of Recognition, centering on the phenomenology of non-dual consciousness. Let us examine these notions in further detail.

In the *PT*, it is Bhairava who instructs the Goddess in the secret of the Heart and its all-powerful *mantra, SAUḤ*. Bhairava is the form of Śiva encountered in the *PT* and in many of the other revealed texts in nondual Kashmiri Śaivism. The term Bhairava derives from the root *bhī* (to be afraid) and the related adjective *bhīru* (fearful, timid).[14] By a curious process of inversion, Bhairava comes to mean that which is terrifying and frightful. Depictions of him show a sinister, fanged face often surmounted by writhing and venomous serpents that convey the fury of the god of death who is also, paradoxically, the god of transformation and release.[15]

The myth tells us that Śiva punishes the creator god, Brahmā, for his sin of arrogance by cutting off one of his heads with the nail of his left thumb. Now guilty of the sin of Brahminicide, Śiva as Bhairava Bhikṣātana is condemned to wander, begging for alms and carrying Brahmā's skull, which remains attached to his hand. The naked skull bearer of Kāpālika, carrying the trident, draped in sinuous serpents, and accompanied by dogs, serves as the expiatory of Śiva's sin. The skull finally drops off when Bhairava atones for his sin by entering the precincts of the holy city of Benares.[16]

Many powerful Tantric themes are packed into the figure of Bhairava. This skull-bearing transgressor who is fearful and terrible resonates with the ascetic cremation-ground culture of heterodox and transgressive groups who sought power through control of and possession by hordes of frightening goddesses.[17] The figure of Rudra-Bhairava, especially when he is connected with the Yoginīs, Śākinīs, or Mātṛkās, alerts us to the deeply transgressive tradition that the *PT* verses inherit. With roots that go at least as far back as the early Pāśupatas and Kāpālikas,[18] this cremation-ground culture then flourishes in the cult of the Yoginīs, powerful *śaktis* (energies) who came to inhabit actual women through a state of possession and with whom the male initiates ritually copulated in order to produce the commingled sexual fluids of the sacrificial liquid (*argha* or *kuṇḍagolaka)*[19] offered back to these deities. Moreover, children born from the rituals were said to be "born from the *yoginī*" (the phrase occurs in *śloka* 10). Abhinavagupta himself was said to be "born of the *yoginī*" that is, conceived during his parents' practice of a later form of this very same sexual ritual.[20]

The examination of these eroto-mystical or sexo-yogic elements takes us beyond our current scope. It is important to note that in the move from text to commentary—in the shift from *āveśa sādhana* to *samāveśa sādhana*—these powerful ritual themes are in no way eradicated by the superimposition on them of the ideology of nondual consciousness. This is clearly evident from the coded descriptions of the *kula-yagā* or secret ritual given by Abhinagagupta in the chapter 29 of the *Tantrāloka* (*TA*).[21] Here, elaborating on his own left-handed ritual, one encounters the same theme of imbibing of the fluids that emerge from the mouth of the *yoginī,*[22] a multivalent sexual reference with important alchemical components.

Thus, as a result of the interpretive strategies of Abhinavagupta, the term Bhairava (or *bhairavatā,* or *bhairavasvarūpa*) expands beyond its mythic and personified identity and comes to stand for the Ultimate itself, the huge abyss of the unbounded and uncontainable light of consciousness. To attain Bhairava in this yogic sense is to enter into the experience of the all-encompassing and nondual reality of ultimate consciousness. In the hands of this authoritative expositor of the Tantra, the older ritually embedded conceptions become the synthetic Trika-

Kaula which, permeated with nondualism, transforms these older cults of possession into a yogic of left-handed Tantra. Dominated by an overarching inquiry into the power of Ultimate consciousness—of Bhairava conjoined with the Goddess—Abhinavagupta's commentaries transmute the external goddesses into the frenzied energies that emanate from the absolute reality and the secret ritual into an occasion for the *sādhaka*'s recognition of Bhairava as constituting the true inner identity.

Here I would like to explore two themes in which unfold the meaning of Abhinavagupta's formulation of what we are calling the *samāveśa sādhana.* Essentially, the *samāveśa sādhana* may be said to occur in two phases. In the first, the practitioner progresses in the absorption *into* Bhairava. By pronunciating the *mantra,* the *sādhaka* experiences progressive interiorization that finally reveals the reality of the nondual consciousness in the state of *turīyā* (highest state) or the inwardly enclosed *samadhi* (profound meditation). As this state is continuously pursued and assiduously consolidated, there is a second phase of the *samāveśa sādhana.* In an apparent directional reversal, Bhairava—as the ultimate unbounded consciousness—begins to be absorbed into the finite levels of the mind, senses, and body of the practitioner. In the first phase, the nondual consciousness is located *within* the deepest layer of being as the transcendent principle, the supreme Bhairava beyond the sequence of the thirty-six *tattvas* (principles of matter)—beyond the vibratory matrix, beyond the emergent *kula* (body)-explicate[23] of relative reality. In the second phase, the entire display of thirty-six principles, the whole vibratory field, the *kula*-explicate, is invaded by the nondual consciousness to such a degree that it comes to be experienced as floating nondifferently within the ocean of nondual consciousness. Let us look at these two aspects.

In *śloka* 11 of the *PT,* the centrality of pronuncing of the *mantra* is announced. It says, "When the *mantra* has been 'pronounced,' the entire great multitudes of *mantras* and *mudrās* appear immediately before him, characterized by absorption in his own body."[24] Crucial to understanding the process of *samāveśa* through pronunciation (*uccāra*) of the *mantra* are ideas surrounding the Śaivite notion of *spanda* (pulsating life) that view reality as composed of an infinitely complex vibratory web.[25] Tantric Śaivism insists that the vibratory energies that compose physical reality are themselves condensed manifestations of ultimate consciousness. Śaivite tradition also suggests a unifying continuity between the realms of physical reality, the activities of sense perception, and all forms of interior awareness. All are seen as phenomenal manifestations of the ultimate consciousness that exists enmeshed in a complex vibratory matrix.[26]

Within the *anuttara* (supreme), there occurs continuously a subtle pulsation that does not alter the stillness of the absolute. This is the *spanda* that animates the ultimate consciousness. Employing a variety of metaphors, the tradition glosses *spanda* by the term *sphurattā,* the scintillating pulse of the supreme light that continuously trembles with its own innate incandescence. In sonic terms, the *spanda* is glossed as the *nāḍa* (tone vibration), the subtle but powerful resonance echoing through the supreme. In an important metaphoric shift, supreme consciousness is likened to the ocean of Soma (*amṛta*), the nectar of immortality flowing in liquid streams or waves.[27]

In cosmogonic terms, it is the primordial *spanda* that continuously manifests the emergence of space and time and all visible universes. The supreme *spanda* releases a vibrating spectrum of energies that originate within the supreme (*anuttara*). As the infinitely fast vibration of the *anuttara* systematically coalesces and condenses into progressively slower and thicker vibrations, tangible, perceptible forms emerge from the void and formlessness of the ultimate consciousness. These apparently solid appearances are called cognitions (*parāmarśa*) and they are understood as complex interference patterns that arise in the intermerging crosswhirl of energies created by the interaction of vibratory consciousness within itself. Indeed, in the first part of the *PTlv*, Abhinavagupta takes up the explication of the sonic vibratory matrix in terms of the phonemic structure of Sanskrit. It is precisely within this ideology of vibratory matrices that Abhinavagupta interprets the original *śāktis*—the *mātṛkās*—as "the mighty troop of the *Śākinīs*" (*śloka* 15, *PT*). Thus *spanda*, which is the very life to the supreme light of the unitary consciousness, animates and discloses the unfolding multiplicity of phenomena that are contained within the infinite potentiality of that light.[28]

At the same time, *spanda* unifies and encompasses all that has emerged within its primordial embrace and reenfolds endlessly the manifested totality back into the supreme light of consciousness. The unfolding/enfolding reality is the *hṛdaya*, the expanding and contracting Heart of consciousness from which all things ebb and flow. In describing the Heart, Abhinavagupta makes the fundamental equation of his exegetical transformation of the concept of Bhairava; he says:

> The Heart is the subtle vibration of the triangle which consists of the incessant expansion and contraction of the three powers, and it is the place of repose, the place of supreme bliss. This very Heart is the Self of Bhairava, of that which is the essence of Bhairava, and of the Blessed Supreme Goddess who is inseparable and non-different from Him.[29]

Far removed from the original fanged deity of the earlier ritual conceptions, Bhairava thus emerges as the all-encompassing reality, the absolute thateffortlessly contains all manifestational realities.

Implicit within Tantric Śaivism there are a variety of spatial metaphors indicating the relative positioning attention within this vibratory matrix: *above* and *within* indicate the subtler forms of vibration that correspond to inwardly absorbed awareness; *below* and *outside* point to the cruder and more condensed forms of the physical world. From the innermost subtle above, the outer forms are nourished and sustained, rooted to the primordial source-vibration. Connecting the outer forms to the formless, ultimate consciousness, there stands the branching vibratory matrix, the web of pulsating light, or resonant sound, or liquidly flowing energies, and it is these that make up the extended body of the *sādhaka*'s consciousness.[30] Thus, from the relatively superficial activities of sense perception to the progressively subtler forms of inner awareness, there spans a unified spectrum of levels of the *spanda* that lead inward until the most delicate and powerful tendrils of individuality merge with the infinitely fast vibration of the ultimate consciousness.

All of these ideas inform the notion of the pronunciation of the *mantra,* which leads to the great vision of the *śaktis* and the recognition of Bhairava. To pronounce the *mantra,* then, is to begin the great inward traverse of this spectrum of vibratory frequencies that will lead the *sādhaka* deeper into the absorption that reveals the interior presence of the multitude of powers, and that finally disclosed Bhairava—the supreme, undifferentiated consciousness—as the deepest and most authentic identity of the practitioner.

In this way, in the traditional progression of *sādhana,* Bhairava first becomes accessible in the enstatic state of *tūriya,* which the advanced *yogin* stabilizes by gaining proficiency in the *nimīlana* or closed-eyed *samādhi.* However, contrary to earlier yogic notions, for the Tantrin the journey of consciousness does not terminate in this introvertive condition; indeed, the practitioner attempts to entice the absolute consciousness from its self-enclosed state. The *sādhaka* wishes to activate a dancing blissfulness within the initial, flat voidness of pure, contentless consciousness. It is clear that Abhinabagupta's commentary on the *PT* verses is informed by, for example, the teachings of the *Vijñāna-bhairava-tantra* (*VBh*), which prescribes the secret and subtle gestures of awareness that will unfold and magically expand the experience of this enclosed *samādhi.*[31]

The *VBh* urges the *yogin* to be alert during everyday situations—listening to the notes of a song, observing the flow of the breath or powerful emotions (e.g., fear, anger, or great happiness) or when waking yields to sleep; there may occur a sudden, flashing expansion, a surging efflorescence of consciousness that is the manifestation of Bhairava.[32] As the *Śiva Sūtras* state (I.5), *udyamo bhairavaḥ* (Bhairava is the surging expansion).[33] Thus, in his commentary Abhinavagupta addresses the advanced *yogin* who has cultivated an inward and enclosed *samādhi* and urges him to a more daring stance of openness to the hidden presence of Bhairava flashing forth from the most unexpected of places. The openness will initiate the second phase of the *samāveśa sādhana.* Here the practitioner cultivates the open-eyed *samādhi* that will mature into the *bhairavīmudrā* in which the *yogin* bathes in all moments in the perception of unbounded consciousness.[34]

Thus, the *samāveśa sādhana* advises an alternation of introvertive states—in which Bhairava is discovered as concealed in the innermost depths—with extrovertive conditions that reveal the discovery of the omnipresence of Bhairava. In this way, the *sādhaka* is said to emulate the essential pulsation of the *rudrayāmala,* of the expansion and contraction of the Rudra-dyad as they embrace in the Heart of reality.[35]

The body becomes the abode of all divinities, the text tells us. All the *mantras* and *mudrās* come to dwell within the body of the one who pronounces the Heart *mantra.* Thus, in this usage the notion of the body embraces much more than the physical body; it expands to contain the array of the subtle energies of speech, mind, and vital breath that connect the physical body to the absolute consciousness.

In the first two verses of the *PT,* the Goddess implores Bhairava to reveal the great secret of the power that abides in the Heart. His statement of the secret reveals the famous *khecarīmudrā* or *bhairavīmudrā,* the condition of moving in the void of pure consciousness, the undifferentiated consciousness that is Bhairava. While the term *mudrā* ordinarily refers to certain symbolic hand gestures, it is clear that in this context it is more properly translated as a "state of consciousness:" a *mudrā* in this sense is an inner gesture expressive of a state of consciousness. Thus, the practitioner attains the highest and most unimpeded state of consciousness in which all movement occurs solely within the field of the absolute.[36]

In his commentary on this section, Abhinavagupta employs an important alchemical metaphor to explain a second meaning of the term *samāveśa.* Says Abhinavagupta:

> It has been said that if the principle of consciousness obtains the state of being the Heart, then the condition of being free while still alive ensues. Whenever a flowing form is produced by the condition of practice, due to the heating up of the vessel of awareness whose nature is the Heart, that flowing by a regular absorption (*samāveśa*) the levels of body breath and mind, just like quicksilver (*siddharasa*) penetrating into metal, negates the insentiency of breath and mind.[37]

There are interesting links here to traditions of Indian alchemy (*rasāyana*), but what is clearly at stake is an inner alchemy connected to the flow of the transformative power of consciousness liberated by the practice of *samāveśa.* This passage illuminates the invasive absorption of nondual consciousness into the apparently separate individuality of the practitioner. Just as the activated quicksilver transforms base metal into precious substance, so too the outward flowing form of consciousness overtakes the relative body-mind apparatus and works magical transformation upon it. This new status reflects itself not only in terms of a transformed vision of the Self and of the phenomenal universe, but also in the attainment of a divinized condition of physical embodiment. Here, the flowing form of Bhairava increasingly overwhelms the finite self with its limitless power and brings about a progressively and increasingly effortless immersion (*nimajjana*), or reposing (*viśrānti*) in the abyss of the Heart of Bhairava.

Abhinavagupta tells us that the "great entanglement of the sport of existence"[38] arises as part of the astonishment experienced in the supreme consciousness, an astonishment, in this case, that there should be anything at all different from the infinite Self. This great entanglement is filled up with Bhairava, with the directly experienced perception of the Self as the all-pervasive reality both internally and externally. One of the terms that is often encountered in this regard is the notion of appropriation (*svīkartavya*). Abhinavagupta explains, "This cognition of the Heart must be appropriated, made one's own, as a reality that is empty of differences, whose nature is that it appears all at once, devoid of time."[39] By means of this transformative appropriation of all things to Bhairava, the practitioner is said to directly transform the field of experience from night into day. Describing the culmination of this process, Abhinavagupta says:

> When the absorption into the Heart is maintained for four periods of forty-eight minutes, then the totality, whose nature is essentially light, attains the condition of day, and the contraction of the night of *māyā* is destroyed. Then the practitioner with this very body becomes omniscient like Bhairava.[40]

The night of *māyā* (illusion) is the contraction that has given rise to the great entanglement of existence. This night is to be dispelled by the clarifying and expansive absorption into the reality of the Heart of Bhairava that is essentially light. Activated by practice of the *mantra,* the gleaming light of the Heart severs the knots of limitation and contraction to reveal the illuminating vision. Once released, however, this light can in no way be held back: it is unconcealable and unbounded. As it continues to emanate from the inner reality of the Heart, it invades the entire structure of finiteness, transforming its inertness and insentience into the vibrancy and liveliness of the absolute:

> This is the tetrad, the moon and its three parts, the Heart, which, being present and being reposed in one's own Heart whose form is a consciousness of the self, must be projected within oneself in order to obtain an absorption (*samāveśa*) whose nature is that it appropriates the levels of mind, breath, and body. One should place the entire group (*kula*), consisting of the mind, breath, body and senses, so that its one essence is resting on that tetrad, with its inert character having been dissolved, whose principal part is the cognition of the form of that tetrad. Because of the expansion of its light, one will arrive at a state where the *kula* becomes light. In this way the absorption of the tetrad of the emissional power in the levels of body, breath, and so on has been shown.[41]

The "moon and its three parts," the tetrad, refer here to the knower, process of knowing, and the known object all encompassed within the moon, the wholeness of consciousness. The *kula* becomes light, says Abhinavagupta. The opaque and limiting structure of body, breath, and senses is invaded by the expanding light of the Heart. Animated and transformed by the quickening essence of consciousness (the new meaning of the sacrificial liquid offered to the Goddesses), the liberated one becomes Bhairava incarnate in whom even the activities of the senses and the body are radically awakened and divinized.

Thus, in Abhinavagupta's interpretation, *samāveśa* refers to the inner grasping of the *śakti* which opens the *sādhaka* to a state of identity with Bhairava. By uniting with the Goddess, the *sādhaka* is said to be "born of the *Yoginīs* Heart," that is, to be reborn as Bhairava. Caught up in a series of macranthropic experiences, the *sādhaka* truly comes to embody the cosmos. In such a state, the capacity to experience finite objects is not lost; instead, objects are now correctly perceived as "luminous with the play that bestows the fragrance of the Self."[42] The astonishment of this experience involves discovery of Bhairava as the true inner identity and the bewildering perception that this nondifferentiated consciousness is simultaneously at play as a luminosity inherent within all external objects. In this way, the *jīvanmukta* (liberated one) "moves in the Heart," "moves in the void," and experiences all things as having their being within the omnipresent reality of the Heart of Bhairava. The awakened one is surrounded by Bhairava on all sides. What were formerly perceived and improperly evaluated as separate, finite objects (including the body, senses, and mind) have now revealed their true status as Bhairava itself. Fulfilling the meaning of both *bhukti* (enjoyment) and *mukti* (liberation), the *siddha* (one with supranormal powers) dwells in this blissful state of the englobing and all encompassing nondual consciousness.

In the movement from the *āveśa sādhana* to the *samāveśa sādhana,* there occurs an important revalorization of the place of ritual. The direct, meditative absorption in the Heart is said to fulfill the purpose of any ritual.[43] Indeed, the entrance into the Heart constitutes initiation, even if the actual ritual of initiation has not been performed.[44] Moreover, as a result of the direct knowledge of the ultimate reality of the Heart, the practitioner gains essential knowledge about all rituals, even if he does not know their specific rules.[45] The practitioner who has been born of the *yoginī* becomes automatically an expert in the rituals of all schools, not necessarily because he has come to know the ritual regulations of each of the schools in detail, but rather because he comes to know the so-called Method of the Ultimate (*anuttara-vidhi*).[46] Says Abhinavagupta, "with respect to the Ultimate, which is only consciousness, all other things are extraneous."[47]

These are curious statements that seem to indicate a movement in the direction of the transcendence of the need for elaborate ritual. In this particular context, at least, the need for exacting and the complex ritual of the Hindu Tantra seems to be obviated.[48] Nevertheless, in the *PTlv* itself an entire section of the commentary is devoted to a description of ritual procedures (*vidhi*), including sacrifice (*yāga, yajana*), adoration (*pūjā*), and oblation (*homa*). In his comment on this passage, Abhinavagupta concentrates almost exclusively on the notion of appropriation (*svīkaraṇa*). For him, the significance of the ritual is that it involves a process of reducing the external constituents of the ritual to a state of identity with the ultimate reality of the Heart.

> But one may ask: how should he sacrifice properly? With the highest devotion, with reverence and with great faith, all of which grant him absorption. This great devotion consists in effecting the subordination of the finite levels of the body, the vital breath and the subtle body. This subordination consists in accomplishing a state of humble devotion, whose nature is an immersion into the essence of that which results in the removal of those finite levels and the establishment of the superiority of the supreme consciousness, whose nature is the divinity which has been described and is to be sacrificed to.[49]

This passage resonates with the alchemical metaphor explored above. Tantric ritual is here revealed as a mechanism for stimulating the production of the flowing form of consciousness that overtakes the finite levels and transforms them into what they already in essence are—the supreme consciousness. In order to accomplish this esoteric purpose of ritual, the Tantric hero (*vīra*) must have received already the initiatory *śaktipāta* that decontracts his consciousness.[50] Abhinavagupta affirms that only when the contraction of the finite self (*anu*) has ceased is the *vīra* fully qualified to perform, in its truest sense, the ritual. Thus, in a general sense, these rituals serve the *vīra* as a stage extending his inner vision of the unity of all things within Bhairava-who-is-consciousness. It is precisely by appropriating all things to the Heart that the vision of inner unity is extended outward. In these rituals, the *vīra* finds an arena for solidifying the unitive vision acquired during meditative absorption and for extending and expanding this inner vision of unity to include all of the external constituents of the ritual. Ritual serves as a context within which the *vīra* will eventually attain the advanced form of meditative realization known as the extrovertive *samādhi* (*unmīlana samādhi*).

As a result, in the Tantric *sādhana* described by Abhinavagupta, the relationship of meditation and ritual seems to be one of symbiotic interdependence. The successful practice of one deepens and enhances the performance of the other. Synergistically feeding one upon the other, the two wings of external and internal Tantric practice advance the *vīra* along the path of *sādhana.* In so doing, ritual and meditation converge, to merge one with the other, until the boundary between the two categories fades and the distinction between outer practices and inner attainments blurs.

In the *Tantrāloka,* Abhinavagupta describes a meditation using terms and images drawn from a fire ritual. The two fire-sticks are rubbed together in order to inflame the sacred fire-pit of Bhairava. The meditation essentially consists in visualizing the entire universe reduced to the wheel of pure consciousness, and then rehearsing the process by which the entire universe once again emerges. The *siddha* becomes one with Bhairava when he actually experiences the continuous emanation and reabsorbtion of the universe from his own consciousness. Abhinavagupta says:

> Now as for the Supreme, as it is called here, there is a meditation on it. The light, the freedom, whose essential nature is consciousness contains within it all principles, realities, things. This light abides in the Heart. It has been described in this way in the *Triśiro-mata:*
>
> The knower of truth sees that reality within the Heart is like a flower within which are all external and internal things, a flower shaped like a plantain bloom. He should meditate with undistracted mind on the union there in the Heart of the sun, moon, and fire. From this meditation, as from the agitation caused by two firesticks, one comes to experience the oblation fire of the great Bhairava which expands and flames violently in the great firepit known as the Heart. Having arrived at the effulgence of Bhairava, which is the possessor of the powers and full of the powers, one should contemplate its identity with the abode of the knowing subject, the means of knowledge, and the known object.[51]

To achieve the condition of Bhairava, the *siddha* employs ritualized meditations and meditative rituals that serve as arenas for manifesting the state of identification with Bhairava. These practices become the context within which the *siddha* exercises and tests the authenticity of the attainment of the powers of manifestation, maintenance, and reabsorbtion of the universe.

Thus, Abhinavagupta describes the practice of a subtle two-phased absorption that consists of a repeated alternation between a swallowing contraction of the manifested universe into the silent witnessing consciousness and the releasing expansion of the universe once again from this void of consciousness. Describing the essential structure of the Tantric *sādhana* and the posture of the one who abides in Bhairava, the *bhairavīmudrā,* Abhinavagupta says:

> In this way, the whole multitude of paths is effortlessly dissolved in the great wheel of Bhairava which is contained in consciousness. Then—even when all this has come to an end and all that is left are latent impressions—one should meditate on the great wheel which revolves and is the overflowing of the true Self. Because of the dissolution of all that could be burned, and because of the destruction of even the remaining latent impressions, the practitioner should meditate on that wheel as becoming calm, then as pacified, then as tranquil quietude itself. By this method of meditation, the entire universe is dissolved in the wheel, in that consciousness. Consciousness then shines alone, free of objects. Then, because of the essential nature of consciousness, manifestation occurs once again. That consciousness is the

> great Goddess. Continually causing the universe to become absorbed in his own consciousness, and continually emitting it again, the practitioner would become the perpetual Bhairava.[52]

Thus, it is in the dialectical relationship between meditation and ritual, in the repeated alternation between the inner and outer practices, that the *samāveśa sādhana* moves toward its unifying goal.

The Hindu Tantra generates and functions within numerous and powerful oppositions: purity and impurity; popular and elite; high and low; inner and outer; form and formlessness; ritual and meditation; possession and yogic absorption; *dharma* and *adharma;* covertly transgressive and overtly conformist; the pursuit of *bhukti* and *mukti;* the pursuit of *kāma* and *mokṣa;* the states of order and disorder; to name just a few. The condition of embodied divinity, the deified state of the *bhairavīmudrā* seeks precisely to overcome these manifold oppositions.

The one who experiences embodied enlightenment is said to dwell in the universal bliss (*jagadānanda*) as she/he abides in the spiritual posture in which consciousness is both completely introverted and completely extroverted. The posture describes the state one who achieves embodied enlightenment, the *jīvanmukta.* It describes the tasting of the nectar of the bliss of Bhairava that is discovered by the *jīvanmukta* at the innermost depths and in the outermost limits of sensory experience. Indeed, the *bhairavīmudrā* is important because it represents the fullest possible stretch of awareness. In this condition, what the *jīvanmukta* tastes in the innermost depths of consciousness is identical to that which is found as the essence of all the sensory experiences of the so-called objective world. Using the methods of the Tantra, the practitioner finds a way to entice the divine pulsation of consciousness into revealing itself at all times, in all experiences, and under all circumstances. Abhinavagupta ecstatically sings the praises of this state in the *PTv:*

> That in which everything shines and which shines everywhere, O awakened ones, is the one brilliant quivering gleam, the Supreme Heart. That which is the abode of the origin of his own world, expanding and contracting at the same time, he rejoices in his own Heart. He should worship the vibrating Heart which appears as cosmic manifestation; thus the Heart should be worshiped in the heart, in the *suṣumṇa* passage where one will encounter the great bliss of the pair of Śiva and Śākti.[53]

Like the serpent wound around the *liṅga,* the spiraling embrace of consciousness with itself, always first implodes centripetally into the dark star, the great void at the Heart of all things. Here nothing that is not infinity itself can gain a foothold. Here all limitations and identifying characteristics of individuality are bewilderingly and fiercely stripped away. Who dares to enter into this abyss—the abode of the deepest embrace of Bhairava and of the Śakti—must truly be a renunciate, must have courageously abandoned all things to a sacrificial yielding into the all-consuming fire of Bhairava.

Yet the Heart is also the illuminating, perpetual supernova always joyfully exploding outward. At the highest level, it does so through the all-encompassing and illuminating vibration of the supreme *mantra* of consciousness, the great *OṂ*, which is also the great *mantra AHAṂ*. In this primordial cry, Bhairava-Śiva perpetually announces the realization of recognition "I am Śiva" or a "It is Śiva that is the great I AM, the great 'I' consciousness of reality" (*Śivo'ham*). This great *mantra* then fractures itself in the three successive levels of speech, reducing and congealing the hyperfluidity of the vibrating light as it approaches ever closer to human knowabilty. The interplay of the titanic forces that perpetually dwell at the Heart of things is the true domain of this early Hindu Tantra. The perennial intent of the Tantric practitioner is the fascinated emulation of this great play of Bhairava and the Goddess.

The *PT* invites the practitioner to discover the continuous occurrence of this play at the intimate core of life. It prescribes the methods by which the *sādhaka* comes to embody the paradoxical totality of these unimpeded forces within a transformed human life. The text is thought to arise as part of the play, the great dialogue, the blissful intercourse of this divine pair. Bhairava, the horrific, skull-bearing god, sweetly instructs the Great Mother of the Universe in the many and utterly secret (*atirahasya*) methods of the Hindu Tantra. These methods allow the practitioner to validate experientially the otherwise theoretical teaching of the omnipresence of Bhairava.

It is by these developments that this early Hindu Tantra rejects the dry vistas of traditional philosophical debate that seek only the representation of the Ultimate through conceptual truths. It rejects also the renunciation of traditional Indian monasticism, which protectively seeks to isolate the monk from the stain of worldliness. Transcending the dualities of conventional thought and morality, the Tantra demonstrates an outward gesture of embracing delight in all of reality. The Tantric hero pushes outward into spiritual exploration, into savoring the experience of so many varieties of the blissful *ekarasa,* the unitary taste of consciousness. In this way, the Tantric hero delights in all, even the suffering of the ordinary world. In this way she/he becomes the great dancer, the one who in all experiences and at all times relishes the nectar, the taste of the *śivanāndarasa.* Says Abhinavagupta, describing the experience of Bhairava:

> That in which there is no division or limitation, for it flashes forth all round; in which the consciousness is intact—in which consciousness alone expresses itself, whether as knower, means of knowledge, or as known; that which increases and expands by the nectar of divine joy, of absolute sovereignty in which there is no need for imagination or meditation. Śambhu told me that is the universal bliss, *jagadānanda.*[54]

TABLE 1

śloka 9	O beautiful One, the Heart of the Self of Bhairava is the third *brahman.* It is united, O fair-hipped One, with the fourteenth phoneme, and it is followed by the last of the master of the lunar stations. (*S-AU-Ḥ*)
śloka 10	He who is not born of the *yoginī,* who is not Rudra, does not clearly obtain this Heart of the God of Gods, which immediately grants both liberation and union.
śloka 11	When the *mantra* has been "pronounced," the entire great multitudes of *mantras* and *mudrās* appear immediately before him, characterized by absorption in his own body.
śloka 12	He who "remembers" during forty-eight minutes, sealed in the navel, in the *cumbaka*—"kissing pose"—such a man always binds in his own body the host of *mantras* and *mudrās.*
śloka 13	When asked, he can even tell about past and future things. "Pronouncing," that is "remembering," during a period of three hours, the form of the divinity which he desires to reach.
śloka 14	Without any doubt, he beholds before his very eyes that divinity attracted by the powers of Rudra. Practicing remembrance for only two periods of three hours, he becomes one who resides in the ether.
śloka 15	With three periods of three hours, all the Mothers, the powerful mistresses of Yoga, the heroes, the Lords of the heroes, and the mighty troop of the Śākinīs.
śloka 16	All these, having arrived, impelled by Bhairava who gives the sign, grant the supreme perfection or whatever boon is desired.

NOTES

1. For a concise statement on the Hindu Tantra, see André Padoux, "Tantrism," *The Encyclopedia of Religion,* ed. Mircea Eliade (New York: Macmillan, 1987). For references on Hindu and Kashmiri Tantra see the bibliography in Paul E. Muller-Ortega, *The Triadic Heart of Śiva: Kaula Tantrism of Abhinavagupta in the Non-Dual Śaivism of Kashmir* (Albany: State University of New York Press, 1989).

2. I should point out that the distinction between the *āveśa sādhana* and the *samāveśa sādhana* as I employ it here, is not a native category. I make distinction as a way of locating the fine line between the two domains of religious practice and ideology.

3. Abhinavagupta (ca. 950–1014 C.E.) was a Kashmiri Brahmin known for his contributions to the development of Indian aesthetic theory. He was also one the most illustrious representatives of Kashmir Śaivism. He was a prolific writer, with some forty-four works attributed to him. In his *Parātrīśikā-laghuvṛtti (PTlv)* (roughly, *The Short Gloss on the Supreme, the Queen of the Three*), he presents his most concise statement on Tantric *sādhanā.*

4. See note 20 for problems on the *Rudra-yāmala-tantra* (*RYT*).

5. See: *Parātrīsikā-laghuvṛtti,* ed. Jagaddhara Zadoo, Kashmir Series of Texts and Studies 68 (Srinagar: Research Department, Jammu and Kashmir Government, 1947), (*PTlv*); *Parātrīṃśikā-vivaraṇa,* ed. Mukunda Rama, Kashmir Series of Texts and Studies 18.

(Srinagar: Research Department, Jammu and Kashmir Government, 1918), (*PTv*); *La Trentina della Suprema,* trans. Raniero Gnoli (Turin: Boringhieri, 1978), (*PTv*); *La "Parātrīśikālaghuvṛtti" de Abhinavagupta,* trans. André Padoux, Publications de L'Institut de Civilisation Indienne, fasc.38 (Paris: Editions E. de Boccard, 1975), (*PTlv*); *A Trident of Wisdom,* trans. Jaideva Singh (Albany: State University of New York Press, 1989), (*PTv*).

6. For example, see George Feuerstein, *The Yoga-Sūtra of Patañjali: A New Translation and Commentary* (Kent, Eng.: Wm, Dawson & Sons Ltd, 1979).

7. In *Triadic Heart,* I explore the concept of the Heart (*hṛdaya*) as the symbolic focus of the Tantric *sādhanā* prescribed by Abhinavagupta; included there is a translation of the *PTLv.* The *PTlv* gives direct access to the theoretical and practical bases of the obscure Kaulas who contributed directly to Tantric formulations focusing on trangressive sacrality and the importance of the unmediated experience. Much of the present essay is based on my understanding of the *PTlv* to which the reader is referred.

8. See Abhinavagupta, *Tantrāloka Āhnika* 13 for a discussion of the nature of the divine descent of the energy of grace (*śaktipāta*). Ed. Mukunda Rama and Madhuasūdan Kaul, Kashmir Series of Texts and Studies, nos. 23, 28, 29, 30, 35, 36, 41, 47, 52, 57, 58, 59 (Srinagar: Research Department, Jammu and Kashmir Government, 1918–1938).

9. See Table 1 for a rendering of these verses.

10. Abhinavagupta, *PTlv,* commentary on *ślokas* 11–17; Ortega-Muller, 12.

11. Abhinavagupta, *PTlv,* commentary on *ślokas* 11–17; ibid., 11–14.

12. See the discussion of this topic in verses 1–18 of the *Vijñāna-bhairava-tantra: With Commentaries by Kṣemaraja and Shivopadhyaya,* Mukunda Rana, Kashmir Series of Texts and Studies 8 (Srinagar: Research Department, Jammu and Kashmir Government, 1918), (*VBh*).

13. For example, see Abhinavagupta, *PTlv,* commentary on *ślokas* 33–34; Ortega-Muller, 24–26.

14. See Monier-Williams, *A Sanskrit-English Dictionary,* 758 and 767.

15. For representations of Bhairava, see Stella Kramrisch, *Manifestations of Shiva* (Philadelphia: Philadephia Museum of Art, 1981).

16. See Diana L. Eck, *Banaras: City of Light* (Princeton, N.J.: Princeton University Press, 1982), 107–109; and Elizabeth Chalier-Visuvalingam, "Bhairava's Royal Brahminicide: The Problem of the Māhabrāhmana," *Criminal Gods and Demon Devotees,* ed. Alf Hiltebeitel (Albany: State University of New York Press, 1989).

17. See Alexis Sanderson "Śaivism and the Tantric Traditions," *The Worlds Religions,* ed. Stewart Sutherland (London: Routledge, 1988), 660–704.

18. See David N. Lorenzen, *The Kāpālikas and Kālāmukhas* (Berkeley: University of California Press, 1972).

19. See: Abhinavagupta, *Tantrāloka,* chapter 29, 14–16 and Jayaratha's commentary.

20. The text, in its closing verse, claims connection to the *Rudra-yāmala-tantra.* Goudriaan and Gupta demonstrated that there are two published texts that are linked to the *RYT* (*Uttara-tantra* and *Anuttara-tantra*), neither of which is linked to the verses commented upon in the *PTv* and *PTlv.* There are as many as fifty texts that claim to derive from the *RYT,* of which the earliest are the *Parātrīṃśika* verses and the *Vijñāna-bhairava;* see

Teun Goudriaan and Sanjukta Gupta, *Hindu Tantric and Śākta Literature* (Wiesbaden: Otto Harrowitz, 1981), 47–48.

21. See Raniero Gnoli's translation in his *Luce Delle Sacre Scritture,* (Turin: Unione Tipografico-Editrice Torinese, 1972), 680–714.

22. For example, see: Abhinavagupta, *Tantrāloka,* chapter 29, 124b–126.

23. For an exploration of application of the terms "explicate" and "implicate" in this context, see Muller-Ortega, "Tantric Meditation: Vocalic Beginnings," *Ritual Speculation in Early Tantrism: Studies in Honor of André Padoux,* ed. Teun Goudriaan (Albany: State University of New York Press, 1992).

24. Note that there are different versions of these verses in the two Sanskrit texts of Abhinavagupta's commentaries on them in *PT* and *PTlv.* While the differences do not affect verse 11, they do affect the numbering of the verses as well as slight differences in the text of some verses.

25. On *spanda,* see Mark Dyckowski, *The Doctrine of Vibration: An Analysis of the Doctrines and Practices of Kashmir Śaivism* (Albany: State University of New York Press, 1987).

26. On these notions, see Muller-Ortega, "Tantric Meditation."

27. For further exploration, see: Muller-Ortega, *Triadic Heart,* 142ff.

28. Ibid., 118ff for more details.

29. Abhinavagupta, *PTlv,* comment to verse 9; Muller-Oretga, *Triadic Heart,* 213–14.

30. See for example Abhinavagupta, *PTlv,* commentary on *śloka* 9, where the term *śarīra,* body, appears to be used in just this complex fashion.

31. See: Jaideva Singh, *The Yoga of Delight, Wonder and Astonishment: A Translation of the Vijñāna-bhairava* (Albany: State University of New York Press, 1991); and Lilian Silburn, *Le "Vijñāna Bhairava,"* Publications de L'Institut de Civilisation Indienne, fasc. 15 (Paris: Editions E. de Boccard, 1961), (*VBh*).

32. On Bhairava in the *VBh,* see verses 11–13, 23, 25,84–86, 108, 110, and 127.

33. See: Jaideva Singh, *Śiva Sūtras: The Yoga of Supreme Identity* (Delhi: Motilal Banarsidass, 1979), 29.

34. On the *bhairavīmudrā,* see: *VBh śloka 77;* and Abhinavagupta's *Tantrāloka* chapter 23.

35. On the concept of *rudrayāmala,* see Muller-Ortega, *Triadic Heart,* 111, 125, and 173.

36. On the concept of *mudrā* more generally see Abhinavagupta's *Tantrāloka* chapter 23.

37. See Abhinavagupta, *PTlv* commentary on *ślokas* 11–16; Muller-Ortega, *Triadic Heart,* 215–17.

38. Abhinavagupta, *PTv;* Muller-Ortega, *Traidic Heart,* 186 and 284.

39. Abhinavagupta, *PTlv,* comment on *ślokas* 33–34; Muller-Ortega, *Triadic Heart,* 229–31.

40. Abhinavagupta, *PTlv,* comment on *ślokas* 35–36; Muller-Ortega, *Triadic Heart,* 231–32.

41. Abhinavagupta, *PTlv,* comment on *ślokas* 33–34; Muller-Ortega, *Triadic Heart,* 229–30.

42. Abhinavagupta, *PTv;* Muller-Ortega, *Triadic Heart,* 185.

43. Abhinavagupta, *PTlv,* comment on *ślokas* 19–21a; Muller-Ortega, *Triadic Heart,* 218–19.

44. Ibid.

45. Ibid.

46. Ibid.

47. Ibid.

48. Sanderson, "Śaivism," 681.

49. Abhinavagupta, *PTlv,* comment on *ślokas* 29–32; Ortega-Muller, *Triadic Heart,* 226–28.

50. See Abhinavagupta, *Tantrāloka* 13 for discussion of *śāktipata.*

51. Abhinavagupta, *Tantrāloka* 5, 19b–25a; Ortega-Muller, *Triadic Heart,* 157.

52. Abhinavagupta, *Tantrāloka* 5, 27b–53; Ortega-Muller, *Triadic Heart,* 197–8.

53. Abhinavagupta, *PTv,* comment on *śloka* 32b; Ortega-Muller, *Triadic Heart,* 186–87.

54. Abhinavagupta, *Tantrāloka* 5, 50–51, rendering by Jaideva Singh, *The Doctrine of Recognition* (Albany: State University of New York Press, 1990), 109.

12

Tantric Incantation in the *Devī Purāṇa*: *Padamālā Mantra Vidyā*

Lina Gupta

Embedded in the rich mythology of the Śākta text called the *Devī Purāṇa* is a potent incantation, the *Padamālā Mantra Vidyā.* In this paper, I discuss the *Devī Purāṇa* and particularly its use of the *Padamālā Mantra Vidyā,* a Tantric *mantra vidyā* (incantation of mystical knowledge) that is central to the Vāmācāra Śākta Tantra tradition. Although the *Padamālā Mantra Vidyā* seems to be one of the later interpolations added to the core text of the *Devī Purāṇa,* it nonetheless instructs us in our search for the roots of Tantra. The *Devī Purāṇa*[1] is an ancient and authenticated text belonging to the body of work called the Upapurāṇas. The renowned scholar R. C. Hazra notes that the *Devī Purāṇa* is not mentioned in the eighteen Mahāpurāṇas; however, the *Ekāmra Purāṇa* includes it as one of the eighteen Upapurāṇas.[2] Raghunandan in his *Malamāsatattva* also identified the *Devī Purāṇa* as one of the eighteen Upapurāṇas.[3] The text offers discussions on a wide range of subjects including cosmography, astronomy, astrology, divination, and medicine, to name a few. It also furnishes information about the different incarnations of the Devī, her original or essential nature, her various manifestations, her functions and activities, her connections with Śiva and other deities. Devī is, however, the primary focus of the text along with the sixty-four *vidyās* (types of knowledge) that she confers on devotees. While references to Devī or Śakti abound in the Mahāpurāṇas and Upapurāṇas, in no other text is the supremacy of the Devī so firmly established as it is in the *Devī Purāṇa.* The work was composed specifically in the Vāmācāra Śākta tradition because it focuses on the worship of Devī in her most terrifying forms as Kālī, Durgā, Cāmuṇḍa, et al. Vāmācāra Śākta rituals follow sacred codified texts that contain secret Tantric rites. The other branch of Śāktas, the Dakṣiṇācāras, worship the tranquil goddesses Sarasvatī, Lakṣmī, and a pacified form of Durgā.

Most of the Śākta Purāṇas are believed to have been written in the southeastern part of Bengal and Assam, particularly in Kamarupa and Kamakhya. The *Devī Purāṇa* contains a large number of Bengali words and grammatical peculiarities of the Bengali language; for this reason, Bengal seems likely as the place of origin. The text, however, is a compilation of work by many people of various periods and possibly from other regions. Its various compilers seem to have been familiar with different parts of India, e.g., Kamarupa, Kashmir, Simhala, etc.

Despite the difficulties presented to the reader of this text, one recognizes the significance of the work for worshiping the goddess. Although considered an Upapurāṇa, it, nonetheless, is recognized as an important text for the correct performance of many Vedic rituals as well as Tantric ceremonies. The authority of the text was confirmed by writers such as Śaṅkarācārya (seventh century C.E.) and the astronomer Bhāskaracārya (tenth century C.E.), who consulted the *Devī Purāṇa* on various matters. Vallālasena, in his *Dānasāgara* (twelfth century C.E.), commented on the influence of the *Devī Purāṇa's* Tantric injunctions on Hindu religion as did the Smārta Raghunandan, a devotee of Lord Gaurāṇga, in the fifteenth century C.E. Most important, the *Devī Purāṇa* is recognized for its contributions to the ritual worship of Durgā;[4] it is used for the most important part of Durgā Pūjā, the ritual that is performed on the the penultimate night of the Nava Rātri celebration.

Worship of the goddess is not unique to the *Devī Purāṇa*. Certainly, Vedic texts mentioned the names of several goddesses and referred to their powers; but the central deity of the *Devī Purāṇa* is not like the seemingly benign goddesses of the Vedas. In contrast, she is a fierce and dangerous divinity who fights and destroys her enemies. She is also, unlike the Vedic goddesses, viewed as the supreme universal power or Śakti; she is second to none.

The Goddess of the *Devī Purāṇa* clearly exhibits two distinct origins: she is both non-Vedic and Vedic. Her non-Vedic character is evinced by the location of her home in the Vindhya Mountains, an area where the Pulindas, Śavaras, Kirātas, Varvaras, and Kāpālins, aboriginal and immigrant tribes who lived on roots and dressed in bark, made human sacrifices to female deities.[5] It is the fiercesome tribal aspect of the Devī that is central in the *Devī Purāṇa* and that became prevalent in India's classical period. Classical references to her aboriginal origins abound in the lyrical compositions of many famous poets and writers. For example, Kālidāsa in his *Kumārasambhava* and *Raghuvaṁśa* writes of the frightening Saptamātṛkās and Cāmuṇḍa. Bāṇabhaṭṭa in his *Harṣacarita* informs us that as Durgā she is worshiped in a forest temple under the control of a Dravidian hermit and, in his *Kādambarī,* he tells of the goddess of the Śavaras as one who is worshiped with human sacrifice. Daṇḍin in his *Daśakumāracarita* speaks of the Goddess Caṇḍika who is worshiped in a temple where the hunters (Śavaras) sacrifice boys in order to gain sorceric powers. Subandhu writes of the bloodthirsty Kātyāyanī in his *Vāsavadatta Devī.* In the *Kathāsaritsāgara,* Somadeva tells the story of Jīmūtavāhana who was captured by thugs who then took him to a Śavara village in order to sacrifice him to Durgā.

When was the *Devī Purāṇa* written? It is difficult to determine the exact date of the text; but, from the internal evidence, it may be said that the book postdated the early Buddhist period because the text identifies Buddha as one of the ten incarnations of Viṣṇu and refers to the Jainas as a heretical sect. Varāhamihira of sixth century C.E. cited the contents of the *Devī Purāṇa* in his *Bṛhatsaṁhita;* thus, we can postulate that the main body of the text must have been formulated after the sixth century B.C.E. and before the sixth century C.E.

The question is, when did the initial compilation of the materials in the *Devī Purāṇa* begin? In the seventy-third chapter, the *Devī Purāṇa* employs two words, *horā* and *drekkāṇa,* in relation to a discussion on the hours and days. The *Pārāśarā Horā* which was written between the twelfth and tenth centuries B.C.E. discusses the same two words, as does Varāhamihira, centuries later, in the *Bṛhatsaṁhitā.* In addition, the *Devī Purāṇa* refers to various other customs, rites and practices that were neither prevalent in Purāṇic times nor acknowledged in other Purāṇas. In other words, the textual evidence contains antique words and refers to customs that had been abandoned by the time of writing the other Purāṇas. Thus, the evidence suggests that the core of the *Devī Purāṇa* was written before the compilation of the other Purāṇas.

In the first chapter, the *Devī Purāṇa* refers to itself as being "*Vedānta-tattva-sahitā;*"[6] a phrase claiming that the text contains the Vedic truth and the essential meaning of the Vedas. In addition, Vedic influence is obvious in its injunctions, *Nyāsa, mudrā,*[7] *mantra, homa,* and *kuṇḍas.*[8] In particular, the *Padamālā Mantra Vidyā* incantation is referred to as "*Vedasiddhāntakarma Pratipādanī,*" that is, it conforms to the injunctions of Vedic laws and principles.[9] Such characterizations assert attempts at synchronized realizations of the Brahman, the Ultimate Reality, in the form of the Goddess.

Throughout the text and integrated with the Vedic elements are irrefutable Tantric components such as particular rites, customs, oblations, invocations, incantations, utterance of mystic syllables, and applications of sorcery. Some of the rites may have originated in part in the Vedic-Brāhmaṇic tradition. It seems obvious that the *Devī Purāṇa* relied on the Vedas to a certain extent, yet gravitated toward Tantrism as a way to assert power by way of magical ritualistic acts. According to the *Devī Purāṇa,* performance of the *vidyās* bestows magical powers such as the Tantric eight powers *(aṣṭa siddhi)* on the *sādhaka.*[10]

It is possible to postulate a tentative framework for the origination of the text; germination possibly was based on the religious practices of the pre-Vedic aboriginal tribes, both indigenous and immigrant. Devī worship as found in the first three Vedas might have inspired redaction of an early section of the *Devī Purāṇa* sometime in the first few centuries B.C.E. through which the aboriginal material was reinterpreted. Subsequently, various topics from the *Atharva Veda* were integrated into the work; in fact, the *Devī Purāṇa* recognizes the *Atharva Veda* as authoritative and as its guiding source.[11] Various interpolations and additions augmented the text during the next few centuries as Tantrism spread and was sanctioned throughout India. The final redaction of the *Devī Purāṇa,* which by this time was encyclopedic in scope, must have occurred about the time of Varāhamihira's *Bṛhatsaṁhitā* in the sixth century C.E.

The *Devī Purāṇa* speaks of sixty-five types of *vidyā,* the most important being the *Kāmikā, Padamālā, Aparājitā, Mohinī, Mṛtyuñjaya, Puṣpaka, Khaḍga, Māla, Aṅgana,* and *Guṭika.* Any one of these *vidyās,* when successfully performed and practiced, can confer magical powers on the *sādhaka* and bring liberation from earthly bondage. Here, we will focus only on the *Padamālā Mantra Vidyā,* which also is known by various other names in the *Devī Purāṇa* (*Atibhairava Padamālā,*[12] *Bhairava Vidyā,*[13] *Padamālā Mahā Vidyā,*[14] *Padamālā,*[15] *Mantramālā* or *Mantrapada,*[16] *Naravimohine Vidyā* and *Cāmuṇḍa Padamāline Mahā Vidyā*[17]).

Here we are concerned particularly with the *Padamālā Mantra Vidyā,*[18] a magical spell used by Śiva to invoke the Devī so that she might engage in the legendary destruction of the demon Ghora. The text relates that the incantation is Atharvavedic in origin and that it was revealed in ten hundred thousand verses to Viṣṇu by Śiva. It eventually was transmitted to the sage Agastya who narrated the story of its divine origin to King Nṛpavāhana.[19] The *Padamālā Mantra Vidyā* consists of thirty-two *mantras* that are used to invoke the presiding deity Cāmuṇḍā and to obtain the *sādhaka's* goals. Because the exceedingly powerful thirty-two germ-syllables (*bīja mantras*) have been deliberately excluded by the editor, only explanations of the purposes and effects of performing each incantation are provided.[20] They are as follows:

1. By taking the vow (*vrata*) of a hero (*vīra*), while muttering the first *mantra* four hundred thousand times, the *sādhaka* achieves veneration and popularity (*sammato bhavati*).
2. By performing the second *mantra,* the *sādhaka* separates his subtle body from his physical body in order to visit a cremation ground (*śmaṣāna pravesanam*).
3. By obtaining success in the performance of the third *mantra,* the worshiper minimizes the required hours for chanting other *mantras* (*mantrābalambanam*).
4. The fourth *mantra* empowers the *sādhaka* to repel all arms hurled by others (*sarva śastra stambhanam*).
5. By owning the power of the fifth *mantra,* rain can be stopped at will (*vṛṣṭi vāranam*).
6. By achieving success in the performance of the sixth *mantra,* the *sādhaka* develops the power to vanish and reappear at will (*antardhāna karaṇam*).
7. The seventh *mantra* empowers the *sādhaka* to have control over all forms and all bodies of water (*jala sādhanam*).
8. The eighth *mantra* enables the *sādhaka* to free himself from all types of weapons (*śāstramokṣanam*).
9. The ninth *mantra* helps to cut through all obstacles (*sarva vighna nivāranam*).
10. By performing rituals in accordance with the tenth *mantra,* the wor-

shiper can spread epidemic diseases among his or her enemies (*mārī praveśaṇam*).

11. By constant chanting of the eleventh *mantra* during confrontation, an enemy's weapons can be paralyzed (*parasainya stambhanam*).
12. By repeating the twelfth *mantra,* the *sādhaka* persuades the deity to churn (the contents of) a skull for attracting spiritual wine (*kapālamathanam samasta madyākarṣanam*).
13. By chanting the thirteenth *mantra,* it is possible to attract women (*strīyākarṣaṇam*).
14. By repeated utterance of the fourteenth *mantra,* killing someone can be accomplished from a distance (*visarjjanam*).
15. By reciting the fifteenth *mantra,* the power of a sword can be subdued (*khaḍga stambhanam*).
16. By successful chanting of the sixteenth *mantra,* one can achieve magical control over all animals and other beings (*sarvasattva vasikaranam*).
17. By repeating the seventeenth *mantra* properly, the action of other *mantras* can be subdued (*paramantra cchedanam*).
18. By the power achieved from applying the eighteenth *mantra,* a female Tantric companion will become available (*bhairavīkaraṇam*).
19. With the successful repetition of the nineteenth *mantra,* Devī is pleased to grant whatever the aspirant desires (*svayaṁ devyā asādhyam sādhayati*).
20. With the power of the twentieth *mantra,* the evil influence of planets and stars can be repelled (*grahagahasayanam*).
21. The twenty-first *mantra* when muttered successfully attracts spirits (*āvesanam*).
22. The twenty-second *mantra* when chanted properly causes a spirit to be smeared with ash and made to dance (*bhasmanā nṛtyāpayati*).
23. By repeating the twenty-third *mantra,* adverse symptoms of any kind can be driven away (*upasarganivāraṇam*).
24. The twenty-fourth *mantra* endows the Tantric powers of sorcery (*kāpālika sādhanam*).
25. Successful repetition of the twenty-fifth *mantra* agitates all the sense-organs (*ripu kṣobhanam vaśikarañca damarukeña*).
26. The twenty-sixth *mantra,* repeated properly with proper oblation, enables one to make another insane (*unmatta homeṇa unmatti karaṇaṁ*).
27. By chanting the twenty-seventh *mantra,* one causes another to be bitten by a snake (*sarpairdaṁśāpayati*).
28. With the power of the twenty-eighth *mantra,* the aspirant inspires another to dance (*nṛtyāpayati*).
29. By muttering the twenty-ninth *mantra,* the aspirant feeds delicious and sumptuous food to others (*bhuñjayati*).

30. By chanting the thirtieth *mantra* with proper Tantric oblation, one obtains the power to hypnotize women (*mocāpayati*).
31. With the power achieved from the thirty-first *mantra,* the *sādhaka* achieves power to burn down a city (*puradahajananam*).
32. The thirty-second *mantra* bestows power on the *sādhaka* to purge all types of fevers (*sarvajvarāveśakaranam*).

These are the merits of the *Padamālā Mantra Vidyā* provided they are uttered according to the directions specified in the *Devī Purāṇa.* Sitting in the cremation ground, wearing a black garment and a black garland, a *sādhaka* repeats each one of the thirty-two mantras eight thousand times while performing proper oblations and other ritual requirements. As a result, he/she is able to create a unique verbal charm or spell to produce the desired effects.

In addition to the thirty-two specific achievements of the *Pamadamala Mantra Vidyā,* the *Devī Purāṇa* mentions an additional one hundred eight goals attainable through chanting the powerful incantation. For example, the sin of Brahmanicide can be nullified by a single utterance of the incantation and, whether chanting or listening to the *mantras,* one is assured of receiving merit equivalent to a bath in the holy river or equal to the performance of all rituals.[21] In fact, all ailments and harmful situations are remedied by the *Padamālā Mantra Vidyā* when uttered with utmost devotion and according to prescription.

The *Devī Purāṇa* tells us that the *vidyā* is not limited to any particular group of people, but the text cautions that agnostics or those without reverence for the Devī and, most important, those who lack control over the senses should not be given this incantation.[22] The text emphasizes that this *vidyā* is the *Mahāvidyā,* the Supreme Knowledge, the sum and substance of all *mantras* and Tantras; as such it empowers material and spiritual success, that is, *bhukti* and *mukti.* Each part of the *mantra* is uniquely and individually powerful. When parts of the *mantra* are chanted separately, a *sādhaka* is rewarded with a specific earthly goals (*bhukti*); when rendered in full, the *Padamālā Mantra Vidyā* leads to *mukti.* To understand the connection between the individual and combined effects of the *mantra,* it is necessary to recognize that, with completion of each section, the reciter changes internally as well as externally. With each attainment of a material nature, caused by uttering one section of the *Padamālā Mantra Vidyā,* one gains added insight into one's own being and the nature of reality. The unified power of the thirty-two *mantras* surpasses the limited power of the individual *mantra* and liberates the aspirant from all ignorance. The significance of the full *mantra* becomes clearer as one understands the importance of sound within the Tantric paradigm in which the human body is a microcosm of the material universal macrocosm; both are produced by the power of the original sound called *nāda,* which eternally permeates and pulsates throughout the cosmos. The ultimate goal of human life, according to Tantrism, is to internalize the cosmos and unify the inner vibrations with the outer. That is, to be self-realized is to internalize one's own being by traveling back to the original sound; thus, emphasis is placed upon sound and the efficacy of *mantra.* When macrocosm and microcosm become one through repetitions of *mantras* or intensified thought in the form of sound, the adept becomes empowered.

One can better understand the nature and origin of the *Padamālā Mantra Vidyā* by recognizing the resemblance of some of the *mantras* to certain rites and practices addressed in Vedic literature. Two hymns of the *Ṛg Veda* describe a rite that is efficacious in getting rid of a co-wife or controlling a husband.[23] Other references in the *Ṛg Veda* pertain to healing[24] and destruction.[25] Both the *Taittirīya Saṁhitā*[26] and *Taittirīya Brāhmaṇa*[27] refer to practices to win someone's love or favor. Without doubt, the precursors of many later Tantric incantations and spells can be found in the Vrātya Book of *Atharva Veda.*[28] In this chapter, mysterious hymns praise Brahman as the heavenly Vrātya who is none other than the great God (Mahādeva) Rudra (Īśana); the heavenly Vrātya is the macrocosmic counterpart of the microcosmic earthly Vrātyas, who belonged to certain aboriginal tribes. The special cult of the Vrātyas[29] practiced mystical spells, incantations, prayers, sorcery, and necromantic practices.[30] Possibly in the eighth century B.C.E., the Atharvavedic Aṅgirasa were involved in practices that in a later time would be called Tantric. In the fifth century B.C.E., the Buddha encountered Atharvavedic Brahmins engrossed in spells, charms, and rituals; he called them Atharvanikas because of their preoccupation with sorcery.[31] By the time of Emperor Aśoka, cross-cultural relationships and contacts had greatly expanded and the Atharvavedic cult was enriched by the further contributions from the Vrātyas and indigenous tribes and influences from immigrant Huṇās, Pāṣaṇḍins and others.

While we need to exercise caution in postulating direct influences, there are similarities among the specified functions of *Padamālā Mantra Vidyā* and certain Vedic *mantras.* However, the *Devī Purāṇa* specifies that the *Padamālā Mantra Vidyā* is "*Atharvavedokta,*"[32] meaning that it conforms to injunctions in the *Atharva Veda* or enables one to perform a significant number of rituals prescribed in the text.[33] Many of the *mantras* of the *Padamālā Mantra Vidyā* closely resemble passages from the *Atharva Veda Saṁhitā.* Specific correspondences are as follows:

Padamālā Mantra Vidyā	*Atharva Veda*
Verse 2	V, 20–21
4	III, 1–6
11	III, 1–6; V, 20, 21
14	III, 25
20	VII, 4
32	VI, 9; XXIX, 5

While certain passages from the *Atharva Veda* may have inspired some sections of the *Padamālā Mantra Vidyā,* there can be no doubt that the *mantras* are credited with the type of inordinate potency that is attributable only to Tantrism. The *Devī Purāṇa* asserts that the *Padamālā Mantra Vidyā* is a *mahāvidyā* that guarantees success in all actions. Its power is singular because it contains the essence of all the texts and scriptures disclosed by Śiva in the *mūlatantra* (root of Tantra).[34] It seems likely that many of the thirty-two separate *mantras* of the *Padamālā Mantra Vidyā* have been influenced by Vedic texts and *mantras,* particularly the *Atharva Veda;* but, as noted above, the *Padamālā Mantra Vidyā* also contains non-Vedic elements.

Two words used in the *Padamālā Mantra Vidyā* paticularly clarify the connection between Tantric *mantras* and rituals as well as illuminate the antiquity of some Tantric practices; they are *kapalāmathana* and *madyākarṣaṇa. Kapālamathana* is a compound of two words *kapāla* (skull) and *mathana* (churning). The *kapāla* or skull cup is an essential implement for Tantric ritual. An explanation of its importance is provided in the fifth *skandha* of the *Devī Bhagavata Purāṇa* wherein Śiva, having become angry with Brahmā for telling a lie, cuts off his head. Part of his penance for the sin of Brahmānicide required that Śiva use Brahmā's skull *(kapala)* for alms. Reenacting the myth, the Kāpālikas and the followers of Vāmācāra Śākta Tantra schools use a skull cup for alms. The same myth also informs us that Śiva is the origin of the Tantrism.[35] Later Kāpālikas and Vāmācāras practiced sitting in a cremation ground and using wine-filled skulls for oblations. Drinking the spiritual wine (*kāraṇa-vāri*), it was believed, destroyed earthly bondage (*māyā*) and the eight hindrances (*aṣṭapāśa*) to liberation. The historical Buddha noted Atharvavedic Brahmins who where engrossed in rituals utilizing skulls (*cavasisa manta*)[36] and, particularly, those who predicted the future by tapping on skulls (*kapāla kotani*).[37] He specifically referred to a contemporary Atharvavedic Brahmin, a possible native of Bengal named Vaṅgisa, who was adept at skull tapping.[38] Such references leave little doubt that the ritual use of skulls was known in both the *Atharva Veda* and in the Tantric tradition. The skull-tapping ritual was a practice particularly prevalent in Bengal and upper Assam, the region where most of the Vāmācāra texts have been found.

The word *madyākarṣaṇa* is the compound of *madya* (wine) and *ākarṣaṇa* (to attract). These two compound words explain the ritual acts that correspond to the twelfth incantation. In order to receive the Devī's blessing, the aspirant must offer her a skull filled with wine. Churning the wine in the skull combined with repeated utterance transforms the ordinary physical wine into spiritual liquor, an oblation suitable for the Devī. Like the nectar of the gods, this spiritual liquor becomes a source of immortality for the *sādhaka.* After offering the wine to the Goddess, the aspirant drinks it, and thereby is able to transcend the *tamasic* to the *sattvic* state and remain in an eternally blissful condition.[39] The *Kulārnava Tantra* informs us that this ritual awakens the serpent power (*kulakuṇḍalinī*) that remains dormant in the pelvic center (*mūlādhāra cakra*).[40] The awakened power rises up the spinal cord, piercing the remaining *cakras* of the spinal cord including the final *brahmarandhra cakra* that is controlled by the pineal gland (*candra granthi*). Once the serpent power reaches this *cakra,* a secretion called *amṛta* (nectar) is released. The nectar then flows from the brain to the aspirant's tongue and, once imbibed, the *sādhaka* is absorbed in ecstasy (*ānandasudhāpānarato naraḥ*).

The wine in the skull cup has a vital role in Tantric ritual because it helps stimulate the experience of *Kuṇḍalinī.* Once important in early Vedic ritual, the use of wine was abandoned at a later time and, thus, was absent from all Hindu ritual with the exception of the Vāmācāra Śākta practices. For the Vāmācāra Śāktas, wine was one of the five necessary ritual ingredients (*pañcatattva* or *pañcamakāra*). In Tantra, *madya* is a *mahādāna* or a great gift that generates the state of Śiva, the equivalent of *mokṣa. Madya* symbolically removes *aṣṭapāśa,* the eight afflictions of bondage, and opens the path to liberation. By imbibing ritual wine, one symbolically consumes the entire universe, an expression not to be taken literally, but one that is a metaphor for becoming so spiritually extended that the entire universe can be contained within the self.[41] Also, *madya* is described symbolically as the nectar essence of the union of Śiva-Śakti flowing into the highest cerebral region.[42]

In each of the thirty-two different *mantras* of the *Padamālā Mantra Vidyā,* Devī is addressed by a different name.[43] Each indicates the way in which she is perceived by her devotees when performing the concomitant rituals. The names refer to Devī's appearance and identities when she destroys the demons. Altogether the thirty-two names portray the presiding deity Cāmuṇḍa as she embodies the essence of *Padamālā Mantra Vidyā* or vice versa. These thirty-two names respectively are the following:

1. In the first *mantra,* Devī is addressed as Bhagavatī Cāmuṇḍa, meaning the goddess who slaughtered the demons Caṇḍa and Muṇḍa.
2. In the second *mantra,* Devī is called Śmaśanavāsinī, a name that refers to someone who resides in a cremation ground.
3. In the third *mantra,* Devī is invoked as Khaṭvāṇgakapālahaste, a deity who holds a rib bone and a human head.
4. The epithet of the fourth *mantra* is Mahāpreta Samāruḍhe or one who is mounted on ghosts or great spirits.
5. In the fifth *mantra,* Devī is addressed as Mahāvimānamālākule, one who is well decorated with garlands and is seated on a form of flying transportation.
6. In the sixth *mantra,* Devī is called Kālarātri, referring to an entity who is like the darkest night.
7. In the seventh *mantra,* she is Bahugaṇaparivṛte or someone surrounded by innumerable attendants.
8. In the eighth *mantra,* Devī is hailed as Mahāsukhe Bahubhuje, meaning many-handed blissful goddess.
9. In the ninth *mantra,* Devī is addressed as Ghanta Damaru Kiṇkininādaśabda Bahule; in this guise, she is adorned with a bell, a percussion

instrument covered with skin, and ornaments producing rhythmic sounds.

10. In the tenth *mantra,* Devī is called Aṭṭattahāse or someone who roars with frightening laughter.
11. In the eleventh *mantra,* Devī is visualized as Ca Kāranetre, one who has squinting eyes.
12. In the twelfth *mantra,* Devī is called Lalanājihve, referring to her lolling tongue.
13. In the thirteenth *mantra,* Devī is invoked as Bhrukuṭimukhi referring to the pronounced frown on her face.
14. In the fourteenth *mantra,* Devī's name is Huṁkārabhayatrāsinī, someone who scares others with her bellowing voice.
15. In the fifteenth *mantra,* Devī is Sphurita Vidyūtsamaprabhe or a deity as beautiful as streaked lightning.
16. In the sixteenth *mantra,* Devī is Kapāla Mālā Veṣṭita Jaṭamukuṭa Śaśāṅkadhārinī, one holding a moon in her matted crest and adorned with a wreath of skulls.
17. In the seventeenth *mantra,* Devī is venerated as Aṭṭahāse, a term reminding the devotee of her roaring laughter.
18. In the eighteenth *mantra,* Devī is called Bibho, a reference to the all-pervading Cāmuṇḍā.
19. In the nineteenth *mantra,* Devī is recognized as Vicce; here she is black, fierce, infallible, and a giver of blessings.
20. In the twentieth *mantra,* Devī is addressed as Huṁ Huṁ; in this embodiment, she mutters *huṁ* as a *bīja mantra* and bestows the four aims (*puruṣārtha*) of life.
21. In the twenty-first mantra, Devī is Daṁstrā Ghorāndhakārinī, meaning one with dreadful teeth and creatrix of a dark abyss.
22. In the twenty-second *mantra,* Devī is addressed as Sarvabighna Vināśinī in order to convey her power to destroy all obstacles.
23. In the twenty-third *mantra,* Devī is Urdhakeśī, a term that refers to her spiked hair.
24. In the twenty-fourth *mantra,* Devī is called Ulukavadane, one with a frightening owl-like face.
25. In the twenty-fifth *mantra,* Devī is addressed as Karaṁgamālādhārinī; it describes her as holding a garland of water pots (*kamaṇḍalu*).
26. In the twenty-sixth *mantra,* Devī is invoked as Vikṛtarūpinī, the goddess with a hideous face.
27. In the twenty-seventh *mantra,* Devī is addressed as Kṛśnabujaṅga Veṣṭitaśarīre or one whose body is encircled with a black snake.
28. In the twenty-eighth *mantra,* she is Pralamvaṣṭhi, the one with pendulous lips.

29. In the twenty-ninth *mantra,* Devī is addressed as Bhagna Nāsike, one who has a broken nose.
30. In the thirtieth *mantra,* Devī is invoked as Cipiṭāmukhe; the names refers to someone who has a sunken face.
31. In the thirty-first *mantra,* Devī is addressed as Kapilajaṭe Jvālāmukhī, a deity with tawny complexion and matted hair.
32. In the thirty-second *mantra,* Devī is addressed as Rakṭākṣi Pūrṇamayā or one who has blood shot eyes.

Whether used separately or together, these thirty-two epithets depict a fierce and abhorrent vision of the goddess, she who is the presiding deity of the *Padamālā Mantra Vidyā.* According to the description of her physical features, she is as beautiful as lightning (and possibly as swift and unpredictable) and, at the same time, hideous and frightening like an owl with a sunken face, a profile suitable to her wrathful countenance on the battlefield. Her complexion is tawny or black; she has squinting bloodshot eyes, a broken nose, pendulous lips, a lolling restless tongue, and dreadful teeth, features attributable to the goddess Cāmuṇḍa. The shining sharp teeth are indicative of her aggressive and dangerous nature. Her hair is either matted or spiked and is decorated with a crescent moon, an attribute that connects her with Śiva. Her adornments enhance her violent image, that is, a garland of skulls and a snake. Her methods of transportation are appropriate for her fearsome role: she is mounted on ghosts and moves about on some sort of flying conveyance. Her violent nature is characterized by a bellowing voice and roaring laughter. She is prepared for the ultimate battle against demons and thus is arrayed with a full range of frightful characteristics. War is horrifying and her appearance merely mirrors the situation; it is meant to instill fear in her opponent. Suitably paralyzed from horror, her opponent loses the battle.With the *huṁ* of the *bīja mantra,* she energizes herself for war. Normally beautiful when she grants boons to adepts, the exigencies of war require that she takes on an abhorrent appearance.

Three of Devī's names given in the *Padamālā Mantra Vidyā* are particularly evocative, that is, Kālarātri, Khaṭvāṅga, and Kapālahaste. In the sixth incantation, she is Kālarātri, an epithet used to indicate her awful appearance and terrifying disposition. The first part of the word, *kāla,* is a masculine noun denoting time. Time, as perceived by Vedic seers, is where everything takes place; in fact, it is the framework in which all of creation unfolds. Vedic seers conceived of *kāla* as being a powerful deity; the deified Kāla was the creator and sustainer of the universe.[44] Everything that is created and preserved also must be destroyed by and in time; thus the Vedic image of Kāla as the devourer of all things is significant and was syncretized with Rudra, the Vedic god of destruction.[45] Ultimately Kāla became Mahākāla and Rudra became Śiva and the two were fused in the Purāṇic and Tantra literature.[46] According to the *Mahānirvāṇa Tantra,* during the dissolution of the universe, Kāla or Mahākāla devours the entire universe, but the supreme goddess who is the spouse of Mahākāla or Śiva even engulfs Kāla and hence is known as Kālī.

In the *Devī Māhātmyam,*[47] Kālī is called Cāmuṇḍa, the goddess of the *Padamālā Mantra Vidyā,* the terrifying deity associated with the ultimate dissolution and destruction of the demon Ghora. The word is a feminine noun referring to the darkness after sunset. According to the *Rātrisūkta* of the *Ṛg Veda,*[48] the sage Kuśika while absorbed in meditation realized the enveloping power of darkness and invoked Rātri as the all-powerful goddess. Thus, the darkness after sunset was deified and was invoked by sages to deliver mortals from all fears and earthly bondage. Later she was identified with various goddesses; in the *Atharva Veda,* Rātridevī is called Śiva or Durgā, the consort of Śiva.[49] In the *Bṛhad Devatā,* Vāgdevī was identified with Sarasvatī;[50] but, elsewhere the name Rātri identified Sarasvatī, goddess of knowledge and wisdom who delivers the ignorant from bondage.[51] In the Purāṇas, Kālarātri signifies Raudrī, the goddess who kills the demon Ruru and Kālī-Cāmuṇḍa who kills the demons Caṇḍa and Muṇḍa.[52] Rātrī, then, was the agent of destruction and eliminator of oppressive forces and ignorance.

Addressing the Devī as Kālarātri in the *Padamālā Mantra Vidyā* serves two purposes: (1) to invoke the appropriate deity for the task at hand; and (2) to empower the *sādhaka* with the devouring quality of Kāla and the all-consuming quality of Rātri. Thus, the presiding deity of the *mantra* will eliminate all obstacles and grant success to the devotee. In addition, the word *kālarātri* in Tantra refers to the darkness of night, a state normally frightening to ordinary individuals but beneficial to worshipers of the Supreme Goddess. Here the word *Kālarātri* does not refer to the entire night but rather to different hours of darkness. Each time of night, according to Tantric tradition, is under the sway of a particular terrifying goddess who grants a particular desire to the aspirant.[53] When Kālarātri is invoked in the sixth *mantra* of the *Padamālā* ritual, the *sādhaka* seeks the power to vanish and reappear at will, an ability that removes one of the eight afflictions called *aṣṭapāśa* in Tantra.

Similarly, Devī's names in the third *mantra* of the *Padamālā Mantra Vidyā,* Khaṭvāṅga and Kapālahaste, grant the power to cut through the spells inflicted by others. The ramifications of these two names can be understood in light of a myth narrated in the *Ramāyāṇa* in which Devī appeared as Rakteśvarī, a wrathful form of the Supreme Goddess, to destroy the demon Vīrasena in response to the prayers of King Dilipa (also called Khaṭvāṅga). Having killed the demon, Devī drank his blood from his severed head.[54] While the word *khaṭvāṅga* ordinarily refers to the leg of a bed, in Hindu myth it also signifies a skull attached to a rib bone; as such it is a menacing, deadly weapon. In a story from the *Ramāyāṇa,* it was used as an alternate name for King Dilipa and possibly it referred to one of his accoutrements of war. The *Vāmaṇa Purāṇa* relates that Kālī, dressed in a tiger skin and adorned with a garland of human skulls, holds a *khatvāṅga.*[55] The *khatvāṅga* appears in myths in which Kālī is called upon to save humans from a peril that only she can eliminate.

Likewise, Kapālahaste, the third name of interest here, refers to one who holds a *kapāla* or skull. In this invocation, Cāmuṇḍa is identified with the deity Rakteśvarī of the *Ramāyāṇa.* In the *Devī Purāṇa,* Śiva intones the *Padamālā Mantra Vidyā* so that the Goddess will come forth to destroy the virtually invulnerable demon Ghora. Addressing her as Kapālahaste and Khaṭvāṅga, he calls forth her deadliest form. Ontologically the *sādhaka,* by ritually uttering the two names, also evokes Devī's most powerful aspect, that which obliterates obstacles to the attainment of *bhukti* and *mukti.*

According to the *Devī Purāṇa,* mere recitation of the *mantras* is ineffectual without performing the proper ritual (*siddhisādhana*) with its regulations and restrictions (*bidhi*), repeated muttering (*japa*), loud chanting (*kīrtana*), and silent utterance of the mystical germ-syllables (*bīja mantra*). The thirty-two *mantras* are performed along with special invocations and concentration on the particular deity at a specified time and at a particular location. Specifically, Devī worship must occur on the fourth (*caturthī*), fifth (*pañcamī*), eighth (*aṣṭamī*), ninth (*navamī*), eleventh (*ekādaśī*) days of the full moon and full moon days. Rituals performed on the eighth, (called Mahāṣṭamī) and the ninth (called Mahānavamī) days of the full moon are particularly efficacious. Their designation as *mahā,* meaning great, indicates their status as the holiest times for worship. In addition and as prescribed by the *Devī Purāṇa,* the Goddess is worshiped on the first day (*pratipada tithi*) of the month of Āśvina (sixth month of the Hindu calendar) for nine days, in the month of Caitra (March 14 to April 13) and, on the ninth day of the lunar fortnight, various animals are sacrificed and devotees offer their own blood for attainment of specific goals. Sacrifices of flesh and blood also should be made on the ninth day of lunar fortnight of Jyaiṣṭha (16 May to15 June). Devī Cāmuṇḍa is not worshiped at the home altar or even in a temple; rather worship is performed in a cemetery or a cremation ground. As is typical in Tantrism, the ritual performance of the *Padamālā Mantra Vidyā* exhibits a distinct structure that can be grouped into the following categories: (1) the prerequisites, (2) the preparation, (3) the procedure, and (4) the performance. The very specific and controlled ritual is as dynamic as it is complex; its delineation in the *Devī Purāṇa* offers unique insight into the heart of the Tantric tradition.

Proper initiation (*dīkṣā*) by a competent *guru* is the primary and inviolable requirement for performance of the *Padamālā Mantra Vidyā;* its success, in fact, is contingent on an initiation. Tantric scriptures designate that a *śiṣya* (aspirant), before performing rituals, must undergo initiation. Śākta teachings, in particular, are transmitted directly from *guru* to disciple because secret knowledge may be heard, deciphered, and retained only by the competent and dedicated.

According to Śākta tradition, no ritual can be performed without the *bīja mantra.* Because *bīja mantras* are never written or disclosed in public, they can only be learned directly from a *guru.* Conforming to this tradition, no edition of the *Devī Purāṇa* provides the *bīja mantras* for any one of the sixty-five *vidyās* discussed in the text. Such potent secret information can be revealed only to one who has been properly prepared. The *Rudrayāmala* clarifies the significance of initiation; in a conversation between Śiva and the Goddess, Śiva explains that an uninitiated aspirant neither achieves success (*siddhi*) in Tantra performances nor liberation.[56] The *Devī Purāṇa* asserts that, without proper *dīkṣā*, all efforts are futile and, unless both the *guru* and *initiate* are competent, all *mantras* are fruitless.[57] Furthermore, both the *guru* and *śiṣya* are cautioned about their mutual selection of each other. The *guru* must have full mastery, that is, have the ability to advise on various types of *vidyās*, a judicious temperament, and most important, the capacity to remove the disciple's doubts. The *Kulārṇava Tantra* adds that a competent *guru* is one who is actively involved in the unbroken tradition of Tantra, that is, that which originated with Śiva and has been handed down from generation to generation; it also affirms that a competent *guru* is well versed in the *mantras* and is one who guards the traditional doctrine.[58] Because the *guru* is successor to the divinely originated knowledge, the disciple regards the *guru* not as an ordinary human, but as a deity. If the *guru* is a male, he is worshiped as Śiva; if female, she is adored as Śakti. As one who confers divine knowledge, the *guru* restrains or removes the darkness of bondage from the devotee; thus, the deeper significance of a *guru* does not refer merely to the ability to teach, direct, and guide, but also to the capacity to cause the disciple to internalize his/her identity, purpose, and meaning of life. Thus, a person with the power to remove another's bondage is no ordinary human.

As to the initiate (*śiṣya*) of the *Padamālā Mantra Vidyā*, the *Devī Purāṇa* asserts that there are no gender or caste specifications; the knowledge is accessible to anyone who adores the goddess, but success depends on the student's preparation through initiation. A disciple must rely solely on the *guru* and be prepared to surrender everything to the *guru*.

In Tantric *dīkṣās*, the *guru* confers divine knowledge and, as a consequence, destroys the initiate's ignorance or sin. The purpose of the *dīkṣā* then relates to the two roots *da* (to give) and *kṣa* (to destroy). Tantric initiation, regardless of the sect, is a complicated procedure. Some aspects of Tantric initiations appear to be greatly elaborated versions of tribal initiation rites that still prevail in parts of India. Such rites traditionally were a rite of passage and a symbolic rebirth wherein an experienced elder led the young into adulthood. The lack of caste and gender requirements for Tantric initiation is distinct from Vedic initiation, which is limited to the first three castes; such liberalism may underscore the Tantric connection to tribal practices.

A second prerequisite for participation in the *Padamālā Mantra Vidyā* ritual is internal and external preparation. Internal preparation begins with specific mental and physical practices (*aparihārya prārambhik*) involving cleansing the mind of negative impulses and inclinations of a debasing nature. The *Devī Purāṇa* specifications are typically Tantric in that the *sādhaka* must prepare mentally (*bhāva*) in order to grasp the significance of Tantric regulations (*vidhe*), perform ritualistic practices and strenuous physical exercises and utter germ-syllables (*bīja mantra*).[59] External preparation involves living on alms (*bhikṣānna bhōjana*), following specific religious rules and taboos in relation to food habits, behavior, time and space (*puraścaraṇa*). Also the *Devī Purāṇa* specifies that preparation for the *Padamālā Mantra Vidyā* requires the *śiṣya* to make a vow called *vīravrata* (literally hero's vow). Ordinarily the word *vīra* refers to someone who is courageous, but within the context of Tantrism, the term indicates a being who through discipline and mental preparation (*bhāva*) has evolved beyond the afflicted state of ordinary humans (*paśu*). Only by following strictly prescribed procedures including control of the senses, cleansing the self of negative inclinations, meditation, penance, and following the ways of justice and truth can a person transcend the *paśu* state to become a *vīra.* Having taken the vow, the seeker then becomes a *vīra sādhaka.* The term *vīra* is derived from *vī* (freedom from) and *ra* (passion or desire).[60] While in the state of *vīra,* the seeker must be devoid of desires, ignorance, and worldly activities; perform the required Tantric rites; and conform to the scriptural injunctions.[61] The *vīra* state is one that requires great moral effort and the courage to confront endangering situations and steadfast pursuit of spiritual success (*siddhi*). One of the most grueling of the Vāmācāra Śākta practices performed by the *vīra sādhaka* is the *nilasadhana.* On a special night, the *sādhaka* must sit on a corpse in a deserted location such as a cremation ground, riverbank, or pond and offer an oblation of consecrated flesh (*mahāmāṁsa*) to the fire deity. Through successful completion of the rite, he transcends to the highest state wherein he/she is united with the deity.

According to the *Devī Purāṇa,* the *sādhaka* must perform the *Padamālā Mantra Vidyā* only when wearing black clothing (*kṛṣṇa vastra*) and a black garland, a string of black beads for chanting *mantras.* He/she also must be anointed with a special black paste *(kṛṣṇa anulepanan)* on the forehead and body. The black paste made from the residual ash of sacrificial alters and clarified butter. Special types of honey and black sesame are to be used for the oblations. At the end of the ritual, the *sādhaka* eats the consecrated meat that has been offered to the *Devī.* Ingredients used in the performance of the *Padamālā Mantra Vidyā* are those typical of Vāmācāra Śākta Tantric rituals. In particular, two types of specially prepared honey are required. Preparation begins with extracting the juice directly from various flowers and canes; the juices are fermented, mixed together, and kept in sealed containers for an extended period of fermentation. Honey thus prepared is carefully combined in three specific ways and is categorized as spiritual liquor (*kāraṇavāri*) which has *sattvic, rajasic,* and *tamasic* natures.

Another of the requirements for performing the *Padamālā Mantra Vidyā* is the offering of consecrated flesh or *mahāmāṁsa.* The sacrifice is prepared from eight types of meat sacred to the goddess—human, cow, ram, horse, buffalo, boar, goat, and deer. After offering the *mahāmāṃsa* to the goddess, the *sādhaka* is required to eat it. Vedic texts mention sages who, in their ritualistic performances, used certain animal meats for oblations and afterward ate the meat as a blessing from the divine.[62] But it is only the Vāmācāra Śākta rituals that require offering *mahāmāṃsa* to the deity. In Tantrism, the spiritual liquor represents Śakti, the Goddess as energy, and the meat represents Śiva. When taken together, radiant bliss and *mokṣa* are realized by the *sādhaka* while in a living state.[63]

The actual performance of the *Padamālā Mantra Vidyā* ritual consists of three parts—ritual offerings, physical actions or movements, and vocal aspects. Various oblations include offerings of the *mahāmāṃsa,* black sesame seeds (*kauṇḍāgni homa*), spiritual water (*kāraṇavāri tarpaṇa*), clarified butter, and the three special types of honey (*trimadhu tarpaṇa*). The physical actions are comprised of visualization of the presiding deities on different parts of the body (*nyāsa*), drawing special diagrams on a birch leaf (*yantra maṇḍala* on *bhurja patra*), carrying a talisman that includes the deity's name or a particular *mantra* (*kavaca*), practicing hand or finger gestures needed for spiritual attainment (*mudrā*), and practicing breathing exercises (*prāṇāyāma*). Simultaneously, the *sādhaka* must fulfill the vocal requirements of the ritual, that is, chant spells (*mantroccārana*), utter germ syllables (*japa*) and repeat the thirty-two *mantras* eight thousand times in fulfillment of what is known as the *puraścaraṇa.*

The *puraścaraṇa* primarily refers to the repetition of *mantras.* Although in Hinduism there are various types of *puraścaraṇa,* in Tantric *sādhana* it is the foremost act. The success of the *Padamālā Mantra Vidhya* rests on the specific number of repetitions of the *mantras;* particularly efficacious, repetition ensures the likelihood of attaining the goal. Although normally *mantras* are repeated to propitiate a deity, in this ritualistic context, the repetitions call forth the appropriate aspect of the deity. The five stages of *puraścaraṇa* are: (1) muttering the *japa* germ syllables and repeating *mantras;* (2) *homa* (oblations to the ceremonial fire); (3) *tarpaṇa* (offering spiritual water or liquor to the deity); (4) *abhiṣeka* (ablution and consecration of the deity; (5) *virprabhojana* giving Brahmins the food offered to the deity. In addition, there are elaborate rules and restrictions for performing the *puraścaraṇa.* In general, twelve injunctions (*dvādasaite dharmaḥ*) are followed to achieve success in muttering *mantras* (*mantrasiddhidan*).[64] Thus not only is the *sādhaka* required to chant the thirty-two mantras of the *Padamālā Mantra Vidyā,* but he must do so according to the *puraścaraṇa* requirements as well.

The *Devī Purāṇa,* while not considered a full-fledged Purāṇa, is, nonetheless, a work of great authority on the worship of Devī. Steeped in Tantric lore, rich in incantations and ceremonial hymns, and filled with ritual prescriptions, the text is invaluable. Certainly the work provides fertile ground for the study of the origins of Tantrism in general and more specifically the origins of Śākta Tantrism. Many of the features of its myths and rituals harken back to an antiquity rooted in non-Vedic aboriginal rites, as well as the Vedas, notably the *Atharva Veda.* We may deduce from various sources that worship of goddesses as described in the first three Vedas inspired the initial compilers of the *Devī Purāṇa* to compose the nuclear portion in the early centuries B.C.E.; and toward the end of the first century B.C.E., elaboration and interpolations on the *Atharva Veda* augmented the original core. When Tantrism emerged as a distinct religious path in the late Epic period, the *Devī Purāṇa* was expanded and became the authoritative Purāṇa concerning worship of the Goddess in her most dreadful Tantric manifestation. The completed encyclopedic work, replete with intricate Tantric rituals must have been completed about the time of Varāhamihira (sixth century C.E.) or soon thereafter. Central to its Tantric character is the *Devī Purāṇa's* inclusion of the sixty-four types of *vidyās,* the most powerful of which is the *Padamālā Mantra Vidyā.* It is the *master ritual* for the attainment of the highest spiritual goals and one that demands the utmost seriousness and dedication from its performers.

NOTES

1. Five different manuscripts of the *Devī Purāṇa* are known; three of these manuscripts are written in Devanagiri and two in Bengali script. There are serious discrepancies among the five versions The *Devī Purāṇa* at our disposal has only the second of four original chapters (*pādas*). In addition to the three missing *pādas,* the *bīja mantras* or the germ syllables, the most significant part of the *mantras* are missing from the text. The editors of the published versions caution that the *bīja mantras* have not been included because they can be uttered only by informed practitioners. Two publisheded editions of the *Devī Purāṇa* are *The Devī Purāṇa,* rev. ed., ed. Ācārya Pancanan Tarkaratna (Calcutta: Nava Bharat Publishers, 1975); and ed. Puspendra Kumar Sharmā (New Delhi: Shri Lal Bahadura Shastri Kendriya Sanskrita Vidyāpeetham, 1976).

2. R. C. Hazra, *Studies in the Upapurāṇas* 2 (Calcutta: Sanskrit College Research Series, 1963), 2:71.

3. Ibid., "Influences of Tantra on the Tattvas of Raghunandan," *Indian Historical Quarterly* 9 (1933): 678–704.

4. Cf. The *Bṛhatnāva yadiya Purāṇa,* ed. Hrishikesh Shastri (Calcutta: Bibliotheca India, 1891); the *Kālikā Purāṇa,* 2nd rev. ed., ed. Pañchanan Tarkaratna (Calcutta: Nava Bharat Publishers, 1977), chs. 59–60; and *Devī Purāṇa,* chapter 21, 22, 23, and 60.

5. *Mahābhārata.* IV:6 (Virāṭa-parvan) and VI:23 (Bhīṣma-parvan); See *The Mahābhārata,* trans. J. A. B. van Buitenen (Chicago: The University of Chicago Press, 1973, 1975, 1979).

6. Sharmā, ed., *Devī P.* 1:55.

7. Ibid., 7:65–66 and 88.

8. Ibid., 1:55; 7:22; and 8:6.

9. Ibid., 9:62–64.

10. Ibid, 39:27–39.

11. "*Devīpurāna Atharvadipananim,*" ibid., 9:64.

12. *Devī,* p. 9:49.

13. Ibid., 9:50.

14. Ibid., 9:52

15. Ibid., 9:53

16. Ibid., 9:66.

17. Ibid., 9:70.

18. Ibid., chapter 9.

19. Ibid., 2:14–24.

20. Ibid., 9:67–68.

21. Ibid., 9:73.

22. Ibid., 9:74.

23. *Ṛg Veda* (hereafter *RV,* ed. Bijon Bihari Goswami (Calcutta: Haraf Prakasani, 1987), 10:145 and 159; Cf. Maurice Winternitz, *History of Indian Literature,* 2 vols. (Calcutta: University of Calcutta, 1962), 1:156.

24. *RV* 10:162.

25. *RV* 1:191; 6:52; 7:50, 104.

26. *Taittirīya Saṁhitā,* 2.3.10; see *The Veda of the Black Yajus School, Taittirīya Saṅhitā,* Harvard Oriental Series, ed. Arthur Berriedale Keith (Cambridge, Mass.: Harvard University Press, 1914).

27. *Taittirīya Brāhmāna,* ibid., vol. 18 2.3.1.

28. *Atharva Veda,* ed. Bijon Bihari Goswami (Calcutta: Haraf Prakāśanī, 1988).

29. Hazra, *Upapurāṇas,* 2:65–67.

30. M. Winternitz, *A Concise Dictionary of Eastern Religion* (Oxford: The Clarendon Press, 1919), 137.

31. *Jātaka,* 7 vols., V. Fausbol (London: 1877–1897), 2:21, 33, 217 and 4: 436.

32. *Devī P.* 9:62–64.

33. Ibid., 9:69.

34. Ibid., 9:65.

35. G.Tucci claims greater antiquity for the Tantras than that of the Kāpālikas, *Journal of the Asiatic Society of Bengal,* 26 n.s. (Calcutta:1930):128ff. Cf. ". . . genuine Tantras can be proved to have existed before the seventh. century A.D. and the "Kāpālikas . . . " Similarly, Winternitz assessed "that some of the elements of Tantrism are already found in earlier works;" see *History,* 2:599.

36. *Vinaya Piṭaka,* ed. Herman Oldenberg (London: 1879–1883), 2:15

37. *Mūla Sarvāstivāda Vinaya,* ed. Nalinaksa Dutta (Calcutta: 1942–1950), 2:80.

38. *Theragāthā Commentary of Buddhaghoṣa* (Srilanka: Simon Hewavitarne Bequest Publication, n.d.), 2:192.

39. *Kaulmārga Rahasyam,* Bangiya Sahitya Parisat Series 76, ed. Satish Candra Vidyābhusana (Calcutta: Bangiya Sahitya Parisat Publishers, n.d.), 32.

40. *Kulārṇava Tantra,* ed. Sir John Woodroffe and M. P. Pandit (Delhi: Motilal Banarsidass, 1984r), 5:107–108.

41. Ibid., 5:125.

42. Ibid., 5:31, 32, 39, 108, 109, etc.

43. Devī P. 9:70.

44. *AV, Kāla Sūkta,* 19:53:6–9.

45. *Pāśupata Sūtras,* Trivandrum Sanskrit Series 143 (Trivandrum: University of Travancore, 940), verse 2:3.

46. *Karpūrādi Stotra* (*Hymns to Kālī*), Tantrik Texts 9 (Calcutta: n.d.), 2.

47. *Devī Mahatmyam,*, ch. 5.

48. *RV* X:127:1–8.

49. *AV* XIX: 4, 5, 3

50. *Bṛhad-devatā,* Harvard Oriental Series 5, 6, ed. Arthur Avalon (Cambridge, Mass: 1904), 2:74–77.

51. *Sarasvatī,* ed. Amulyacaran Vidyābhūṣaṇa (Calcutta:1933), I:61.

52. *Varāha Purāṇa* (Mathura: Gita Press, n.d.), chapters 90–96.

53. Various Tantric and Purāṇic texts enumerate the list of *kālarātris* during which one of the Dasamahāvidyā (Ten manifestations of the Supreme Goddess) presides.

54. *Ramāyāṇa,* ed. J. M. Mehta and others (Baroda: Oriental Institute, 1960), *Yuddha Kaṇḍa.*

55. *Vāmana Purāṇa,* ed. Anand Swarup Gupta (Benares: All-India Kashiraj Trust, 1968), chapter 2; *Srimad Devībhāgavatam, skandha* 5; Pranab Bandyapadhyaya, *Mother Goddess Kālī* (Calcutta: KLM Pvt. Ltd., 1993), 69.

56. *Rudrayāmala,* ed. Jīvānanda Vidyāsāgar (Calcutta: 1892), *Uttara Taranga,* 3rd *patala.*

57. *Devī P.* chapter 125.

58. *Kulārṇava Tantra* 13:38–112.

59. *Kaulāvalīnirnaya of Jñānasiddhi,* Tantric Text Series 14, ed. Arthur Avalon (Calcutta: n.d.), 4:4–7.

60. *Kulārṇava Tantra* 17:25.

61. *Parāsurāma Kalpa Sūtra,* Gaekwad Oriental Series 22, pt. 1 (Baroda: n.d.), 5:22.

62. *Aśvalāyana Gṛhya Sūtram,* ed. Kunhanraja (Calcutta: Adyar Library Publication, 1937), 2:24; cf. *Gobhila Grhya Sutram,* pt. 1, ed. Candrakanta Tarkalamkara (Calcutta: 1908), 3:10:15–34.

63. *Rudrayāmala, Uttara Taranga* 26.

64. *Gautamīya Tantra,* Rashik Mohan Chattopadhyaya (Calcutta: Chattopadhyaya Publisher, 1888), chapter 14.

CONTRIBUTORS

Douglas Renfrew Brooks, University of Rochester, New York.

- *The Secret of the Three Cities: An Introduction to Hindu Śākta Tantrism* (Chicago: University of Chicago Press, 1990).
- *Auspicious Wisdom, The Texts and Traditions of Śrīvidya Śākta Tantrism in South India* (Albany: State University of New York Press, 1992).

Robert L. Brown, University of California, Los Angeles, and Los Angeles County Museum of Art.

- *The Dvaravati Wheels of the Law and the Indianization of South East Asia* (Leiden: E.J. Brill, 1996)
- Editor, *Ganesh: Studies of an Asian God* (Albany: State University of New York Press, 1991).

Thomas B. Coburn, St. Lawrence University, Canton, New York.

- *Encountering the Goddess: A Translation of the Devī-Māhātmya and a Study of Its Interpretations* (Albany: State University of New York Press, 1991).
- *Devī Māhātmya: The Crystallization of the Goddess Tradition* (Delhi: Motilal Banarsidass/South Asia Books, 1984).

Teun Goudriaan, Vakgroep Oosterse Talen en Culturen, Rijksuniversiteit te Utrecht, Utrecht.

- *Hindu Tantrism,* with Sanjukta Gupta and Dirk Jan Hoens (Leiden: E.J. Brill, 1979).
- *Hindu Tantric and Śākta Literature,* editor with Sanjukta Gupta (Weisbaden: Otto Harrassowitz, 1981).
- *The Sanskrit Tradition and Tantrism,* editor (Leiden: E.J. Brill, 1990).

Lina Gupta, Glendale College, Glendale, California.

- "Kālī, The Savior," *After Patriarchy: Feminist Transformations of the World Religions,* ed/ Paula M. Cooey, William R. Eakin and Jay B. McDaniel (New York: Orbis, 1991).
- "Hindu Women and Ritual Empowerment," *Women and Goddess Traditions,* ed. Karen l. King (Minneapolis: Augsburg Fortress, 1997).

Katherine Anne Harper, Loyola Marymount University, Los Angeles.

- *Seven Hindu Goddesses of Spiritual Transformation: The Iconography of the Saptamatrikas* (Lewiston, N.Y.: The Edwin Mellen Press, 1989).

- "Daiunzan Ryoanji Sekitei—The Stone Garden of the Mountain Dragon's Resting Place: Soteriology and the Bodhimandala," *The Pacific World: Journal of the Institute of Buddhist Studies,* New Series, 10 (1994).

Dennis Hudson, Smith College, Northhampton, Massachusetts

- "The Ritual Worship of Devī," *Devī, The Great Goddess: Female Divinity in South Asian Art,* ed. Vidya Dehijia (Washington, D.C.: Arthur M. Sackler Gallery, Smithsonian Institution, 1990.
- "The Courtesan and Her Bowl: An Esoteric Buddhist Reading of the Manimekalai," *A Buddhist Woman's Path To Enlightenment,* ed. Peter Schalk, Historia Religionum 13 (Uppsala: Acta Universitatis Upasaliensis, 1997): 151–90.

M. C. Joshi, Former Director General of the Archaeological Survey of India, New Delhi

- "Tantrism and Womanhood," *Indian Horizons* 34/1–2 (1985): 40–41.
- "Śākta Tantrism in the Gupta Age," *Aruna Bharati: Professor A. H. Jani Felicitation Volume,* ed. B. Data (Baroda: Oriental Institute, 1983): 77–81.

David Lorenzen, Colegio de Mexico, Mexico City

- *The Kāpālikas and Kālāmukhas: Two Lost Śaivite Sects,* 2d rev.ed. (Delhi: Motilal Banarsidass, 1991).
- *Kabir Legends* (Albany: State University of New York Press, 1996).

Thomas Mc Evilley, Rice University, Houston, Texas

- "An Archaeology of Yoga," *RES* 1 (1981).
- *The Shape of Ancient Thought: Studies in Greek and Indian Philosophies* (New York: Allworth Press, forthcoming 2001).

Paul Muller-Ortega, Universtiy of Rochester, New York.

- *The Triadic Heart of Siva* (Albany: State University of New York, 1989).
- *Meditation Revolution: A History and Theology of the Siddha Yoga Lineage* (Delhi: Agama Press, 1997).

André Padoux, Centre National de la Recherche Scientifique, Paris

- *Vāc: The Concept of the Word in Selected Hindu Tantras* (Albany: State University of New York Press, 1990).
- *Le Coeur du la Yoginī. Yoginīhṛdaya, avec le commentaire Dipika d' Amrtananda* (Paris: College de France, 1994).

Richard K. Payne, Institute of Buddhist Studies at Graduate Theological Union, Berkeley, California.

- *The Tantric Ritual of Japan: Feeding the Gods, The Shingon Fire Ritual,* Sata Pitaka Series, 365 (New Delhi: International Academy of Indian Culture and Aditya Prakashan, 1991).
- *Re-Visioning "Kamakura" Buddhism,* editor, Kuroda Institute Studies in East Asian Buddhism, 11 (Honolulu: University of Hawaii Press, 1998).

GLOSSARY

Āgamas—traditional religious texts of non-Vedic origin often associated with Śaivism.

Bhukti—enjoyment, domination, a practical goal in Tantrism.

Cakra—a wheel; the discus carried by Viṣṇu; mystical centers located in the human body.

Ḍākinī—minor female deity; semidivine sorceress.

Darśana—literally seeing or viewing; also used to designate various Hindu schools of worship.

Dīksā—a consecration or initiation ritual.

Guṇa—the three qualities that make up matter, namely: *sattva*—knowledge and intellect; *rajas*—passion, physical and mental activity; and *tamas*—mental and physical passivity.

Kālāmukha—a Tantric cult centered on the left-handed worship of Śiva.

Kāpālika—a Tantric cult centered on the left-handed worship of Śiva.

Kaula—one who performs Tantric left-handed (*vāmācarā*) rites.

Kuṇḍalini—the latent energy located at the base of the spine. The awakening and raising of the Kuṇḍalinī represents spiritual liberation (*mokṣa*).

Liṅga—the male generative organ, a symbol of divine creation when associated with the *yoni.*

Maṇḍala—a complex diagram used in ritual.

Mantra—a sequence of syllables with or without meaning

Mātṛkās—the divine mothers; a class of goddesses; in yoga, symbols of the cakras.

Mokṣa—spiritual release or freedom.

Mukti—the same as *mokśa.*

Mudrā—symbolic hand gesture; in Tantra may refer to an entire ritual.

Nāḍī—in yoga, channel through which energy flows through the subtle body.

Nityā—the sixteen-fold division of eternal goddesses of the Srividya School.

Sādhaka—a Tantric practitioner.

Sādhana—the road to spiritual emancipation or domination; ritual practice for achieving a particular goal.

Śākta—a devotee of divine energy (Śakti) as personified by the Goddess.

Śakti—the divine energy that is personified as being female, the Goddess.

Siddha—a yogin who has acquired *siddhis* or supranormal powers, sorcerer.

Śrīcakra—a sacred diagram consisting of nine triangles and representing the creative aspect of the Goddess.

Śrīvidyā—a particular *mantra;* sacred knowledge of the Goddess; a cult dedicated to the Goddess.

Śrīyantra—same as *Śrīcakra;* a sacred diagram consisting of nine triangles and representing the creative aspect of the Goddess.

Śruti—hearing, sacred knowledge of the Vedas.

Vidyā—true knowledge; in Tantrism, a specialized type of divine or esoteric knowledge.

Yantra—sacred diagram possessing occult powers; in Tantric meditation, the residence of the deity.

Yoginī—a female divinity, sometimes protective but more often a sorceress; a female practitioner of Tantrism.

Yoni—female generative organ; a symbol of divine creation especially when associated with the *liṅga.*

INDEX

U

V